D0026313

bread baking

bread baking

An Artisan's Perspective

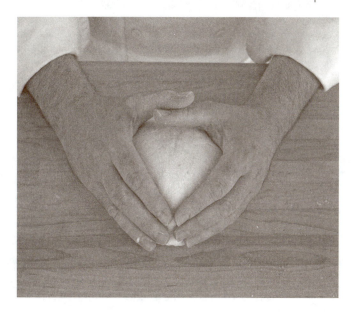

Daniel T. DiMuzio

WILEY

JOHN WILEY & SONS, INC.

Photography on pp. iii, 48, 58, 59, 81, 83–90, 114, 115, 149, 150, color insert following p. 50: pp. 2–5, 7, 8, color insert following p. 114: p. 5 (bottom) by Hilary Hunt Amaro

Photography on pp. 15, 42, 43, 64, 70, 79, 91–95, 106, 123, 124, 132, 175, 191, 192, color insert following p. 50: pp. 1, 6, color insert following p. 114: pp. 1–4, 5 (top), 7, 8 by Daniel T. DiMuzio

This book is printed on acid-free paper. ♾

Copyright © 2010 by John Wiley & Sons, Inc. All rights reserved.

Published by John Wiley & Sons, Inc., Hoboken, New Jersey.

Published simultaneously in Canada.

No part of this publication may be reproduced, stored in a retrieval system, or transmitted in any form or by any means, electronic, mechanical, photocopying, recording, scanning, or otherwise, except as permitted under Section 107 or 108 of the 1976 United States Copyright Act, without either the prior written permission of the Publisher, or authorization through payment of the appropriate per-copy fee to the Copyright Clearance Center, Inc., 222 Rosewood Drive, Danvers, MA 01923, 978-750-8400, fax 978-646-8600, or on the web at www.copyright.com. Requests to the Publisher for permission should be addressed to the Permissions Department, John Wiley & Sons, Inc., 111 River Street, Hoboken, NJ 07030, 201-748-6011, fax 201-748-6008, or online at http://www.wiley.com/go/permissions.

Limit of Liability/Disclaimer of Warranty: While the publisher and author have used their best efforts in preparing this book, they make no representations or warranties with respect to the accuracy or completeness of the contents of this book and specifically disclaim any implied warranties of merchantability or fitness for a particular purpose. No warranty may be created or extended by sales representatives or written sales materials. The advice and strategies contained herein may not be suitable for your situation. You should consult with a professional where appropriate. Neither the publisher nor author shall be liable for any loss of profit or any other commercial damages, including but not limited to special, incidental, consequential, or other damages.

For general information on our other products and services, or technical support, please contact our Customer Care Department within the United States at 800-762-2974, outside the United States at 317-572-3993 or fax 317-572-4002.

Wiley also publishes its books in a variety of electronic formats. Some content that appears in print may not be available in electronic books.

For more information about Wiley products, visit our Web site at http://www.wiley.com.

Library of Congress Cataloging-in-Publication Data:
DiMuzio, Daniel T.
  Bread baking: an artisan's perspective / Daniel T. DiMuzio.
    p. cm.
  Includes bibliographical references.
  ISBN 978-0-470-13882-3 (cloth)
  1. Bread. 2. Cookery (Bread)   I. Title.
  TX769.D56 2009
  641.8'15—dc22
  2008021437
Printed in the United States of America
10 9 8 7 6 5 4 3 2 1

Contents

7 Proofing and Retarding _____ 105

8 Baking _____ 121

9 Rich and Laminated Doughs _____ 137

10 Creating Dough Formulas _____ 155

Preface

It took a while, but good bread now holds almost the same status in the culinary world as great wine. Twenty years ago, you'd have been hard pressed to find a decent baguette anywhere outside of New York or Berkeley. Today, we can find good bread in most cities, even if it takes the form of par-baked loaves that are finished in grocery stores. Some artisan bakers sneer at these breads, but their flavor and texture is often pretty good, and sometimes they are better than what passes for artisan bread in local bakeries.

Which leads to the question: What makes bread good? Can we identify good bread in some way that makes it easy for people to know immediately that what they're buying is among the best stuff available?

Many artisans have tried, but it seems that we can't. The consensus among bakers profiled for this book is that there is no longer any meaning in the term *artisan bread*. That label was a mark of distinction ten or fifteen years ago, but marketing specialists at mega-groceries and bakery café chains have co-opted the term. There are no laws in the United States that prevent them from doing so, even though the bread that they sell may not be worthy of special attention. Plenty of genuine artisans are still out there making great bread, but great product cannot be distinguished with simple terminology.

So the proof isn't in the name, or a shiny oven on display, or the quality of the marble on a bakery's sales counter. The only real evidence of artisanship in bread baking is in the flavor and texture of the bread itself. That flavor and texture are usually the result of production processes designed by knowledgeable craftspeople. What may surprise you is that these craftspeople can now be found not only in boutique bakeries but also medium-sized wholesale operations and even large-scale manufacturers who take their commitment to the craft seriously and find the people and tools needed to succeed. The most important aspect of making high-quality bread isn't the embrace of old-fashioned techniques but rather the identification of what's *essential* among those techniques and the acceptance of the need to use those procedures, whatever the inconvenience or cost.

This book is meant to aid bakers or students who take bread seriously and who wish to begin their quest for craftsmanship in bread baking. Any real mastery of the subject takes time, of course, and it is only with experience and the personal assistance of well-trained baking professionals and instructors that artisanship can finally be achieved. We do believe, though, this book can help you get started.

Text Organization

The first chapter of *Bread Baking: An Artisan's Perspective* provides a brief history of bread making and highlights the importance that bread has played—with no exaggeration—in the development of human civilization. The rest of the chapters in this book are organized to resemble the production process associated with baking bread.

Chapters 2 through 8 take the readers sequentially through the subjects that bakers must consider when learning how to make bread. Ingredient selection is first, with a discussion of how ingredients affect fermentation and dough structure, followed by an introduction to baker's math and formula layout. Next, important concepts in mixing dough, fermenting it, shaping it into loaves, and retarding or proofing the loaves before baking are discussed. Finally, I outline how to judge when bread is ready for the oven and identify the critical aspects of scoring, loading, and baking bread to achieve the appearance, height, and textures appropriate to different types of bread.

Chapter 9 is devoted to the subject of *vienoisserie*—that is, sweet yeasted doughs that include lots of butter or are laminated with butter. Large quantities of fat, sugar, and eggs can have significant effects upon the rate of fermentation and the structure of dough, so these issues are tackled in a dedicated section. Laminating procedures are explained, and common pastries made from these doughs are demonstrated.

Chapter 10 is unique, since it requires readers to reflect on the principles and techniques learned previously in the book and apply them as they create their own formulas. Here, readers will discover that dough formulas are more than just lists of ingredients and batch sizes. Scenarios illustrate how principles associated with ingredient selection, mixing, and fermentation can affect attempts to create formulas that are "in balance."

Following the main chapters in the book, there are four Advanced Topics. The first three cover flour milling, wheat composition, advanced baker's math, and an in-depth look at fermentation, which will be of interest to bakers who want to know more about those subjects. The final Advanced Topic, which briefly discusses the creation of decorative dough pieces, will be of great interest to bakers and pastry students who want to take a more creative approach to the baking process. These Advanced Topics are included to provide information to bakers, students, and instructors wishing to further explore areas included in the main chapters of the text. An appendix of formulas follows the Advanced Topics. Within this section formulas are organized alphabetically. Most formulas include batch sizes for both 5-quart and 20-quart mixers. Metric and U.S. measurements for the ingredients listed are also provided.

Following the appendix of formulas, the reader will find a useful glossary of all highlighted terms in the text and an index of subject matter covered in the chapters.

Aspiring bakers will find this book to be of great use in providing a framework for their pursuit of artisanship in bread baking.

Text Features for Students

In an effort to make this book as accessible as possible to the reader, several features are included to enhance the content included in each chapter:

◆ **Learning Outcomes** are listed at the start of each chapter and provide a road map for students. These learning outcomes help students to focus on key content within each chapter to ensure their mastery of the principles and techniques presented.

◆ **Artisan Baker Profiles** of successful owners and bakers that have had an impact on the industry are included at the end of Chapters 2 through 10. The artisan bakers profiled provide their insights on the artisan bread baking industry and also offer pearls of wisdom to baking students planning to venture into the bread baking industry.

◆ **Baking Formulas** emulate the artisanal perspective on bread baking. Baking formulas are included within the Lab Exercises and Experiments at the end of some chapters and also in an appendix of formulas at the end of the book. The goal of these formulas is to provide flexibility by providing various batch sizes using 5-quart and 20-quart mixers, and including baker's percentages and U.S. and metric measurements. The procedures are organized to reflect the production process associated with baking bread. All of the formulas included in this text have been thoroughly tested for accuracy.

◆ **Sidebars** appear throughout each chapter, breaking up the content into manageable chunks for readers so they're not overwhelmed. These sidebars provide students with more background on particular topics to help them organize each chapter's content in a logical way.

◆ **Lab Exercises and Experiments** appear at the end of several chapters and help students put the concepts presented in the chapter into practice. By preparing the formulas provided, they see the theories in action and think critically about how using various techniques, methods, and ingredients affect the characteristics of the finished product (e.g., mixing rustic dough, hand mixing vs. mechanized mixing, etc.).

◆ In addition to the resources provided in the book, there is a **Student Companion Website (*www.wiley.com/college/dimuzio*)** that includes electronic versions of all the formulas listed in the appendix. The formula creation worksheets included in Chapter 10 are also available electronically so students can use them when creating formulas with one or two pre-ferments.

Flexibility for Instructors

Bread Baking: An Artisan's Perspective provides instructors with a flexible approach to the content and allows for customization when teaching this particular topic. Because so many instructors are faced with a limited number of hours to teach key concepts, each chapter of this book presents key material and then, where appropriate, advanced topics are covered in the Advanced Topics section at the end of the book.

RESOURCES FOR INSTRUCTORS

An **Instructor's Manual** (ISBN 978-0-470-25727-2) includes suggested course syllabi, chapter outlines, teaching tips, additional lab exercises and experiments, and answers to the questions for review at the end of each chapter. The Instructor's Manual also contains approximately 20 multiple-choice questions and one or two short-answer essay questions for each chapter.

The **Instructor's Companion Website** (www.wiley.com/college/climuzio) includes password-protected electronic versions of the Instructor's Manual and Test Bank. All of the formulas included in the appendix of the text are also included for quick reference.

Acknowledgments

My parents were always supportive of my interest in bread baking, and, though they are now deceased, I must thank them for their encouragement and willingness to eat anything I placed before them. I think that my mother in particular would have taken great satisfaction in seeing this book published.

My brothers, sisters, in-laws, nephews, and nieces have all given me valuable feedback on the breads I've baked. Thankfully, they usually loved the stuff, and I value the honest opinions they provided because they have always taken food as seriously as I do. And—believe me—you haven't encountered unvarnished analysis until your bread has been sampled by a five-year-old kid.

There's really nothing you can read in this book that I alone invented. All knowledgeable artisan bakers learn their craft from people who have greater knowledge than they did at some point. I have been privileged to learn from some of the best in this business—either in person or from their writings—and I cannot give enough credit to them for imparting to me the principles that make up this very work. Among them have been Michel Suas, Lionel Vatinet, Eric Kayser, Jeffrey Hamelman, James MacGuire, Didier Rosada, and Thom Leonard. Just listing them like that makes me feel very humble and fortunate to have learned from the greats. Thom Leonard, especially, of WheatFields Bakery Café in Lawrence, Kansas, provided technical editing for many of the chapters and Advanced Topics, and the book is much better for his constructive criticisms.

Thanks to all the talented bakers and bakery owners who agreed to be profiled for this book. Their observations about baking and the bakery business should prove valuable to students considering the profession.

I would also like to acknowledge the thoughtful feedback that the reviewers provided during their reviews of various phases of this manuscript:

John Angeline, Bucks County Community College; Luis Dall, Maryland Country Caterers; Vincent Donatelli, Ashville-Buncombe Technical Community College; Stephanie Johnson, Elgin Community College; Melina Kelson-Podolsky, Kendall College; Holly A. Pugliese, California Culinary Academy; David Ricci, Johnson & Wales University; James Usilton, Atlantic Cape Community College; Jean Yves Vendeville, Polly's Hospitality Institute.

Thanks also to the students at Culinard who assisted in any way in the testing of formulas, creation of decorative sculptures, and the photography for the book. They are, in no particular order: Avery Lowe, Charlotte Song, Wilma Yu, Jennifer Harvey, Patrillo White, Heather Guarino, Barbara Higgins, Anna Plummer, Jessica Little, Kim Chism, and Aimee Watkins. I actually couldn't have put this together without them.

I'm grateful to Chef Antony Osborne for allowing me to use the facilities at Culinard for research, test baking, and all the photography. His support proved invaluable in making the book a reality.

My agent, Neil Salkind, offered wise counsel to me on many occasions. Thanks, Neil, for re-orienting me when necessary.

I was lucky to be referred to Hilary Hunt Amaro when I was seeking a photographer for this book. I took a number of the photos myself, and I think my photos were just fine, but it is Hilary's photos that stand out for their consistent quality. She took what seemed like ordinary work and made it seem interesting or even beautiful. She was excited to be involved in the project, and her enthusiasm showed in her work. I recommend her highly.

I also would like to express my deep appreciation to the editors at John Wiley & Sons for the opportunity to put these years of observation into written form. In particular, I wish to thank Cindy Rhoads for her consistently good suggestions for making things clear, and for making this amateur author seem readable to his audience.

chapter 1

The History of Bread Making

Learning Outcomes:

- Identify the many critical junctures in world history related to society's need for bread.

- Describe the evolution of bread from its primitive origins through its modern-day form.

- Identify the key role wheat plays in the development of leavened bread.

- Define fermentation.

- Understand the evolution of the short, intensive, and improved mixing methods.

- Discuss how artisan bread baking evolved as a reaction to misguided baking techniques.

A Brief History of Bread Making

For many of us, bread is what we use every day to hold the ham in our sandwich or the butter on our toast, and we don't give it much more thought.

This is a very different perception than that of people just a few generations ago. For them, bread was the staple of most meals, or even the means of sustaining life itself. Bread served these purposes for thousands of years.

Bread's Impact on Basic Survival

Bread used to be so important to everyday existence that its scarcity or abundance could affect the history of kingdoms and empires. You've probably read about epic struggles for existence, wars of succession, and the overthrow of governments in your high school or college history classes. A surprising number of these events illustrate the historical and cultural importance of bread. This chapter demonstrates that the bread we take for granted today was once not only an accompaniment to dinner—bread was power.

A Cornerstone of Civilization

THE SUMERIANS

The *Sumerians*, for instance, who 10,000 years ago ruled over an area in what is now Iraq, could lay claim to being the world's first true nation because they devised more efficient methods of organized agriculture. Better organization meant more grain for bread produced by fewer people. Nomadic life gave way to settled agrarianism, which allowed for the development of skilled artisans, bureaucrats, and a professional military. Villages grew into towns and then cities. All this happened because wheat for bread was plentiful and more time was available to accomplish things of greater magnitude within their civilization.

The evolution of specialized trades and businesses would have been critical before the Sumerians could establish a strong central government. As far as we can tell from archaeological records, they used their prosperity to expand their power all over the area known as the *Fertile Crescent* (today's Middle East) and established what came to be viewed as the world's first true empire.

FROM ANCIENT ROME TO THE FRENCH REVOLUTION

The *Roman* rulers of antiquity (200 B.C.–A.D. 400) famously kept their citizens content and supportive by providing "bread and circuses"—that is, free bread and gladiatorial entertainment. King Louis XVI of France should have studied that lesson before the French Revolution (1789–1799), when a period of famine made bread both expensive and difficult to obtain. France's starving population eventually was so outraged that revolutionaries overthrew the thousand-year-old monarchy. It's been said that King Louis XVI's wife, *Marie Antoinette*, on hearing that mobs in Paris were incensed by the scarcity of bread, commented, "Then let them eat *brioche*" (later mis-

The Evolution of Fermentation

The first person to discover fermentation may also have discovered the first hangover. Archaeological evidence suggests barley was used to make beer long before leavened bread was a reality. In fact, the ancient Egyptians often located their breweries and bakeries in the same building.

Eventually, the Stone Age people made pots from clay and were able to boil their grains into a sort of mush or porridge. By today's standards, this porridge was probably not appealing in taste or texture. It would have been coarse, with many bits of chaff from the grassy stalks. It almost certainly had no salt, and sugar was unknown at the time. This mush could sustain life, though, and the ability to store grains for long periods enabled people to stock up when they were available in the wild.

People eventually discovered that by slamming a round rock in their hand onto a flat rock on the ground, they could smash open grains and shorten the time necessary for the seeds to absorb water and make porridge. This process represents the first known method of milling flour. By the late Stone Age, people were making flour using a special concave saddle stone placed on the ground, and finally they moved to a more elaborate mortar-and-pestle arrangement, with the large mortar carved from stone or wood and the pestle made from a long length of hard wood (see Figure 1.1).

Figure 1.1 In modern-day Zambia, villagers still use an ancient method of crushing grain to make their family's porridge: a mortar and pestle. Courtesy of IStock Photo.

translated as "cake"). Her iconic words were remembered as a symbol of the disparity between the suffering peasants and the indifferent royals.

BREAD AFFECTS POLITICS TODAY

Bread has affected politics more recently in Russia and Eastern Europe. Former communist governments in these regions sometimes put a hold on bread prices, or even rolled them back, to keep their citizens from revolting. The Soviet Union became defunct for a number of reasons, but long lines for bread in government bakeries didn't generate sympathy for the party in power.

As we examine the past, then, it isn't an exaggeration to say that bread is central to the development of civilization. Indeed, it would be hard to imagine life without it.

How Bread Began

The evolution of bread is tied to the evolution of human life. Multiple species of *yeast* and *bacteria* were among the first plants and animals to appear on Earth. When larger species evolved and moved to land three billion years later, the yeast and bacteria fed on them when they died. Those single-celled organisms were hard at work degrading large pieces of organic matter before wheat or any other grain appeared. So fermentation was certainly around by then and was essentially a process of decomposition. We define *fermentation*, then, as the breakdown of organic substances by yeast and bacteria.

ROASTED GRAINS = ROASTED GRASS SEEDS

In the Stone Age, people gathered grasses from the wild and probably first consumed their seeds by roasting them over a fire. They eventually learned to distinguish one grass from another and selected only those with the biggest seeds or the best flavor. Among those chosen were the early varieties of barley, oats, and, possibly, einkorn and emmer.

Bread: An Accidental Creation

We can only speculate about when the first breads were made, but it is believed they resulted from people accidentally spilling bits of porridge onto the hot stones of a hearth. They wouldn't have thrown away the results; food was hard to find. They probably ate the crisped little disks and found they liked them enough to continue making them. It's likely these first breads were coarse, dense pancakes. If you made them and baked them dry, you could carry them with you to work or to hunt, with no need to start a fire or boil water to make them palatable.

These first pancakes almost certainly didn't rise as they baked. Fermentation was well established throughout nature, and pots of porridge that had been kept too long must have occasionally gone over. But, as far as archaeologists can tell, the sort of grain mush that captured gas from wild yeasts was not yet commonly made. The fermentation of porridge also produced alcohol, of course, and people must have discovered its inebriating effects at some point. Archaeologists believe fermentation was used to make grain-based beverages, like beer or ale, before leavened bread was common. In truth, the mash for brewing beer and the porridge for making bread were nearly the same thing, with the beer mash just being a lot wetter.

BREAD THAT RISES

By 4000–3500 B.C., though, evidence suggests Egyptian slaves were working with bread made from grains that acted differently than barley or oats. If a batch of porridge made with this grain was left out a few days, it would grow in size. When it was baked on hot stones, it grew even further, billowing into short, pillow-shaped loaves. Those grains were the early ancestors of today's bread wheat. It is thought they are related to *einkorn* or *emmer*, which can still be found growing in the same areas today.

The critical difference between the flour made from early wheat and that made from grains like barley or oats was that wheat contained some unique proteins that could combine with water to form a more complex protein called *gluten*. Gluten had the ability to capture the gas produced during fermentation, and it could stretch to accommodate the gas as it accumulated. Other grains didn't contain enough of the right proteins to form gluten, so, while they could be used to make flour for bread, their flours would not make dough that could capture gas.

It is quite possible, even probable, that other societies within the Fertile Crescent were using similar forms of wheat by this time (see the Sumerians, above). This doesn't mean other grains for bread were no longer used. The Egyptians, we know, continued to use barley for bread well into the Roman era, and the Greeks, who learned of leavened bread from the Egyptians, left written records of how much they loved the taste of barley bread, just as they enjoyed the taste and texture of the newer wheat loaves.

THE ROMAN GUILDS

Ruins from the Roman cities of Pompeii and Herculaneum (see Figure 1.2) show that, in the year A.D. 79, Roman cities featured combination bakery/milling shops, where wheat (possibly a type of durum) was ground into flour and used to make bread for everyday consumption. At this time, those who practiced the craft of bread baking formed a *guild*, which was a legally sanctioned group of professional craftsmen. Their mills were still made of stone but were fairly large, and they were turned by two or more men (probably slaves). Then, as before, the possession of bread-making wheat was what really gave power to both emperors and their bureaucrats. When rulers were challenged in ancient Rome, the usurpers sometimes attempted to capture the fields where wheat was grown—it was the harvest that sustained life and bestowed title upon the rulers.

Figure 1.2 The ruins of an ancient Roman bakery in the city of Pompeii, Italy, dating from about A.D. 70. Notice the hand-powered mill on the right and the wood-burning oven on the left. Courtesy of IStock Photo.

A BASTION OF SLOW CHANGE

It may be difficult to believe, but from the fall of the Roman Empire to almost the start of World War I—about 1,400 years—bread making didn't change as much as you might expect. Some advances in the numbers of water-powered and wind-powered mills occurred, but wheat flour was still milled by means of chiseled, closely fitting stones. To get anything like white flour, you needed to pass the milled whole wheat through a progressively finer set of mesh or silken screens—a process only the wealthy could afford. Even then, the actual flour color would have been light tan or gray.

Ovens were still wood- or coal-fired and completely hand-loaded. No refrigeration was commonly available, so, although commercial yeast was produced by the late nineteenth century, there was no reliable way to distribute it very far from the yeast factory. Naturally leavened starters—*levain* to the French, sourdough to the English—remained the most common means of leavening bread in bakeries throughout Europe.

THE APPRENTICESHIP SYSTEM IN FRANCE

The guild of bakers in France continued to use the same apprenticeship system it had devised centuries before. When a boy was in his early teens, his family arranged for a master baker to take him on for training. He lived in the baker's home, usually located above the bakery itself, where he was housed and fed, with little or no wages, as he learned how to knead dough in large troughs. More experienced men then shaped the loaves and watched the ovens. After a few years, the apprentice was either promoted within the ranks of that bakery and made real wages, or he would move on as a journeyman baker for another employer.

Workdays were quite long—12 hours or more—and the typical bakery was a basement hovel where a wood-fired oven, a wooden bench, and a dough trough competed for space with the bakers themselves. Wonderful aromas surrounded the baker during his shift, but the work was hard, the wages were low, and the profits for the owners were marginal at best, given the government price controls since the Middle Ages.

The Parisian Croissant

In the late Renaissance, the Turks were besieging the city of Vienna, in the Austrian Empire. Bakers then, as now, usually worked through the night, and some bakers working in a basement heard loud digging noises outside their bakery as they were making their bread. They alerted the Austrian military commanders, who discovered the Turks digging tunnels under the city walls. The Austrians were able to surprise the Turkish soldiers and defeat them. In appreciation of the pivotal role the bakers played in surprising the Turks, the Emperor commissioned them to create a simple, sweetened yeast roll shaped like the crescent in the Turkish flag.

Viennese bakers who migrated to France in the 1800s brought with them the tradition of crescent-shaped rolls. By the 1920s, some bakers in Paris used a laminated dough (like puff pastry) that was yeasted to create the croissants, and the so-called Parisian croissant was born. Both the laminated croissant and the classic baguette first appeared in Paris in the same decade. They are almost certainly the two most iconic (and imitated) French bread products in the world.

Mechanized Bread Making

By the end of the nineteenth century, attempts were made to bring the baking profession into the industrial age. Steam-powered dough mixers were displayed at a technology exposition in Paris in 1889, but they were never widely adopted—possibly because they were judged by bakery owners as impractical or too revolutionary. Because electricity was not available for use in refrigeration, it was also not commonly available for powering mixers.

ELECTRIC MIXERS FINALLY APPEAR: THE SHORT MIX METHOD

A good deal changed after World War I. Electrical service became available in most large towns and cities, creating a market for mixers powered by electric motors. Early electric mixer models were fairly slow. They worked only on one speed, and the dough they created was not much different in consistency from that mixed and developed by hand. The chief advantage in these early machines was that they saved a huge amount of manual labor. They may have also saved a bit of time, but the entire process from mixer to oven wasn't remarkably shorter. It still took 4–5 hours of bulk fermentation until bread dough was mature and strong enough to shape at the bench. This was the only option available to bakers then, and the technique had no name at the time, but it was later called the *short mix* or *traditional method*.

POWERED MIXERS MEET BETTER INGREDIENTS

In the early 1920s, the advent of powered mixers was accompanied by the introduction of better-quality commercial yeast and white flours that were stronger and more affordable. While stone mills weren't completely discarded, steel roller mills ground most of the flour used in French bakeries. The baguette and the Parisian croissant had made their debut in Paris by this time. The Parisian croissant married the technique of butter-laminated puff pastry with what had been merely a sweetened, yeasted crescent roll. Baguettes probably were related to *pain viennoise* or Viennese bread, which featured a technique of boosting the power of manufactured yeast by placing it in a slurry of equal amounts of water and flour. This method was associated with bakers who had immigrated to France, some of whom had worked in Vienna. This slurry, a type of *pre-ferment*, sat for 5 hours or more and was later added to any remaining flour and water to complete the mixing of the actual bread dough. Because many of the Viennese who worked with French bakers were originally of Polish descent, this wet pre-ferment came to be called a *poolish*.

Direct Mixing Method

By the 1930s, many bakers were taking advantage of the stronger yeast strains available by eliminating the step of creating a pre-ferment for baguette dough. This came to be known as the *direct method*, because bakers were able to avoid the trouble of feeding a levain or mixing a poolish ahead of time (for more information on the subject of pre-ferments, see *Chapter 5*). Even with these changes, the time necessary for making baguettes was really not less than before, so direct mixing might actually be seen as a variation on the short mix or traditional method. The convenience of not making a poolish still required an extended bulk or *primary fermentation*. The yeast produced gas faster, but the dough still had to gain strength through long fermentation and a series of folds.

World War II and Its Aftermath

Virtually the entire European continent was consumed by war from 1939 to 1945. White flour became less and less available. Bread bakers in France and elsewhere had to use higher-extraction wheat flour (nearly whole wheat) and added barley, rye, and other flours to make their supply of flour go farther. By the time the war ended, the scarcity of flour for bread was so acute that bakers sometimes added sawdust to make enough dough for their customers.

PROSPERITY RETURNS

While the postwar economic boom did not happen overnight, some prosperity was returning to France, and the bakery profession was on its way to recovery by the early 1950s. During the rebuilding that occurred in this decade, electricity became available even in parts of the countryside that had never had it before. Bakeries in the countryside began to acquire the same types of mixer used by bakers in the cities and larger towns. Making bread dough completely by hand became less and less common, but the quality of bread was as good as ever because the dough was still fermented for long periods.

FRANCE AND FRENCH BREAD BECOME "MODERN"

By the mid-1950s, a new type of mixer featuring both low and high speeds made its appearance in the French bread baking community. This new type of mixer allowed bakers to combine ingredients on the lower speed and then change to the higher one to develop the gluten faster than before. When using the high speed option for 8–12 minutes or more, this mixer could produce dough that was lighter in texture than any previously made, and its loaves had impressive volume. The loaves also had a much whiter crumb, and, though few people seemed to notice at the time, their taste was much blander than bread made by hand or with the older, slower mixers. The increase in gluten strength obtained using this new mixer before the dough even left the mixing bowl was a persuasive consideration. Bakers liked how dough mixed for a long time on high speed could gain maturity quickly—in as little as 30 minutes. Bakery owners embraced the prospect of making two or three times as much bread in about the same amount of production time as before.

The Intensive Mix Method

By the mid-1960s, most bakeries in France were using the new mixers. With the more powerful equipment came the adoption of the high-speed mixing technique, eventually named the *intensive mix*, which shortened the bulk fermentation, or *pointage*, so it was almost more of a rest period for the dough than a true fermentation. Millers began to mix small quantities of fava bean flour into their normal bread flour, which whitened the crumb of bread and accelerated the oxidation process that strengthened the dough. Bakers used greater quantities of yeast to ensure dough was gasified quickly for the new, almost no-time fermentation technique.

PAIN CHAUX

Customers seemed to love the new style of baguette, and it became customary for them to patronize the bakery two or three times a day to purchase warm loaves, or *pain chaux*, straight from the oven. They almost had to, if they wanted fresh texture, because the cottony loaves staled in a matter of hours. Several theories exist for how a product with such mediocre flavor and poor keeping qualities could come to dominate the bread market, with its novelty when compared to the dark, dense breads of recent wartime, the appeal of warm bread being available several times a day, and the sense of modernity or progress it conveyed were among them.

The reasons for small shop owners to invest in the new equipment went beyond merely making more money; industrial bakeries were appearing, with the capacity to produce tens of thousands of loaves per day. If the little guys were to survive and keep their prices for bread competitive with these newcomers, they had to make more bread in less time with fewer people on staff. Some present-day artisans would question the wisdom of those decisions, but—at that time—few people saw the quality as an issue. Bigger, lighter loaves (eventually termed *pain blanc*) actually seemed better to many consumers, and the option of buying warm bread three times a day seemed to outweigh any trifling issues of flavor or color.

Unfortunately for those bakers, the movement toward a new style of bread was just part of a new attitude toward the role of bread in an average consumer's diet. Bread consumption was on the decline during the 1950s and 1960s, and the loss of quality in the same period did nothing to stop the trend. Many bakery owners who simply couldn't compete with bread factories or more mechanized small bakeries had to close their shops. The number of bakery operators in France has continued to decline; Steven Kaplan provides evidence in *Good Bread Is Back* (Duke University, 2006) that from 1960 to the year 2000, the number of operators in France dropped from 55,000 to around 33,000, and bread consumption per capita went from perhaps 300g (12 oz) per day to about half that. These small operators who mechanized the bread process were honest working men who were trying to preserve their craft in the face of increased competition from large industrial bakeries. They were trying to save their lives and their means of making a living. Most of us probably would have made the same choices these small bakery operators made at the time to save our livelihoods. It may be fair to say, though, that this trend toward mechanization, when combined with industrialized bread production, was largely responsible for the decline in French bread quality and the drop in the number of bakery operators.

Rescue Arrives—The Improved Mix Method

By the late 1970s and early 1980s, many bakery operators and consumers realized bread quality was not as good as it had been 20 or 30 years earlier, but they didn't know why. Bakers became acutely aware of the drop in individual bread consumption, and studies were initiated to determine exactly what made modern bread so unappealing.

At that time, Raymond Calvel was a professor of baking at a milling school in Paris called l'École Française de Meunerie. He had been among the most vocal critics of the intensive mixing practices that had overtaken the French baking community. In his books and technical articles, he proposed that the lack of taste in modern baguettes resulted from short (or even nonexistent) bulk fermentations, as well as a mixing process that destroyed the important pigments in flour while oxidizing important fatty acids. He recognized bakers would never return in large numbers to completely manual production methods, so he went about devising a mechanical mixing and fermentation technique that preserved the aromas and flavor of bread without sentencing bakers to a life of endless waiting.

BETTER BREAD IN THE SAME SHORT TIME

The method he created later became known as the *improved mix method*. It combined some of the accelerated gluten development of the intensive mix method with as much of the flavor, color, and crumb structure as possible. It featured a short mix (3–4 minutes) on first speed with another short period on second speed (3–5 minutes, using a spiral mixer). If the mixer had removable bowls, the baker could pre-mix the flour and water for only about 20 minutes before adding the salt and yeast and continuing on second speed. As the mixture rested, the baker utilized the rest time to begin assembling another dough in a different bowl, or performed other tasks. The use of a simple pre-ferment such as leftover baguette dough (*pâte fermentée*) could jump-start the development of bacteria and organic acids, which shortened the primary fermentation and development of maturation to just 60–90 minutes.

The improved mix method enabled bakers to make better-tasting bread with good volume, nice color, and a crumb that approached that of traditional mix methods. The time expended to make bread from start to finish remained essentially the same as using the intensive mix method. In the early 1970s, Julia Child credited

ARTISAN BAKER PROFILE

Amy Scherber

Amy's Bread, New York, New York

Amy Scherber moved to New York City after graduating from St. Olaf's College in Minnesota. She initially pursued a career in marketing, but after just three years she realized her obsession with food needed a professional outlet. She left her job and enrolled at the New York Restaurant School, then gained experience as a line cook and pastry chef at the famous Bouley Restaurant in Manhattan.

Amy's interest in bread led her to seek bakers in France who would allow her to work with them and learn firsthand the techniques necessary for making outstanding loaves. These hands-on experiences were her central inspiration in developing the traditional philosophy her bakers practice today. Among the bakers who have influenced her outlook are Bernard Ganachaud, Eric Kayser, Christian Vabret, and Didier Rosada.

Amy opened a tiny 650-square-foot shop in the Hell's Kitchen neighborhood of Manhattan in 1992, where she initially prepared everything—from mixer to oven—in just one room. Even in New York City, traditionally prepared handmade breads were hard to find at that time, so the community embraced her new business, and it was not long until she had to find a new facility to accommodate the growing demand for her baguettes and *pain au levain*. She opened her second location in the Chelsea Market district in 1996, where most of the baking takes place today. Her company has now grown to six locations in Manhattan, and her staff has ballooned from five people at the original spot to over 100 bakers, administrators, and sales staff. Though they now make thousands of loaves every day, her bakers continue to shape every one of them by hand and to uphold as much as possible the traditions she learned in France.

She has written *Amy's Bread* (William Morrow, 1996) together with Toy Dupree, and has another book forthcoming as of this writing. Amy and her bread have often been featured on television shows such as *Martha Stewart Living* and *Emeril Live*. She has been nominated twice by the James Beard Foundation for pastry chef of the year, and she serves on the advisory board of the Bread Bakers Guild of America.

IMPRESSIONS OF ARTISAN BREAD BAKING AS AN INDUSTRY

People who succeed as you have in this business are often confronted with the dilemma of maintaining standards of exceptional quality while building their business and increasing their production levels. How do you do it?

As the business grows, you can see when the product suffers from taking on too much business. Then you have to figure out how to improve the production process to bring back the quality. You can add another shift of bakers to make more of the product later so it is not all done at once. You can change your equipment to accommodate a different-size batch, such as purchasing a bigger mixer, or add staff to make things go faster. These all cost more money than using machines, but the initial investment in machines is also very expensive. It can be done, but it is up to the managers of the bakery to maintain a standard of quality if they are growing their business. I think you just have to catch up and hit a plateau for a while, and then grow again when you have stabilized the team and the production. That is how we do it.

What are your thoughts on prospective artisan bakers? What characteristics or personality traits do you look for in prospective employees that will increase their potential for hire? Are there any traits that might exclude them?

An employee that seeks out the bakery with a well-researched cover letter and a personal visit, as well as a follow-up call and repeat visit, is usually someone we really want to hire. The person who brings in a tattered book of recipes they made when they worked somewhere else is a no-hire because I don't want them to steal my recipes after they work for me, and I don't want them to make someone else's bread in my bakery.

Do you have any pearls of wisdom for the bakery and pastry students reading this book?

Stay in each job at least two years to really learn what goes on in that bakery, as long as you are being treated properly, and be willing to do anything that needs to be done. You will definitely move up and learn more if you are willing to do everything.

Calvel for his insights on the taste of bread and for instructing her and her coauthor before they wrote their iconic *Mastering the Art of French Cooking, Volume II.*

Renewed Interest in Great Bread

It might be said that since the late 1980s there has been a renewed interest in good bread among French consumers and the bakers who serve them. Much of the bread in France is still made using intensive mix methods, but a growing number of bakery owners offer alternatives. Bakers such as Lionel Poilâne (who died tragically in 2002) and his brother, Max Poilâne, each maintained bakeries that, sometimes against fashion, used the high-extraction brown flour and sourdough methods of France's past, while avoiding baguettes altogether.

Other artisans have resurrected the baguette as a symbol of proud bread making. A number have risen to prominence; among the best-known are Jean-Luc Poujauran, Eric Kayser, Dominique Verbron, and Basil Kamir. These bakers are competitors who have achieved near-celebrity status. They each have their own ideas about how to achieve the "best" flavor and texture, but they have at least one thing in common: a commitment to using technological advances with caution while making the best bread possible.

THE BREAD BAKERS GUILD IS ESTABLISHED

This revival of good bread-making practices has spread through some other parts of Europe and has even made its way to North and South America, Australia, and Japan. Within the United States, an organization arose in 1993 to meet the needs of a nascent artisan bread movement. This organization was formed by professionals and home bakers who viewed their craft as an institution that needed nurturing, education, and support. They named the organization the *Bread Bakers Guild of America*, and it continues to uphold its mission by offering opportunities for the exchange of important ideas through conclaves, seminars, and informative newsletters. More information about the Bakers Guild can be found at www.bbga.org.

Summary

Until quite recently, bread was the most important source of sustenance among people in the Middle East, North Africa, Europe, and the Western hemisphere. The availability of bread ingredients such as wheat and other grains played a significant role in determining the history of nations from biblical times through the fall of communism.

Milling methods and mixing technology didn't change significantly for several millennia, but by the early twentieth century, bakers began to consider the possibility of incorporating more advanced milling and mixing methods into their production. The machines they adopted were purely beneficial at first, but by the 1950s, more powerful mixers had a destructive effect on the quality of bread in France. About three decades later, an artisan movement came about that aimed to reclaim the reputation of French bread and raise the consciousness of passionate bread bakers throughout the rest of the Western world. Artisan bakers believed that while successful business practices are necessary for any bakery to survive, they would not abandon sound principles of bread making for the sake of production and profitability.

Key Terms		
	Sumerians	*guild*
	Fertile Crescent	*pain viennoise*
	Romans	*pre-ferment*
	Marie Antoinette	*poolish*
	yeast	*direct method*
	bacteria	*primary fermentation*
	fermentation	*intensive mix*
	einkorn	*pointage*
	emmer	*pain chaux*
	gluten	*improved mix*
	short mix	*pâte fermentée*
	traditional mix	*Bread Bakers Guild of America*

Questions for Review

1. How was the greater availability of wheat for bread a factor in the growth of Sumerian civilization?

2. What grain enabled Egyptian bakers and others to make leavened bread?

3. What substance was used to make most grain mills through the early nineteenth century?

4. What reasons did Raymond Calvel provide for the deterioration of bread quality through the 1960s and 1970s?

5. How did the pre-ferment called *poolish* get its name?

Questions for Discussion

1. How can you choose between a really good baguette and one that is poorly made?

2. Where do you go to purchase bread? Would you pay a bit more or make a special trip to an artisan bakery if you're confident the product is better?

chapter **2**

Ingredients and Their Effects

Learning Outcomes:

- Identify the characteristics associated with the interaction among the most important ingredients in bread making: flour, water, yeast, and salt.

- Learn about the origins of wheat and why it is preferred over other grains for bread flour.

- Identify the three parts of the wheat berry most important to millers and bakers.

- Understand how changing even one ingredient in a formula can have both intended (primary) and unintended (secondary) effects on the bread.

- Learn how flour is milled and why the method of milling can create important differences in flour.

- Identify the essential nutrients found in wheat.

Ingredients for Baking Bread

Flour and water are the only two ingredients absolutely necessary to create bread. These ingredients were probably the only things *Neolithic man* used to make the first loaves of bread ever eaten.

Of course, bakers today don't limit themselves to these two ingredients. A large number of other ingredients have found their way into bread through the years, and the changes they have produced range in character from subtle to enormous.

Those changes are often more complex than first imagined. Putting salt in a dough formula, for example, doesn't only add flavor to the bread (*its primary effect*) but also affects the mixing time for the dough, how long the whole mass should be fermented, the length of the loaf's final proof, and the keeping qualities of the finished loaf (all—from this point of view—*secondary effects*). Determining the ingredients to include or how much of each to use can be perceived as a casual process, but for predictable results, you have to do more than just pick what you like and add it to your dough. In this chapter, you'll eventually see that, when it comes to ingredient selection, one item doesn't simply get added to another but may actually *change* the other.

We discuss fundamental characteristics of typical bread ingredients in this chapter. Planning a sensible list of ingredients for your own formulas is discussed in *Chapter 10*.

The Most Important Ingredient: Flour

While wheat flour has been the preferred choice in many cultures for about 2,000 years, this wasn't always the case, and in some of today's applications it still isn't. Chickpea flour, for instance, has been used to make flatbreads in Asia and the Mediterranean region for centuries. If you go to certain parts of Italy and France today, you'll still find *cecina* and *socca,* which are examples of these. Centuries ago, corn (also called *maize*) was selected for cultivation in the Americas, probably because grains like wheat weren't native to the hemisphere. The Mexican tortillas, tamales, and pure corn bread found in the American South today are examples of contemporary breads that hail from a wheat-free tradition.

Although we don't often think in such terms, flour can come from a number of very different sources. For instance, it can come from grinding unconventional foods like potatoes or beans. In most cases, though, when we discuss making bread, we are talking about flour made from a grain or a combination of grains, such as wheat, rye, corn, or barley. In fact, today it's almost always a given that, when we refer to *flour* in a recipe, with no other descriptors, we're talking about flour made from wheat only (see Figure 2.1).

FLOUR DEFINED

Flour can be defined as the powder or particles that result from the crushing or milling of starchy seeds, grains, tubers, or legumes. In the Stone Age, flour that came

Figure 2.1 Heads of winter wheat growing in a field near Davis, California.

from grains crushed by hand using rocks would have been quite coarse and mealy. Ancient Egyptians used stones that were chiseled and shaped purposely for milling to enable them to produce flour that was much finer in consistency. For approximately the next 6,000 years, this was the basic method used to mill flour. The steel rollers invented during the latter half of the nineteenth century helped produce even finer flour, much more like what we see today. Mechanized sifters were also used in conjunction with the steel rollers to remove as much bran and germ as possible (for more on the history of milling, see *Chapter 1*).

Wheat Dough Can Inflate

While a number of grains are used to make bread today, only wheat (and, to a slight degree, rye and barley) has the stuff necessary to create a membrane that retains the gas bubbles formed during *fermentation*. As we mentioned in *Chapter 1*, fermentation is the breakdown of organic substances by yeast and bacteria. Wheat flour's ability to capture the gases from fermentation and thereby leaven bread is the reason it has become the preferred grain for bread making in so many cultures.

The Wheat Berry

If you look at the cross section of a grain of wheat (also called a *wheat berry*), illustrated in Figure 2.2, you'll see the three basic components of the seed that concern

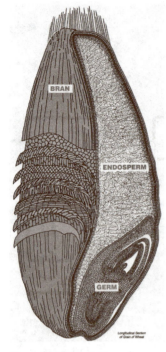

Figure 2.2 Cross section of a wheat berry. Courtesy of Wheat Foods Council.

bakers: the germ, the endosperm, and the bran. The *germ* is the smallest of the three, and, if the berry were actually planted in soil, this is the part of the grain that would grow into a seedling. It constitutes only 2–3% of the seed's total weight and contains most of the natural oils. Small amounts of sugars, minerals, and vitamins are also found here, as well as some water-soluble proteins. The germ is highly nutritious. Unfortunately, the oils in the germ can turn rancid in a matter of days or weeks, depending on temperature and storage conditions, so it's usually removed during milling to provide greater shelf life to the flour. If you wish to add wheat germ to your dough, you can buy it in its isolated form from many bakery suppliers.

The *bran* looks like a shell around the germ and endosperm and accounts for 13–17% of the weight of the seed. It is formed mostly from layers of cellulose, and its general function is to offer a water-permeable protective coating for the wheat berry until it finds suitable soil, moisture, and warmth for sprouting. Even though the bran is essentially indigestible, it provides a good deal of fiber and contains important minerals as well. If we want to make high-rising and light-textured breads, however, the bran can pose a problem, as flour with bran makes for heavier loaves and a denser texture. If you don't mind this—and lots of people don't—you can select *whole wheat flour* to make all or some of your breads, because it contains all three parts of the grain. Alternatively, you can add *wheat bran* purchased separately from a miller or bakery distributor.

The largest share of the berry's mass is formed by the *endosperm*, which consists mostly of starch, water-insoluble proteins, and a class of carbohydrates called *pentosans* (which are a type of gum). Together, they make up 81–84% of the berry. The endosperm's function within the seed is to act as food for the embryo (the germ) as it nears sprouting time. While this is nature's intention, farmers and millers intervene by harvesting the berries and grinding them into flour before sprouting occurs.

Other grains have different shapes and colors than the wheat berry, but their basic cross section wouldn't look remarkably different from Figure 2.2. Generally speaking, they are surrounded by cellulose, contain starch and proteins, and their germ can sprout into a new plant if it finds the right environment.

Wheat Classification

Millers and wheat farmers have devised a classification system in North America to help them predict the likely performance characteristics of wheat shipped to market. The system comprises three factors that are correlated with a particular crop before it is sold or turned into flour.

PROTEIN CONTENT

The first classification evaluates the grain's protein content. About 80% of the protein in a wheat kernel can form *gluten*, so determining how much protein is in a wheat berry can tell you what sort of application is appropriate for the type. *Hard wheat* is the term applied to varieties that are high in protein (10–18%). They are called that because a hard wheat berry is actually quite difficult to break. *Soft wheat* is the term applied to varieties that are lower in protein (8–11%). Higher-protein wheat is generally considered suitable for flour to be made into bread and bagels by the retail baking industry. Lower-protein varieties are usually considered appropriate for cakes, pastry, cookies, and crackers. The protein level of wheat and its potential gluten levels in flour are certainly related, but they are not precisely the same thing.

Keep in mind that about 20% of the proteins in the wheat berry are water soluble and do not form gluten at all.

KERNEL COLOR

The second classification has to do with the grain's actual color. The terms *red wheat* and *white wheat* are used to describe the appearance of the grain's bran and color of flour made from the whole grain. Red wheat is the more common type, but the number of farmers growing white wheat has grown significantly in the last decade. Consumers who prefer to eat bread made from whole wheat find that the whiter bran is less bitter than the red, and, in some cases, the comparative lack of color makes whole wheat white varieties more marketable to consumers who have been raised on white bread.

HARVEST SEASON

The third common classification identifies the season in which the grain was grown. *Spring wheat* is planted in the spring and harvested in the fall. Berries from spring wheat are almost always hard, and the flour from them usually is very high in protein. *Winter wheat* is sown in the fall, lies dormant during the winter, and then resumes growth during the spring. It is harvested in late spring or early summer. Both hard and soft wheat varieties can have a winter classification.

Before wheat is marketed, it might acquire a label like *hard red winter*, *soft white winter*, or *hard red spring* (see Table 2.1). Artisan bread bakers favor hard winter wheat flour (10–15% protein) the most, and it is grown in both red and white varieties. Winter wheat sold in the United States generally has gluten-forming proteins that have a good balance of strength and extensibility, tolerance to long mixing, and tolerance to long fermentation.

Spring wheat (12–18% protein) is usually much higher in protein, which, at first, might seem like a desirable trait, but the gluten from spring wheat is often too strong and resistant to extension, making it a poor choice for many hand-shaped breads. If dough has higher gluten levels, it must be mixed longer to achieve a desired level of development. However, a longer mix time can incorporate too much oxygen into the dough and cause the destruction of desirable carotene pigments. These yellowish pigments are a significant source of aroma and flavor in simple hearth breads. Last, the higher protein content of spring wheat tends to make the bread crust tough and leathery, and, ironically, can reduce the volume of bread dough and cause it to be too inextensible to rise well.

TABLE 2.1 Wheat Classification

Variety	Protein Content	Kernel Color	Planting Season	Harvesting Season	Typical Use
Soft red winter	8–11%	Red	Fall	Early summer	Cake, pastry flour
Soft white winter	8–11%	White	Fall	Early summer	Cake, pastry flour
Hard red winter	10–15%	Red	Fall	Early summer	Bread flour
Hard white winter	10–15%	White	Fall	Early summer	Bread flour
Hard red spring	12–18%	Red	Spring	Fall	Bread flour, high-protein flour
Durum	14–16%		Spring	Fall	Semolina, durum flour

For more in-depth information about the composition of flour, its important characteristics, and the milling process, see *Advanced Topic #1.*

Other Grains

ALTERNATIVE WHEAT VARIETIES

Durum is a variety of wheat grown principally in Italy, parts of the Middle East, and North America. The coarse meal ground from it is generally called *semolina* to distinguish it from the more finely milled *durum flour.* It is very high in protein, and the durum wheat berry is unusually hard. It has much more *beta carotene* than typical bread wheat, so it produces flour or meal that is decidedly yellow in color. It is prized for use in making dried varieties of pasta, and the strength of its gluten gives that pasta its characteristic chew. Durum has also been used to make bread in Sicily and other parts of southern Italy for centuries. Some artisan bread shops feature semolina breads with rustic, fanciful shapes. Mixing dough with semolina or durum flour can be a challenge, as it takes longer than normal bread flour to absorb water, and its tolerance to long mixing is not good. Bakers who wish to use durum flour or semolina are well advised to give their dough a rest period (see *autolyse* in *Chapter 4*), and they should be conservative in estimating how long the dough should mix on second speed. Using normal bread flour for at least half the total flour weight extends the dough's tolerance to mixing.

Spelt is a variety of wheat known as *farro* in Europe. It does contain gluten, and its flour can be used to make leavened bread. However, it is weaker than modern bread wheat so generally does not provide the height or volume characteristic of conventional bread. Some people who experience intolerance to gluten (*not* people with celiac disease) find they can digest spelt bread more easily than ordinary wheat bread. The legendary Parisian baker Lionel Poilane is thought to have used a measureable amount of spelt flour in his famous sourdough *miche.*

Kamut® is a brand name for a wheat variety thought to have its origins in the Middle East. It is now grown in Montana and parts of Alberta, Canada. As spelt does, Kamut has a form of gluten that supports leavened bread but lacks strength and volume when compared to conventional wheat dough. According to legend, the berries used to grow Kamut came from ancient Egyptian tombs. Agronomists disagree, believing people in the Egyptian countryside kept this obscure, possibly ancient wheat variety around in much the same way gardeners maintain strains of heirloom tomato.

RYE

Rye has long grown in parts of northern and eastern Europe where the growing season is too short for much success with wheat farming. It can be blended with a lot of white flour to create breads with a grayish crumb and relatively light interior, or it can form the majority flour in a formula and produce loaves with greater density and an earthy aroma. It has just a tiny bit of gluten—practically none—and the rest of its endosperm is so different from wheat that the doughs made from rye have a set of mixing, shaping, and handling requirements all their own. See *Chapter 4* for more discussion about these unique requirements.

Rye is commonly marketed in North America as dark, medium, white, or whole rye flour. Coarser choices such as rye chops, rye meal, and pumpernickel are all made from whole rye. Dark rye is milled from the outside of the rye berry, has the darkest color, and is least tolerant to mixing, but it has the deepest flavor. Medium is probably the most commonly available type of rye flour. It has moderate color and decent flavor, and it is comparatively easy to handle. White rye is milled from the center of the rye berry and has the lightest color and least flavor, but is sometimes prized by bakers in large northeastern U.S. cities for use in deli-style rye breads with light color and texture.

VARIETY GRAINS

Almost any other grain can be added to a dough formula. You'll find them marketed by some distributors as whole berries and mixtures of berries (five-grain, nine-grain, etc.), as cracked varieties, as meal, and as flour. Instead of grinding them into flour, many bakers cover dried grains in water overnight and use this *soaker* in their dough the next day. A soaker is a mixture of cracked or whole grains with water that is left to soften for a time before final use. Often the water is boiled just before adding it to the grains. Grains typically utilized this way include corn, rice, barley, oats, wheat berries, rye berries, quinoa, flax, and buckwheat.

Water

It might seem unnecessary to touch on common water as an ingredient, but it has critical effects on dough making. Yeast and bacteria, as all life, cannot thrive without sufficient water. In fact, just adding or subtracting water from a dough or preferment can have profound effects on the rate and type of fermentation. Amylase is an enzyme that is critical to successful fermentation, and it cannot degrade starch into sugars without sufficient water (see *Chapter 5* for more information on water's effects upon yeast, bacterial, and enzyme activity).

The structure of bread dough can also be manipulated by changing its water content. Gluten itself does not form in the absence of water. An excess of water creates an ideal environment for enzyme activity, which weakens the gluten bonds and sometimes creates stickier dough. Also, dry dough tends to be stronger, with a close, cottony crumb, while extra water can ensure a more extensible dough, with large, irregular holes and a chewy texture.

SOURCE OF WATER

Some artisan bakers—often they are home bakers—use only spring water in their dough because they wish to avoid the chlorine or other additives that might seem to make the water less pure. There is no harm in this practice, of course, but it is not a practical solution for most professionals because packaged water is expensive. Most artisan bakers use common tap water and, except in rare cases of contamination of the water source, this is usually fine. Levels of chlorine or other chemicals are not likely to be high enough to negatively affect fermentation, and there are rarely any significant problems in using it. Even so, it's important to note that the mineral content of hard tap water or well water can give dough somewhat greater strength, and those same minerals are actually beneficial to a fermentation. A lack of minerals in soft water tends to lengthen fermentation times and may give dough an unusual level of extensibility.

It is common for professional artisan bakers to install filtration systems for their water supply if they feel their water is too hard or has off flavors, or if they and their customers have strong feelings about the issue of additives in water. A lack of strength from too-soft water in bread dough can be addressed by extending fermentation times or adding sets of folds during the bulk fermentation. (For more on the subject of fermentation and dough strength, see *Chapter 5*.)

Salt

We might assume salt's role in bread making is centered on flavor, but that thinking is shortsighted. Salt can certainly be used to enhance the flavor of other dough ingredients, but its effects on the various dough processes are numerous and must not be overlooked.

TIGHTENS GLUTEN

When salt is added to a dough, it tightens the gluten structure and adds strength. This improves the ability of the dough to capture and hold the carbon dioxide gas from fermentation, and it ensures the loaf will have good volume. Some bakers hold back their salt until the end of the mixing process to avoid making the dough too strong too soon, thereby shortening the overall mixing time. While that technique can shorten your workday by a few minutes, it has side effects that might preclude its use by educated artisans. Salt is a natural antioxidant, and if we subtract salt from a bread dough being mixed at high speed, the rate of oxidation in the dough is dramatically increased. Most of the carotenoid pigments may be destroyed before the salt is added, thereby significantly reducing the flavor and aroma components associated with them.

SLOWS FERMENTATION AND ENZYMES

Even small amounts of salt slow the rate of fermentation and enzyme activity in bread dough and pre-ferments. This is because salt crystals are *hygroscopic*, which means they tend to draw water away from their environment. When salt crystals and yeast cells are competing for the same water, salt wins, which slows yeast's life processes significantly.

Adding small amounts of salt can be useful in avoiding overfermentation in pre-ferments, but the final level of salt in bread dough these days is typically limited to 1.8–2.2% of flour weight, with 2% being the norm. While a lack of salt in dough can lead to a bland flavor profile, anything more than 2.2% is likely to make the bread taste too salty. There should be enough salt in bread to bring out its natural flavors, but there are practical limits to using it to manipulate fermentation and enzyme activity. (For more information on the evolution of salt as an ingredient in bread dough, see p. 21.)

Salt's hygroscopic nature has another important effect on bread. Even after a loaf is baked, the presence of salt tends to maintain its moisture content and thereby discourages staling in dry environments. On the other hand, in humid areas, the salt in bread may absorb water from the atmosphere and promote soft or even soggy crust development.

Salt Is a Recent Addition to Bread Dough

People have known that salt enhances the flavor of foods for thousands of years, but, strangely, salt didn't make its way into many bread recipes until the late seventeenth century. We may never know exactly why, but food historians speculate that, because salt was often a regulated and taxed commodity throughout history, it was too much of an added expense for bakers to use. In any case, if you travel to the regions of Tuscany or Umbria in Italy today, you will still find rustic breads that have little or no salt. Some Middle Eastern flatbreads, as well, leave out the salt, and this practice may reflect their historical origins. Some artisan bakers place a great deal of emphasis on the source of their salt, often insisting it be sea salt. In fact, even salt mined from land-based deposits originated from an era when the entire earth was covered by seawater, so, from at least one perspective, all salt is sea salt. Whether your source for salt is the sea beds of Mediterranean beaches or the bakery aisle of your local supermarket, you might be wise to ensure its crystals are fine in size and easily dissolved.

Some bakers use only sea salt in their dough, either because they like its flavor more or they perceive it to be purer than typical table salt. There are even sea salts with specific geographic origins on the market; these typically command high prices due to the labor involved in extracting them or because of the scarcity of the salt itself.

SOURCE OF SALT

There are certainly some differences in the composition of various salts on the market. Some contain additives (like iodine or anticaking agents) courtesy of the manufacturer, and others contain naturally occurring minerals already bonded to the salt crystals themselves. When they are used in cooking applications, some sea salts seem to impart nuances to the flavor of certain dishes, possibly due to their mineral content, or perhaps because the larger crystal sizes characteristic of some types are easily perceived by the palate. In any case, when salt is used in bread dough, its relatively small quantity within the formula means that any subtle differences in the flavor profile of exotic salts are unlikely to be detected by the customer. There is little or no demonstrated benefit to using more expensive salts to affect dough strength, fermentation, or bread flavor. Even so, some artisan bakers choose to use it because their customers assume sea salt is in some way purer or because the bakers wish to help sustain the work of fellow artisans in the salt business.

If you do choose to use some sort of special salt, you may wish to ensure it comes in a fine crystal. There are table salts and sea salts sold by bakery distributors that are marketed this way. Fine crystals dissolve easily in most doughs, while large crystals must be dissolved separately in the water to be certain no unincorporated crystals remain in the finished dough.

Yeast

Yeasts were among the earliest forms of life on earth. They are considered a type of fungus, although their single-celled nature would seem to lump them with other primitive one-celled organisms that don't fit neatly into defined parts of the plant and animal kingdoms. There are thousands of known species, but there is often just one that concerns us as bread bakers: *saccharomyces cerevisiae*, which prefers to feed on sugars such as glucose, fructose, sucrose, and maltose. While it can feed directly on foods that are high in sugar, such as ripe fruits and vegetables, honey, beets, and cane sugar, it can also feed on sugars converted from plant starch by the enzyme amylase. Yeast cells produce their own enzyme, *zymase*, to help them obtain energy from those sugars, leaving behind the by-products *carbon dioxide* and *alcohol*.

The first fermented bread doughs were inoculated with various wild yeasts, and by saving small portions of that raw dough and feeding it more flour and water, the bakers of antiquity were able to create leavened breads on a regular basis. Wild yeasts are literally everywhere—in the air, on the ground, or almost any place you look. It is speculated that most of the yeast cells in a sourdough starter originated from the outside of the bran layer in wheat berries. If yeasts are not surrounded by food and water, they go into an inactive state that enables them to survive for years without actually dying. When they find an acceptable environment, they are reinvigorated and can resume their life process—commonly known as *fermentation*.

These fungi were the essential engine that powered the leavening process for thousands of years, although, until the late nineteenth century, bakers were unaware of their existence. It was only then that microscopes were available to biologists, who could then gain a more complete understanding of how yeasts feed themselves and increase in number. Commercially produced strains of yeast, grown in and separated from a medium of water and molasses, became available to the baking community not long thereafter. By the 1920s, bread made with this commercial yeast—*saccharomyces cerevisiae*—was sold commonly alongside traditional loaves made from wild sour cultures.

By the 1950s, scientists isolated and successfully cultivated certain strains of saccharomyces cerevisiae that could act faster than others, thereby reducing the time necessary to wait for dough to build up sufficient gas before shaping. Today, there are even more vigorous strains that, unfortunately or not, can be counted on to help bring dough from mixer to bench in less than 15 minutes.

YEAST CLASSIFICATIONS

So-called *fresh yeast* represents, more or less, the first type of yeast that was manufactured for bakers. It can come in a number of forms: *cream yeast* (which is in a liquid state), *crumbled yeast*, and *compressed yeast* (formed into individually wrapped 1- or 2-lb blocks). Its chief advantages are that it dissolves and goes to work quickly and that it survives freezing better than other types. Its biggest disadvantage is that it is highly perishable, with a stated shelf life of only 21 days after manufacture, under refrigerated conditions. At that point, it gradually loses potency until its performance would be described as unpredictable.

Active dry yeast was created to help solve the storage and shelf life limitations of fresh yeast. By surrounding live, active cells with dead cells and removing most of their moisture, yeast manufacturers were able to provide a reliable source of yeast activity that could be kept in sealed packages for a year or more after manufacture. Because most of the water is removed from active dry yeast, you only need to use about half the weight of yeast called for in formulas that specify fresh yeast. Its chief advantage is that it can be stored unopened for at least a year and sometimes two. Another possible plus is that the dead yeast cells in the product produce a type of protein called *glutathione*, which can act as a natural relaxer in bread dough that is otherwise too tight and inextensible. Its chief disadvantage is that it must be resuscitated in 4–5 times its own weight in warm (100–110°F) water, which is then subtracted from the quantity of total water in a bread formula. The time for blooming or proofing the yeast in warm water is around 10 minutes, which can add an inconvenient extra step for bakers in a hurry to complete their production.

Instant dry yeast combines the ease of use of fresh yeast with the convenient storage of active dry yeast. There is no need to dissolve it first in warm water; in fact, the manufacturer prefers that you mix it first with the flour before adding any liquids. The conversion factor versus fresh yeast is even a bit lower. You need to use just 33–40% as much instant yeast as you would fresh yeast in any formula to get a similar rate of fermentation. The storage requirements are the same as for active dry yeast, so you can keep plenty on hand without worrying about a loss in potency.

A subcategory of instant yeast is labeled *osmotolerant yeast*. This has been specially developed to work well in dough formulas that have very little moisture or that feature a large amount of sugar (totaling more than 12% of the weight of the flour). Examples of breads that are often well paired with this yeast are croissants, Danish, and brioche.

Sweeteners

Most sweeteners do much more than sweeten bread. Sugar in all of its forms (table sugar, honey, molasses, and others) is probably added in most cases because of its effect on flavor, but its secondary effects on fermentation and dough strength can make the process of adding any of its forms fairly tricky. While it is true that sugar acts as food for yeast, its hygroscopic nature (see "Salt") draws a lot of moisture from the dough, and, at levels of 12% of flour weight or higher, it ties up so much water that the yeast don't have enough moisture available to maintain their typical rate of fermentation. So, at levels below 12%, sugar can help increase the rate of fermentation, but at higher levels, it actually begins to slow it. To counteract the slowing effect of high sugar levels on fermentation, bakers must use proportionately more yeast in their formulas. It is common to see yeast percentages in very sweet breads that are 2–4 times higher than those of typical unsweetened breads.

At about the same level of concentration (12%), sugar also begins to have a noticeable slackening effect on the dough, leaving it with gradually less strength as quantity is increased. Sugar actually tenderizes bread dough by interfering in the creation of strong gluten bonds. While that tenderizing effect can be desirable at times, truly large amounts of sugar may destabilize bread dough completely, resulting in flat loaves with poor volume. The strategy for combating this effect on dough structure is covered in *Chapter 10*.

Fats and Oils

You may already know that ingredients like butter, margarine, and vegetable oil have a tenderizing effect on bread or pastry dough. Fat literally shortens gluten strands as a dough is mixed. This phenomenon is called the *shortening effect*. If you have experience making pie dough, you may also know that the way you add fat to a dough can have a great effect on its texture. Working butter completely into pie dough creates the shortest or most tender dough, while adding it in larger pieces creates a flakier dough. In both cases, fat tends to weaken the dough structure considerably, and, while this is desirable in pie or tart dough, it usually isn't when mixing bread dough. We love the flavor and silky texture fats can bring to bread, but we generally still want yeasted breads to have height and a reasonably light texture. Strategies for incorporating large amounts of fat into a dough while preserving dough strength are discussed more fully in *Chapter 10*.

Butter clearly has better flavor than most other solid fats, such as margarine and vegetable shortening. It also melts easily on the palate (unlike shortening), so it feels more pleasant in the mouth. It is also quite expensive. Still, in most artisan bread applications, butter remains the solid fat of choice. It isn't the easiest one to work with, because its narrow range of plasticity (60–70°F) means you can't spend a lot of time laminating croissant dough. Butter demands that we work quickly and efficiently with it. But we come back to it again and again because its flavor and mouthfeel are far superior to most other solid fats.

Oils are often included in bread dough. You can add interesting aromas and flavor by using fragrant olive oil in a focaccia, or (if you have the budget) you can use more exotic products like walnut oil to add complexity to your loaves. It's also possible to use more neutrally flavored oils like soybean or canola oil to add a bit of tenderness to a bread crumb, as we typically see with challah.

Milk Products

Fresh milk is only 85–88% water, so you shouldn't simply substitute it on a one-to-one basis with water when designing a dough formula. Whole milk and many cheeses contain some butterfat, so, like butter, they can have some small tenderizing effect on bread dough. It is more common for large bakeries (including many artisan bakeries) to use dried nonfat milk because it is less perishable than fresh milk, takes up less space in the bakery, and doesn't require refrigeration. Milk contains the same destructive protein as dead yeast (glutathione) that can degrade gluten strength in dough, so treating milk to deactivate glutathione is often recommended before using it in bread dough. *High-heat dried milk* is heated to 190°F before drying and packaging, and its glutathione is thereby deactivated. Neither fresh milk nor any other form of dried milk can make the same claim, so scalding them to over 180°F may be advisable if you need to avoid the relaxing effects of glutathione.

Milk also contains important solids like lactose (milk sugar) and some proteins. The proteins in milk can accentuate a browning process that's present in baking all breads, called the *Maillard process*. This is discussed in greater detail in *Chapter 8*.

Eggs

Whole eggs are about 75% water, so, as with milk, bakers must be careful not to simply substitute one for the other. Whole eggs are net tougheners, which means that, although the yolk contains fat, enough proteins are present in eggs to more than compensate for any tenderizing effects in the yolk.

ADD STRENGTH

Whole eggs typically are included in a bread formula to add strength to dough, together with a bit of color and flavor. If strength is all you want, then egg whites may be added alone, or you can use separated egg yolks to add richness and color to the bread crumb. Whole eggs and egg yolks are also useful in another way—as emulsifiers. Lecithin is a natural emulsifier in egg yolks that holds added fat in suspension with the moisture in dough. This is especially important in high-fat breads like brioche.

EGG OPTIONS

Many artisan bakers prefer to use whole shell eggs, as they contain no additives and fit comfortably within a product lineup that focuses upon natural ingredients.

However, many bakers, artisan or not, choose frozen or refrigerated pasteurized egg products because of their ease of use, their smaller storage requirements, or because pasteurized egg products are less liable to harbor harmful microorganisms. It is difficult to generalize about the comparative performance characteristics of fresh eggs and pasteurized eggs in bread dough. There can be obvious differences in using either of them with pastry or confections—many of the differences have to do with flavor—but bakers who use pasteurized egg in bread feel its performance is comparable to that of fresh eggs. The pasteurized products do seem to function well in providing structure and emulsifying properties to dough, and their presence in dough seems less obvious than it would in a custard or meringue. If you need to mix 200 lb or more of challah dough, the prospect of shelling hundreds of eggs by hand may influence your decision.

Nuts, Seeds, Grains, and Dried Fruits

Raisins are probably the most commonly used dried fruit when making bread. Black raisins of various sizes seem to dominate, but golden raisins such as sultanas can add extra sweetness and subtle complexity if you choose to use them, either by themselves or as part of a mixture. Some bakers soak raisins in water or some other liquid to plump them before use, and others just add them to dough as they are. In either case, add raisins toward the end of the mixing time when you have already achieved the gluten development you wish. They should be added on first speed only to ensure as little breakage as possible. Other options for dried fruit include apples, apricots, cranberries, figs, dates, or just about any other dehydrated fruit you can find. Pay attention to additives (such as preservatives or sweeteners) used to maintain their color or make them less tart.

Nuts usually are at their best as a bread ingredient when they are toasted first to enhance their aromas. Walnuts, almonds, pecans, and hazelnuts are often prepared this way. Some seeds, such as sunflower or sesame, can be treated the same way. There is really no limit to which seeds can be used, but the most common are probably sesame, poppy, caraway, sunflower, flaxseed, and fennel (though a little bit there goes a long way). It might be fair to say that dry seeds and nuts are best added to bread dough toward the end of the mix, as with raisins, on first speed only. You might find that when adding raisins and nuts to the same dough, the chance of breaking the raisins is lower if you add the nuts first and incorporate them for a few seconds, and then follow with the raisins.

Using Whole Grains

If whole cereal grains (or even cracked grains) are used in dough, they are often soaked in water to cover overnight. The quantity of water is generally completely absorbed by the grains. This grain-and-water mix is called a *soaker*, and any water calculated to be added to the soaker itself is considered separately from the water used to hydrate the flour in bread dough. Some formulas call for a soaker to be added at the start of the mixing process, while others ask you to wait until the end of mixing to minimize any weakening effect the soaker may have on dough structure.

ARTISAN BAKER PROFILE

Thom Leonard

WheatFields, Lawrence, Kansas

Artisan bread baking became a national phenomenon in the early 1990s, but certain pioneers of the craft's revival in the United States were already working at making great bread as far back as the 1970s and 1980s.

Thom Leonard is one of those people, and he has been baking hand-shaped breads professionally since 1973. He might be described as a Renaissance man among artisan bakers, as he is equally knowledgeable about such diverse subjects as farming, flour milling, miso production, and writing. In particular, his knowledge of wheat equals that of a cereal chemist. He authored *The Bread Book* (East West Health Books, 1990), which describes how to grow your own wheat, mill it, and turn it into bread that is truly your own. (Thom's favorite strain of wheat is an heirloom variety called Turkey Red.) He has also written many articles on bread making and gardening for various journals.

He started baking professionally in 1973, but his acquaintance with European-style bread making mostly occurred at the Baldwin Hill Bakery in central Massachusetts, where he worked in the early 1980s. It was there he became acquainted firsthand with the natural leavening techniques he would use in making whole wheat pain au levain in a wood-fired oven. Thom's commitment to all-natural bread baking represents just one facet of what for him is a desire to lead an entirely sustainable lifestyle.

He is unusual, perhaps, in his equal appreciation of two sometimes divergent schools of thought in French bread baking principles. One was exemplified by Professor Raymond Calvel, who focused on the citified, all-white French baguette, and the other was championed by Lionel Poilane, who only made rustic country-style loaves from high-extraction flours and didn't sell baguettes at all.

Thom has been the owner and operator of several bakeries, and he is now the general manager and head baker at WheatFields, which he cofounded in Lawrence, Kansas, in 1995. There he sells breads based on both artisan schools of thought, including well-crafted baguettes and expertly made multigrain pain au levain.

IMPRESSIONS OF ARTISAN BREAD BAKING AS AN INDUSTRY

Can we define artisan bread? If so, what makes it distinctive, in your opinion?

I don't really like the term *artisan bread*. A baker may be an artisan, but the bread made by him or her is not; perhaps *artisanal* would be the correct adjective. An artisan is one who does skilled work with the hands. In today's world of marketing catchphrases, no matter what we decide it means, someone else will define it differently to meet their needs.

Did you have any preconceptions about the artisanal bread business (or any aspect of the bread business) that were altered by your later experience?

I could not have imagined that there would be nationally distributed artisanal bread that rivaled or surpassed the quality of much of the locally produced bread or that this would be the main competition.

What would you say are the philosophical underpinnings of your bakery?

We use only certified organic flour from a farmer-owned and -operated mill, and we bake our bread in a wood-fired oven.

What are your thoughts on prospective artisan bakers? What characteristics or personality traits do you look for in prospective employees that will increase their potential for hire? Are there any traits that might exclude them?

Methodical orderliness wins lots of points. A degree in baking arts from an established culinary program shows commitment. Lack of attention to personal hygiene and grooming gets negative points.

Do you have any pearls of wisdom for the bakery and pastry students reading this book?

Stay focused on the basics. Understand the process; practice the skills; go to bed early.

Herbs and Spices

You can use your favorite herb when making bread. Fresh varieties are likely to do a better job here than dried ones, although some dried herbs, like rosemary and oregano, can be substituted if need be. For some herbs, such as basil, the fresh version is really all that will do. When you run out of fresh basil it's best, perhaps, to use no basil at all. In any case, when to add the herbs is really up to the baker. Adding them early in the mixing process is no problem if you don't mind some green color in your dough; adding them toward the end of the mix is fine as well. Using olive oil in conjunction with herbs is common but optional. One caveat might be appropriate here: Be careful which herbs you use together, and use discretion when adding them, as a subtle addition can be more pleasing than overdoing it.

We can't generalize too much about using spices, as they're all different from one another, but exercising caution in both the quantity used and the timing of addition may be warranted. Cinnamon is used commonly in sweet breads, but it has a destructive effect on yeast, so adding it directly to dough can be risky. Making a paste or smear out of sugar, butter, and cinnamon and using it as a filling helps avoid the dangers of adding cinnamon to the dough itself. Small quantities of nutmeg and cardamom can be found in some formulas for Danish dough, where they seem to cause no problem at all.

Summary

While bread can be as simple as a mixture of flour and water, other ingredients can add nuances of taste or texture that make it more appealing. When using other ingredients, though, keep in mind that each addition can complicate how the entire dough will perform during mixing, fermentation, shaping, and baking. The most important ingredient choice is the type of flour. Wheat flour must be chosen for leavened breads, but other grains and even legumes are milled and used to make traditional favorites that aren't leavened at all.

Key Terms

Neolithic man	autolyse
primary effect	spelt
secondary effect	farro
fermentation	miche
wheat berry	rye
germ	soaker
bran	hygroscopic
whole wheat flour	zymase
wheat bran	carbon dioxide
endosperm	alcohol
pentosans	fresh yeast
gluten	cream yeast
hard wheat	crumbled yeast
soft wheat	compressed yeast
red wheat	active dry yeast
white wheat	glutathione
spring wheat	instant dry yeast
winter wheat	osmotolerant yeast
durum	shortening effect
semolina	high-heat dried milk
durum flour	Maillard process
beta carotene	

Questions for Review

1. What are the only two essential ingredients necessary to make bread?

2. What quality makes wheat unique among cereal grains?

3. What are the three basic parts of the wheat berry?

4. What part of the wheat berry accounts for most of its mass?

5. What two basic proteins unite to form gluten?

6. How is hard wheat different from soft wheat?

7. Describe the effect of salt on fermentation.

8. Describe the complex effect of sugar on fermentation.

9. Which type of yeast is more perishable, compressed yeast or instant dry yeast?

10. Whole eggs have both fat and proteins in their makeup. Are they considered net tougheners or net tenderizers when viewed in terms of dough strength?

Questions for Discussion

1. Using organic flour in artisan bread baking is becoming increasingly common. Why do you think bakers and their customers are willing to pay more for flour that performs similarly to the type that is not certified organic?

2. Do you use sea salt when you cook? when you bake? You might already know that sea salt can cost 10–15 times as much as plain baker's salt. Do you think the extra cost can be justified from a business standpoint?

3. Do you think customers are willing to pay more for baked products that feature expensive ingredients and a lot of manual labor?

Lab Exercise & Experiment

*I*n the *Appendix of Formulas* there are two versions of the formula for challah—one is less sweet (normal), while the other is more so. If you make a small batch of each type, you will probably notice differences in fermentation rate, extensibility, the feel of the dough, proofing time, final volume, and the definition of the braids.

Note that, because the sugar level is higher in the sweeter version, the recommended bake temperature for those loaves is about 10 degrees lower than for the "normal" challah (a discussion on why this is so is located in *Chapter 8*). If you wish to see the noticeable effect on the rate of browning when sugar levels are increased, you may bake both types of challah at the higher temperature, but the sweeter loaves will brown more quickly, and they might not be completely baked at their centers when the loaf has browned completely. You may wish to bake some of the sweeter ones at the higher temperature and the remaining sweeter loaves at the recommended lower temperature to highlight the significant differences brought about by simply changing the sugar levels by a few percentage points. (A fuller explanation of the use of percentage relationships in expressing ingredient quantities is included in *Chapter 3*.)

1. Describe any noticeable differences, record them, and determine why they occurred.

2. You may decide that, while you like the flavor of one type, you prefer the looks or handling characteristics of the other. Are the side effects that take place when we alter a single ingredient inevitable, or are there strategies we can sometimes use to minimize them?

CHALLAH (NORMAL)

STRAIGHT DOUGH	Metric		U.S. Measure		Formula Baker's %
	(1X)	(4X)	(1X)	(4X)	
	5-Qt Mixer	20-Qt Mixer	5-Qt Mixer	20-Qt Mixer	
Bread flour	650g	2600g	1 lb 6.0oz	5 lb 8.0oz	65%
High-gluten flour	350g	1400g	12.0oz	3 lb 0.0oz	35%
Water	330g	1320g	11.2oz	2 lb 12.9oz	33%
Whole eggs	150g	600g	5.1oz	1 lb 4.4oz	15%
Egg yolks	60g	240g	2.0oz	8.2oz	6%
Vegetable oil	80g	320g	2.7oz	10.9oz	8%
Sugar	70g	280g	2.4oz	9.5oz	7%
Salt	20g	80g	0.7oz	2.7oz	2%
Instant yeast	7g	28g	0.2oz	0.95oz	1%
TOTAL YIELD	**1717g**	**6868g**	**3 lb 10.4oz**	**14 lb 9.5oz**	

NOTE: The yeast quantity listed in the formula is intended for bakers who use the short mix method. A dough mixed with the intensive mix method should receive a yeast percentage around 0.7%, while the yeast percentage for an improved mix dough would be more appropriately set at 0.4%.

GOAL TEMPERATURE: 77°F (25°C). You may have to use water as cold as possible to arrive anywhere close to the goal temperature. See directions for calculating correct water temperature in *Chapter 4*.

MIXING METHOD: Choose the intensive mix method (p. 196), but be careful not to overmix or overheat the dough. If the dough is too warm after mixing, cover tightly and hold in a refrigerator until it cools sufficiently.

FERMENTATION: 45–60 minutes.

SCALING: Scale all your strands first and then roll them all, or have a team work on scaling and rolling strands simultaneously, braiding loaves as they go.

1. Four-strand loaf—6 oz (170 g) per strand.
2. Three-strand loaf—8 oz (225 g) per strand.
3. Knotted rolls, 1½–3 oz (45–85 g) per small strand.

SHAPING:

1. Drawings that demonstrate braiding techniques are in *Chapter 6* on pp. 96–99.

2. Three loaves per parchment-covered full sheet tray is recommended, spaced evenly on the tray. Egg-wash loaves immediately both after panning and then just before going into the oven to get a superb shine.

PROOFING: 60–75 minutes at 80°F and 80% humidity. Allow space for growth during proofing between trays on the rack.

BAKING:

1. 350–375°F (175–190°C), or even less if premature browning is an issue; 25–40°F less for rack or convection ovens.

2. When ready (see *Chapter 7*), load the trays into the oven. No scoring is necessary, and no steam should be used, but remember to egg-wash the loaves a second time just before baking them.

3. You may wish to double-pan the loaves if you are baking in a deck oven—too much bottom heat can cause excessive browning on the bottoms of the loaves.

COOLING: Cool (without crowding the loaves) on a rack with wire shelves.

CHALLAH (SWEET)

| STRAIGHT DOUGH | Metric | | U.S. Measure | | Formula Baker's % |
| | (1X) | (4X) | (1X) | (4X) | |
	5-Qt Mixer	20-Qt Mixer	5-Qt Mixer	20-Qt Mixer	
Bread flour	650g	2600g	1 lb 6.0oz	5 lb 8.0oz	65%
High-gluten flour	350g	1400g	12.0oz	3 lb 0.0oz	35%
Water	330g	1320g	11.2oz	2 lb 12.9oz	33%
Whole eggs	150g	600g	5.1oz	1 lb 4.4oz	15%
Egg yolks	60g	240g	2.0oz	8.2oz	6%
Vegetable oil	80g	320g	2.7oz	10.9oz	8%
Sugar	120g	480g	4.1oz	1 lb 0.3oz	12%
Salt	20g	80g	0.7oz	2.7oz	2%
Instant yeast	7g	28g	0.2oz	0.95oz	1%
TOTAL YIELD	**1767g**	**7068g**	**3 lb 12.1oz**	**15 lb 0.3oz**	

NOTE: The yeast quantity listed in the formula is intended for bakers who use the short mix method. A dough mixed with the intensive mix method should receive a yeast percentage around 0.7%, while the yeast percentage for an improved mix dough would be more appropriately set at 0.4%.

GOAL TEMPERATURE: 77°F (25°C). You may have to use water as cold as possible to arrive anywhere close to the goal temperature. See directions for calculating correct water temperature in *Chapter 4*.

MIXING METHOD: Choose the intensive mix method (p. 196), but be careful not to overmix or overheat the dough. If the dough is too warm after mixing, cover tightly and hold in a refrigerator until it cools sufficiently.

FERMENTATION: 45–60 minutes.

SCALING: Scale all your strands first and then roll them all, or have a team work on scaling and rolling strands simultaneously, braiding loaves as they go.

1. Four-strand loaf—6 oz (170 g) per strand.
2. Three-strand loaf—8 oz (225 g) per strand.
3. Knotted rolls, 1½–3 oz (45–85 g) per small strand.

SHAPING:

1. Drawings that demonstrate braiding techniques are in *Chapter 6* on pp. 96–99.

2. Three loaves per parchment-covered full sheet tray is recommended, spaced evenly on the tray. Egg-wash loaves immediately both after panning and then just before going into the oven to get a superb shine.

PROOFING: 75–90 minutes or sometimes longer at 80°F and 80% humidity. Allow space for growth during proofing between trays on the rack.

BAKING:

1. 330–350°F (165–176°C) or even less if premature browning is an issue; 25–40°F less for rack or convection ovens.

2. When ready (see *Chapter 7*), load the trays into the oven. No scoring is necessary, and no steam should be used, but remember to egg-wash the loaves a second time just before baking them.

3. You may wish to double-pan the loaves if you are baking in a deck oven—too much bottom heat can cause excessive browning on the bottoms of the loaves.

COOLING: Cool (without crowding the loaves) on a rack with wire shelves.

chapter **3**

Basic Baker's Percentage (Baker's Math)

Learning Outcomes:

- Understand how a formula expressed in percentage relationships instead of ingredient weights can offer a likely snapshot of the fermentation, flavor, texture, and handling characteristics of a given dough.

- Resize formulas using the same percentage ingredient relationships.

- Recognize typical amounts (expressed in percentages) of salt and yeast in bread dough.

- Recognize typical hydration rates, expressed as percentages.

- Understand how to use percentage expressions of ingredients in a formula to describe a bread dough to a fellow baker.

An International Language for Bakers

Statistics show that even though culinary students work with math every day, many dislike it.

Still, common tasks like looking at the clock, paying your bills, and figuring out how much fuel is left in your gas tank all require math. While you aren't using advanced math for these calculations, you are performing basic calculations. These basic calculations are the foundation for *applied math*. You use applied math continually throughout life as a practical tool for organizing your daily routines so you have more control over how everything turns out.

That is essentially why bakery managers and pastry chefs use what's called *baker's percentage* (or *baker's math*). You may realize by now that making bread successfully on a consistent basis is a more complicated and precise process than you had imagined. Baking always presents unpredictable challenges, but by mastering baker's percentage you can help yourself gain control over much of what is happening in your daily production. For instance, it can:

1. Give you an immediate, numeric snapshot of how wet your dough will be, the texture it will have, how it will handle at the bench, how it will ferment over time, and even how it will probably taste.

2. Help you troubleshoot problems in product quality by zeroing in on abnormalities that may be apparent.

3. Aid you in designing formulas that are in balance, with less guesswork or trial and error involved.

4. Enable you to fix scaling errors by changing batch sizes when necessary to maintain a formula's proper ingredient ratios.

5. Allow you to customize batch sizes to get close to the minimum dough you need and avoid unnecessary waste.

6. Provide a common language for discussing bread formulas with other bakers in a concise, easily readable form.

It's All in the Percentages

Look at the two formulas for a *straight dough* presented in Table 3.1. (A straight dough is a dough mixed using no pre-ferments or starters. For more about what defines a straight dough, see *Chapter 5*.) Each has the same list of ingredients, but the quantity of individual ingredients used and the total weight for each dough are very different.

One of the formulas in Table 3.1 is for making French baguette dough, and the other is for making an Italian-style ciabatta dough. Even though each of these classic breads has the same ingredients, the quantities for each ingredient are different. It mostly comes down to the water level in each one—ciabatta dough is generally wetter than baguette dough. Can you tell with just one look at these ingredient lists which dough is which?

TABLE 3.1 Two Formulas for Straight Dough

DOUGH #1		DOUGH #2	
INGREDIENTS	Weight (g)	INGREDIENTS	Weight (g)
Bread flour	1377	Bread flour	2156
Water	1060	Water	1488
Salt	28	Salt	54
Instant yeast	10	Instant yeast	12
TOTAL BATCH	2475g	TOTAL BATCH	3710g

You probably can't (at least not in a glance), because the list of weights, without any interpretation, doesn't tell you very much. You may have had the instinct (correct, in this case) to mentally divide the weight of the water in each formula by the weight of its flour, to assess quickly which dough is wetter. The answer to your calculation would be expressed as a decimal and represent the *fraction* or *proportion* of the flour weight that was represented by the water weight. This water level in a dough is referred to as its *hydration rate*. If the hydration rate for one of these formulas is higher than for the other, the formula with the higher hydration rate must be for ciabatta, which we already said would be wetter.

Technically, we can leave the hydration rate expressed as a decimal, but it is more useful when analyzing a formula to convert the decimal to a percentage. To do that, simply multiply the decimal by 100 and add a percentage sign. For example, if we divide the water weight of Dough #1 by its flour weight, we could express it using the equation below:

$$1,060\text{g water} \div 1,377\text{g bread flour} = 0.7697893 = 0.77 \text{ (rounded)}$$
$$0.77 \times 100 = 77\%$$

The hydration level for Dough #1, then, is 0.77, which can also be more usefully expressed as 77%.

Look at the identical formulas in Table 3.2, where we've divided the water weight by the flour weight in each and expressed the percentage answers next to the weights themselves. We've also expressed the weight of bread flour in each formula as 100%, as that is the standard being measured against the water weight in each formula.

TABLE 3.2 Weight versus Percentage of Ingredients in Formulas

DOUGH #1			DOUGH #2		
INGREDIENTS	Weight (g)	%	INGREDIENTS	Weight (g)	%
Bread flour	1377	100%	Bread flour	2156	100%
Water	1060	77%	Water	1488	69%
Salt	28		Salt	54	
Instant yeast	10		Instant yeast	12	
TOTAL BATCH	2475g		TOTAL BATCH	3710g	

We can see the hydration rate for Dough #1 is 77%, which is greater than that for Dough #2, at 69%. Because ciabatta is wetter than baguette dough, the ciabatta formula must be Dough #1.

It can also be useful to express the weights of the salt and the yeast as percentages of the flour weight, as they tend to fall within certain narrow ranges, and the percentages can quickly alert you as to whether or not these formulas have suitable salt and yeast quantities. So we'll calculate those percentages as well, and list them in Table 3.3.

DOUGH #1
28g salt ÷ 1,377g bread flour = 0.020334 = 0.02 (rounded)
0.02 × 100 = 2%

10g yeast ÷ 1,377g bread flour = 0.0072621 = 0.007 (rounded)
0.007 × 100 = 0.7%

DOUGH #2
54g salt ÷ 2,156g bread flour = 0.0250463 = 0.025 (rounded)
0.025 × 100 = 2.5%

12g yeast ÷ 2,156g bread flour = 0.0055658 = 0.006 (rounded)
0.006 × 100 = 0.6%

TABLE 3.3 Calculating Percentages of Salt and Yeast Quantities in Formulas

DOUGH #1 CIABATTA			DOUGH #2 BAGUETTE		
INGREDIENTS	Weight (g)	%	INGREDIENTS	Weight (g)	%
Bread flour	1377	100%	Bread flour	2156	100%
Water	1060	77%	Water	1488	69%
Salt	28	2%	Salt	54	2.5%
Instant yeast	10	0.7%	Instant yeast	12	0.6%
TOTAL BATCH	2475g		TOTAL BATCH	3710g	

Note that in Dough #2 (the baguette), the percentage of salt is higher than in Dough #1 (the ciabatta). The percentage of salt in a bread formula is usually 1.8–2.2%, with 2% salt being the most common for breads today. The level of salt in Dough #2 is 2.5%, and even though just a 0.5% difference might not be considered critical when we're analyzing water or flour levels, it is a significant difference when we're talking about either salt or yeast.

The amount of salt or yeast in dough may seem tiny, but that is precisely because it doesn't require much salt or yeast to make a big difference in your dough. Changes of even 0.1% or 0.2% in their level can be noticeable in the rate of fermentation or in the taste of the final loaves, so staying within recommended ranges is probably wise. The baguette dough (Dough #2) would be noticeably salty when compared to the ciabatta dough (Dough #1), so an adjustment down to 2–2.2% is probably to be recommended.

To adjust the salt in the baguette dough, we could calculate 2% of 2,156g flour, which is 43g (rounded), and then substitute that for the 54g salt already listed, which is too high to keep the dough formula in balance. If we had not calculated the percentage levels of salt in those two formulas, we would never have known the baguette dough needed adjustment.

Note that the yeast *percentage* in the baguette dough is smaller than that for the ciabatta dough (0.6% versus 0.7%), even though the actual weight of yeast in the baguette dough is greater (12g versus 10g). The baguette dough, because it has the lower percentage of yeast, will almost certainly ferment more slowly than the ciabatta.

It isn't the actual weight of salt or yeast that matters so much when you're comparing two formulas—the *percentage* content is what truly matters. The dough with the greater *percentage* of yeast in its formula will be the one that ferments faster. If we had not calculated the percentage levels of yeast in those two formulas, we would never have known which dough was likely to ferment faster. When you're determining the sequence of production for any baking day, knowing which breads are likely to ferment fastest can be the difference between having a smooth production or surviving a stressful one.

Changing Batch Sizes

Some bakeries will precalculate the correct weights of ingredients to use in formulas and print them in a manual the mixer uses when calculating how much dough is needed to fill orders. The pages in the manual often feature formulas that look like the ones in Table 3.4.

TABLE 3.4 Sample of Correct Weights of Ingredients to Be Used in Formulas

BAGUETTE DOUGH					
BATCH SIZE YIELD (@375G)	1X 18 LVS	1.5X 26 LVS	2X 36 LVS	2.5X 44 LVS	3X 54 LVS
Bread flour	4000g	6000g	8000g	10000g	12000g
Water	2720g	4080g	5440g	6800g	8160g
Salt	80g	120g	160g	2000g	240g
Instant yeast	28g	42g	56g	70g	84g

The person operating the mixer can certainly use these generic batch sizes, and the dough should turn out as expected nearly every time. If orders for baguettes on a given day total only 45 loaves, however, should the mixer make the 2.5X batch and short an order to prevent waste, or go ahead and make the 3X batch to get 54 loaves?

It's true there is almost always some scaling error when bakers divide dough at the bench, so a little extra dough is fine, but technically, that's almost 9 more loaves in dough than the bakery will get paid for baguettes that day, which can really add up through the day and into the week.

If the bakery mixes 9 batches of other dough that day of similar size and round that far up to cover the orders, the result could easily be 70 or 80 loaves more than can be sold. That's almost 15% of production headed for the dumpster before any bread even goes out on delivery!

This sort of batch sizing is common in bakeries, but if you are familiar with using baker's percentage, you can get much closer to the exact size batch of each variety you need every day. This gives you a real advantage in controlling your food cost and ensuring your bakery's profit margins. (It also helps you keep your job or even argue for a pay raise!)

DETERMINE THE BATCH SIZE YOU NEED

To get a more precise formula that matches the size of the order you need to fill, first calculate the total weight of dough you would need to make exactly the number of loaves specified in your order. For instance, if the total number of baguettes ordered for a given day is 75, and baguettes are scaled at 375 grams, multiply those two numbers to determine the total weight needed:

75 baguettes × 375g per baguette = 28,125g dough

You could theoretically just use that weight to calculate your formula, but that would require your bench crew to cut at precisely 375 grams for every baguette piece they portion. You probably realize this is impossible if they are to move through portioning quickly. For practical reasons, then, you might realistically expect about 5% cutting loss, and it is a good idea to go ahead and add 5% (or whatever your typical cutting loss may be) to the size of your batch to allow for this inevitable margin of error. So by adding 5% to the weight of the previous batch size, you get:

28,125g dough × 105% = 28,125 × 1.05 = 29,532g dough (rounded up)

To determine the relative percentages of ingredients associated with the baguette dough in Table 3.4, we can start by borrowing the weights for one of the batches listed. It doesn't actually matter which batch we choose, because the percentage relationship of each ingredient weight and its corresponding total flour weight are the same for every batch. We arbitrarily select the 1X batch weights to calculate those percentages, but, again, we could have chosen any one of the columns listed in the table. We have listed the weights and the percentages that should correspond to them in Table 3.5.

TABLE 3.5 The Percentages Listed under Baker's Percentage Are Determined by Dividing the Weight of That Ingredient by the Weight of the Flour Used for That Batch Size

BAGUETTE DOUGH		
INGREDIENTS	Baker's Percentage (%)	Straight Dough Weight (g)
Bread flour	100%	4000
Water	68%	2720
Salt	2%	80
Instant yeast	0.7%	28
TOTALS		6828g

For example:

$$4{,}000g \div 4{,}000g = 1.00 = 100\%$$

$$2{,}720g \div 4{,}000g = 0.68 = 68\%$$

$$80 \div 4{,}000 = 0.02 = 2\%$$

$$28 \div 4{,}000 = .007 = 0.7\%$$

Find the Total Flour Weight: Using the *Percentage Sum*

No matter what size batch we wish to make, if we want to make the same dough, the percentage relationship between its ingredients will not change. So we can use the same percentages listed for the 1X batch size (6,828g) and apply them in a

TABLE 3.6 Percentages for Larger Batch Size

BAGUETTE DOUGH		
INGREDIENTS	Baker's Percentage (%)	Straight Dough Weight (g)
Bread flour	100%	?
Water	68%	?
Salt	2%	?
Instant yeast	0.7%	?
TOTALS	170.7%	29532g

customized batch meant to get the size we need (29,532g) with little unnecessary scrap dough. We have filled in those percentages along with the larger batch size in Table 3.6.

Notice we have also totaled the percentages listed in the table. If you divide your desired batch size by the sum of the ingredient percentages in any formula, you will arrive at the weight of total flour required for that batch size. *Total flour* refers to the total weight of flour required for a formula, whether you use one type of flour or more than one. For example:

29, 532g dough ÷ 170.7% = 29,532 ÷ 1.707 = 17,301g total flour (rounded up)

For the sake of brevity, we refer to the sum of the ingredient percentages in any formula as the *percentage sum*. This concept is referenced frequently when using baker's percentage in this book, so it should be well highlighted and reviewed often. In the totals line, in the Baker's Percentage column in Table 3.6, the percentage sum is 170.7%, or 1.707 expressed as a decimal number.

FINDING THE REMAINING WEIGHTS

If we then take the weight of flour obtained in the previous calculation and insert it on the bread flour line in Table 3.6, we can multiply that number by each of the remaining ingredient percentages, one after the other, to find the weight for the larger batch we need. For example:

17,301g flour × 68% = 17,301 × 0.68 = 11,765g water (rounded up)

17,301g flour × 2% = 17,301 × 0.02 = 346g salt (rounded down)

17,301g flour × 0.7% = 17,301 × 0.007 = 121g instant yeast (rounded down)

The resulting ingredient weights are posted in Table 3.7. This is the list of ingredient weights that will give us the batch size we need.

TABLE 3.7 List of Ingredient Weights for Particular Batch Size

BAGUETTE DOUGH		
INGREDIENTS	Baker's Percentage (%)	Straight Dough Weight (g)
Bread flour	100%	17301
Water	68%	11765
Salt	2%	346
Instant yeast	0.7%	121
TOTALS	170.7%	29533g

Discrepancies in Batch Size

Notice the total weight listed in Table 3.7 is 1g higher than for that listed in Table 3.6. Because we round the weights listed to the nearest gram, we occasionally obtain minute differences between the total weight we were aiming for and the actual sum of the individual weights listed in the formula. As long as the extra (or missing) gram is associated with the flour or water weight listed (and it is), this will not make a significant difference in the characteristics of the dough you are making.

The total weight above, for illustration, is more than 65 lb in American units, and the 1g discrepancy we find in the calculation represents about 1/28 ounce, or a factor of 0.00003%. More flour than that still clings to your scoop after you measure it, so this is not a quantity worth obsessing about when you make your calculations.

To get as close as possible to the desired batch weight, however, and to minimize the occurrence or size of discrepancies in your calculations, you should never round the percentage sum you use. The total of percentages listed in Table 3.7, for example, is 170.7%. We do convert that to 1.707 when we calculate our ingredient weights, but we do not round it at all. This keeps discrepancies in the calculations to a minimum and usually prevents them altogether. It is advisable and convenient, though, to round all your ingredient weights to the nearest gram where practical. The weight of a gram is so minuscule that, in the case of mixing most bread dough, fractions of a gram should usually just be rounded up or down.

One exception to this principle is when you are making a very small amount of pre-ferment (such as poolish or sponge—see *Chapter 5*) and the yeast quantity needed is a fraction of a gram. In that case, even half a gram's difference in yeast could cause too rapid a fermentation, so you should calculate those tiny quantities to the tenth of a gram.

When You Have Two or More Flours

We just illustrated that dividing desired batch size by the percentage sum determines the weight of total flour in your batch. It is important to emphasize that the idea we are referring to here is the *total* flour weight in the formula, a critical distinction when a formula has more than one type of flour. An example of this idea is illustrated in Table 3.8.

The bread dough represented by the formula in Table 3.8 is typically called *pain de campagne*, or (loosely translated) "country bread." It features two flours—white bread flour and rye flour. The method to determine total flour in this batch is the

TABLE 3.8 Determining Total Flour Weight in the Formula

COUNTRY BREAD (*PAIN DE CAMPAGNE*)		
INGREDIENTS	Baker's Percentage (%)	Straight Dough Weight (g)
Bread flour	90%	
Rye flour	10%	
Water	68%	
Salt	2%	
Instant yeast	0.7%	
TOTALS	170.7%	29533g

same as for the baguette dough formula in Table 3.7, but with one additional step. For example:

29,533g (batch size) ÷ 1.707 (percentage sum) = 17,301g (*total* flour)

Because the batch size in Table 3.8 (country bread) is the same as that for Table 3.7 (baguette dough), the total flour for each batch is the same. Still, the amount of bread flour in the country bread is only 90% of the total flour for that batch, so we cannot simply take the weight of total flour for the country bread and plug it into the bread flour box in Table 3.8. We must separately calculate the weight of the bread flour and the rye flour, using the weight of total flour as a starting point.

17,301g (total flour) × 90% = 17,301 × 0.9 = 15,571g *bread flour* (rounded up)

17,301g (total flour) × 10% = 17,301 × 0.1 = 1730g *rye flour* (rounded down)

We can now calculate the remaining ingredient weights for the formula:

17,301g (total flour) × 68% = 11,765g water (rounded up)

17,301g (total flour) × 2% = 346g salt (rounded down)

17,301g (total flour) × 0.7% = 121g instant yeast (rounded down)

Now we can plug the weight for each ingredient into the grid in Table 3.9.

TABLE 3.9 Calculating Ingredient Weights for a Formula

COUNTRY BREAD		
INGREDIENTS	Baker's Percentage (%)	Straight Dough Weight (g)
Bread flour	90%	15571
Rye flour	10%	1730
Water	68%	11765
Salt	2%	346
Instant yeast	0.7%	121
TOTALS	170.7%	29533g

The best way to master the use of baker's percentage in designing bread formulas is to use the technique every day you make dough. The logic of the system will become apparent to you through repeated use.

In the advanced topic on baker's math in the back of this book, we apply what you have learned about analyzing straight doughs with baker's percentage to formulas that use pre-ferments.

Summary

The only way that a single glance at a dough formula can tell you much about a dough's characteristics is if the ingredients contained are expressed as a set of percentage relationships between the flour and each of the remaining ingredients. As long as the relationship between those ingredients does not change, the dough will remain the same no matter what size batch you choose to prepare.

Becoming familiar with the concept of baker's percentage allows a baker to easily resize formulas, catch percentage irregularities in salt or yeast before scaling, adjust water levels precisely, and create formulas that will probably be in balance even before testing. When your formulas are in balance, you can predict their performance and stay in control of your daily production.

Key Terms		
	baker's percentage	*hydration rate*
	baker's math	*total flour*
	straight dough	*percentage sum*

Questions for Review

1. If you want to make the same baguette dough you made yesterday but want a larger batch size, will the percentage relationships between all the ingredients change?

2. What is the typical range for salt content in modern bread dough?

3. What is the typical range for instant yeast content?

4. Which dough will ferment faster—one hydrated at 68% or one hydrated at 74%? Which one is wetter?

chapter 4

Mixing Methods

Learning Outcomes:

- Understand the history and evolution of dough mixing.

- Identify the two most important stages in the dough mixing process.

- Describe the physical changes that occur in dough as it mixes.

- Distinguish among the three basic mechanical mixing methods.

- Recognize the advantages and disadvantages of utilizing an autolyse.

- Identify how hand mixing and machine mixing affect dough characteristics differently.

- Recognize how changing the ingredients in dough helps determine the mixing technique used.

The First 10,000 Years: Hand Mixing

In the late nineteenth century, a French baker's apprentice would have worn himself ragged making bread dough, but it was simple work: Put water in a wooden trough, add flour to thicken the mixture, and set it aside to rest for a while. Then, fold it over and over on itself many, many times.

This procedure was similar to the method successfully employed by Egyptian slaves during the age of the Pharaohs. However, a few things did change: The type of wheat flour used by the early Egyptians was from a different, weaker strain, and milling practices in the 1870s made for less bran in the flour than the French baker's apprentice used. It is also important to note that salt wasn't added to the list of basic ingredients until the late seventeenth century. Still, the essential method for combining all these ingredients into a semisolid mass really hadn't really evolved much from the time of Moses to the nineteenth century.

Two Stages in the Dough Mixing Process

Both the Egyptian slave and the baker's apprentice may have recognized two distinct stages in the process of mixing bread dough from wheat flour. First, we combine the liquid and solid ingredients to form a homogenous mass. During this initial stage, the starch and proteins present in the flour absorb water (or *hydrate*) and begin to adhere to one another in an unorganized way. Then, bonds develop between certain simple proteins that are *insoluble*, which means they will not dissolve in water. These proteins, *glutenin* and *gliadin*, begin to form long, fairly tangled chains. At this point, the dough is a bit lumpy and acts more like a liquid than a solid, and it might seem unlikely it would ever hold a defined shape. To illustrate what the dough looks like at the end of this *incorporation* stage, see Figure 4.1a.

After this first stage, when the hydration of the starches and proteins is complete, we begin to develop the gluten. By simply turning the mass of dough over and over on itself, we are able to coax the pile of tangled proteins and starches into a smoother, more solid mass that results from the gluten strands unwinding and becoming organized into a weblike framework. The rough, thick liquid we had a few minutes ago begins to adhere to itself so well that it looks and feels more like a solid. This split

Figure 4.1a Incorporation of ingredients.

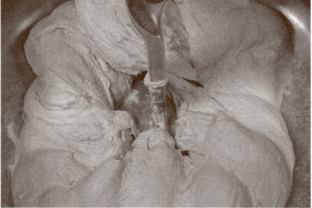

Figure 4.1b Development of gluten.

Tenacity Versus Elasticity

I t is important to distinguish between the terms *tenacity* and *elasticity* in reference to dough because they are not precisely the same, even though their definitions seem to refer to similar qualities. Also, many people mistakenly believe the term *elastic* refers to a substance's ability to be stretched, when it actually describes a quality where, for instance, a baguette that is being stretched seems to retract or snap back *after* it has been extended.

personality exhibited by wheat-based dough is a result of its *viscoelastic* properties. That is to say, bread dough made from wheat flour can exhibit the physical characteristics of both a liquid *and* a solid. Figure 4.1b illustrates how the dough looks after completion of this *development* stage.

Dough Transformation During Mixing

There are some important terms that describe the viscoelastic properties of bread dough. They include *viscosity*, which refers to dough's ability to resist flowing like a liquid, and *elasticity*, which is the tendency for the dough to snap back upon itself after it has been stretched. *Tenacity* describes the tendency for dough to resist flowing or stretching at all. *Extensibility* is what we call the ability of bread dough to be easily stretched without retracting to its original shape. And the term *plasticity* alludes to a seemingly contradictory combination of some of the qualities defined above—it describes any substance's ability to be manipulated and molded into a desired shape, different from its original form, which it holds.

When bakers made bread by hand, the amount of time they spent developing the gluten was determined by the characteristics or viscoelastic properties they wished the dough to achieve. From a more practical standpoint, the time spent might also be limited by the endurance of the baker's back muscles. *Overmixing*, a condition in dough where it has been mixed too long and completely loses its elasticity, would have been almost impossible.

What Does Overmixing Do to Bread Dough?

I f dough is overmixed, the bonds between the gluten-forming proteins begin to break down, and the proper balance that has been achieved between elasticity and extensibility can come undone. Once this happens, dough becomes too extensible, much like taffy, and it loses some of its ability to hold the air that enables it to rise. Figure 4.2 illustrates this concept.

While the nineteenth-century apprentice mixed all his dough by hand, the practice of mechanical mixing was imminent. Eventually, the evolution of mechanical mixing altered the baker's profession irrevocably. Powered mixers were widely adopted because of the work they helped save and because of the improvements in quality of life they allowed. It is also important to note that the mechanization of the dough mixing process affected the bread baking culture in ways that were not anticipated. In retrospect, this impact was not always to the benefit of bread baking as a craft.

Figure 4.2 Overmixed dough. Courtesy of French Baking Machines (FBM).

Precursors to Mechanized Mixing

In the late nineteenth and early twentieth century, four major developments converged and significantly influenced the emergence of mechanized mixing. The first of the four developments was more effective milling machinery that could produce greater quantities of white flour with gradually less bran. The second was the commercial availability of faster-fermenting types of yeast. The third was the increasing availability of electricity for powering the new dough mixing machines. The fourth was the

French government's continued practice of regulating the price of bread. As the costs of rent, flour, and labor would rise, bakery owners were not allowed to recoup their higher costs through higher bread prices. The financial pressure to make more bread with less expense pushed bakers to embrace mechanization as their personal salvation, thereby helping them keep their bake shops afloat.

Mechanization Arrives: The Short Mix Method

The first large-scale promotion of French mechanical mixers was at the Universal Exposition of 1867 in Paris. They were steam driven, and, because bakers of the era didn't find them practical, they were not widely accepted. By the early 1920s, though, electric power was becoming commonly available, and the first electric mixers began to be widely adopted. They were not fast, but they were convenient to use and saved a great deal of manual labor, so their wider acceptance within the profession made sense.

One popular type of early electric mixer was the two-armed mixer. It mixed gently and slowly, essentially mimicking the motion of hand mixing. Because the agitation was gentle, the resulting dough was fairly close in characteristics to that produced completely by hand.

The dough formula used with these early mixers was similar to that used for hand mixing in that it was very wet and designed to undergo 4 or 5 sets of folds before the dough would be strong and easy to handle. Because of this, the first widely adopted electric mixers may not have saved much production time. Their advantage was rather that they accomplished most of the dough's incorporation of ingredients and some of the gluten development while saving the baker from what had previously been an exhausting and tedious task. The mixing technique associated with this first style of machine later came to be known variously as the *short mix*, the slow mix, or the traditional method and featured 12 to 15 minutes at low speed. One type of early mechanical mixer is pictured in Figure 4.3.

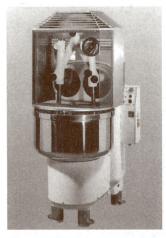

Figure 4.3 A modern version of a fairly old design: the two-armed mixer.

Intensive Mix Method

More powerful mixers emerged by the mid-1950s and were gradually adopted within the French baking community (see Figure 4.4). Because these mixers had two or even three speeds, the development of the dough's gluten could be achieved more rapidly and completely right in the mixer bowl, without need for long periods of bulk fermentation. During a dough's bulk fermentation, it achieves *maturity*, where a balance of viscoelastic properties such as elasticity and extensibility are created and provide for ease of dough handling. Gluten strands that were previously knotted and underdeveloped align themselves into a smoother, stronger dough. This dough maturity can happen almost passively over time, with possibly 4 or 5 sets of punches and folds contributing to the realignment of the gluten, but that takes at least 4–5 hours to complete.

Mechanically mixing the dough for longer periods on high speed can accomplish a similar realignment with no need for long fermentation to finish the job. Instead of waiting 4–5 hours for a traditionally mixed dough to be easily handled,

Figure 4.4 A modern planetary mixer, which is much more powerful than the two-armed mixer pictured in Figure 4.3. It's an all-purpose workhorse found in many bakeries. Courtesy of Hobart Corporation.

the baker could mix 8–15 minutes on high speed and have the dough ready for division in 30–60 minutes.

For the most part, bakers were happy about these advancements. While they were previously accustomed to 12–16-hour workdays, they could now arrive at work later in the morning and still get baguettes done in time for the morning rush. More importantly, up to three full cycles of baguettes could be mixed, shaped, and baked before the end of the business day. Bakers were able to make and sell much more bread in a given amount of time than when they used slower mixers. Undoubtedly, this efficiency made bakery owners embrace what they called *pétrissage intensifié*—the *intensive mix*—as the production method of choice from the late 1950s through the early 1980s.

When using the intensive mix method, ingredients were incorporated into a homogenous mass using the first speed setting for 3–5 minutes. Once the flour was fully hydrated, second speed was used to continue mixing the dough for another 8–15 minutes (in extreme cases, even 20 minutes), during which time the gluten in the dough developed completely and the mass reached nearly full maturity. After only 30–60 minutes, the batch was brought to the bench and divided into portions. The finished baguettes were then shaped and baked, and, because the yeast was also faster than in the old days, the entire cycle of mixing through baking took place in

Figure 4.5 An oblique or fork mixer has a free-spinning bowl and a two-pronged agitator that can run at both low and high speeds, unlike the old-fashioned two-armed mixer. It is gentle on dough as it mixes, but the resulting mix times are prolonged when compared to a spiral mixer, and the operator runs some risk of incorporating more oxygen into the dough for that reason. Courtesy of French Baking Machines (FBM).

less than 4–5 hours, compared to perhaps 7–10 hours previously. Examples of more powerful multispeed mixers are illustrated in Figures 4.5 and 4.6.

Bakers were able to produce three complete batches of baguettes, beginning to end, and have warm bread available to their customers for breakfast, lunch, and dinner. In essence, these machines made for less work, the dough matured in less time, and the total sales of bread every day helped make up for the artificially low prices mandated by the national government.

The bread produced with this method was also radically different in appearance than baguettes made with the short mix. Sheer size was the most obvious change: The volume with the intensive mix baguettes was much greater than before. Their crust was much thinner; the texture was cottony, and the crumb structure was much more homogenous than with the previous style. Also, the crumb color was transformed from an ivory or yellowish tint to a bright white.

Because the weight was the same but the volume was much greater, the density of the final product was much less. This lack of density made for what was then a

Figure 4.6 A modern spiral mixer. Many artisan bakers see the spiral mixer as the choice that allows speed of production while maintaining control of oxidation and kind treatment of the dough. Courtesy of French Baking Machines (FBM).

unique eating experience for customers used to handmade or short mix baguettes. It also made for a much shorter shelf life—3–5 hours—but when customers were conditioned to come in two or three times a day for *pain chaux* ("hot bread"), the shelf life problem was less important. While there were several advantages to the intensive mix method, one aspect of its use did not endear it to more traditional bakers and their customers: It had almost no flavor.

The Improved Mix Method

By the mid 1960s, the French began lamenting publicly that the taste of bread just wasn't what it used to be. Food scientists and bakery technicians began to research why this might be so. Using modern technology, they compared the characteristics of similar dough samples at a microscopic level and found that dough made with the intensive mix method featured a much lower level of organic acids than the dough made with the traditional mix method. They also determined these organic acids were primarily responsible for the flavor and aromas associated with a great-tasting loaf of bread. The reason for the lower acidity in the intensively mixed dough was that its short fermentation period didn't allow enough time for important types of bacteria to produce lactic and acetic acids as by-products. These acids not only affected the flavor of the dough, which was important, but also had a reinforcing effect on the dough's strength. The various effects of organic acids during fermentation are discussed more thoroughly in *Chapter 5*.

Research also determined that mixing for too long a period or too intensively produced a crumb that was bleached out and absent of color. Just as with a meringue, the effect of whipping the dough intensively within a bowl made the crumb color turn white, as it became *overoxidized*. Intensive mixing destroyed the *carotenoid pigments* responsible for the yellowish or ivory tint present in white flour. Intensively mixed bread dough was often mixed to a dry consistency, as it required no folds for development. Between the drying of the dough and the rough handling from so much mixing, the crumb structure became much more homogenous and cottony, with few large air pockets (*alveoli*) present to provide texture.

Telling bakers that the cure for tasteless bread was mixing less and working more might have been time wasted. The practical advantages of using mixers to achieve shorter periods of dough maturation were abundantly clear, and the money invested in equipment had already been significant. Going back to slower methods and longer workdays was not viewed with enthusiasm. Faced with the choice of better bread with more time invested or lower-quality bread made in less time, many bakers chose the latter.

Experts such as Raymond Calvel had studied the problem of reconciling the need for better bread with the desire of bakers to have a life outside of work. In the 1960s, he and others like him developed a hybrid mix method later known as the *improved mix* method (*pétrissage amelioré*). Calvel decided to incorporate select elements of traditional mixing such as a rest period, or *autolyse* (see sidebar), and the use of preferments (see *Chapter 5*) with more restrained use of the second speed setting of the mixer. By using poolish, sponge, or old dough (*pâte fermentée*) as a primary source of organic acids, the bulk fermentation of the entire final dough could be shortened to 1–2 hours with no real sacrifice of flavor.

What Is an *Autolyse?*

When Professor Calvel developed the hybrid mix method, later known as the improved mix method, during the 1960s, he most likely drew on his knowledge of mixing and fermentation techniques from his early days as a baker and instructor in the 1920s.

He used *pâte fermentée* (pre-fermented dough) because its long period of fermentation allows enough time for its bacteria to create accentuated amounts of lactic acid. This inclusion of acid before the final fermentation started allows the baker to obtain strong dough and good-tasting bread in only 1–2 hours of bulk fermentation (compared to about 5 hours in a short mix).

Another element Calvel advocated was the use of a defined rest period, or *autolyse*, between the incorporation of ingredients on first speed and the gluten development on second speed. The interval of rest was typically 20–30 minutes. When the dough is allowed to rest

Figure 4.7a A dough that has been mixed on first speed only in a planetary mixer for 4 minutes, before a 20-minute autolyse rest period. It is lumpy and tears easily.

Figure 4.7b The same mixed dough after a 20-minute autolyse rest period. It has smoothed considerably and can be well stretched before tearing.

Is There a Best Mixing Method?

The improved method may seem the best option for serious bakers who are concerned about both the quality of the loaves *and* maintaining efficient production schedules. This method enables bakers to make good-tasting, nice-looking loaves in a reasonable period. Should we conclude the improved mix method is always the best?

The answer to this question can be complicated. To get a snapshot of the characteristics produced in bread by the three defined mixing methods, see Table 4.1. From an artisan's standpoint, the improved method is probably the best way to make a baguette with nice volume that also possesses good qualities of taste, color, and interior structure. But we can't simply say that it is the *best* method for all baguette

What Is an *Autolyse?* (Continued)

without agitation, the gluten-forming proteins in the flour begin bonding and organizing on their own in a completely passive manner. As a result, the dough does not need to be turned so much by the mixer's hook. Less turning translates to less air being absorbed by the dough (oxidation), thereby preserving the precious carotene pigments in the flour. An illustration of the passive dough development enabled by an autolyse can be found in Figures 4.7a and 4.7b.

The other major advantage of using the autolyse period during mixing is that in the temporary absence of salt during this period, the enzymes in the flour can become much more active. Protease, especially, can work to degrade some of the elasticity that might result from using large amounts of pre-ferment, and this subtle weakening of the protein bonds makes the baguette dough much more extensible.

The major disadvantage of utilizing an autolyse or rest period is that you must wait 15–20 minutes before the enzymes you are encouraging have sufficient effect on the dough. This intermission in mixing can be inconvenient or even inefficient if you don't want to be stumbling over a number of bowls containing partially mixed dough. (Mixers with nonremovable bowls pose an even bigger dilemma if including the autolyse.)

Many artisan bakers still embrace the autolyse for at least some of their dough mixing because of the distinct advantages it offers. Still, its benefits in terms of color, extensibility, and even flavor are sometimes outweighed by longer production times and more complicated schedules. The use of poolish or liquid levain instead of autolyse, for instance, can add both flavor and extensibility to baguette dough while enabling a shortened mix time and no down-time at all.

If the dough were to ferment for only 1 hour, though, it would still need substantial gluten development to occur in the mixer. Calvel found that by reducing the mix time on second speed to only 3–4 minutes (instead of the typical 10–15 minutes), the dough would still receive considerable gluten development prior to entering its bulk fermentation stage. By adding one set of folds during the fermentation and by using enough pre-ferment to supply a lot of organic acids, a baker could mix, ferment, shape, and bake a load of baguettes in 4½–5 hours. That compared favorably to the 7–10 hours necessary to make baguettes using the short mix method, and it was almost as brief as using the intensive mix method. The improved mix method seemed to offer a practical alternative to those bakers who recognized the failings of the intensive method but who were not willing to go back in time and ignore the advantages created by more modern equipment.

The bleached-out color and tight crumb structure that characterized intensively mixed baguettes were essentially absent in loaves made using the improved mix method. The flavor was good, the volume was still quite acceptable, and the shelf life of a loaf was improved when compared to the intensive product. It seemed that Professor Calvel and his like-minded colleagues had found the ideal mechanized mix method for French bread—one that combined the positive aspects of machine mixing (better volume, shorter fermentation time) with the desirable traits resulting from traditional mixing (good flavor, creamy color, and open crumb structure).

---

making, because the short mix method also makes baguettes of excellent eating quality and superior color, even if their volume isn't as impressive as that of bread made with improved mixing.

TABLE 4.1 The Three Comparative Mixing Methods for French Bread

	SHORT MIX	INTENSIVE MIX	IMPROVED MIX
Flavor, aromas	Very good	Bland	Good
Crumb color	Very yellowish	Very white	Yellowish
Crumb structure	Very open	Very closed	Open
Volume	Smallest	Best	Good
Shelf life	Best	Poorest	Good
Required folds	3–4	None	1–2

Also, baguettes aren't the only type of bread bakers want to sell. Hearth loaves like *pain de campagne, pain au levain,* and San Francisco–style sourdough probably favor a texture with characteristics similar to that of baguettes, but what about *pain de mie* (sandwich bread), brioche, or challah? These are breads for which a close crumb structure is entirely appropriate. Also, the amount of butter and sugar added to a bread such as brioche requires a dough that is stronger than what we obtain with the improved mix method. An intensive mixing process can help provide that strength while allowing for the inclusion of such rich ingredients.

So, rather than perceiving the three mix methods as good or bad in absolute terms, we should make it a point to associate each method with the types of bread that may benefit from their appropriate application.

We must also recognize there are not literally only three mix methods available to the bread baker. Any combination of low-speed and high-speed mixing is theoretically possible. Still, anyone who develops formulas for bread should understand that these three mixing methods are historic, well-defined reference points for the purposes of comparison and analysis. The qualities you obtain from whatever customized mix method you develop may yield results outside the precise parameters described for each mix method in this chapter. A thorough knowledge of the three classic mix methods gives you much-needed insight into how your bread behaves and how you can alter the results if you choose.

Special Circumstances or Exceptions

The mixing methods already described can be used as points of comparison for just about any dough. Baguettes were selected for our discussion because they have played an important role in the history of artisan-style baking and because they continue to act as a sort of measuring stick for bread mastery in any bakery.

Of course, in some scenarios, simply mixing 5 minutes on first speed and 3 minutes on second speed won't produce great results. These may be good time estimates for baguette dough, but they might lead to disaster if you are mixing brioche or Vollkornbrot, for example. In this section, we briefly describe factors that can significantly affect the mixing time or mixing method best suited to your dough. Many of these factors are associated with the ingredients included in the formula. We now discuss characteristics of these ingredients.

FLOUR

Flours can vary a lot in their protein quantity. Protein quantity can be measured fairly accurately by the miller, whose specification sheets tell you whether the protein levels are within the limits you've requested. Higher-protein flours (13–14%) form more gluten within a batch of dough, and they require more mixing than moderate-level flours (11–12%) if a baker is to achieve sufficient, comparable development. Lower-protein flours (9–10%) perform in just the opposite way and require that you stop the mixer earlier than would be appropriate for dough made from moderate-protein flour.

Rye flour is particularly low in gluten-forming proteins. The level is so low, in fact, that when mixing bread dough that is high in rye flour, we consider the rye flour itself to have no gluten at all. If a dough formula is one-third rye flour, for instance, the lower overall level of gluten might dictate that we mix that dough for 1–2 minutes less than we would for a baguette dough of similar batch size and consistency. Higher percentages of rye flour dictate proportionately less mixing on second speed. Some types of rye bread feature formulas with 100% rye. These doughs are generally mixed on first speed for only a few minutes before they are removed from the mixer and immediately divided.

Another aspect of working with rye flour can complicate a mixer's job: Rye is high in *pentosans*, a type of carbohydrate that is different from starches. Pentosans absorb a great deal of water through the early stages of mixing (up to 15 times their own weight), but they are by nature quite fragile in structure. They aren't durable enough to withstand much high-speed mixing, and after just 3–4 minutes on second speed they can begin to break down and render their absorbed water back into the dough. This is sometimes the cause of the excessively sticky rye doughs bakers dread. Another cause is the comparatively high soluble-sugar levels in rye flour.

Because rye dough features lower levels of gluten and higher levels of pentosans, any dough that contains a high percentage of rye usually requires more careful mixing for less time than required for white dough.

WATER

Flour can only absorb so much water before the resulting dough begins to act more like a liquid than a solid mass. Any water not fixed by the proteins and starches in the dough is referred to as *free water*, and the more free water there is in a dough formula, the longer the dough will require mixing to achieve sufficient gluten development.

A number of white breads with Italian origins (such as *pane Pugliese* and *ciabatta*) have what are called *superhydrated doughs* as their basis. Their water content can be extremely high—74–84% is common—potentially producing floppy dough that can be difficult to mix in a short amount of time. One coping strategy developed by bakers is called the *double hydration method*. In this method, the water is added in two stages instead of all at once at the beginning of the mix. Enough water is added before mixing to bring about a consistency similar to that of a moderately wet baguette dough. The remaining water is added later, after the gluten is sufficiently developed. The second addition of water can be mixed in on first speed to ensure the dough is not overmixed or overoxidized.

SALT

Salt's effect on dough mixing is that it strengthens the gluten bonds, thereby extending the amount of time necessary to develop the gluten in dough. It also functions as an antioxidant, effectively reducing the loss of carotene pigments and precious flavor components during mixing.

Some bread bakers prefer to hold back any salt addition until mixing is nearly finished in an effort to shorten the mix time during production. If bakers do hold back adding the salt, the dough may absorb much more oxygen than normal, and overoxidation may occur before the salt is added. Flavor and color can be seriously compromised this way, so, in the interest of maintaining good quality, it is optimal for a baker to add the salt toward the beginning of the mixing cycle.

An exception to this principle occurs when you incorporate an autolyse into your mixing procedure. During an autolyse, salt is held back until the rest period is over in order to encourage an increase in enzyme activity. Because no high-speed mixing occurs before or during the autolyse, the dough's color and flavor can still be preserved in the temporary absence of salt. Before the remaining mix at high speed commences, the salt in the formula should be added to maximize its antioxidizing effects.

BUTTER, SHORTENING, AND OILS

Even small amounts of fat added at the beginning of mixing tenderize bread dough to some degree. Fats interfere somewhat with glutenin and gliadin joining together to form gluten during the initial mixing stage, and are said to *shorten* the gluten strands. This effect is, in fact, the derivation of the term *shortening*. Biscuits, scones, and shortbread provide examples of the tenderizing and shortening effects of fats on gluten structure.

Large amounts of fat added at the beginning of dough mixing can yield bread that is flaky or dense instead of springy and light-textured. For instance, the typical strategy for adding a lot of butter to a batch of brioche dough is to mix the dough *without* the butter until the gluten is developed (intensively, in this case). Once the dough is smooth and strong, you then change back to first speed on the mixer and add the butter in pieces, mixing it in slowly until it is completely incorporated. Using this method creates a light and feathery-textured loaf that belies its rich ingredients.

SUGAR

Sugar is *hygroscopic,* which means that sugar crystals absorb water from their environment. At levels below approximately 12% of the weight of the flour, sugar usually poses no serious problems if it is added at the beginning of the mix. However, at concentrations above 12%, sugar quickly absorbs so much water from the mix that many of the gluten-forming proteins don't have sufficient water to link up and form gluten. As a result, the sugar slackens and tenderizes the dough so much that it possesses poor structure and might not rise as much as you would wish.

If your formula's sugar percentage is high, one way of addressing this problem is to add the sugar in stages. If you add only about one-third of the sugar at the beginning of the mix, then add another third after a few minutes, and add the remaining quantity a few minutes later, you give the gluten time to form and develop before the sugar can interfere too much with the dough's strength. Ideally, a bit of water is added with the sugar addition to ensure the sugar dissolves completely during mixing.

RAISINS, NUTS, SEEDS, AND GRAINS

Any dried fruit should be incorporated into dough carefully, and generally at the end of the mix. Hold back the raisins or similar fruits and mix the dough completely without them. Then add the raisins, using first speed only, until they are evenly mixed in. Plumping the fruit in water, rum, or other liquid before use is optional. Keep in mind, if the raisins are not soaked ahead of time, they will draw a significant amount of water away from the dough and possibly make the dough drier than it was before the addition of the raisins.

Nuts and seeds can also be safely mixed into dough after the gluten structure is developed. Some bakers prefer to add seeds toward the start of a mix cycle. You may wish to try both methods and see whether you can tell a difference in the structure of your dough.

If whole grains are added to bread dough, they are almost always soaked in a large amount of water well ahead of time. It is not unusual to devote an entire day to soaking whole grains in order to soften them and make them easier to chew. It is a good idea to actually measure the amount of water you add to this *soaker* and to incorporate this measurement as a component separate from the amount of water already specified in the formula.

Controlling Dough Temperature

When we mix bread dough (especially a series of different doughs), we strive to control the rate of fermentation the dough undergoes after it leaves the mixer. Some doughs require different ideal temperatures than others; we refer to the optimal dough temperature after it leaves the bowl as the *goal temperature.*

Why do we bother with this? There are at least two important reasons. First, by keeping the dough's temperature at a moderate 75–77°F in most cases, we can maintain the levels of strength and balance of flavors we wish (see *Chapter 5* for more information about why this is so). A second critical reason is that when a dough's temperature during bulk fermentation varies by even a couple of degrees from the goal temperature, it can ferment either much more slowly (when too cool) or much faster than normal (when too warm).

Those differences in the rate of fermentation cause you to either take the dough to the bench later than normal because it isn't ready on time or take it for division much sooner than you had expected. This, in turn, leads to less predictable final proof times, and you may have some loaves ready to go into the oven before you have unloaded the batch before them.

In short, unless you control the dough's temperature, you don't know when it will be ready, and you can't plan your production schedule easily. You might inadvertently create an unmanageable mess, and you might lose hundreds of pounds of product.

So how can we control the dough's temperature? The factors that most influence the final dough temperature after mixing are the temperature of the flour, the temperature of the room (which affects the temperature of the mixer bowl), any friction created during mixing, the temperature of any large mass of pre-ferment used, and, finally, the temperature of the water in the mixture. Of all these factors, only the temperature of the water is easy to control before you begin your mix.

There are two common methods of calculating the water temperature necessary to obtain the goal temperature you want for your dough. One is intended for use with straight doughs (which use no pre-ferment), and the other is meant for use with doughs that contain significant amounts of pre-ferment (where 20% or more of the total flour is contained in the pre-ferment). Doughs with smaller amounts of pre-fermented flour can probably be accommodated with the calculation meant for straight doughs, but you can try both methods yourself and see what works for you.

An explanation of the two methods of calculating water temperature to arrive at a given goal temperature for bread dough is contained in Table 4.2, together with examples of calculations.

Controlling Dough Temperature (Continued)

TABLE 4.2 Calculating Water Temperature

By calculating and controlling the ideal temperature of the water you use to make bread dough, you can get close to the ideal temperature (goal temperature) of the dough for purposes of bulk fermentation and proofing. By controlling the dough's temperature, you can more easily predict how fast it will produce carbon dioxide gases and how soon the finished loaves will be ready for baking.

Yeasted dough is a living thing that reacts to its environment, but you can usually control its growth and flavor development by controlling its temperature. To do so, you must determine the following criteria:

1. Determine your *goal temperature* for the final dough (usually 75–78°F).

2. Determine your *base temperature*, in one of two ways:

   a. If you are mixing a straight dough, multiply the numerical value of your goal temperature by 3.

   goal temperature × 3 = base temperature

   b. If, instead, you are using a large quantity of pre-ferment (such as old dough), multiply your goal temperature by 4.

   goal temperature × 4 = base temperature

3. Measure the following temperatures and subtract them from the base temperature: the flour, the pre-ferment (if used), the environment (room temperature or surface of the mixer bowl), and an appropriate friction factor. The result of the calculation is your desired water temperature.

   Example:

   a. For a straight dough (no pre-ferment): Your goal for the final dough temperature could be 75°F. The room temperature (and that of the mixer bowl) today is 77°F, the flour is 75°F, and your friction factor has been 25°F. To calculate the desired water temperature for this batch of dough, we write down the following:

   75° (goal temperature) × 3 = 225°F (base temperature)

   225°F − 77°F − 75°F − 25°F = 48°F

   base temp. − bowl temp. − flour temp. − friction temp. = desired water temp.

   b. For a dough made with a pre-ferment: Your goal for the final dough temperature is 75°F. The temperature of the room (and the mixer bowl) today is 77°F, the flour is 75°F, and the pre-ferment used is 70°F. Your friction factor has been 25°F. To calculate the desired water temperature for this batch of dough, we write down the following:

   75°F (goal temperature) × 4 = 300°F (base temperature)

   300°F − 77°F − 75°F − 70°F − 25°F = 53°F

   base temp. − bowl temp. − flour temp. − friction temp. − pre-ferment temp. = desired water temp.

Important Notes:

   a. The bowl temperature and the room temperature are not always the same, as the thermostat in a bakery measures the temperature of the air. It is the mixer bowl that transfers heat or cold most quickly to a dough, so it may be wise to bring your thermometer into contact with the bowl's surface and see if there is a difference. After one or two batches of dough have been mixed, the temperature of the bowl is raised a bit and stabilizes somewhat.

   b. The temperatures for the room (or bowl), flour, and pre-ferment can change somewhat every day, so measure them every day.

   c. The friction factor should theoretically be the same every day, but, in this author's experience, it can vary a bit over long periods of time, which may be related to the changing seasons. This would make no sense unless we accept that the "friction factor" is also a reflection of influences other than friction, strictly speaking. This method of water temperature calculation is simple to use, and yet it has its flaws.

   d. For a planetary mixer, there is usually 25–30°F friction factor, depending on the season of the year, the size of the batch, and the length of mixing time. It increases with larger batches and longer mix times and decreases with smaller batches and shorter mix times. Consequently, the temperature of the water you should use every day will probably change. Don't ever assume it will remain the same from one day to the next—do the calculation every day!

4. After mixing bread dough, measure its temperature to see if you arrived at the goal temperature. If the dough temperature is higher than the goal, then the friction factor you used was probably too low and should be increased by the difference you just found. A dough temperature that's lower than the goal suggests your friction factor was too high, and should be reduced for the next batch.

ARTISAN BAKER PROFILE

Dave Fox

Blue Baker, College Station, Texas

Dave Fox is probably one of very few Ivy League graduates who decided to make a living by working with bread dough. He graduated in 1997 from Dartmouth College in Hanover, New Hampshire, with an idea that he might like getting into the restaurant business. His focus was on fine dining, and between gaining a culinary education at the New England Culinary Institute and some practical restaurant experience, he found he most enjoyed working with baked goods.

As he worked for other restaurant operators, Dave learned quite a bit about the financial end of running a business, and he gained insights into important aspects of restaurant design. In May 2001, he was given the opportunity to finally open his own place, and Blue Baker was born in the university town of College Station, Texas.

IMPRESSIONS OF ARTISAN BREAD BAKING AS AN INDUSTRY

What do you like most about the bread business?

I am in this field because I really enjoy making things and seeing people enjoy what's been created. On the one hand, baking relies on basic ingredients and simple processes where even my two-year-old can participate. And yet, bread baking can be extremely complex and features thousands of variables—all of which can change.

Any other bakers who were your inspiration?

A book that early on left the greatest impact on me is Daniel Leader's *Bread Alone*.

What are your thoughts on the future of the artisan bread business?

I feel the greatest challenge is that people want what is convenient. Buying bread at a grocery store is easy, and that makes operating a standalone retail bakery challenging, except in urban locations with high population density. I think successful operators will either focus on wholesaling to groceries and restaurants or move toward opening bakery/cafés. One thing I notice is that many guests are becoming more educated about bread, and their tastes are gradually more discriminating. Both of those trends should help our field grow.

Summary

Mixing dough by hand remained a remarkably unchanged process for several millennia after the discovery and cultivation of wheat. The process had two primary goals: first, to create a thoroughly hydrated and homogenous mixture, and second, to reorganize the joined gluten strands into a smoother, stronger mass that could be divided and shaped into loaves that would hold their shape. Dough that has reached the state where it can be easily cut and shaped had reached what was called *maturity*.

When mixing by hand, that state of maturity required 5 hours or more of folding and fermenting after the dough was initially combined and kneaded. The first electric mixers saved a lot of that work, but the time required for dough to reach maturity remained about the same. The mixing technique employed by the first powered mixers was called the *short mix method*.

Faster and more powerful mixers were adopted in France by the 1950s, and the mechanical development they could achieve on high speed allowed for much less fermentation time being necessary to achieve dough maturity. The baguettes these machines created were lighter in texture, whiter in crumb color, and lower in flavor than those made by traditional means. The new technique for mixing a long time on high speed came to be known as the *intensive mix method*.

By the 1980s, many bakers and their customers began to miss the deeper flavors of the older, more traditional mixing methods. Bakers were mostly resistant to going back entirely to the old ways, so Professor Raymond Calvel and others researched methods to combine the convenience of high-speed mixing with the taste and texture that resulted from slower, traditional mixing. Calvel developed what was later called the *improved mix method*, which featured less mixing on second speed and the use of pre-ferments to achieve good eating characteristics as well as dough maturity in about the same overall time as that used by the intensive method.

The three mixing methods described here should act as reference points for those bakers wishing to develop their own formulas and procedures. Any combination of slow-speed and high-speed mixing is theoretically possible, and different types of bread can benefit from different mix methods. The likely effects of mixing for less time or more time are well illustrated by these examples, and an understanding of what changes occur and why they occur is essential to any serious student of bread baking.

Key Terms

hydrate	*intensive mix*
insoluble	*pain chaux*
glutenin	*overoxidized*
gliadin	*carotenoid pigments*
incorporation	*alveoli*
viscoelastic	*improved mix*
development	*autolyse*
viscosity	*pentosans*
elasticity	*free water*
tenacity	*superhydrated dough*
extensibility	*double hydration method*
plasticity	*shorten*
overmixing	*hygroscopic*
short mix	*soaker*
maturity	*windowpane test*

Questions for Review

1. What are the similarities and differences between how bread dough was made in ancient Egypt and in nineteenth-century France?
2. Explain the goals of each of the two stages of mixing.
3. What does it mean if a dough is overmixed? How is this different from dough being overoxidized?
4. What three basic mechanical mix methods are used in France? What sort of bread does each method produce?
5. What are some of the important technological and economic developments in France that preceded the onset of mechanized mixing?
6. How does rye flour pose a challenge when it is present in a dough formula? What precautions must a mixer take when rye flour is part of the formula in order to avoid creating problems with the dough?

Questions for Discussion

1. Is there a "best" method for mixing bread dough? Explain your answer.
2. Are we limited to the three classic mixing methods when deciding how to mix bread dough? Why is it important to know the three classic mixing methods?
3. What ingredients, including those not mentioned in this text, might give you reason for concern when mixing bread dough?

Lab Exercise & Experiment #1: Mixing a Rustic Dough

To get a sense of how significant the changes that evolved with the mechanization of bread baking were, it is helpful to make at least one simple variety of bread by hand. The formula given here is designed to make a type of bread called *pain rustique*, which is essentially an easily formed, nearly unshaped loaf. It is cut from a larger mass of dough that has been fermented in bulk for several hours following its initial mix.

PAIN RUSTIQUE—HAND METHOD

	Metric		U.S. Measure		Formula Baker's %
	(1X)	**(4X)**	**(1X)**	**(4X)**	
	5-Qt Mixer	**20-Qt Mixer**	**5-Qt Mixer**	**20-Qt Mixer**	
STRAIGHT DOUGH					
Bread flour	600g	2400g	2 lb 2.0oz	8 lb 8.0oz	**100%**
Water	450g	1800g	1 lb 9.5oz	6 lb 6.0oz	**75%**
Salt	13g	53g	0.8oz	3.0oz	**2.2%**
Instant yeast	2g	8g	0.1oz	0.5oz	**0.4%**
TOTAL YIELD	**1065g**	**4261g**	**3 lb 12.4oz**	**15 lb 1.5oz**	

GOAL TEMPERATURE: 77°F (25°C). See directions for determining correct water temperature in *Chapter 4*.

MIXING BY HAND:

1. Add all the ingredients and mix with your hands until they are homogenous. The dough will be wet—don't add extra flour.

2. Cover the tub and allow the mixture to rest for about 15 minutes.

3. After the rest period, give the mixture a set of folds as you would any baguette dough, even though the dough may seem unmanageable. Repeat these rest periods and sets of folds 4 or 5 times until the dough seems to be more elastic and less fluid.

SCALING:

1. Gently empty the tub of dough onto a well-floured bench and rearrange the dough so its shape is rectangular and its thickness the same throughout.

2. Cut a strip of dough as wide as you want your loaves to be. Then cut for length. Keep the dough portions as rectangular as you can and rest them temporarily on floured proofing boards as you proceed. Keep the proofing boards with the portions covered as you proceed.

3. Standard loaves—8–16 oz (450–525 g).

SHAPING:

1. The portions are not so much shaped as they are stretched slightly. Stretch each loaf into a rectangle 8–10 inches long and place on well-floured couche with pleats between each row of 2 loaves.

2. With this bread, you may wish to leave any small pieces of dough sitting on top of the larger rectangle because the loaves will be flipped upside-down just before loading them in the oven.

PROOFING: 45 minutes at 80°F and 80% humidity. If a proofer is not available, cover the rack holding the boards and keep as close to 80° as possible.

BAKING:

1. In a deck oven—475–500°F (245–260°C).

2. Load the ciabatta on your peel or mechanical loader, flipping them upside-down as you do so to expose the attractive veined look of the flour clinging to the underside.

3. Insert the loaves with a few seconds of steam. No scoring is necessary.

4. 25–30 minutes for loaves, 12–15 minutes for rolls. Be sure to vent the oven after the first 10 minutes of baking. Shorter bake times tend to leave too much moisture in the loaves and will soften the crust; longer times may make for a thick crust and a dry interior.

COOLING: Cool (without crowding the loaves) on a rack with wire shelves.

Figure 4.8a Mixing dough by hand; during hand mix.

Figure 4.8b Dough after hand mix.

When this formula is closely followed, the resulting bread is actually quite appealing in flavor and texture and may serve as a standard for comparison as you prepare variations of historical French mixing methods.

After you have combined the ingredients and allowed the dough to rest, this dough's most prominent feature is its wetness, as it looks more like heavy pancake batter than workable dough (see Figures 4.8a and 4.8b). During the nineteenth century, hand-mixed dough was made in fairly large batches weighing more than 100 lb. Folding it over and over on itself in a wooden trough was the primary means of gluten development, and the mass grew gradually stronger with every set of folds. Trying to accomplish these folds many times over would be almost impossible if the dough were very stiff. Nineteenth-century bakers didn't use a lot of water in dough just to cut their costs—they were also trying to save their backs.

The rustique dough is folded every 20 minutes or so; after 4 or 5 sets of folds, it is set aside a few more hours to allow it to develop the flavor and structure needed for cutting and final fermentation (proofing). Figures 4.9a–4.9d illustrate the method for developing gluten by folding the dough mass. Notice how much the appearance and form of the dough changes over time as it is folded.

Figure 4.9a Folding dough at 20 minutes.

Figure 4.9b Folding dough at 40 minutes.

Figure 4.9c Folding dough at 60 minutes.

Figure 4.9d Folding dough at 80 minutes.

After the dough is cut into portions, it should be handled fairly gently. The pieces are usually ready for the oven in less than 1 hour.

The finished loaves come out of the oven looking like roughly cut pillows, but what they lack in their outside appearance they more than possess in flavor, color, and open crumb structure. There were certainly prettier loaves made in the 1800s, but the eating characteristics of this bread should give you a good idea of what the standards for flavor and texture may have been before mechanized mixing came along and changed everything.

Lab Exercise & Experiment #2: Comparing the Three Mixing Methods

If you have performed Experiment #1, you have seen how a hand-mixed dough that is wet enough can produce loaves that are wildly open in texture and have good flavor.

To understand how the mechanization of mixing changed things over most of the twentieth century, we will now make baguettes from three separately mixed doughs; one represents the short mix method, another the intensive method, and the third the improved method. Using the baguette formula featured here, make three batches of dough and ferment them appropriately until they have reached full maturity. Note that each method has a different recommended time for bulk fermentation. Also note that the appropriate amount of water to add for each method is probably different. For instance, an intensively mixed dough typically uses 2–4% less water than a typical improved mix dough, and short mix dough uses proportionately more water than the improved mix dough.

The photographs in Figures 4.10a through 4.10c illustrate a method for testing the level of gluten development using any of the three mix methods. Figure 4.10a features a short mix dough that is similar in many respects to a dough made by hand. We observe that the dough tears before we can stretch it into any sort of membrane; it is considerably underdeveloped and will require 4 or more sets of folds over 4–5 hours to achieve the strength necessary for dough maturation. Baguettes made from this dough will have minimal volume but optimal taste, an open crumb, and a yellowish crumb color.

In Figure 4.10b we see a major contrast in the development of the gluten, as we can stretch the dough easily into a thin, translucent membrane. This dough has been intensively mixed. While it could probably withstand more mixing before losing elasticity altogether, it is so developed now that baguettes made from it will have a close crumb structure and a crumb color that's fairly white from the extra oxygen incorporated during long mixing. The bulk fermentation time is much shorter than for the short mix—only 30–60 minutes—and the volume of these loaves can be impressive, but that convenience and size come at the cost of lost flavors and aromas.

Figures 4.10a–c The stretch or "windowpane tests" for the three basic dough mixing methods: Figure 4.10a illustrates a windowpane test for a short mix bread dough; Figure 4.10b illustrates a windowpane test for an intensive mix bread dough; Figure 4.10c illustrates a windowpane test for an improved mix bread dough.

Figure 4.10c shows us testing the development of an improved mix dough. It does admit some light, and it stretches without tearing, but the cloudiness and veined look inside the gluten window tell us that while the dough is more developed than short mix dough, it has certainly not achieved an intensive level of development. This is as it should be for this defined state of dough development. This dough will produce baguettes with good volume, though not as accentuated as for the intensive mix baguettes. The crumb structure will be moderately open, and the crumb color will retain much of the yellowish tint characteristic of the short mix method. The flavor will still be good, and it can attain maturity in 2 or 3 hours (1 hour with enough pre-ferment)—longer than for intensive baguettes, but much less than the short mix baguettes, which take a much longer time to make.

Compare and contrast the resulting baguettes from each batch for the following characteristics: creamy color, size of air pockets (*alveoli*), overall volume, taste, texture, moistness, and keeping qualities. Based on your findings, do you agree with Professor Calvel's assertion that the improved mix method provides the best solution for efficient production of attractive, enjoyable baguettes?

BAGUETTES—DIRECT METHOD

	Metric		U.S. Measure		Formula Baker's %
	(1X)	**(4X)**	**(1X)**	**(4X)**	
	5-Qt Mixer	**20-Qt Mixer**	**5-Qt Mixer**	**20-Qt Mixer**	
STRAIGHT DOUGH					
Bread flour	1000g	4000g	2 lb 3.0oz	8 lb 12.0oz	**100%**
Water	700g	2800g	1 lb 7.5oz	6 lb 2.0oz	**70%**
Salt	20g	80g	0.7oz	2.8oz	**2%**
Instant yeast	3g	12g	0.1oz	0.4oz	**0.3%**
TOTAL YIELD	**1723g**	**6892g**	**3 lb 11.3oz**	**15 lb 1.2oz**	

NOTE: The yeast quantity listed in the formula is intended for bakers who use the short mix method. A dough mixed with the intensive mix method should receive a yeast percentage around 0.7%, while the yeast percentage for an improved mix dough would be more appropriately set at 0.4%.

GOAL TEMPERATURE: 77°F (25°C).

MIXING METHOD: Short mix, intensive mix, or improved mix—see pp. 195–196.

BULK FERMENTATION: See directions associated with the mix method chosen, pp. 195–196.

SCALING: See options, p. 196.

SHAPING: See directions in *Chapter 6*.

PROOFING: See directions, pp. 196–197.

BAKING: See directions, p. 197.

COOLING: See directions, p. 198.

chapter 5

Fermentation

Learning Outcomes:

- Define fermentation.

- Identify the food source and by-products of yeast fermentation in bread dough.

- Identify the food source and by-products of bacterial fermentation in bread dough.

- Identify the three enzymes of most concern to bakers.

- Understand the nature and function of the three enzymes of most concern to bakers.

- Distinguish between living and nonliving participants in the process of fermentation.

- Predict the likely effects on both flavor and structure of bread dough when manipulating fermentation.

- Define pre-ferment.

- Identify the four pre-ferments with manufactured yeast and the two pre-ferments with wild yeasts that are most commonly used in making artisan-style breads.

Fermentation: A Process of Transformation

Fermentation can be defined as the breakdown (or decay) of organic substances by yeast, bacteria, or molds. When scientists describe a substance as *organic*, they mean it contains carbon atoms in its molecules. While some organic substances can be made synthetically, we tend to think of them as matter that makes up living things or that is produced by living organisms.

Many foods you may eat every day come about as a result of fermentation. Cheese is usually produced by having certain molds and bacteria act on curdled milk solids. The type of cheese you end up with depends on factors like what milk you use, the temperatures used during fermentation, and the exact mold or bacteria you selected to ferment the curds. Yogurt is another fermented milk product; it results from milk's inoculation with lactic bacteria that makes it thicken and become noticeably sour.

Wine is usually fermented grape juice, though any fruit can be used. The yeast on the outside of grape skins (often called the *bloom*) was used through most of history to ferment the juice, but most winemakers today use commercially produced strains of yeast for tighter control over fermentation. Beer and ale are produced from a fermented liquid grain mash (generally from barley or wheat) and, as with wine, brewers today use selected commercial strains of yeast, though the wild yeasts clinging to the barley hulls were the agents used to make beer since the Stone Age.

You might think of fermented bread dough as a more solid form of beer. That may sound ridiculous, but it isn't—the yeasts involved in fermenting both bread and beer are often the same species, and when mixed with water and grain (or flour), they produce the same by-products: alcohol and carbon dioxide. *By-products* are the waste products created during fermentation of organic matter.

Does Fermentation Create or Destroy?

Of course, fermentation isn't always a food-friendly process. If you wait too long to use a bottle of milk, bacteria in the liquid eventually causes the milk to go sour. Leftover fresh or canned tomatoes can get bubbly and generate alcohol within days, producing a sort of tomato wine we didn't expect. And old bread or cheese will go moldy some day, despite our efforts at preservation. Fermentation itself cannot be characterized broadly as a beneficial or a hazardous process. It simply occurs, naturally and inevitably, but if we can control it, it can also occur predictably.

So whether fermentation of flour results in spoiled grain mash or useful bread dough depends on your personal perspective. In a certain sense, it is both. Regardless of how we view them, microbes move along on their mission, as they have in one form or another for 3 billion years. They frustrate us when we try to store foods for long periods, but they can also be harnessed to create excellent foods on their own. Bread is certainly one of them.

Fermentation of Bread Dough

Technically speaking, dough fermentation begins as soon as flour, water, and either yeast or bacteria all come in contact with one another. For practical purposes, though, professionals treat dough fermentation as a segmented, well-defined production process that proceeds as follows: *bulk fermentation, intermediate proofing,* and *final proofing.*

Bulk fermentation is the term applied to the period just after dough has been mixed and during which the dough is allowed to mature before division into portions. Typically, it can vary in length from 0–15 minutes for so-called no-time dough to 4–5 hours or more for some traditional baguettes or sourdough. Artisan bakers typically develop some of the viscoelastic properties of bread dough (see *Chapter 4*) mechanically as they mix the dough, but they allow much of the development to occur passively during long bulk fermentation, as the organic acids produced by bacteria work to strengthen and flavor the dough. Many industrial bakeries try to circumvent the time devoted to bulk fermentation by mixing bread dough for more time and getting greater strength that way, or by combining longer mix times with the use of chemical dough conditioners. While these conditioners in dough can mimic the handling qualities developed during long fermentation, they cannot replace the flavors organic acids provide, and their presence on an ingredient label may suggest to many consumers that the baker cares less about food quality than about convenience in production.

Intermediate proof (sometimes called *bench proof*) is the name of the rest period between dough division and loaf shaping in which just-handled portions can relax and inflate a bit before being stretched and molded. This period is usually 15–30 minutes.

We define *final proof* as the period of fermentation after shaping in which the loaves are allowed to grow in size to much of their potential before they are placed in the oven. Breads made with manufactured yeast usually proof in 45–90 minutes, but some artisan-style breads (especially sourdough varieties) have a conventional final proof that exceeds 3–5 hours.

Fermentation actually proceeds throughout the entire dough-making process, even through the first 10 minutes or so of baking loaves in an oven. Defining specific fermentation periods is useful, though, as it provides a framework for better analysis of the process and allows us to identify segments where different types of fermentation occur.

OTHER STAGES OF FERMENTATION

Two other important periods of dough fermentation don't fit as neatly into the definitions given in the preceding section. The first of these is *pre-fermentation*, where a certain fraction of flour and water from a formula are combined and fermented well ahead of the time the final dough is mixed. The general purpose of *pre-ferments* is to provide flavor, strength, and keeping qualities to bread dough without requiring a long bulk fermentation time. Not all bread formulas call for a pre-ferment, so this stage of the dough fermentation process is essentially optional.

The remaining period of fermentation is the interval between the insertion of loaves into an oven and the time the yeast cells die from the rapidly increasing loaf temperature. Yeast dies at about 139°F, but until that temperature is reached, yeast fermentation proceeds at a much accelerated rate. This causes a rapid rising effect on the loaves during the first few minutes of baking—5–10 minutes, in most cases—

and the effect is referred to as *oven spring*. Only when the yeast cells are dead can fermentation be said to have finished.

Yeast Fermentation: Produces Carbon Dioxide and Alcohol

Yeasts are one-celled organisms classified as a type of fungus. You might be more familiar with larger examples of fungi, such as mushrooms or truffles. Fungi can be viewed as plants, but they have no chlorophyll, so they must subsist directly on the decaying remnants of once-living organisms. In the case of mushrooms or truffles, dead trees often serve as a food source for the plant. With yeasts, however, the source of food is simple sugars, such as glucose, which can be found ready for use in many types of plant matter—such as fruit juices—or which can be converted from the starches present in grains and root vegetables. Figure 5.1 illustrates the various types of manufactured yeast available, and Table 5.1 compares their advantages and disadvantages. Notice that the granules of active dry yeast are visibly larger than those of the instant dry yeast. All of these types can work well in most breads when you know how much to use and how best to add them. What mostly distinguishes them, besides their appearance, is their comparative shelf life, their moisture content, and their ease of use.

After consuming simple sugars, yeast cells produce the *by-products* (or waste products) *carbon dioxide* gas and *alcohol*. There are countless species of yeast on Earth, but we usually try to propagate only one when fermenting bread dough. Its scientific name is *saccharomyces cerevisiae*, and it is the same species of yeast usually used today to ferment both wine and beer. It and other yeasts reside naturally on the skins of grapes and the bran coating of cereal grains such as wheat. When the grapes are crushed or the wheat berries are broken and mixed with water, the yeasts resurrect themselves and begin to feed on the sugars dissolved in the grape juice or mashed grains.

Figure 5.1 Choices in manufactured yeast, clockwise from the top of the photograph—compressed (fresh), instant dry, and active dry.

TABLE 5.1 A Comparison of Features in Using Different Types of Manufactured Yeast

Yeast Type	Method of Addition	Conversion Factor	Shelf Life	Comments
Fresh (compressed)	Dissolve in batch water	None	3 weeks after date of manufacture if refrigerated	Easy to use, best choice if dough to be frozen
Active dry	Bloom in warm water first	Use half as much as fresh (50%)	1 year after manufacture if unopened	Dead yeast cells produce glutathione—relaxes dough
Instant dry	Add directly to flour	Use 40% as much as fresh	1 year after manufacture if unopened	Easy to use and store no blooming, no refrigeration

Since the time of the ancient Egyptians, some societies have used the foam that can form on top of brewing beer in their bread. This foam contains yeast cultures that essentially lost their wild nature and can be used to create loaves with greater lightness and less density than those made from wild sourdough cultures. Until electrical service and refrigeration became common, though, commercial yeast distribution was prohibitively costly and limited to bakeries within a short distance from a brewery. The wild yeasts in sour cultures were the predominant form of yeast leavening in bread through the late nineteenth century.

Bacterial Fermentation: Produces Organic Acids

Bacteria are primitive one-celled organisms placed within the Monera Kingdom. The types of bacteria common in bread dough consume the same simple sugars used by yeast cells. The primary by-products of bacteria in dough fermentation, though, are two types of *organic acids*: *lactic acid* and *acetic acid*. Lactic acid is also found naturally in milk, and, in concentrated form, it produces the tangy flavor we find in yogurt. Acetic acid is found in all varieties of vinegar and is more sour than lactic acid.

ORGANIC ACIDS PROVIDE STRENGTH AND FLAVOR

The types of bacteria that produce these acids can thrive in temperatures of 50–90°F and are collectively referred to as *lactic bacteria*. As bakers, we are concerned with two categories of lactic bacteria: *homofermentative bacteria* and *heterofermentative bacteria*.

These names may seem hard to pronounce and even harder to remember, but it is important to identify them and explain a bit about their behavior. Yeast must be regulated to control how fast dough rises, but the bacteria, primarily, determine how well your dough will mature and how good the bread will taste. If you want your bread to develop good handling properties naturally and to taste good, you must pay as much attention to the quantity and type of bacteria in your dough as you do to the activity of yeast.

This is, perhaps, the one concept in artisan-style baking that escapes bakers who look for easy, time-saving ways to make bread. Unfortunately, bacterial fermentation almost always proceeds more slowly than yeast fermentation—much more slowly. Scientists have successfully isolated strains of the yeast *saccharomyces cerevisiae* that can speed carbon dioxide production considerably. Lactic bacteria, though, have so far been much less cooperative; the bacteria in bread dough we make today probably aren't different from those present in the time of Moses.

HOMOFERMENTATIVE BACTERIA: PREFER A WETTER AND WARMER ENVIRONMENT

Homofermentative bacteria prefer environments that are wet and moderately warm—perhaps 70–95°F. Their chief by-product during fermentation is lactic acid, which is fairly mild in its sourness compared to the sharper acids contained in lemon juice or vinegar, for instance. Homofermentative bacteria can survive in somewhat drier conditions and within other temperature ranges, but they do best in the warmer range specified in the preceding section.

HETEROFERMENTATIVE BACTERIA: PREFER A DRIER AND COOLER ENVIRONMENT

Heterofermentative bacteria do better in somewhat drier and cooler environments; they prefer temperatures of about 50–65°F. They produce both lactic acid *and* acetic acid as by-products, as well as a small amount of carbon dioxide gas. Acetic acid, as previously mentioned, is also found commonly in vinegar, and its flavor profile is much sharper than that of lactic acid. Heterofermentative bacteria can survive in some numbers at different temperatures than specified and in wetter environments, but drier and cooler situations favor their reproduction and their ability to ferment bread dough.

Nonliving Organic Substances: Esters and Enzymes

When the acids from bacterial fermentation encounter the alcohol produced by yeast fermentation, another category of organic substances is generated by their re-action. These substances are called *esters*, and they are thought to be responsible for a significant amount of the pleasant aromas generated in bread dough. While esters are produced from the by-products of living organisms like bacteria and yeast, they are not themselves a type of living substance.

Enzymes are specialized organic compounds that act as catalysts in certain micro-biological reactions, such as fermentation. More simply put, they are chemicals that act to break down certain organic substances, such as starch or protein, and that act of destruction affects both the speed of fermentation and the strength of the dough. Again, though they are organic compounds, they are not actually alive. Three specific enzymes are of most interest to us as bakers: *amylase*, *zymase*, and *protease*.

The foremost of these may be *amylase*, the enzyme responsible for the breakdown of starch into simple sugars. Not much sugar is naturally present in wheat flour—it is mostly composed of starch. Without sufficient amylase, yeast cells and bacteria can soon run out of food, and neither carbon dioxide gas nor organic acids can build up enough to make bread that rises high and tastes good.

▲ A variety of flours and meals used in making bread, clockwise from the top: whole wheat flour, high-gluten flour, cornmeal, cracked wheat, all-purpose flour, semolina, and medium rye flour, with bread flour in the center.

▼ Clockwise, from lower left: Liquid Levain, Firm Levain, and Poolish.

▲ Baguettes fully proofed in couche.

▼ Baguettes.

Boule scoring technique.

Rosemary/Olive Oil Boules after baking, scored as shown in previous series of photos.

Alternative boule scoring technique.

San Francisco Sourdough made with no manufactured yeast and shaped as boule and as a long bâtard.

Auvergnats made from Pain de Campagne, baking in the oven.

Auvergnats cooling on a rack.

Bleu Cheese with Toasted Walnuts, shaped as a small boule. The cheese crumbles are folded into the dough, rather than mixed into the dough, to prevent them from disintegrating.

A variety of Pain au Levain. Notice the wildly open crumb.

Double Raisin with Toasted Walnuts, shaped as a short bâtard. Notice how the crumb turns a purple hue from the walnut skins in the dough.

Baguette dough variations, clockwise from left: epi couronne, boulot, baguette (with straight epi behind), bâtard, diagonal cross-section of baguette.

Zymase is an enzyme that breaks down simple sugar (or glucose) into alcohol and carbon dioxide. Yeast cells produce their own zymase so, unlike amylase, its level doesn't require adjustment before millers send their flour out for use by bakers. It is important to remember that while yeast cells using their zymase can break down sugar, the yeasts still need amylase to be already in the flour to break down starch into sugar itself.

Protease is an enzyme that breaks down protein chains. Strictly speaking, it does not affect fermentation, but it does act upon proteins in dough as the dough ferments. As we discussed in *Chapter 2*, the gluten strands in bread dough are composed of two simpler proteins, glutenin and gliadin, that join in the presence of water and give bread dough its structure and its ability to capture and hold carbon dioxide gas. Protease acts to break apart these chains of proteins, which weakens the dough's strength somewhat. This effect can be beneficial to a baker who wants to stretch baguette portions made from dough that's too strong. The protease degrades gluten strength enough that loaves can be extended more easily from their unshaped portions. Keep in mind, though, that protease continues to degrade gluten strength over time, so loaves that must be held in a proofer or refrigerator for long periods risk collapsing on themselves if strength is reduced too much or too quickly.

More detailed discussion of the nature of the fermentation process can be found in *Advanced Topic #3*.

Manipulating Fermentation: Time, Temperature, and Hydration

Just about all bread dough contains the saccharomyces cerevisiae yeast (*S. cerevisiae*) and both types of lactic bacteria, whether the dough is made with manufactured yeast or raised by a sourdough culture. Many of the wild yeasts in sourdough, as well as the manufactured variety sold by bakery suppliers, actually belong to the *S. cerevisiae* species, though they represent different strains. The lactic bacteria in fermented dough tend to build up more noticeably in sour cultures and the breads made from them, making their presence more obvious, but they are also present in commercially yeasted bread dough used to make mildly flavored loaves like French baguettes and typical sandwich bread.

There are methods we can use to alter the numbers of yeast and bacteria in dough during fermentation, or to vary the amount of by-products they generate. By controlling the population of microorganisms and their fermentation activity, we can promote the bread characteristics they produce in flavor, texture, and aromas.

CHANGING THE TIME

Manufactured yeast cells process sugars much more quickly than do bacteria, so their numbers within the dough grow much faster, initially, and yeast by-products dominate the fermentation process in its early stages. Wild yeasts in sour cultures work more slowly than their commercially made cousins, but even they can surpass bacteria in a race to consume sugar. A bread dough made with manufactured compressed yeast (see *Chapter 2*) at about 1% of the weight of the flour used probably needs only 1½–2 hours to produce sufficient carbon dioxide to leaven the dough and make acceptable bread. We need 3–4 hours, though, for enough lactic bacteria to accumulate to produce enough acid to make bread dough taste very good.

CHANGING THE TEMPERATURE

Increasing the temperature of bread dough or of the environment in which it is fermented has a dramatic effect on yeast fermentation by increasing the rate at which yeast cells consume simple sugars. Gas production increases, as does alcohol production. The effect of increased temperature on bacterial fermentation is to increase the proportion of homofermentative bacteria and the by-product they produce, which is the milder lactic acid. So increasing the temperature of a dough or its environment speeds alcohol and gas production (the rising of the dough) while maintaining a milder flavor profile.

Decreasing the temperature of the dough slows yeast activity considerably; even a drop of 2–3°F can make a noticeable difference. The bacteria that thrives at lower temperatures is the heterofermentative variety, which produces both lactic and the sharper-flavored acetic acid. So lowering the temperature of a dough or its environment reduces the rate of alcohol and gas production while increasing the acidic flavors it will exhibit. It should be noted, though, that the mere presence of lactic or acetic acid in dough does not transform it into sourdough. Sourdough bread has elevated levels of lactic bacteria from the considerable amount of concentrated sour culture in its formula. Breads leavened with manufactured yeast, which are typically not sour at all, also have populations of lactic bacteria, but their numbers are lower, and their effect on flavor, while considerable, is definitely more subtle.

CHANGE THE HYDRATION

Increasing the water in a bread dough formula enables the yeast to move about more freely in their consumption of simple sugars. The faster they can move, the faster they can eat, so increasing the water in a dough or pre-ferment increases the rate of yeast activity and the gases and alcohol yeast create. Lowering the quantity of water does just the opposite.

The effect of different water levels on bacterial activity is more complex. Homofermentative bacteria, like yeast cells, favor higher levels of water in bread dough. Heterofermentative bacteria, with their sharper-flavored acids, thrive in a somewhat drier environment. So increasing water levels in a dough increases homofermentative activity and promotes milder flavors, while decreasing the water favors heterofermentative activity and creates higher levels of the sharply flavored acetic acid.

Pre-Ferments: How to Shorten Fermentation Time While Increasing Strength and Flavor

We mentioned previously that bacteria need time to develop in number and contribute their acids to the strength and flavor profile of bread dough. Unlike yeast, they can't be hurried along, and bread-making procedures that ignore that fact are usually doomed to create bland, uninteresting loaves.

There are successful strategies for shortening the bulk fermentation of a batch of dough, however, that produce mature doughs just as full of flavor as the long-fermented types they mimic. By fermenting a portion of the flour and water used in a bread formula as much as a day before, we can use that as an ingredient in the final dough to obtain the increased levels of bacteria and organic acids responsible for strength and good flavor. These mixtures of flour and water that are fermented ahead of when the final dough is mixed are called *pre-ferments*. They are of two general types: *pre-ferments with manufactured yeast* and *natural pre-ferments*.

PRE-FERMENTS WITH MANUFACTURED YEAST

Poolish is the pre-ferment devised by Polish bakers in the nineteenth century to jump-start older, weaker varieties of commercial yeast. Traditionally, it is made from half flour and half water by weight, with a small amount of yeast that allows for a savings on ingredients while providing for an extended fermentation time that ensures enough bacterial development. Typical fermentation time for a poolish is 5–18 hours, though some bakeries use even longer times. Its wet makeup promotes rapid yeast development, higher proportions of lactic acid, and greater enzyme activity. While it is historically the pre-ferment of choice for baguette production, its wetness can make controlling its fermentation a tricky business, and poolish is the pre-ferment that requires the greatest level of experience to manage successfully.

Sponge is often the name applied to stiffer mixtures of flour, water, and yeast that are fermented ahead of time. The hydration level of sponges made from North American flour is usually 60–63%, and they can be fermented for 5–24 hours. Their dry consistency, compared to poolish, makes for a much slower development of yeast activity and much lower risk of overfermentation. It also yields a higher level of acidity than does poolish, making for somewhat more noticeable flavor enhancements and greater dough strength. The increase in dough strength is terrific if you need it, but extra-long loaves like baguettes can be harder to shape if you use sponge, so its appearance in baguette formulas is probably not recommended.

Biga is, historically speaking, the name applied to stiff pre-ferments used in Italy to flavor bread dough and give their weaker flours greater strength. Its characteristics are similar in many respects to sponge, but the hydration of biga can range even lower, to 50–55%, and it usually features more yeast than does sponge. Its extremely dry consistency makes it an ideal environment for heterofermentative bacteria and the sharp acetic acid they produce. It is an ideal pre-ferment for use with extremely wet final doughs, as its higher acid levels can strengthen wet dough while its dry nature reduces the development of excessive enzyme activity.

Old dough (called *pâte fermentée* by the French) is, as the name suggests, leftover bread dough held back from a previous batch and used as an ingredient in a later batch. It is generally wetter than a sponge but much drier than poolish. Its biggest difference from either of those other pre-ferments is that it contains salt. It is, after all, just leftover bread dough, and it is often not distinguishable from the bread dough to which it is added. Old dough in industrial bakeries is sometimes called *re-run*, which refers to its purpose there: the reutilization of dough that would otherwise be thrown away. Artisan bakers, though, realize the benefits of using old dough can be even greater than saving money. Its effects on flavor and dough maturity are similar in many ways to that created with sponge, and, as an additional benefit, it is possible to use old dough that was mixed as part of a batch of standard bread dough used for loaves that very day. Larger quantities of old dough, though, probably should be mixed as a separate batch—just like any pre-ferment—and old dough kept for more than 3 hours should be refrigerated after 1 hour at room temperature until it is finally used. That can be complicated for a high-volume baking operation if refrigeration space is limited. Old dough, when used in measured quantities and handled with respect, can create great flavor in a final dough in much less time than straight dough can. If handled casually or inconsistently, however, the flavors created are inconsistent at best.

Natural Pre-Ferments

The first pre-ferments probably weren't thought of as pre-ferments at all. They were leftover dough—as with old dough—but these were pieces of *sourdough* held back from a batch of bread made that day and saved for adding the next day to another batch. No commercially produced yeast was used in this process. Ingredients for a sourdough starter are pictured in the color insert following page 50.

This was the most common method of bread leavening from the days of the ancient Egyptians through the late nineteenth century, so it was an integral part of bread making in its day, not just an optional procedure used to add flavor or dough strength. As this technique evolved, a leftover piece of sourdough was fed 2 or 3 times with additional flour and water to enable it to grow in size and leavening power before its incorporation into bread dough made the next day. These feedings before final use in another dough are sometimes referred to as *elaborations*.

Different cultures applied different names to this naturally yeasted process. German-speaking peoples called it *sauerteig*, the Italians referred to it as *lievito naturale*, and the British usually used the term *barm* to refer to a sourdough culture. The French use the term *levain* to identify a sourdough process, and that is the one we use here. While the precise flours used may differ and the names vary even more among nations, the underlying process is essentially the same, and the principles applied are more similar than they are different.

Two basic types of levain are now used by the French, with artisan bakers choosing one or the other depending on where they were trained or which tradition they choose to uphold. The oldest type is probably the *firm levain*, which is similar in consistency to the sponge from manufactured yeast described previously. The hydration range of firm levain is 55–60% when using North American flours, and the reason it is made dry is to slow the fermentation and allow only 2 or 3 feedings before it is used to make bread. Wetter mixtures would ferment more quickly and would possibly require more attention from a baker to ensure they would not overferment. Keep in mind that through most of bread-making history, levain was not optional but actually necessary for making leavened bread, and there were no refrigerators around to keep a pre-ferment from getting out of control.

Figures 5.2a–5.2e illustrate generating a firm sourdough culture. The initial culture pictured in 5.2a was held for 24 hours at 85°F. The feedings that occurred afterward were all made with white bread flour and held at 70°F.

The other type of levain used by some French bakers is known as *liquid levain*, and, as its name implies, it is mixed at the consistency of a liquid, much like poolish (which

Figure 5.2a Sourdough culture after combining ingredients.

Figure 5.2b The same culture after 24 hours of fermentation.

Figure 5.2c After 48 hours of fermentation.

Figure 5.2d After 5 days of fermentation.

Figure 5.2e After 10 days of fermentation.

Generating and Maintaining a Sourdough Culture

There are numerous ways to create your own sour culture for bread making. As we made clear in the opening of this chapter, fermentation goes on everywhere around us; the only challenge is to find the microbes you want and isolate them so you can use their abilities to transform dough over and over.

Some books on bread baking encourage the baker to seek yeast and bacteria from sources like buttermilk, potato water, organic grapes or just outdoor air. All of those choices can serve as starting points for fermentation, and they may offer dramatic evidence of life in short order. Still, because the culture will be supported eventually by flour and water only, we can presume that most of the microbes present at the beginning of those fermentations will be gone in a matter of days. A levain that was started with grapes crushed in water shows vigorous fermentation in just a day, but the yeast present on the outside of the grapes are less likely to thrive in a medium of flour and water, and the initial burst of microbial activity might be attributed to the simple sugars present in the juice itself. If we feed the culture a daily diet of bread flour and water, the microbes most likely to survive and thrive are those that prefer such a regimen, and these are more than likely be the same microbes already present on the bran in whole-grain flours.

For this reason, we suggest that starting with a flour mix that is high in bran and in naturally present fermentable sugars nearly always gives good results, provided the baker is willing to pay attention to details and patient enough to await the results. Even starting with flour and water only, the baker has numerous choices, but for the sake of simplicity we chose the method outlined in Table 5.2 to illustrate one possible way to obtain a fairly firm sour starter, known as *levain* in France.

We start with a half-and-half mixture of whole wheat flour and medium rye. Both of these flours are easily available in most bakeries across the United States, so they require no special ordering. The whole wheat flour is rich in bran, so it provides a high likelihood of success in inoculating the culture with the yeast and bacteria we seek. It is also high in mineral content, which helps the culture thrive. Rye flour is high in fermentable sugars that can provide immediate nutrition to the wild microbes, and its high amylase content ensures much of the starch in both flours is converted to sugars as the culture ferments. Mix these flours in a clean container with enough warm water (perhaps 90°F) to make for a 90% hydration, and hold the mixture, covered, at an ambient temperature of about 85°F for around 24 hours. We have never had an instance where this method did not work. Attention to the details described above, though, is paramount to success. Lower hydrations and lower temperatures can still succeed, if allowed time, but the evidence of success is slower to come.

After the first day, we begin to feed the culture twice a day with white bread flour and much less water—only a 60% hydration—and we hold the mixture at a much lower temperature of only 70°F. The combination of these significant changes works to eliminate those yeasts and bacteria that are not tolerant of them, and, by the process of elimination, the species we desire start to dominate all others.

Initially, the aromas produced by the culture may seem unappetizing, but this is because literally hundreds of different yeast and bacteria are present at this time, and they all are adding their various by-products to the mix. As we make the changes described above, we see the aromas change dramatically. By the time 10 consecutive days of proper maintenance and feeding has elapsed, the culture is near to the stabilized *levain* we are looking for. The aromas produced by then are a combination of alcohol and noticeable acidity, with other aspects (like fruitiness) that contribute complexity to the whole.

After only 5 days, the level of gas production in the culture is so obvious you could probably use it to leaven bread. At this point, though, the selection of the most desirable yeasts may not be complete. The culture also may not seem very sour at this point—it is common for the build-up of bacterial activity and acidity to require 10 days or more.

If you wish to promote more yeast activity in your culture, feed it 3 or even 4 times a day, though you may want to use smaller feedings. Once-a-day feedings can work if the feeding is large enough, but wild cultures can benefit from the stirring that occurs at feeding time, which expels carbon dioxide while incorporating oxygen. Cultures fed and stirred only once a day do not benefit as often, which can result in lower yeast activity and higher acidity. The aromas that come from the culture itself may also not be as complex.

Maintaining a culture at a lower temperature slows yeast activity while increasing the levels of acetic acid. If this sourer profile is what you seek, then holding the levain there may be fine, but there are limits to how much you can chill a culture being maintained for immediate use. Anything below 50°F is probably risky, as most yeasts we need for bread making don't thrive at those temperatures. For practical reasons, many home bakers (and even some professionals) keep sour starters in their refrigerator at some point. It is thought by many artisan bakers that such colder temperatures actually damage the culture, but experience indicates the damage may be temporary. If re-

Generating and Maintaining a Sourdough Culture (Continued)

frigeration of the culture is necessary for extended periods, two practices may be advisable: Continue to feed the culture at least twice a week for a few hours at room temperature to maintain viability, and resume twice-a-day feedings at 70°F at least 2–3 days before its use in baking. Keeping the culture refrigerated is probably not the best option for professional use, but operations that close 1 or 2 days a week may have few alternatives.

TABLE 5.2 One Possible Schedule for Generating and Maintinaing a Firm Sourdough Culture

Ingredients	Amt. of Ripe Culture to Add	Flour to Add	Water to Add	Holding Temperature, Covered	Time to Next Feeding
Day 1	—	100g med. rye 100g whole wheat	180g @ 90°F	85°F	24 hrs
Days 2–10	100g	100g white bread flour	60g @ 66–70°F	70°F	12 hrs

Many possibilities exist, including different flours or hydrations, different feeding intervals, and different holding temperatures. Larger and/or more frequent feedings promote more yeast activity and less acidity, while smaller and/or less frequent feedings create less yeast activity and greater acidity. Temperature affects the culture as well; warmer temperatures encourage yeast activity and milder acidity, while cooler temperatures slow yeast activity and produce a more sour flavor profile.

is fermented with manufactured yeast). Its origins may be debated, but by the late nineteenth century in France, bakers who used levain to make their bread may have realized that by making a sort of slurry from their firm levain well before use, they could encourage the growth of wild yeast cells and the homofermentative bacteria that produce lighter-textured breads and less sour flavors when compared to bread made from firm levain. We do know that this method of liquefying levain was used for making baguettes and other breads by the early twentieth century. Its use was eventually displaced by the adoption of poolish as an easier method by many bakers. Since the early 1990s, bakers like Eric Kayser in Paris have resumed using liquid levain as an alternative to poolish and other yeasted pre-ferments in their bakeries. It produces more acidic overtones than poolish, of course, but its liquid consistency makes for less heterofermentative bacteria than in firm levain, so its flavor is less sour than that associated with firm levain. More liquid also means more wild yeast activity, so sourdough breads made with liquid levain can achieve more lightness than breads made only with firm levain. Liquid levain can be used in smaller proportions with commercial yeast to make breads with flavor profiles that are complex and fruity with no sourness at all, and its higher enzyme activity can make the extension of baguettes occur more easily.

ARTISAN BAKER PROFILE

Alison Pray

Standard Baking Company, Portland, Maine

Alison Pray worked in the restaurant and catering industry for 12 years before applying for a baker's position at the Clear Flour Bread bakery, in the Boston area, in 1992. She had become fascinated by the craft of bread as practiced by village bakers, and she dedicated herself to learning as much as she could from Clear Flour's owners, Christy Timon and Abe Faber.

In 2002, Alison and her business partner decided to open their own bakery in Portland, Maine. They named it the Standard Baking Company, and the quality of their all-natural breads and pastries has led to critical praise from such notable sources as the *New York Times* and Jane and Michael Stern's Roadfood.com. Alison has been a member of the Bread Bakers Guild of America since 1995, and she serves on the Guild's Advisory Board.

Her bakery's most popular menu items are the baguette, a rustic Italian bread, and various laminated pastries. The bakery produces approximately 2500 pounds of bread dough and hundreds of pastries each week.

IMPRESSIONS OF ARTISAN BREAD BAKING AS AN INDUSTRY

Did you have any preconceptions about the artisan bread business (or any aspect of the bread business) that were altered by your industry experience?

Before working my first bakery job, I had this image of bread baking as a quiet, contemplative process. The reality of working in production baking was much more like a restaurant kitchen than a meditation, although you do get to have more solitary work during quiet hours than in a restaurant.

What are your thoughts on the future of the artisan bread business?

I think we'll continue to see much more growth in the artisan bread business. Large companies like Panera and La Brea are exposing millions of people to the concept of fresh-baked, high-quality bread. Neighborhood bakeries are continuing to open in small towns and city neighborhoods. We've seen small established bakeries investing in new equipment, or perhaps opening second and third locations, enabling them to become more regional than local. I'm noticing more and more backyard bakeries opening too, part-time bakers who sell their baked goods at co-ops and farmer's markets.

As the larger companies become more successful, this will invite competition, so I expect to see more franchise or conglomerate-owned bakeries. At the same time, I believe small neighborhood bakeries hold a unique place in our culture. As the pace of most of our lives is accelerating and we feel obligated to multitask constantly, stopping at a neighborhood bakery for only one item is like stepping back in time. I think more and more people are choosing to buy locally, not only for the difference in quality but just as much for the experience of connecting with others.

What's the biggest make-or-break cost factor of running a successful artisan bread shop?

Labor cost.

What are your thoughts on prospective artisan bakers? What characteristics or personality traits do you look for in prospective employees that increase their potential for hire? Are there any traits that might exclude them?

We hope to find people with a passion or strong desire to learn about the process of bread baking. We would be less likely to consider people who think of baking as easy or who think they've already learned everything there is to know about it.

Summary   *Fermentation* can be defined as the breakdown of organic substances by yeasts, bacteria, or molds. It is by nature a process of degradation, but, under controlled environmental conditions, it can create other foods or beverages that are valued or even prized. Bread is among them.

Professional bakers identify three important stages of dough fermentation: bulk fermentation, intermediate proofing, and final proofing. Fermentation proceeds throughout the life of a dough, though, right on through the first minutes of baking in an oven.

Yeast and bacteria are the living microorganisms that cause dough fermentation. Nonliving organic substances like enzymes also participate in degrading starch and proteins. The major by-products of yeast fermentation are carbon dioxide and alcohol, while the major by-products of bacterial fermentation in dough are lactic acid and acetic acid. It is the yeast that primarily leavens a dough, but it is the bacteria that create acids that promote strength and flavor in bread. The most important enzymes present in bread dough are amylase, zymase, and protease.

We can manipulate the amount of time, the degree of temperature, and the amount of water (hydration) used during fermentation of bread dough to change its flavor and strength characteristics. By using pre-ferments in dough formulas, we can add certain characteristics of strength or flavor to a final dough without waiting the usual 4 or 5 hours for a straight dough to come to maturity. The important categories of pre-ferments in artisan baking are pre-ferments with manufactured yeast and natural pre-ferments. Examples of pre-ferments with manufactured yeast are poolish, sponge, biga, and old dough. Examples of natural pre-ferments are firm levain and liquid levain.

Key Terms

fermentation	homofermentative bacteria
by-products	heterofermentative bacteria
bulk fermentation	esters
intermediate proof	enzymes
final proof	amylase
pre-fermentation	zymase
pre-ferments	protease
oven spring	pre-ferments with manufactured yeast
yeast	natural pre-ferments
carbon dioxide	poolish
alcohol	sponge
saccharomyces cerevisiae	biga
bacteria	old dough
organic acids	elaborations
lactic acid	firm levain
acetic acid	liquid levain
lactic bacteria	

Questions for Review

1. How can fermentation be both a process of decay and a process of creation?

2. What are some common foods and beverages, other than bread itself, that are products of fermentation?

3. What are the three stages of fermentation identified by professional bakers?

4. What sort of environment favors the development of yeast activity? What sort of by-products do yeast produce?

5. What sort of environment is preferred by homofermentative bacteria? How is the environment preferred by heterofermentative bacteria different? What by-products do each of them produce?

6. What are the three enzymes of most importance to bread bakers? Are enzymes alive?

7. How can we change the rate of yeast activity in bread dough? How do we control the numbers and types of bacteria in dough?

8. Why is it important to develop bacterial activity in bread dough during fermentation?

9. Can we shorten bulk fermentation time in bread dough while preserving dough strength and a good flavor profile?

10. How are wetter pre-ferments different from drier pre-ferments in their overall effect on flavor and dough strength?

11. Do natural pre-ferments contain yeast?

Questions for Discussion

1. Scientists have isolated faster strains of yeast that can sufficiently inflate bread dough in 30–60 minutes. Their attempts at speeding production of acids by bacteria have so far met with no success. Most North American bakeries don't take the time to ferment dough long enough to give it good, naturally derived flavor. To do so, they would have to raise the prices for their bread, as most artisans do already. Is it the industry's reluctance to do things less efficiently that keeps them from making better bread? Or is it the consumer's unwillingness to pay the higher price that results from taking more time?

2. Artisan-style attention to long fermentation and great bread baking is still around, but its face has changed since the early 1990s. How has the availability of great bread evolved in your area? What form does it take, and how available will it be 10 years or so from now?

Lab Exercise & Experiment

Scale and mix two batches of the following formula for *pain de campagne* (French country-style bread).

PAIN DE CAMPAGNE					
	Metric		U.S. Measure		Formula Baker's %
	(1X)	(4X)	(1X)	(4X)	
	5-Qt Mixer	20-Qt Mixer	5-Qt Mixer	20-Qt Mixer	
STRAIGHT DOUGH					
Bread flour	900g	3600g	1 lb 11.0oz	6 lb 12.0oz	**90%**
Medium rye flour	100g	400g	3.0oz	12.0oz	**10%**
Water	680g	2720g	1 lb 4.4oz	5 lb 1.6oz	**68%**
Salt	22g	88g	0.7oz	2.6oz	**2.2%**
Instant yeast	3g	12g	0.1oz	0.4oz	**0.3%**
TOTAL YIELD	**1705g**	**6820g**	**3 lb 3.2oz**	**12 lb 12.6oz**	

Options:

You could use a pre-ferment to make this dough, if you wish. With sponge, biga, or old dough, limit pre-fermented flour in the formula to 35% or less. The high enzyme levels in poolish make it less risky at 25% or less. Firm levain works reliably up to 30% or so, but liquid levain can create stickiness at anything above 18–20%.

The use of any pre-ferment reduces significantly the time necessary for the dough to reach maturity.

GOAL TEMPERATURE: 77°F (25°C).

MIXING METHOD: Short mix, intensive mix, or improved mix—see pp. 195–196.

BULK FERMENTATION: See directions associated with the mix method chosen—pp. 195–196.

SCALING: See options, p. 196.

SHAPING: See directions in *Chapter 6*.

PROOFING: See directions, pp. 196–197.

BAKING: See directions, p. 197.

COOLING: See directions, p. 198.

Keep as many variables as possible at the same value, except for total fermentation time allowed before division. This means water temperature, the size and type of container, the place where you ferment the dough, and so forth should be the same for each batch.

Ferment the first dough for 3 hours if possible, giving the dough 1 fold at the midpoint.

Scale, mix, and ferment the second dough as you wait for the first to complete its bulk fermentation. Ferment it for 1 hour with 1 fold at the midpoint, and then divide it into pieces of the same size (500g or 18 ounces should be adequate). After their intermediate or bench proof, shape them into short bâtards, proof them, and bake them at approximately 430°F, taking note of the dough's handling characteristics, strength, ease of shaping, the appearance of the scoring, and the final appearance of the shaped loaves.

When the 3-hour dough has completed its bulk fermentation, divide it in the same manner as the 1-hour dough and handle it in exactly the same manner. Keep a record of the comparative handling characteristics of the two doughs, using such criteria as stickiness, smoothness, strength, extensibility, gas levels, plasticity, proofing time, and final appearance of the raw loaves and the baked loaves.

What differences do you see? Are there any differences in taste? What happened in the extra 2 hours that might have made the 3-hour dough act differently from the 1-hour version? Has this changed your understanding of what effects long fermentation can have on the characteristics of bread dough?

chapter 6

Division and Shaping of Loaves and Rolls

Learning Outcomes:

- Recognize important precautions in dividing and handling bread dough and the portions you cut from it.

- Become familiar with the objective of shaping loaves and rolls.

- Be able to shape a round loaf.

- Be able to shape an oval or log-shaped loaf.

- Be able to shape a baguette.

- Be able to shape small round or oval rolls.

Giving Form to Dough

You may remember that some breads, like pain rustique (see *Chapter 4*), are not shaped much at all after their dough is divided into portions. They are cut into squares or rectangles and merely transferred to parchment or a linen *couche* to rest and reinflate a bit before they bake (*couche* refers to a length of linen cloth that is floured, pleated, and used to hold raw loaves and support them as they proof). That particular variety is reflective of a rustic baking tradition when bread was more for sustenance than anything else, and the chore of giving shape to very wet pieces of dough might have seemed more trouble than it was worth. We now appreciate the unique texture and open crumb possible with bread that hasn't been shaped, so varieties like *pain rustique* and *ciabatta* still hold a treasured place on bread menus at most artisan-style bakeries in North America.

Since the early days of baking leavened breads, most varieties have gradually taken on a more refined appearance and are shaped more carefully—sometimes even elaborately. Some of these shapes seem more practical for certain applications—like making sandwiches, or serving at dinner—while other shapes are rooted in tradition or even have religious overtones. While the reasons for selecting a shape can vary widely, both operators and consumers realize that giving recognizable shape to breads makes them more appealing in appearance and therefore more marketable.

Shaping gives direction to the growth that results from capturing and holding the gases from fermentation. We can cut and leave dough in a fairly formless blob, as we do for *pain rustique* and *ciabatta,* or we can try to pull the dough's skin around itself in a manner that gives a defined shape to the loaf and tends to produce greater height and better volume.

The First Step: Division

There is most definitely a right and a wrong way to go about dividing and handling dough portions before you shape them. If you do it correctly, the crumb will eventually have the texture you intended and the portions will provide a vehicle for quick, consistent shaping. If you are too casual about it, the loaves will vary quite a bit in size, the crumb will be unpredictable, and the final form of each loaf will vary greatly.

DON'T USE MORE FLOUR THAN YOU NEED

First, you must decide whether your dough is very wet, moderately wet, or firm in consistency. The wetter the dough, the more flour must be on the bench surface before the dough tub is emptied onto it. Ciabatta (see page 210 in the *Appendix of Formulas*), for instance, is extremely wet and requires a heavy veil of flour on the bench before you invert the tub and dump the dough. Baguette dough is moderately wet and requires some flour, but you should not use more than will keep it from sticking to the bench. Dough for challah or bagels may not require any flour on the bench at all, since it is fairly firm in consistency. The infinite variety of breads prevents us from giving any more specifics, but the underlying principle is this: Use only enough flour to keep the mass of dough and the portions from sticking to the bench—no more. If you use an excessive amount of flour on the bench when dividing dough, the excess flour will be folded into the portions but never really absorbed by the dough itself. The unincorporated flour will be visible and leave somewhat unappetizing streaks in the final loaves, so minimizing the use of flour on the bench to what you absolutely need is a practice worth learning.

ARRANGE YOUR BENCH TO PROMOTE EFFICIENT WORKFLOW

Minimizing the amount of lateral movement involved in cutting the dough and holding it as it undergoes its *intermediate proof* (see *Chapter 7*) takes less effort on your part and allows you to work much faster. For this reason, you should arrange the bench ahead of time and plan your workflow.

Empty your dough from its tub directly in front of the spot where you plan to stand at the bench. You might place the dough at one end of your bench, your scale next to it, and your proofing boards or bench-proofing area just beyond that and within reach of the scale. This arrangement should minimize the movement necessary to divide the dough mass and move the portions to where they will be pre-shaped and held to await final shaping. Figure 6.1 illustrates the arrangement just described. Every bakery has its own idiosyncrasies and design limitations, so you must plan the most sensible model for your own workflow. The dough cutting, pre-shaping, and holding should proceed in one direction to increase efficiency and minimize unnecessary body movement.

Figure 6.1 A baker's bench with the dough, a balance-beam scale, and proofing boards set up in a logical workflow.

DIVIDE THE DOUGH INTO STRIPS, THEN INTO PORTIONS

Dividing dough by hand with a baker's balance (see Figure 6.1) is common in artisan bread bakeries. Some larger bakeries choose to use heavy hydraulic dividers that minimize the compression of the dough's crumb. These can certainly speed the division of dough, but you may notice a certain loss of openness in the crumb of hearth loaves, and these expensive machines are a justifiable expense only for bakeshops doing a large volume.

In some dividers used by bread factories, the dough mass is literally sucked through a narrow channel by vacuum pressure before a large blade shears off portions. Bakeries operated by artisans should avoid using this type of divider. This vacuum-driven process does significant damage to the dough's structure and risks compressing the crumb to an unacceptable degree.

Some very large bakeries now use low-stress (or no-stress) dividers that use gravity, computers, and high-tech laser beams to measure and cut dough on a continually moving conveyor belt. These dividers are truly amazing and do very little damage to the crumb of the loaves, but they can cost 2–4 times as much as a typical deck oven and are affordable for only *very* high-volume bakeries. So it is necessary for you to learn hand division.

When you flip the dough tub to empty it, place the dough mass directly in front of you, within easy reach. This way, you won't have to stretch your arms to cut the dough, which will tire you quickly and slow your pace. Start by cutting the dough with your bench knife into wide strips—probably 4–5 inches, depending on the size of the portions you need (small rolls can be cut from much narrower strips of only 2 inches or so). Then, cut the strips into rectangular portions, weighing each as you go, and add or subtract a small amount of dough to obtain the weight you need.

If you find you are using more than one large chunk of dough together with one or two small pieces to get to the correct weight, start cutting the large chunks a bit larger to begin with to reduce the time needed to cut the total dough mass. A sense of urgency when dividing is necessary to make short work of the process. You may find this awkward at first, but if you start looking closely at the size of the correctly weighed portions you have cut, you should get a better idea of how much dough to cut initially from each strip. When you become more experienced, you can cut quickly and get to within a half-ounce of your desired portion weight on the first try. Keep in mind that as you cut your portions, you must handle the dough gently.

PRE-SHAPE THE DOUGH PORTIONS

After you have cut your dough mass into the proper-sized portions, you typically put them through what is called *pre-shaping*. When you pre-shape a piece of dough, you give the piece a very light turning, folding, or rounding to provide a shape that, when rested, can be easily finessed into its final form. Little force should be applied to the dough portion as it is pre-shaped. If you tighten the gluten too much by using too much force during pre-shaping, you risk tearing it, and the pre-shapes may be so tense that, even after a 20-minute rest, you may not be able to extend the dough as much as you would like during final shaping.

Figure 6.2 shows some common shapes for bread dough, along with the form their pre-shaped piece usually takes.

Notice the boule (the round loaf) and the boulot (the short loaf with the tapered ends) are both simply pre-shaped as lightly formed rounds. Both the baguette and the bâtard can be pre-shaped as cylinders. The remaining steps for completing

Figure 6.2 Pre-shaped representations and finished shapes. In the top row, from left to right, a lightly rounded pre-shape and the final shapes that come from it: a finished round (or *boule*, in French) and a finished *boulot*, or football shape. In the second row, from left to right: a cylinder pre-shape and the final shapes that come from it: a finished *bâtard*, or log, and the classic baguette.

the shaping of these loaves is presented shortly. One point that bears repeating is that little tension is created during the pre-shaping process. Further, in the case of hearth loaves, you should handle the dough gently enough so it doesn't lose any of its open crumb structure. Many pan breads made from intensively mixed dough are handled quite differently, as the goal in producing them is to eliminate large holes in the crumb. A more aggressive amount of deflation and tightening can actually help prevent large holes (called *alveoli*) in sandwich breads such as *pain de mie*, where they are not desirable.

KEEP THE PORTIONS COVERED

After the portions are pre-shaped, they must be covered to prevent a dry skin from forming on their exterior. If you choose to rest the portions on your wooden bench, you might choose to cover them with linen cloth, or possibly cloth and then plastic. Laying plastic sheeting directly on dough portions can be risky, as the dough may

TABLE 6.1 Loaves and Pre-Shapes

Type of Loaf	Pre-Shaped Form	Suggested Intermediate Proof or Rest (approx.)
Round (boule)	Round	10–15 minutes
Oval (boulot)	Round	15–20 minutes
Log (bâtard)	Cylinder	15–20 minutes
Baguette	Cylinder	20–30 minutes

stick to it. If you use proofing boards to hold your portions, flour the boards first and then place the boards with their pre-shapes on a covered speed rack as they undergo the intermediate proof. Leave space between the portions on your boards, thereby preventing them from growing together as they rest.

The total time you devote to the intermediate proof depends on how long it takes for your pre-shaped portions to relax enough to complete the shaping process. Round loaves (*boules*) can usually be completed after only 10–15 minutes of rest. A *boulot* (oblong, tapered loaf) probably needs 15–20 minutes before it can be shaped and tapered without any danger of tearing it. *Bâtards* (short logs with squared ends) also need 15–20 minutes in most cases, but *baguettes* (long, thin loaves shaped like a strand) often take 20–30 minutes before they are ready for final shaping. The more you tighten during pre-shaping, the longer you must wait to do the final shaping, in most cases. Baguette pre-shapes take the longest time to relax because the loaves have to be stretched so far before they are finished. A comparison of typical rest times for loaves and pre-shapes is found in Table 6.1.

Other factors can affect how long the portions require rest, such as dough hydration (wet dough is more extensible and needs less rest), dough strength (elastic dough needs *more* rest), and enzyme activity (dough with a lot of protease activity is more easily extended and requires less rest). Only experimentation with your own dough varieties can tell you how long you need to allow portions to rest before doing the final shaping.

Shaping Loaves and Rolls

Once your pre-shaped portions have relaxed sufficiently, you can proceed with their final shaping. The following photographs provide a general introduction to the craft of shaping bread. However, there is no substitute for real experience and personal instruction in learning how to shape. The photos and captions are presented as a mere suggestion. Also, there are variations on the methods illustrated. You should defer to the method demonstrated by your instructor when you run into situations that require further explanation or example.

ROUND SHAPE

The round loaf is possibly the easiest shape to master, though there are important points to consider before you decide a round has been shaped properly. These points are outlined in the procedure for shaping a round loaf in which a pre-shaped round portion of dough is about to undergo the steps for final shaping.

Procedure for Shaping a Round Loaf

1. Lay the dough portion on the bench in front of you so the seam is facing up. Flatten it somewhat, patting out the excess gas (if any), while leaving it inflated enough to preserve its open crumb structure.

2. Fold the edges of the flattened portion in toward the middle, holding them there with your fingers as you do (see Figure 6.3a). Four folds or so are usually sufficient; the exact number is not important, only that you gather the edges of the flat round portion toward the middle. Press or pinch the edges together lightly (see Figure 6.3b) and then turn the portion over so the gathered edges are down against the bench and the smooth side of the portion is now up.

3. You can see the round beginning to take shape. All that is left is to pull the skin on the outside of the dough down toward the bottom, where you gather it together and create a central seam that resembles the navel on an orange. To do this, cup your hands around either side of the dough and begin to pinch its bottom against the bench surface, alternately pushing the loaf away from you and pulling it toward you, moving in a circle as you go (see Figures 6.3c–6.3e).

4. You must monitor how the loaf is shaping as you apply tension to its bottom and vary the pressure you apply and the direction you push or pull to react to what you see before you. Some improvisation or variation in technique is natural from baker to baker, but the basic principle of pulling the skin down toward the bottom of the loaf without tearing it remains a constant.

5. Once the loaf is shaped (see Figure 6.3f), place it seam-side down on a floured proofing board or seam-side up in a round proofing basket (*banneton* or *brotform*—see *Chapter 7*). When you have finished shaping the portions or have filled a rack with shaped loaves, place them as soon as possible into a proofer, or keep them covered and in an environment as close to 80°F as possible.

Figure 6.3a

Figure 6.3b

Figure 6.3c

Figure 6.3d

Figure 6.3e

Figure 6.3f

TAPERED OR OBLONG SHAPE

The tapered or oblong shape is similar in some ways to a log shape, and some bake-shops simply form their portions first into logs and then taper the ends to get an oblong shape. If you feel confident using this method, it is acceptable, but you may want to try the following method, which uses a round pre-shaped dough and produces loaves that are a bit easier to distinguish from logs.

The illustrations in Figures 6.4a–6.4f show how to make the proper folds necessary to finish a tapered or oblong loaf.

Procedure for Shaping a Tapered or Oblong Loaf

The illustrations in Figure 6.4a–6.4f show how to make the proper folds necessary to finish a tapered or oblong loaf.

1. Start with the round pre-shape turned over on your bench, seam-side up. Flatten it by patting it a few times lightly, but do not completely deflate the dough (see Figure 6.4a).

2. Place your hands under the far side of the dough circle and fold in toward the middle of the piece, leaving the far edge of the newly folded portion curved as you press down lightly on the edges you have gathered in the middle (see Figures 6.4b and 6.4c).

3. Now, curve your hands to match the contour of the far edges and fold the dough toward you once or twice again (dough that is extensible can be folded down more than dough that exhibits elastic or bucky qualities). As you are folding the dough down this time, take the far, curved edge of the piece and make it meet as closely as possible with the curved edge of the dough closest to you (see Figure 6.4d).

4. The long line where the two curved edges now meet will be the seam on the underside of the loaf (see Figure 6.4e). Rap the seam lightly with the base of your hand to seal it securely (see Figure 6.4f), and then place the shaped loaf either seam-side up in an oblong proofing basket (*banneton* in French, *brotform* in German) or seam-side down in a pleated couche. Note the boulot is quite plump in the middle and tapered on the ends, which distinguishes it somewhat from the log-shaped *bâtard* we will shape next.

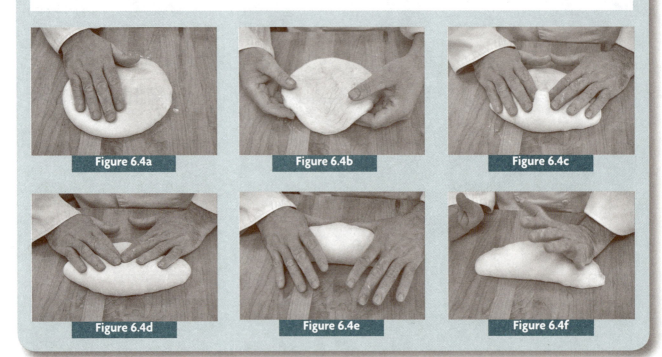

Figure 6.4a   Figure 6.4b   Figure 6.4c

Figure 6.4d   Figure 6.4e   Figure 6.4f

Log Shapes

Short, fat loaves with squared ends, and their slightly longer cousins, are shaped essentially the same way. Refer to Figure 6.5 as a visual guide for shaping dough portions into logs as you follow the steps described in the following procedure.

Procedure for Shaping a Log Loaf

1. Place a pre-shaped cylinder of dough that has relaxed sufficiently on the bench in front of you so its long edges are on the left and right sides and the shorter edges on the top and bottom. Flatten the piece by patting it lightly with your hands a time or two, but be gentle and do not completely deflate the dough piece (see Figure 6.5a).

2. Place your hands under the near edge of the dough and fold it away from you so the edge meets the middle of the piece of dough (see Figure 6.5b).

3. Fold the farther edge of the dough down to the middle in a similar fashion.

4. Use your fingertips to press down on the spot where the two edges meet in the middle, and create a shallow spot that will act as a sort of hinge where you'll make your last fold (see Figure 6.5c).

5. Bring the top edge of the folded piece of dough completely up and over the hinge so it meets and conforms to the straight edge at the bottom of the piece. The long line where the two edges now meet forms the seam at the bottom of the loaf (see Figure 6.5d).

6. Join your thumbs together and push down lightly on the seam while at the same time pushing away from you slightly, which will both close the seam and create slightly more tension around the skin of the loaf (see Figure 6.5e). Lightly rap the seam with the base of your hand to seal it.

7. Place the loaf seam-side up in an oblong shaped proofing basket or seam-side down on a floured, pleated couche (see Figure 6.5f).

8. As soon as you have shaped all the portions, or after you have filled a rack, place the shaped loaves in your proofer or cover them until they are baked.

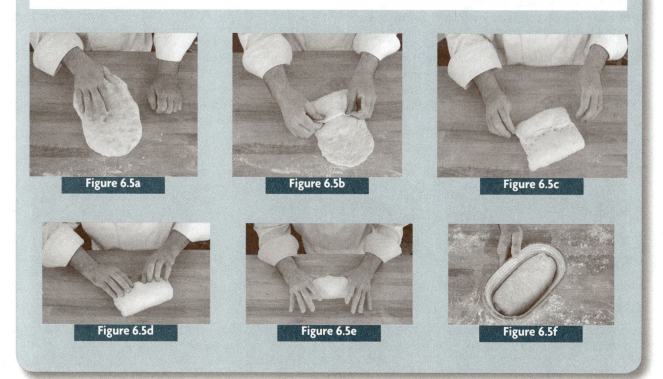

Figure 6.5a

Figure 6.5b

Figure 6.5c

Figure 6.5d

Figure 6.5e

Figure 6.5f

BAGUETTE SHAPE

This is not said to frighten you: Typically, the baguette is the most difficult shape for a baker to master. If you use a dough that is dry and contains chemical relaxers, it is easy to extend a dough piece into a long baguette shape. However, if you use a dough that reflects the origins of true baguettes, which is soft and moderately wet (and sometimes too strong despite that), getting the piece to accept both a series of folds and an exaggerated extension is sometimes challenging. The dough piece requires more handling when shaping baguettes than the other common shapes, and the extended contact between the dough and your hand can cause problems with sticking, tearing, and short tempers.

As a beginner at baguette shaping, you must accept that none of your loaves will look top-notch the first few times you make them. You will become a pro-caliber baguette shaper only if you repeat the shaping technique over and over until you can practically shape them in your sleep. This does not mean you should forego learning how to shape these loaves, but you should realize that few of your first attempts will be perfect, and you should not allow that outcome to dampen your enthusiasm. This book can only provide you with a guide to help get you started; your instructor's lessons and demonstrations are your key to obtaining a comfort level at shaping baguettes. Figures 6.6a–6.6h illustrate the baguette shaping process.

Procedure for Shaping a Baguette

1. Place a pre-shaped cylinder of dough that has relaxed sufficiently on the bench in front of you so its short edges are on the left and right sides and the long edges on the top and bottom. Flatten the piece by patting it lightly with your hands just a few times, but do not completely deflate the dough piece.

2. Place your hands under the far edge of the dough and fold it toward you so the edge meets the middle of the piece (see Figure 6.6a). Then, fold the bottom edge up to the middle in a similar fashion.

3. As you are folding, use your fingertips to press down on the spot where the two edges meet in the middle, and create a shallow spot that will act as a sort of hinge where you'll make your last fold (see Figure 6.6b).

4. Starting at one end, fold the top edge down to meet the bottom edge and seal the edges together with the base of your hand as you go, moving from one end gradually toward the other. Lightly rap the seam with the base of your hand to seal it. When you have finished, you should have a lightly tensioned, sausage-shaped piece of dough (see Figure 6.6c). The long line where the two edges meet and are sealed is now the seam of the loaf.

| Figure 6.6a | Figure 6.6b | Figure 6.6c |

Procedure for Shaping a Baguette (Continued)

5. Turn the dough piece seam-side down and place it in front of you with the ends on the left and the right (see Figure 6.6d).

6. Place the base of one hand (just above the wrist) *in contact with the bench* just in front of the center of the sausage shape. Move your hand forward against the bench, cupped over the dough cylinder but not really pushing down on it (see Figure 6.6e). This will cause your hand to pinch the side of the sausage-shaped piece against the wooden surface of the bench, and it will begin to rotate the cylinder away from you, pulling the skin of the piece back toward you as you rotate the cylinder forward. Stop the motion as you feel the skin get tight beneath your hand; do not pinch outward so far as to tear the dough.

7. Release the base of your hand from the bench surface and put your fingertips in contact with the bench on the opposite side from which you were just working. Pull your fingertips back toward you, always maintaining contact with the bench, and pinch the other side of the sausage shape against the wood surface as you do so. Again, stop the motion when you begin to feel the skin of the piece tighten under your hand.

8. The center segment of the portion where you were just pinching the dough cylinder back and forth should now be much narrower than when you

started. If it is as narrow as the desired diameter of your baguette, you should stop working on that center section and use both hands to narrow the sections just to the left and the right of that area. If it is still a bit too wide or loose, you may repeat the motion back and forth once more to tighten and narrow the diameter a bit more. Any further pinching and tightening of this one small area will result in a crumb structure that is too close and dense at that spot, and the surface of the loaf may tear from being overhandled. Just one or two sets of back-and-forth pinching motion are about all you can do if you want consistent, acceptable results. You will eventually see that you must vary the force you use in pinching the dough against the bench to match the elasticity, extensibility, or diameter of the piece you are trying to shape, and that your goal every time should be to accomplish this tightening and narrowing effect with as few motions as possible.

9. Once the center of the cylinder is tightened and narrowed to the desired diameter, place both your hands on either side of the section you just worked on. Pinch the dough there and narrow those spots on the cylinder the same way you did at the center. Remember: You can use only one or two sets of back-and-forth motion on any one section of the dough, or you might damage the crumb or tear the skin (see Figure 6.6f).

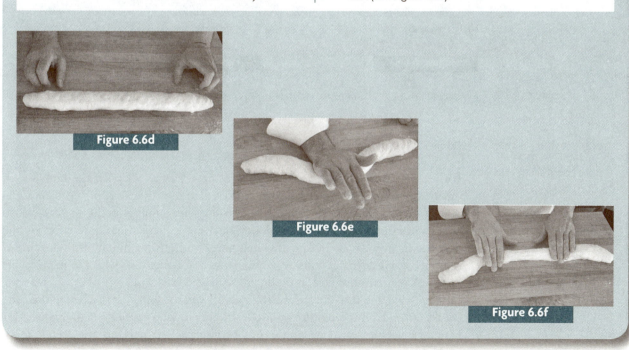

Figure 6.6d

Figure 6.6e

Figure 6.6f

Procedure for Shaping a Baguette (Continued)

10. After you have narrowed the diameter of each segment, proceed to the next adjoining segment, and continue using this method to gradually narrow the cylinder two sections at a time, one under each hand (see Figure 6.6g). Caveats: Do not push outward to either side as you narrow the piece. Just narrow the diameter of each section, release the dough, and move on to the next section. Applying too much pressure in an outward direction as you shape can cause problems with tearing and with making the crumb of the bread too close from being overworked. Just coax the skin of the section down toward the seam of the loaf from both sides, so you can maintain most of the open cell structure in the dough while tightening its exterior and giving the loaf more strength and definition. You will find the loaf's length extends as you work at pinching in the skin from both sides. There should be no need to push outward with your hands to extend the length of the baguette. If the pre-shaped portions resist extension altogether, they may not have relaxed enough before their final shaping. It is also possible the dough pieces were tightened excessively during pre-shaping, or the formula for the dough must be adjusted to allow for greater extensibility (see *Chapter 10*).

11. After you have completed each baguette, place it seam-side down on a floured, pleated couche (see Figure 6.6h) or seam-side down in the channels of a perforated baguette pan. As a last resort, you may place them seam-side down on parchment-lined sheet trays. Perforated baguette pans allow hot air to flow all around the baguettes as they bake, but they prevent the loaves from making direct contact with the hot baking stone in a deck oven, so they are most appropriate for use in a convection or rack oven. Sheet trays may be used in almost any type of oven. Long, slim proofing baskets are available that accommodate baguettes, but they are not as commonly used as in the past when flours were weaker, doughs were wetter, and the raw shaped baguette needed the extra support from a basket to keep it from flattening.

12. After you have shaped all of your portions, or when you have filled a rack with shaped loaves, place them in your proofer as soon as possible, or keep them covered on a rack until they are baked.

Figure 6.6g   Figure 6.6h

SHAPING SMALL ROLLS

Earlier, we mentioned that rolls can be cut from narrow strips of the bulk dough during division, but it is common for bakeries to use some sort of mechanical divider to cut their rolls. The crumb structure of most rolls is going to be close, so using a machine to compress the dough before it is divided has little effect on the final results in most cases. Also, dividing tens of dozens (or hundreds of dozens) of rolls by hand is slow and tedious—so much so that doing it may take so many hours you can't recover your cost in producing them.

Some dividing machines shape the rolls for you too, but, just in case the machine breaks down, it's important for you to learn how to shape a roll. Whether cutting by hand or machine, scaled dough pieces for rolls usually require no pre-shaping at all.

Procedure for Shaping Small Rolls

Figures 6.7a–6.7f illustrate the method for shaping round rolls.

1. For a basic round roll, the goal is similar to shaping a larger round loaf. You want to pull the skin of the dough piece down toward the bottom to form a seam that looks like the navel on an orange. The big difference, of course, is that you must do this on a much smaller scale, with just one hand.

2. Actually, if you have the time, you can flatten the small piece of dough, fold its tiny edges toward the middle, pinch them together, and just finesse the piece into a round shape and place it seam-side down on a parchment-lined sheet pan. Go ahead and try this—you'll see it works.

3. Still, that roll-shaping method is impractical for a busy bakery. If you want to make more than a dozen rolls per day, you must learn a method for roll-making that is faster and therefore more profitable. Place a piece of dough cut to 60–90g (2–3 oz) on a clean bench surface that has no flour or other residue. Cup your right hand over the dough piece (if you are left-handed, you may wish to reverse the technique described here). Start by pushing the piece with the right side of your hand over toward the left side of the work surface (see Figure 6.7a).

4. If you keep the right side of your hand in contact with the bench surface as you push toward the left, the small piece of dough will be pinched between your hand and the bench. This is as it should be. It takes only a split second. Stop when you feel the dough begin to tighten beneath your hand.

5. Remove the right side of your hand so it's no longer in contact with the bench, and place your fingertips in contact with the bench just beyond the dough piece. Pull your fingertips down against the bench and toward you for about 2 inches, pinching the dough in this direction as you do. Stop when the dough tightens beneath your hand (see Figure 6.7b).

6. Release your finger pressure and switch to using your thumb to pinch the tiny dough piece over toward the right, just a few inches. Again, stop when you feel the dough start to tighten beneath your hand (see Figure 6.7c).

7. Release the thumb pressure and use the base of your palm, making sure it's always in contact with the wood, to push the dough piece forward and pinch it against the bench in that direction (see Figure 6.7d). The piece that results from this pinching and shaping might not be exactly round, but you can see that pinching the dough in these four directions pulls its skin quickly

Figure 6.7a

Figure 6.7b

Figure 6.7c

Figure 6.7d

Procedure for Shaping Small Rolls (Continued)

and efficiently toward the bottom of the roll. If you continue to finesse this piece by lightly pinching it over and over in any number of directions, which looks like a continuous circle, you will complete its shaping. Your hand essentially acts like a cage over the piece, pinching the dough first in one direction and then in an infinite number of other directions. As with the round loaf, the seam appears at the bottom of the roll and looks like the navel of an orange. A finished, well-tensioned roll appears in Figure 6.7e.

Figure 6.7e

8. Keep in mind the apparent circular motion of the roll-shaping process is really just an aftereffect of pinching and pulling the piece in all sorts of directions. If you simply move the small dough portion in a circle beneath your hand, you won't create the tightly shaped rolls that you want. You must pinch the dough as it moves in a circle under your hand and pull its skin toward the same spot at the bottom, or you will get a round piece of dough that has no seam (or too many seams) and isn't tight at all.

   To turn the same portions into oblong or tapered rolls (sometimes referred to as *Italian rolls*), initially you use the shaping method used for round rolls, but you don't tighten the roll as much as you would for a finished round roll. Take one lightly tensioned roll in each hand and roll them in alternating fashion both away from you and then toward you, with the dough piece just under your palm. The curved cavity formed by the underside of your hand should help the piece remain fat in the middle. Use your thumb and fingers on either side of your hand to taper the ends as you roll the piece back and forth.

9. After you have shaped enough portions to fill a parchment-lined sheet pan (see Figure 6.7f), place the pan on a covered rack until all pans are ready for loading into a proofer. Depending on how big the rolls become when they are finished proofing, you should arrange them in 3 or 4 long rows of perhaps 5 or 6 rolls per row. Do not leave the rolls or their scaled portions exposed to the air too long. Prolonged exposure to dry air or breezes causes a skin to form on the dough that might prevent you from easily shaping the pieces.

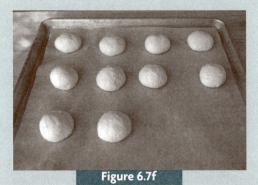

Figure 6.7f

Bread Shapes Can Have Meaning

As bakers have moved mostly away from shapeless blobs toward loaves that are shaped, the idea behind the shapes has sometimes taken on significant meaning.

In Figure 6.8 are examples of loaves from the French countryside that employ shapes reminiscent of what used to be common in their respective areas. Auvergnats, for instance, look sort of like mushrooms, but their name derives from the hats traditionally worn by men in that area of France. The French word *tabatière* can be loosely translated as "pouch," and that loaf does indeed look like some sort of bag.

The Italians have rolls that are shaped like the fingers of your hand, and the Sicilians, in particular, use imagination to create shapes that evoke a coiled snake or the rays of the sun.

In Austria and Germany, bakers make a Christmas bread called *Stollen* that is a variation of breads like brioche. It is folded in a manner to suggest the image of the baby Jesus in swaddling clothes. A formula for making Christmas Stollen is in the *Appendix of Formulas*.

Figures 6.8a–6.8f are a series of photos that illustrate techniques involved in creating certain regional shapes from France, all made from *pain de campagne* dough. While these shapes involve additional steps to complete, they are really just modifications of the basic pre-shapes discussed earlier in this chapter. The extra steps might make them difficult to produce on a large scale, but window and banquet displays can be accentuated by their beauty and variety.

Figure 6.8a is a photograph of a shape called *fendu*. It is characterized by a pronounced crevice or channel that runs down the center of the loaf, and the technique used to create this look can be applied to either round loaves or longer, sausage-shaped pieces. To make a fendu, simply shape a round loaf or a longer loaf and allow it to rest, covered, for 10–15 minutes. Use rye flour or a mixture of rye and white flour to dust the top of the loaf, and then use a long, thin wooden dowel or rolling pin to create a crevice in the loaf. You will probably need to pause and reflour

Figure 6.8a Fendu.

Figure 6.8b Auvergnat.

the crevice before continuing and widening the size of the gap created. A width of perhaps 1½ inches is advisable; anything less might disappear completely during the proof and bake. Either sprinkle the crevice again with more flour, or barely touch up one side of the crevice with a tiny bit of vegetable oil to help ensure separation during the bake. Roll one side of the fendu over toward the other, and proof the loaves upside-down in round baskets or on a pleated, floured couche. Flip right-side up as you load your oven peel.

Figure 6.8b illustrates the creation of mushroom-shaped rolls called *Auvergnats.* Roll 100g (3½ oz) pieces into tight rounds. For each piece, make an additional 15g (½ oz) tiny round, and set the smaller rounds aside to rest, covered, along with the larger rounds, for 5–10 minutes. After the rest period, reround the larger rolls and set aside. Flatten each of the tiny rounds into disks the same diameter as the larger rounds. Using a very light touch with a small brush or your fingertip, draw a *very* thin bead of vegetable oil around the perimeter of each disk. Flip the disks over and place one on top of each larger round, being careful to center them as precisely as you can. Use your finger to push down in the center of each roll, attaching the disk to the top of the roll. Proof these capped rolls upside-down (with the lid on the bottom) in a pleated couche. Flip them over just before baking and load them with the lids on top.

Figure 6.8c shows a buttercup shape. Follow the directions described for Figure 6.8a, but create an additional crevice at right angles to the first one to form a cross-shaped intersection. Round a smaller piece of dough about one-quarter the weight of the piece you have just used for making crevices. Place just a drop or so of vegetable oil at the corners of the larger piece where the crevices intersect, and then rest the smaller round in the center of the loaf. Gather the edges of the loaf together with your hands, holding the small round of dough in the center, and place this loaf upside-down into a floured proofing basket. Proof normally, and then empty the baskets directly onto your oven peel as you load the oven later on.

Figure 6.8c Buttercup.

The loaves are now right-side up, with the smaller round of dough seated in the middle of the loaf.

Figure 6.8d shows two crown-shaped loaves, called *couronne* in French. You will need a ring-shaped basket for each couronne. Make 7–9 individual round rolls of about 170g (6 oz) each, depending on the size of your basket. Allow the rolls to rest, covered, for about 15 minutes, then flatten one of the rolls into a thin disk wide enough to cover the bulge in the center of the basket. Flour the basket, and lay this disk over the bulge so it extends about ½ inch or so beyond the base of the bulge.

Figure 6.8d Couronne de Bordelaise.

Figure 6.8e Fougasse.

Place a bit of rye flour around the edges of this dough disk draped over the bulge in the basket. Now place 6–8 (depending on basket size) of the round rolls in the basket, arranging them evenly around the inside of the ring, with their seams up. Use a sharp knife to cut through the thin piece of dough covering the hump, and make triangular flaps that can be rolled over the seam of each round piece and rested there. Use a drop of water if necessary to keep each flap attached to each round roll. Proof this ring-shaped loaf in its basket, and turn the loaf out of the basket and onto your baker's peel just before loading it into the oven. During the bake cycle, the edges of the thin dough disk separate from the round rolls in the crown, and the final appearance of the loaf is like a flower.

Figure 6.8e shows the classic fougasse shapes that originated in the Provence region of France. Simply let any cylinder pre-shape or round pre-shape rest at least 15–20 minutes before continuing—longer if necessary. After the pre-shapes have rested and they are quite extensible, flatten the pieces completely. The cylinder pre-shapes can now be stretched into a long, relatively narrow piece, and the round pre-shapes can be stretched into large triangles. Make cuts in the flattened pieces, as illustrated in Figure 6.8e, and then stretch them a bit farther to ensure the cuts stay open and don't close during proofing and baking. You may wish to place the stretched pieces on parchment-lined trays (even before cutting them) to make the oven loading go more easily later on. Proof these loaves for about 45 minutes before baking them; they will bake more quickly than most loaves, as they are open in many places and aren't very thick.

Figure 6.8f is a photograph of a tabatière. Allow any round-shaped loaf to rest for 10–15 minutes, covered, before proceeding. Use a narrow wooden dowel or rolling pin to press down onto the loaf as you would for a fendu, except you do so about one-third of the distance from the edge of the loaf instead of in the center. Allow the crevice you've made to relax a moment or two, and flour it with rye flour. Now flatten the smaller third of the loaf and roll it into a flap with round edges. The flap

Figure 6.8f Tabatière.

should be wide enough to easily cover the remainder of the loaf, and it should be fairly thin—about ¼ inch thick. Dot the edge of the flap with a tiny amount of vegetable oil, and fold it up over the remainder of the loaf, creating a sort of half-moon shape with a lid over it. Set them upside-down into floured baskets or into a floured, pleated couche. Proof as you would normally, and then flip them over just before loading them so the flaps are on top.

Examples of all of these loaves after they have been proofed and baked are in the color insert.

BRAIDING

Braiding a number of pieces of dough into a finished loaf can be more time-consuming than most loaf shaping, but the finished loaf often looks quite impressive, even dramatic. Certain traditional breads really must be braided to be authentic in their appearance, such as challah (an egg bread with Jewish origins) and certain varieties of brioche and its derivatives.

Anywhere from 2 to 6 or more strands of dough can be woven to form a loaf. Some decorative loaves result from placing one braided loaf on top of another. It is beyond the scope of this book to provide examples of all possibilities when braiding bread dough, but 3- and 4-strand braids are commonly used in bakeshops to assemble loaves quickly and efficiently.

The Three-Strand Braided Loaf

The illustrations in Figure 6.9 show some of the steps involved in making a 3-strand loaf. This loaf is made using 8 oz (227g) pieces for a total raw loaf weight of 24 oz (680g). You may make your strands lighter or heavier if you wish, but you should roll lighter strands to a shorter length and heavier strands to a longer length than the one described here. Except for the differences in weight and strand length, the procedure is the same.

It is extremely difficult to talk someone through the process of braiding loaves of bread. Some guidance is provided here, but you must rely on the illustrations and the experience of your instructor to help you gain confidence in your braiding technique. Making good-looking braided breads is just as challenging as shaping baguettes. It is unrealistic for you to expect perfect results in a short time, and you will perfect this technique through repetition, so be patient and keep practicing!

Procedure for Making a Three-Strand Braided Loaf

Figures 6.9a–6.9f illustrate the steps in forming a 3-strand braided loaf.

1. Start by extending your 3 scaled pieces of dough into strands 13–14 inches long. Whatever length you choose, make sure all 3 pieces are the same length. You can leave them at the same diameter through most of their length, but tapering their ends makes for a nicer look.

2. Pinch the ends of each strand together and fan them out on their open end so they radiate away from the pinched end, as in Figure 6.9a. You will have 1 strand on the left and 2 strands on the right.

3. Place the far right strand just inside the location of the left strand, crossing over the center-right strand as you do so (see Figure 6.9b). Now, what was initially the far-right strand is located in the center-left of your arrangement, and what was the center-right strand is now on the far right.

4. Take the far-left strand and place it just inside the strand that is now on the far right, crossing over the new center strand as you do so (see Figure 6.9c).

5. Repeat these steps until you have braided the entire length of the loaf. As you approach the end, be careful to keep the strands in the proper order, however short they may be, or you will end up with a sloppy-looking result. Refer to Figures 6.9d–6.9f to see how the braiding is completed.

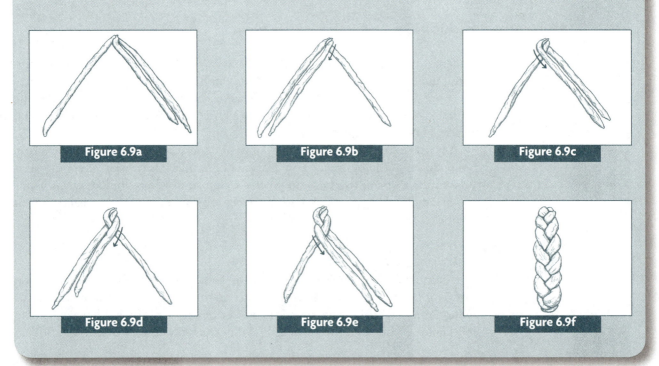

Figure 6.9a   **Figure 6.9b**   **Figure 6.9c**

Figure 6.9d   **Figure 6.9e**   **Figure 6.9f**

Procedure for Making a Three-Strand Braided Loaf (Continued)

6. Tuck the ends under the loaf just a bit, and place the loaf in the center of a parchment-lined sheet pan. You can shape 2 more loaves and place them on either side of the loaf in the center. Locate them between the center loaf and the ends of the pan so they are spaced evenly and will proof and bake later without touching each other.

7. Egg-wash the loaves before placing the tray on a covered rack, and place the rack full of trays in the proofer as soon as possible. Egg-washing the loaves again just before baking is optional, but you will notice a real difference in the shine of the final product if you do so.

The Four-Strand Braided Loaf

The biggest difference between a 3-strand braided loaf and a 4-strand loaf made at the same weight is in their profile. The 3-strand loaf is fairly flat, while most 4-strand loaves stand taller and seem imposing by comparison. So why make 3-strand loaves? They are faster to braid, and it's typically easier to learn the method for doing a 3-strand braid. Four-strand loaves are more impressive, though, and they don't take *that* much more time to produce.

Procedure for Making a Four-Strand Braided Loaf

Figures 6.10a–6.10j illustrate the method for braiding a 4-strand loaf.

1. For a 24 oz (680g) loaf, you need 4 pieces scaled equally at 6 oz (170g). Extend the pieces into strands, but *do not* make them as long as you would for a 3-strand loaf. Ten inches or so is probably sufficient, but make certain all strands are the same length. Taper the ends of the strands as you extend them.

2. Join the ends of 2 strands and lay them in a straight line at a 45-degree angle. Make an *X* shape by joining the other 2 strands, end to end, and laying them on top of and at right angles to the strands already on your bench (see Figure 6.10a).

3. Grab the far end of the strand that lies under the others in the *X* shape. Bring it down toward its opposite member, placing it just inside and away from the opposite strand. Carry the opposite strand up and over to the side where you started. See Figures 6.10b–6.10c to help visualize this process.

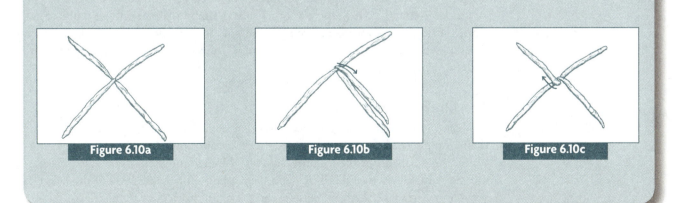

| Figure 6.10a | Figure 6.10b | Figure 6.10c |

Procedure for Making a Four-Strand Braided Loaf (Continued)

4. Use the same procedure to bring the far end of the strands lying on top of the original *X* down toward the opposite side, and flip the strand below back to where the far strand was originally. Refer to drawings in Figures 6.10d–6.10e.

5. Keep repeating this process (see Figures 6.10f–6.10g), nudging the pile of woven strands toward you so the open end of the braid gets gradually closer to you. You must pay close attention to which strand you grab and where you place it as you go, or you will get lost and have to start over. Be careful not to stretch the strands as you braid them, or they will get gradually thinner and one end of the loaf will be much larger than the other.

6. Refer to drawings in Figures 6.10h–6.10j to see how the braiding is completed.

Figure 6.10d   Figure 6.10e

Figure 6.10f   Figure 6.10g

Figure 6.10h   Figure 6.10i   Figure 6.10j

Four-strand braiding is a skill that must be learned as you work under the supervision of an experienced bread shaper who knows several methods for braiding. It is more involved than braiding with 3 strands, but, once you master the technique, you can make 4-strand loaves almost as quickly as 3-strand loaves, and you will instinctively know where to place each end of the strands as you weave them. Remember, this skill is rarely mastered on the first attempt; you must be patient with both yourself and your instructor as you learn it.

The More Elegant Roll

You can use challah dough to make rolls that are a bit more elegant in appearance than a simple small round. They are quite pretty after they have been proofed, eggwashed, and baked, but the maneuver involved in making them does take 2–3 times as long as making a round roll by hand, depending on the skill level of the baker. If you choose to make them, be certain you get a good price for them.

Procedure for Making a Single-Knot Roll

Figures 6.11a–6.11e illustrate the steps in making a single-knot roll.

1. Cut your dough from narrow strips into 2-oz (60g) pieces. For purposes of efficiency, you might want to have one crew member cut pieces of dough as others shape, or use a mechanical roll divider to make this tedious task go quickly.

2. Instead of rounding the pieces, roll them out into very narrow strands, perhaps ½ inch wide and 8–9 inches long.

3. Allow the strand to hang over your nondominant hand in the shape of an upside-down *J* (see Figure 6.11a).

4. Pull the longer end of the piece up and in front of the shorter piece, forming a small loop where the ends overlap (see Figure 6.11b).

5. Bring the longer end behind the shorter one and pull it through to make a loose knot (see Figure 6.11c).

6. Wrap the same longer end back around the shorter one again, essentially repeating step 5 (see Figure 6.11d).

7. Take the other, short end (which so far hasn't been moved) and push it through the front of the center hole in the knot, leaving its tip coming out the back (see Figure 6.11e).

8. Decide which side of the knot looks more attractive or symmetrical and leave that side facing up on a parchment-lined tray. These rolls grow larger than 2-oz rolls from lean dough because of the eggs in their formula, so space them farther apart than you would typical rolls from lean dough. A 4 × 5 arrangement on a full-size sheet pan is probably advisable.

9. Egg-wash the finished rolls as you fill up each tray, and egg-wash them again just before they go into the oven. They will bake much more quickly than full-sized loaves, so use a hotter oven (maybe 400°F), and check the bake after 12–15 minutes to be certain you don't overbake them.

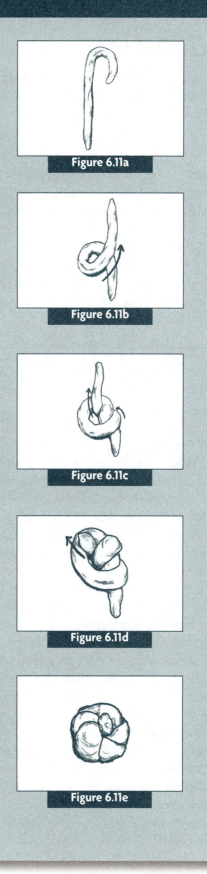

Figure 6.11a

Figure 6.11b

Figure 6.11c

Figure 6.11d

Figure 6.11e

ARTISAN BAKER PROFILE

Ciril Hitz

Department Chair, International Baking and Pastry Institute, Johnson & Wales University, Providence, Rhode Island

Ciril Hitz managed to rethink what he wanted to do with his career more than a couple of times. He intended at first to be an industrial designer, but, after graduating from the Rhode Island School of Design, he switched directions and returned to his native land of Switzerland for 3 years to pursue an apprenticeship in pastry and chocolate work. This apprenticeship seemed like a better fit for him at the time. After obtaining certification, he returned to the Providence area to hone his craft professionally.

Ciril did well in Providence and not long thereafter achieved the rank of head pastry chef and product developer for Hauser Chocolatier. In 1997, he added a faculty position to his resume, teaching classes in the pastry arts as well as in decorative and sculptural breads at Johnson & Wales University.

Peter Reinhart, who has written extensively about bread baking, was also on the Providence faculty at the time. He saw Ciril's exceptional work with decorative bread sculpture, and he encouraged him to compete for a position on the team that would represent the United States in 2002 at the Coupe de Monde du Boulangerie. The Coupe de Monde is held every three years, and it features 12 teams from around the world who compete in the categories of baguette and specialty breads, viennoiserie, and decorative breads. Ciril made the team as the competitor for the decorative breads area. The team won the silver medal, placing behind the Japanese team, and it finished ahead of teams from nations with older bread traditions like Belgium, France, and Switzerland.

Ciril competed at the 2004 Bread and Pastry Championship, where he and his teammate won best of show and where he also won in the category of best showpiece. His star at Johnson & Wales has also been rising; he now chairs the International Baking

and Pastry Institute at the Providence campus. He is often selected as a judge at baking and pastry competitions, and he contributes regularly to magazines such as *Modern Baking* and *Pastry Art and Design*. The latter publication designated Ciril as one of the top 10 pastry chefs in the United States in 2007.

Somewhere in the midst of this growing list of achievements, Ciril found time to create two sets of instructional DVDs, *Bread Art* and *Better Bread*, both of which are available on his website, www.breadhitz.com. He has written a book tentatively titled *Baking Artisan Bread*, which is due for publication in fall 2008.

IMPRESSIONS OF ARTISAN BREAD BAKING AS AN INDUSTRY

Did you have any preconceptions about the artisan bread business (or any aspect of the bread business) that were altered by your industry experience?

For me, the biggest myth was that you can't bake good bread in America. It's simply not true. In fact, many of the artisan bakeries in this country produce bread that rivals the best bread of any European country. The revival of interest in bread baking in this country has increased the quality of bread available and has educated the public. We still have more to do, but I am amazed at how far we have come in a relatively short period.

What are your thoughts on the future of the artisan bread business?

I believe the artisan bread business is in the embryonic stages right now, with some wonderful, strong leaders and models for businesses. I don't want to make any predictions on how it will develop in the years to come, but I do believe there will be growth. Personally, I hope it remains independent and diversified, for the most part.

What are your thoughts on prospective artisan bakers? What characteristics or personality traits do you look for in prospective employees that will increase their potential for hire? Are there any traits that might exclude them?

A willingness to learn and a passion for bread will go far. A know-it-all attitude doesn't help them.

Do you have any pearls of wisdom for the bakery and pastry students reading this book?

I think it's important to stay humble and view every moment as a learning opportunity. Take advantage of chances to interact with other bakers, visit bakeries, and taste different breads. Read. And no matter where you are in life, treat everyone you meet as you would like to be treated yourself.

Summary

Rapid, accurate, and efficient division of bread dough maintains the cost-efficient workflow necessary for profitability in making hand-shaped breads. Immediately after division, dough pieces usually undergo a light pre-shaping that provides a suitable base for finishing the process after the dough has rested. The rest period between dividing and pre-shaping the pieces and the final shaping, which occurs later, is referred to as the *intermediate proof.* This stage is necessary so the dough pieces may be formed or molded shortly afterward in attractive shapes that are symmetrical in appearance and do not suffer from unwanted tears or distortion.

Finally, breads are usually tightened and shaped to turn them into a form that either meets the traditional requirements of classic breads, such as baguettes, or makes them more convenient for specific uses, such as dinner rolls and sandwich bread. During the final shaping process, dough portions are usually folded or tightened in order to pull their skin down around them toward a seam at the bottom. This helps prevent the loaves from flattening excessively during proofing and allows them to achieve greater height in the oven.

Key Terms

couche	*boulot*
intermediate proof	*bâtard*
boule	*baguette*

Questions for Review

1. Why should you be gentle in handling dough portions as you cut them from a dough mass?
2. Why is it necessary to keep pre-shaped pieces and finished loaves covered as you finish making them?
3. What is the purpose of pre-shaping dough portions before they undergo their intermediate proof?
4. Why should you arrange rolls in neat, well-spaced rows as you place them on a parchment-lined sheet pan?

Questions for Discussion

You may realize by now that dividing and shaping loaves by hand is time-consuming and laborious. Machines are available to do the work in much less time.

1. If your bakery were busy enough and you could afford dividing and shaping machines, would you buy them?
2. Is it possible that some machines are acceptable, while others are not? Be specific in your reasoning, and write down your ideas so you can discuss them in class.

Lab Exercise & Experiment

*R*efer to the formula for *pain de mie*, known in English as Pullman bread. Scale and mix two batches of the dough at the same size and with exactly the same ingredients, water temperature, and total fermentation time (usually 1–2 hours).

Divide and pre-shape pieces at a weight appropriate for your particular open-topped baking pans—probably 800–900g, or 28–32 oz. Check with your instructor to be sure what weight to use when dividing the dough. Scale all dough portions at the same weight. Be certain to keep the portions from one batch separate from the other.

When the pieces have rested sufficiently (about 15–20 minutes), shape all the pieces from one batch into short, tight logs and place some of them in conventional bread pans and others onto parchment-lined sheet pans, seam-side down in both cases. As you shape them, slap down aggressively on the dough pieces, deflating them completely, and form them tightly into short, plump logs of equal diameter throughout their length.

Shape the remaining dough less aggressively. Pat out what seems like excessive air, but do not completely deflate the loaves. As you fold and shape them, use moderate tension, but do not pull too tightly as you finish them into short, plump logs of the same diameter throughout. Place them into bread pans and onto sheet pans, as you did with the first batch.

Proof both batches simultaneously, but keep the two batches separately identified, and keep them separated as they bake.

Bake each batch as it appears ready (see *Chapter 7*), but take note of which seems ready first—and then ask yourself why this is so.

When both batches are unloaded from the oven, allow them to cool (if you have time) and then cut open some loaves from each batch for comparison. Note any apparent differences, such as the height of loaves versus their flatness, overall volume, open versus closed crumb structure, or any other point of comparison you may notice.

The only difference in preparing the two batches should have been the way they were shaped. How do you relate the different shaping methods to what you see before you, and how can these observations be applied to how you shape other breads? Is one method always better than the other? Is the first method better for a certain type of loaf, while the second method is suitable for another? Why?

PULLMAN BREAD (PAIN DE MIE)

STRAIGHT DOUGH	Metric (1X) 5-Qt Mixer	Metric (4X) 20-Qt Mixer	U.S. Measure (1X) 5-Qt Mixer	U.S. Measure (4X) 20-Qt Mixer	Formula Baker's %
Bread flour	900g	3600g	2 lb 4.0oz	9 lb 0.0oz	100%
Water	540g	2160g	1 lb 5.6oz	5 lb 6.4oz	60%
Butter, softened	72g	288g	2.9oz	11.5oz	8%
Sugar	45g	180g	1.8oz	7.2oz	5%
Milk powder	54g	216g	2.2oz	8.6oz	6%
Salt	20g	79g	0.8oz	3.2oz	2.2%
Instant yeast	9g	36g	0.4oz	1.4oz	1%
TOTAL YIELD	**1640g**	**6559g**	**4 lb 1.6oz**	**16 lb 6.4oz**	

Variation:

You can use the straight dough above as the basis for an adjusted dough that utilizes a sponge or old dough (see *Chapter 4*). Both pre-ferments are easy to prepare and practically risk-free to use. They add strength to what is already a strong dough, but the flavor is improved noticeably at pre-fermented flour levels of 25–40%.

GOAL TEMPERATURE: 77°F (25°C). See directions for determining correct water temperature in *Chapter 4*.

MIXING METHOD: Use the intensive mix method, described on p. 196.

FERMENTING: About 1 hour.

SCALING: for 13-in. Pullman pan: 32 oz; 17-in. Pullman pan: 44 oz; 9 × 4-in. bread pan: 30 oz. Some variation may result from differences in dough strength or peculiarities of pan size.

SHAPING: Shape as long logs for the Pullman pans and short logs for the standard, open-topped bread pans. Spray both the pans and their lids on the inside surface with pan release before placing shaped dough portions in them.

PROOFING:

1. Slide the lids onto the Pullman pans but leave an opening of about 1 in. or so to monitor the proof. When the crowns of the dough portions reach within ½ in. of the lid, close the lids and bake the Pullman loaves.

2. For open-topped pans, allow the crowns of the loaves to rise above the rim of the pan.

3. The loaves are usually proofed fully 50–70 minutes after being placed in a proofer set to 80°F and 80% humidity.

BAKING:

1. 380–400°F for 45–60 minutes for the closed-top Pullmans (350–370°F for a convection or rack oven); 350–375°F for 30–35 minutes for the open-topped bread pans (310–330°F for a convection or rack oven).

2. The sides of the loaves must be golden brown to support the weight of the crowns.

3. Differences in ovens can produce different temperatures and bake times—be conservative and check loaves earlier than their anticipated finish time.

COOLING:

1. After baking is complete, empty the loaves from their pans immediately or their sides will soften.

2. Cool completely before slicing, and wrap completely after cooling.

chapter *7*

Proofing and Retarding

Learning Outcomes:

- Define the terms proofing, overproofing, underproofing, and retarding as they apply to bread baking.

- Understand the importance of controlling and monitoring the proofing process.

- Recognize when most loaves and rolls are ready for baking.

- Identify the two key factors that lead to overproofing.

- Identify the essential challenge of successful proofing.

- Recognize the three factors that can be manipulated to control gas production during proofing.

- Determine the typical temperature ranges and levels of humidity for ideal proofing of loaves before they are baked.

- Understand how retarding dough or loaves at refrigerator temperatures can allow bakers to organize their bread production and increase their efficiency.

- Specify the names and functions of commonly used smallwares designed for use in proofing hearth loaves.

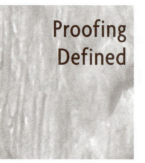

Proofing Defined

Proofing is defined as the period of fermentation between the shaping of bread loaves and the loading of the loaves into the oven. It differs from bulk fermentation because the main goal during proofing is simply to inflate the shaped dough. During the proofing phase of bread production, we increase the dough's volume just enough that when the loaves are placed in the oven, they gradually achieve close to their maximum potential in height.

Judging the Readiness of Proofed Loaves

When you lightly poke a raw loaf of bread with your finger, it will leave an indentation. Look at the photo in Figure 7.1, which illustrates what we mean.

If the loaf still needs more proofing time, the indentation will practically disappear because there is still so much gas pressure and potential for growth in the dough structure. This loaf's condition is described as *underproofed*.

If you have waited too long, then the indentation may remain without springing back at all. The loaf may even collapse because it cannot withstand any more pressure or jostling. This loaf is described as *overproofed*.

With a properly proofed loaf, however, the indentation springs back about halfway, but it remains quite visible after it springs back. This is because the loaf still has potential for growth, but it has inflated considerably and is approaching the time when its structure won't accommodate any more gas. Generally speaking, now is the time to score and load this loaf.

This description can serve only as a starting point in judging when breads are ready to be baked. Your observations of your own breads may vary, to some degree,

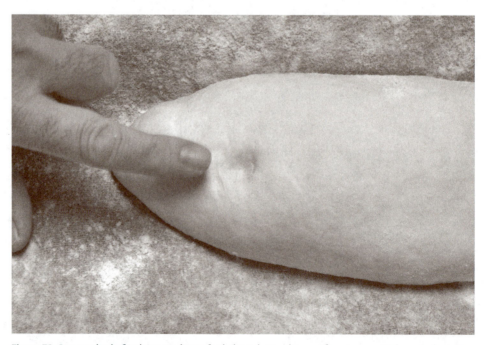

Figure 7.1 One method of judging readiness for baking during the proofing process: Make an indentation and judge the spring-back.

from those recorded above. Only firsthand, repetitive experience with judging the proof enables the baker in charge of this process to make an accurate assessment of whether or not the bread is ready to be baked. It should be expected that bakers who are new to the process will experience errors on their way to expertise, and their learning may actually be accelerated by allowing them to make incorrect judgments (under controlled, experimental circumstances) and then showing them the results.

Proofing versus Bulk Fermentation

While fermentation does progress during proofing, its role in providing flavor or strength to the bread is much diminished at this stage. The flavor development that stems from bacterial activity (see *Chapter 5*) occurs mostly during bulk fermentation. There is not enough time during most proofing cycles to enhance the strength or flavor of loaves, and they don't benefit as much from the mass effect of being left in bulk after mixing.

When proofing is successful, the shaped loaves inflate while retaining just enough potential for growth in the oven. As a result, there is a low risk of collapse during baking.

When proofing is unsuccessful, however, loaves of bread either collapse during the proofing period or are so overinflated with carbon dioxide (CO_2) that they collapse shortly after they are loaded into the oven. When loaves collapse from *overproofing*, the gluten that forms the membranes in the air cells tears because it can no longer stretch and capture the CO_2 generated by the yeast cells in the bread. Once the gluten is destroyed this way, it can't be repaired and the dough must be thrown away.

Some bakeshops use the term "overproofed" to describe bread that has taken on greater size than originally planned, but, unless the loaf actually collapses before the end of baking, it was not truly overproofed. Loaves that get too big without collapsing in the oven might only require that they be scaled at a smaller portion size before shaping and proofing.

Collapse of Overproofed Dough

If a loaf of bread is overproofed, it probably collapsed for one of two reasons (or for both):

1. *Excessive gas production*—The interior of the bread accumulated too much CO_2 gas, and the capacity of the gluten to hold the gas was exceeded.

2. *Degraded gluten bonds*—Enzymes such as protease degraded the gluten bonds within the dough over time, and it collapsed because the bonds grew too weak.

Gas Production in Successful Proofing

Carbon dioxide (CO_2) produced during bulk fermentation and bench proofing (see *Chapter 5*) plays a key role in enlarging the size of air cells in the dough and in stretching the dough so it can be shaped easily. We aim to retain as much of the original cell structure as we can while we divide and shape the dough portions, but by the time loaves are shaped, most of the gas from bulk fermentation has escaped.

The CO_2 created during the proofing process gives final form and structure to the loaves as they bake. *Making sure there is sufficient CO_2 without exceeding the loaf's ability to hold gas is the essential challenge of successful proofing.*

Controlling gas production is possible when we can control the following factors in dough development:

1. The temperature of the dough and its environment.
2. The hydration of the dough.
3. The actual quantity of yeast present in the dough.

Salt can also restrict both yeast activity and enzyme action, but we're limited in using it to control gas production because you can add only so much salt to a dough without ruining its flavor—approximately 2% of flour weight.

Changing the Temperature of Dough

You should remember from *Chapter 5* that changing the temperature of dough or the environment in which it ferments has a dramatic effect on its level of yeast activity. When we reduce the temperature of dough, we reduce yeast activity and the rate at which yeast cells produce CO_2 as a by-product of fermentation. If we do the opposite by increasing the temperature of dough or its environment, then yeast activity and CO_2 production will increase.

The goal temperature for bread dough as it undergoes bulk fermentation is usually 75–80°F. Through experience, knowledgeable bakers have discovered that these moderate temperatures, which are neither too warm nor too cold, are appropriate for developing sufficient yeast activity in dough without hurrying the process too much. In order to achieve these temperatures when the dough has finished its mix, calculate the necessary water temperature based on the friction factor and how warm or cold the flour and the mixer bowl are. These factors are not easy to change, but controlling water temperature is as easy as using ice to chill it or adding hot water to raise its temperature.

For a more thorough explanation of determining the proper water temperature for mixing most bread, see "Controlling Dough Temperature" and Table 4.2 in *Chapter 4.*

In most cases, perhaps, the final proofing of commercially yeasted loaves held at 80°F can be accomplished in 60 to 90 minutes. Still, for reasons of convenience, you may find that delaying the rate of proofing for a few hours may benefit you and your schedule. In this case, you could reduce the rate of yeast activity (and CO_2 production) by lowering the temperature of your proofer, turning it off altogether, or even placing the loaves in a refrigerator. This last option—using a refrigerator—is discussed more fully in "Retarding Loaves of Bread."

You can proof dough at temperatures higher than 80°F, but exceeding 90°F can advance the rate of yeast activity so much that the proof is difficult to control. Proofing at temperatures lower than 80°F is acceptable too, but the proof will require more time. In either case, cover the proofing racks with specially designed plastic bags, or place the entire rack in a dedicated cabinet with temperature and humidity controls. This temperature- and humidity-controlled cabinet is called a *proofer* in the bakery profession, and most professional shops have one.

Where or How Do We Proof?

Under "Gas Production in Successful Proofing," we stated that controlling the temperature and other environmental influences on bread dough helps us control the rate of fermentation and the condition of the loaves as they await baking.

Before electric power became commonly available, loaves either had to proof in the open air of the bakery or, perhaps, in a covered cabinet away from drafts that might encourage the development of a dry skin on the raw loaves.

Modern bakers—even artisan bakers—usually take advantage of modern equipment to aid in controlling the proof. These contraptions—generally called *proofers*—have electrically controlled sensors, heaters, and humidifiers that can create an ideal environment for the loaves as they await the time for baking. Artisan bakers generally set their proofers to 80–85°F and 80% humidity to create a warm (but not hot) environment with just enough humidity to prevent the formation of a dry skin on the loaves that would restrict their growth and mar their appearance.

Proofers are made in many sizes to fit the needs of different bakeries. Some are quite small and accommodate only five or six sheet pans. Both freestanding and built-in proofers usually allow you to roll at least an entire speed rack of product into them—sometimes they accommodate two, four, or even more racks at one time. Still others aren't really appliances at all but rather are heat- and humidity-controlled rooms designed for very large bakeries. At any size, proofers usually have separate controls for heat and humidity, and they must have some sort of door or curtain that can be closed to control the passage of air.

One specialized type of proofer is the *proofer-retarder*. This is equipped with both heating and refrigerating elements as well as a humidifier. Proofer-retarders are generally computer controlled and can be programmed to stop the loaves' growth at temperatures near freezing and then slowly warm them so they are ready for baking at a desired time. Much experimentation and test-proofing is necessary to find a system of chilling and warming that provides safe and predictable behavior in your loaves. Still, once those settings are found, bakers can work almost normal hours by retarding their loaves in the afternoon and returning in the morning to bake them. These appliances are expensive, but if a bakery's sales can justify the expense, they make it much easier for a manager to hire staff and minimize employee turnover.

There is no defined best way to proof loaves. The proofing should be planned, ideally, to meet the scheduling needs of your bakery. Often, depending on how large a production you have, you want your next batch of loaves to be ready for loading right after the previous batch has been emptied from the oven. If the upcoming batch finishes proofing too early, these loaves may overproof before space is available in the oven.

If the upcoming batch hasn't yet properly proofed when the previous batch is unloaded, you may find your oven standing empty and just burning fuel. This situation may increase your utility and labor costs unacceptably. Ultimately, you must experiment with optimal proofing temperatures that help you reliably manage the flow of loaves into and out of your oven efficiently and affordably.

HYDRATION OF DOUGH

You will recall from *Chapter 5* that increasing the hydration of a bread dough or a pre-ferment increases its level of yeast activity. Decreasing the hydration does the opposite by slowing yeast activity and gas production. If you're stuck with a certain temperature while the bread proofs—as when you don't have the luxury of a temperature-controlled proofer—you can change the rate of yeast activity by changing the percentage of water in your bread dough and pre-ferments.

If you must proof your loaves in a simple covered speed rack arrangement at room temperature, be especially aware of the way air moves throughout the room. Your bakery's thermostat may indicate an ambient room temperature of 75°F, for instance, but that doesn't really tell you what the temperature of the air is near your loaves. Especially during the winter, you may notice warm air ends up closer to the ceiling in your bakery while the coldest air collects near the floor. If you have high ceilings in your production area, then most of the warmest air will be above the height of your speed rack, and the colder air will be surrounding your dough. During very cold winter periods, you may wish to avoid using the bottom three or four levels of your speed rack altogether, as the air there is often too cold to promote yeast activity and so dry it may cause a skin to form on the loaves.

Another option is to place sheet trays with wet towels or napkins on them at both the top and bottom of the covered rack. This may at first seem senseless to you, but the natural air currents within the covered rack will help the moisture move around your loaves as they proof.

Yeast Quantity in Dough

The actual quantity of yeast used in the dough also affects the degree of control you have over gas production and yeast activity. Wild yeasts in bread leavened mostly with levain can act very slowly, so reining them in is not usually a challenge. In fact, you may need to raise the temperature of your proofer occasionally, especially during winter months, to get a predictable level of gas production from wild sourdough varieties. Using a liquid levain instead of firm levain in your formulas adds a greater proportion of wild yeast cells to your mix. Just be certain to adjust your formula to balance the water in the liquid levain.

Manufactured yeast can act quickly, so restricting the quantity used in your dough can be critical to gaining control over the final proof. Determining how much to use is, like temperature, a matter of experimentation to find an acceptable level. If you want to proof loaves of bread for about 1 hour at 80°F before they are ready for baking and their dough has bulk fermented for 1½ to 2 hours already, then an instant yeast level of 0.4 to 0.5% *might* be appropriate.

This figure is purely a guideline; there are too many variables in individual bakeshops to be certain it will always be appropriate. Typically, bakers adjust yeast quantities or other formula specifics to experiment with small batches first, and they expect a few failures before finding the right amount. If the proof goes more slowly than planned, you can add a tiny bit more yeast next time. If the proof advances too quickly, cut the yeast back by 0.1 or 0.2 percentage points. Keep in mind that these are reasonable starting points, but the unique conditions of your own bakery may require that you find somewhat different proof times or yeast quantities to achieve your desired result.

The Degradation of Dough Structure

When we say a dough's structure has *degraded,* we mean the dough is actually beginning to deteriorate and come apart. The enzymes present in flour will degrade and destroy any dough over time; it is only a question of when. *Amylase* degrades starch into simple sugars, which can cause stickiness in bread dough, but it is the action of *protease* that poses the biggest challenge to controlling the degradation of dough strength.

You will remember from our discussion of enzyme action in *Chapter 5* that protease works to degrade protein bonds, which include the gluten bonds that give bread dough the strength to hold its shape and capture CO_2 gas. We can manipulate the level of protease activity in bread dough somewhat, but its destructiveness *will* proceed. To control dough degradation, you must control enzyme activity in your dough.

You can slow the yeast activity level of a typical batch of baguettes by simply reducing the amount of yeast in the formula, but reducing the quantity of protease in dough is not as straightforward. Still, a conventional proofing period of 1 to 2 hours for a lean white bread made with manufactured yeast will probably not be affected negatively by the level of protease in the dough. Most North American flours can tolerate such a short period easily without major degradation.

Dough strength can be degraded significantly over longer periods, such as 12 to 24 hours. While that is an unorthodox amount of time to proof finished loaves at moderate temperatures, it is common to do so in a refrigerated environment.

Retarding Loaves of Bread

Retarding might be defined as the use of refrigeration to delay the process of proofing. It can take the simple form of covering a few trays of raw loaves and placing them in a reach-in refrigerator, or it may be as elaborate as using computerized proofers or proofer-retarders to hold entire racks of loaves waiting to be baked.

WHY RETARD LOAVES OF BREAD?

A baker might decide to retard his shaped loaves (instead of proofing them as soon as possible) so he can control precisely when the loaves will be ready for the oven. In a bakery with a small staff, this delay can allow a crew to completely finish the shaping of loaves before any member has to start loading the oven.

Alternatively, a bakery can place loaves in the retarder toward the end of the workday and start the next shift almost a day later by baking those loaves and getting them ready for sale. Instead of waiting an hour or two after shaping the dough and allowing the bread to decide when it will be baked, you can delay the fermentation process significantly and decide when *you* would prefer to bake your bread. Many bakery owners use retardation in their production because it allows for efficiency and control of their operation. Retarding loaves may enable the production shift to occur entirely during daylight hours, which can make it easier for bakery owners to find enthusiastic employees.

UNIQUE CHALLENGES OF RETARDING BREAD

When you retard raw loaves overnight, and no employees are present, it is extremely important to treat the entire process systematically and scientifically to control every aspect of fermentation. If anything starts to go wrong (such as premature growth in the size of the loaves) when no one is around to address the problem, you could lose an entire day's worth of production before the baking staff even arrive.

The essential points for controlling the retarding process are the same as for conventional proofing, but the techniques and the precise settings used differ significantly. You must still monitor the rate of gas production in the loaves as they proof, but you must pay much greater attention to the risk of dough degradation in the loaves as they await their baking time.

Gas Production During Retarding

Strategies for controlling gas production during retardation involve:

1. Reducing dough temperature.
2. Reducing the time of bulk fermentation.

3. Reducing the hydration of the dough.

4. Reducing the quantity of yeast in the dough.

You may notice some similarity between these strategies and those used when proofing loaves of bread conventionally, but the retarding strategies stress the need to reduce enzyme activity and the by-products of fermentation significantly. They also involve severely reducing bulk fermentation time, which is generally not advisable in conventional proofing. Reducing bulk fermentation before shaping and retarding loaves can have a detrimental effect on the flavor of simple breads, but you can use techniques in formulation that counter the risk to flavor and aroma.

Dough Temperature

If you wish to retard loaves for a long period, you should probably reduce the final temperature of the dough to 73–75°F. Reducing the temperature of the dough by 2 to 4 degrees can still provide the right environment for yeast cells to establish fermentation without encouraging a lot of gas production before it is needed.

The temperature inside the retarder (or refrigerator) can be adjusted to deliver a length of retardation that works for your situation. A good starting range for experimenting with this process is 48–52°F. Temperatures much below 46°F can cause the yeast cells to become completely dormant rather than simply slowed down.

Whether you retard in a small refrigerator or a dedicated retarder, you must ensure the variation in temperature and humidity within the cabinet is minimized. Using a refrigerator shared by line cooks or pastry chefs to retard loaves of bread can be frustrating and provide irregular results. Results are more predictable when the refrigerator doors are rarely opened and the loaves inside don't undergo frequent changes in surrounding temperature. Also, if the environment is not humidity-controlled, the trays or racks must be tightly covered with plastic to discourage the formation of a skin on the raw loaves. Again, placing a tray with wet towels on both the highest and lowest levels of a covered speed rack can help reduce the formation of that skin.

Bulk Fermentation Time

If we reduce bulk fermentation time from about 2 hours to 30 minutes or so, the yeast cells are able to begin the fermentation process but don't have much time to generate gas. Air cells can accommodate only so much CO_2 before they break and cause the collapse of the loaves. When retarding loaves, the goal is for the dough to accumulate gas over a long period, so it can be helpful to limit the first period of fermentation to prevent the yeast cells from getting a head start generating gas.

In *Chapter 5*, we discussed how a short bulk fermentation time for bread dough reduces the time for bacteria to generate organic acids responsible for flavor. This is still true, but we can use a pre-ferment to provide the flavor and aromas that might be lacking in dough that undergoes minimal bulk fermentation. It is probably fair to say that firm pre-ferments present fewer risks to retarding finished loaves because they are less enzyme active and won't degrade the gluten of the dough quite as much as a liquid pre-ferment. Nevertheless, liquid pre-ferments can be successfully used in the process of making loaves for a retarding process. Be sure to keep in mind that the higher protease levels will degrade the structure of the dough to some degree and that how much poolish or liquid levain you use in your product may be significantly limited by that effect.

Dough Hydration

You can reduce the level of yeast activity and slow the accumulation of CO_2 in dough by reducing the level of water in your dough formula. For instance, you could reduce the normal hydration in a baguette dough from about 68% for conventional proofing to 65–66% when retarding the loaves a long time. This example is, of course, supplied only for illustration; you would probably have to reduce the hydration of your conventional dough 2–3 percentage points to achieve a successful retardation for loaves baked the next day.

Yeast Quantity

If you reduce the quantity of yeast in your dough formula, you in turn reduce the rate at which CO_2 is produced in the dough. If your baguette dough usually has an instant yeast level of 0.7%, for instance, you would need to reduce its yeast level to 0.2–0.4% if the loaves made from it are to survive a 12–20-hour period of retarding. Again, only experimentation with retarding your own loaves will reveal the yeast level that will work best for you, but that level will almost certainly have to be reduced from the level you use to proof those loaves conventionally.

When working with yeast, you must consider what type of yeast works best when retarding. *Dry instant yeast* and *fresh compressed yeast* both work well when mixing dough for retarded loaves. However, as we discussed in *Chapter 2*, active dry yeast contains a lot of dead yeast cells, and these produce a destructive protein fragment called *glutathione*. Glutathione works like the enzyme protease to weaken the gluten bonds that give dough its strength. These weakening effects are good if you want to reduce the elasticity of conventionally proofed doughs, like baguette dough or laminated base doughs, but when retarding loaves of bread, it might be better to avoid active dry yeast and the glutathione that comes with it.

Dough Degradation in Retarding

As stated previously, the action of protease enzymes is not a factor of concern during most conventional proofing periods, which don't exceed a few hours. Retarding periods can exceed 20 hours, though, so the weakening effect protease has on dough strength is a major concern in retarding.

Here is a list of strategies for controlling the degradation of dough due to enzymatic activity:

1. Mix your dough a bit longer—perhaps only a minute longer—to increase the gluten strength while minimizing the potential effects of overoxidation.

2. Reduce the hydration of your dough to lower the level of enzyme activity and increase overall dough strength.

3. When using pre-ferments, opt for firm varieties instead of liquid types if possible, for the same reasons as in #2.

Specialized Equipment for Proofing and Retarding Loaves of Bread

Figure 7.2 shows examples of smallwares commonly used in bakeshops for proofing and retarding different types of hearth loaves. The linen-lined baskets are French-made

Figure 7.2 An assortment of baskets used in proofing hearth loaves.

bannetons, while the coiled reed models are German-made *brotformen.* Loaves are shaped and then proofed upside-down in the baskets. When they are ready for the oven, the baskets are inverted and the loaves released right-side up onto a peel or loader. All of the baskets shown in Figure 7.2 must be lightly floured before use, and those that are not lined will leave attractive geometric patterns on the finished loaves. Note also the rolled-up linen *couches* set among the baskets. The *couches* are most often pleated and used to line proofing boards that hold baguettes as they proof. Shorter loaves such as *bâtards* and *boulots* are also proofed in *couche* sometimes, but the baskets do make loading those varieties into the oven much faster, even if they are more expensive. For an illustration of baguettes resting in *couche* on a proofing board, see the color insert following page 50.

The plywood board in Figure 7.2 has dimensions similar to those of a typical full-sized sheet pan. One term for this board in North America is a *proofing board* (or *bagel board,* because it is often used to proof bagels overnight in a refrigerator). It can be used to hold dough portions on a rack as they go through their intermediate proof, and it can serve as a surface for holding or proofing finished loaves if they aren't too wet. Finally, it can be used as a rack-sized platform to hold the *couche* material described in the following paragraph.

On top of the bagel board is a wide length of cloth used to hold baguettes and other long loaves as they proof. This cloth, called a *couche,* is usually made from linen canvas. The *couche* is placed on top of a bagel board (also shown in the color insert following page 50) and sprinkled with flour to prevent sticking. The loaves are then placed directly on the couche. While the loaves are placed side by side to be efficient with space, they are just far enough away from each other to allow room for growth and expansion. A pleat is created between each loaf that is high enough to keep the loaves from sticking together when they grow and to help them keep their shape.

Artisan bakers often choose to go through all this labor-intensive preparation of hearth loaves before proofing them so they are able to load each loaf or row of loaves precisely on an *oven peel* when it is time for the bake. An oven peel is (usually) a wide,

▲ Pain au Levain proofing in cloth-covered bannetons.

▼ A wood-burning oven being fired before use.

Loading scored loaves into a wood-burning oven.

▲ Pain au Levain baking in a wood-burning oven.

▼ Whole Wheat Sourdough cooling on a rack.

Shaping sequence for Brioche à Tête.

In the basket, from left to right: Brioche Vendenne, Parisian (partially obscured), and Brioche Nanterre. On the plate: Brioche à Tête.

Croissants.

Assorted Danish, clockwise from bottom left: Danish pocket with raspberry jam, Snail with cheese filling, pocket with pastry cream and fresh blackberry, pinwheel with apricot jam.

Buttercups made from Pain de Campagne cooling on a rack.

Varieties of Pain de Campagne in different regional shapes.

Technique sequence for creating dead dough roses for plaque.

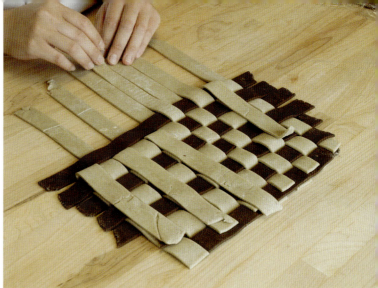

Weaving dead dough by hand.

Creating cornucopia out of dead dough that has been woven by hand.

Twisting dead dough by hand for rope border.

Plaque once assembly is complete (see *Advanced Topic #4: Decorative Dough Pieces* for additional technique shots). The miniature loaves are made from active decorative dough.

Enclosing a foil-wrapped bain marie used as a mold for the base of the centerpiece with dead dough by hand.

Adding twisted rope made of dead dough to the bottom border of the centerpiece base.

Assembling the rooster's tail using dead dough.

Adding the Rooster's feathers using dead dough.

Rooster centerpiece once assembly is complete (see *Advanced Topic #4: Decorative Dough Pieces* for additional technique shots).

▲ A basket and liner made from dead dough, with miniature loaves made from active decorative dough.

▼ A flower box made from dead dough.

flat wooden board attached to a narrow wooden handle, and it is used to slide raw loaves into the oven. Some oven peels are made of metal. A baker generally transfers loaves from the *couche* to the surface of the large peel with a thin 4-inch-wide piece of plywood, referred to either as a *flip-board* or a *hand peel*.

Oven peels differ in size depending on the type of deck oven you use. Bakers generally scatter cornmeal or semolina over a peel before loading loaves onto it; these hard granules act like little ball bearings as you slide the loaves from the oven peel onto the hot stone in the oven. When the loaves have finished baking, they are retrieved with the same oven peel. Your instructor can show you the technique for sliding loaves from the peel into the oven, and for retrieving them afterwards.

Another option for proofing hearth loaves is to place them upside-down (that is, seam-side up) in some sort of basket as they undergo their final fermentation. Two basic types are available from bakery equipment purveyors: *brotformen* and *bannetons*. *Brotform* ("bread mold") is the name given by German bakers to baskets made from coiled willow reeds. *Banneton* is the term used by French bakers for woven baskets with a sewn-in canvas lining. When using either type of mold, you must flour the inside of the basket first to prevent the upside-down loaf from sticking. Place a number of the baskets containing loaves on top of sheet pans or boards and set them on a covered rack before putting them into a proofer or retarder. When the loaves have finished proofing, flip them over onto the peel, score the loaves, and slide the loaves in the oven. *Do not bake the loaves in the baskets.* They are only used to proof loaves and help them hold their shape before baking.

Both brotformen and bannetons come in a wide variety of shapes and sizes. Some very long ones can accommodate baguettes, but most are either round or oval to proof boules and bâtards. Ring-shaped baskets are used to proof crown-shaped loaves. Using brotformen and baskets tends to be more expensive than using linen *couches* (which can also be expensive), and the baskets take up a lot of space on the racks. Still, they have the one considerable advantage of allowing the baker to load the peel and oven quickly with minimal fuss.

Convection ovens and large rack ovens (see *Chapter 8*) don't usually have a stone

Figure 7.3 Examples of metal pans designed for proofing and baking loaves of bread.

for you to load your loaves directly onto. If you have these ovens, going to the trouble of placing baguettes on pleated linen as they proof is probably not worth the effort. In this case, you do not need an oven peel to load loaves into a convection oven or rack oven. Instead, it is more appropriate to place shaped raw baguettes directly on scalloped baguette trays (see Figure 7.3). Then allow the loaves to proof directly on the trays, and load them, tray and all, into the oven when they are ready. If scalloped trays are not available for use in convection ovens, then perforated screens make the next best choice, followed by parchment-lined sheet pans.

If you wish, you may proof rounds and oval-shaped loaves in the same bannetons used for loading deck ovens and flip the baskets onto perforated metal screens or parchment-lined sheet pans, which can then be loaded into a convection or rack oven.

The pan with the sliding lid in the back of Figure 7.3 is called a *Pullman pan*. The pans on the left are probably recognizable to many readers, but notice that some of them are connected in groups of four or five by a metal strap, which is why those units are called *straps*. Connecting them in this fashion makes loading and unloading a large oven full of panned loaves much faster. Also note the pans on the left, which are well used and showing some wear, will color in spots. This coloration is like the patina that forms in sauté pans and woks, and is a natural, harmless development. Under the straps you can see a typical full-sized sheet pan, and on the right is a perforated pan designed to hold baguettes or long rolls if they are baked in a convection oven, which has no hearth.

ARTISAN BAKER PROFILE

Didier Rosada

Uptown Bakers, Washington, D.C.

It would be hard to choose the person who has had the biggest impact on how American artisans make their bread, but if we had to try, Didier Rosada would certainly make the short list. He has been head instructor at the two most influential bread baking schools for artisans in the United States. He has also had a hand in training every U.S. baking team that has competed in Paris for the Coupe de Monde du Boulanger since 1996. The notable gold and silver medals won by these teams attest to the effectiveness of Didier's instruction and training techniques.

Didier apprenticed in his native France from the age of 15, and in 1995 was awarded a *Brevet de Mâitrise*, which is a masters in baking in France. He has worked for Club Med and Bay State Milling, and his acquaintance with the Bread Bakers Guild of America led to him becoming a head baking instructor—first at the National Baking Center in Minneapolis (1996–2002) and then at the San Francisco Baking Institute (2002–2004).

In late 2004, Didier moved to eastern Maryland to become vice president of Uptown Bakers, a leading wholesaler of breads and pastries in the Washington, D.C., metropolitan area. He continues to teach classes occasionally at seminars hosted by the Guild throughout the country, and he owns a bakery consulting business.

IMPRESSIONS OF ARTISAN BREAD BAKING AS AN INDUSTRY

You have never had a job that didn't involve bread baking. Why do you remain in this occupation?

I remain in this unique occupation because it completely fulfills my professional life. Through baking, I was able to day after day create a noble food that people enjoy with their meals. As a teacher and consultant, I shared my passion for this craft. With the experience, I was able to develop my creativity by developing new formulas using different baking processes to obtain the best-quality products possible. Also, the baking community is an extraordinary brotherhood!

Can we define artisan bread? *If so, what makes it distinctive, in your opinion?*

Artisan breads should be made using a traditional process that:

◆ Carefully selects the best and most natural ingredients.

◆ Respects the nature of the ingredients during the process.

◆ Uses a baking process that respects the integrity of the dough.

◆ Uses long fermentation time to optimize dough and bread characteristics.

◆ Uses equipment carefully selected to process the dough without damage.

◆ Bakes the bread under optimum conditions to obtain the best quality in the finished products.

Do you have any insights about how bakers can maintain exceptional quality in their bread as they take on more accounts and need to find ways to efficiently produce more bread in the same amount of time?

Design the bakery to maintain the traditional process (allow enough space for pre-ferments, for example) and select the most appropriate equipment to process the dough under optimum conditions (at the makeup line and the oven, in particular).

Summary

Proofing is the period of fermentation that takes place after loaves are shaped and before they are loaded into an oven. The main purpose of proofing is to inflate loaves with enough CO_2 to maintain their light texture and attractive appearance as they are baked. If loaves of bread collapse before they are completely baked, they are probably overproofed. Making sure enough CO_2 is present to hold the loaves' light texture and attractive appearance while they are baked without stressing the limits of the loaf to hold gas is the essential challenge of proofing bread.

Retarding is a form of proofing that uses refrigeration to delay the proof. You must use precise controls to successfully retard your loaves, because no one is likely to be around to take corrective measures if needed to ensure a high-quality finished product. The points of control can be similar to those for conventional proofing, but the limits of fermentation tolerance can be tested during retardation, and thorough in-shop batch testing is necessary to arrive at workable temperature and ingredient specifications. Only then can a baker reliably control the production of gas and the degradation of dough strength.

Specialized pieces of equipment are available to assist the baker in successfully proofing hearth loaves. They are used primarily when baking on a stone in a deck oven, but some of the equipment can be used for baking in a convection or rack oven as well.

Key Terms

proofing   *proofing board*
overproofed   *bagel board*
proofer   *oven peel*
retarding   *flip-board*
degradation   *brotform*
glutathione   *banneton*
couche

Questions for Review

1. What is the primary purpose of proofing, and what makes it different from other phases of fermentation?

2. What are the two primary causes of overproofing?

3. How is gas production controlled during the proof?

4. How is retarding different from conventional proofing?

5. What are the key strategies for controlling dough degradation during the retarding process?

6. How can using the retarding process provide bakers a more efficient, organized workday?

Questions for Discussion

Some bakers in France and other countries use a synthesized form of vitamin C called *ascorbic acid* to increase the strength of gluten bonds and give them better protection against dough degradation and overproofing. Bakers who hold true to the concept of artisan-style bread making sometimes embrace this technique because it adds strength where and when they need it and is then destroyed in the baking process. When used in quantities of 10–20 parts per million, they argue, ascorbic acid has no effect whatsoever on the taste of the bread, and it is safe for consumption— we consume the chemical safely every time we eat an orange.

Others claim that using ascorbic acid to augment dough strength clutters the dough's ingredient list with unnecessary additives and violates the spirit of using all-natural ingredients in bread baking. Even Professor Raymond Calvel (see *Chapter 4*) was criticized by some French bread experts for his promotion of using ascorbic acid in minute amounts to increase dough strength where necessary.

1. Do you think using a simple vitamin to help prevent loaf collapse during proofing or retardation constitutes a violation of the principle of using all-natural ingredients?

2. If you don't notice any difference in the flavor or quality of the final product, should vitamin C be left out as an ingredient in the formula?

3. Are there alternatives for bakers who wish to improve the strength and fermentation tolerance of their dough without using synthetic ingredients?

Lab Exercise & Experiment

Refer to the following formula for Baguettes—Direct Method and make a batch, following the directions through the time of division and intermediate proofing (bench rest). If you prefer, you may use almost any dough from the formulas listed in the *Appendix of Formulas* at the end of this book. The bread dough chosen is not as important as the concept of observing differences in the final products when they are proofed in different ways. Whichever dough you choose, make sure you use the same mixing method for each batch.

To keep the experiment as simple as possible, shape the dough portions into rounds instead of baguettes. Cut all portions to 20 oz (about 570g), and pre-shape them all precisely the same way. Be certain to shape all your rounds in the same fashion, using the same amount of tension. Place them seam-side down on parchment-lined half-sheet pans, 1 loaf per pan,

Now proof them all in the same proofing cabinet (or covered speed rack), with all the rounds located as closely as possible to the same location on the rack. The temperature in any room (including the inside of a proofer) is actually different depending on distance from the floor or ceiling. Loaves toward the top of a rack usually proof slightly faster than the ones located toward the bottom of the rack because the warmer air resides higher in the room. Locating the rounds as closely as possible to the same spot on the rack helps eliminate differences in temperature that can affect proof.

Test the loaves for readiness after 45–50 minutes, or about 10 minutes before they would normally be ready. The indentation left by your finger should almost disappear, as the tension within the loaf should still be significant. If this is the case, the loaves are described as *underproofed*. Load one of the loaves into your pre-heated oven, scoring it simply with a cross and spraying it heavily with water just before you place it in the oven. (If you use your steam generator after loading the loaf, the generator might not recover in time to provide steam for the next two loaves. Also, repeatedly forcing steam into the oven repeatedly covers previously loaded loaves with moisture, which changes their baking conditions somewhat compared to the last loaf loaded.)

Ten minutes after the first loaf is loaded, check the proof on the remaining loaves. If the indentation still almost disappears, give the loaves a few more minutes of proofing. If the indentation springs back about halfway, then the loaves are just about properly proofed. Place one of these remaining loaves in the oven, scoring it exactly the same way as you did the first loaf. Be certain to spray it heavily with water just before you load it.

About 10–15 minutes after loading the second (properly proofed) loaf, test the proof on the remaining loaf. The indentation left by your finger will probably remain almost completely. Score, spray, and load this last loaf exactly as you did the previous two.

Bake each loaf for precisely the same amount of time—probably 30–35 minutes in a 430°F deck oven (for convection ovens, subtract 25–40°F, depending on brand and type). Let them cool completely before cutting them open, if possible. Compare and contrast the characteristics of the loaves, noting overall volume, cut openings, symmetry in appearance, crust coloration, crumb structure, texture, and overall visual appeal. See also if you can detect differences in flavor among the three loaves (this is why it is best to allow them all to cool completely; the last loaf would taste different than the previous two because it would still be hot and wet inside).

Create a table to record your observations. Try applying your new-found knowledge to the proofing and baking cycles of any breads you bake from this time forward.

BAGUETTES—DIRECT METHOD

	Metric			U.S. Measure		Formula Baker's %
	(1X)	**(4X)**		**(1X)**	**(4X)**	
	5-Qt Mixer	20-Qt Mixer		5-Qt Mixer	20-Qt Mixer	
STRAIGHT DOUGH						
Bread flour	1000g	4000g		2 lb 3.0oz	8 lb 12.0oz	**100%**
Water	700g	2800g		1 lb 7.5oz	6 lb 2.0oz	**70%**
Salt	20g	80g		0.7oz	2.8oz	**2%**
Instant yeast	3g	12g		0.1oz	0.4oz	**0.3%**
TOTAL YIELD	**1723g**	**6892g**		**3 lb 11.3oz**	**15 lb 1.2oz**	

NOTE: The yeast quantity listed in the formula is intended for bakers who use the short mix method. A dough mixed with the intensive mix method should receive a yeast percentage around 0.7%, while the yeast percentage for an improved mix dough would be more appropriately set at 0.4%.

GOAL TEMPERATURE: 77°F (25°C).

MIXING METHOD: Short mix, intensive mix, or improved mix—see pp. 195–196.

BULK FERMENTATION: See directions associated with the mix method chosen, pp. 195–196.

SCALING: See options, p. 196.

SHAPING: See directions in *Chapter 6*.

PROOFING: See directions, pp. 196–197.

BAKING: See directions, p. 197.

COOLING: See directions, p. 198.

chapter 8

Baking

Learning Outcomes:

■ Define oven spring.

■ Identify the reasons for scoring loaves before they are baked.

■ Explain why steam might be used during the first few minutes of baking.

■ Recognize the transitions that take place as raw dough becomes finished bread.

■ Determine when a loaf of bread has finished baking.

Baking Transforms Raw Dough

Baking, like all forms of cooking, is a process of transformation. We take raw bread dough and surround it with intense heat so its starches, proteins, and other organic compounds change from their original state into another we find more appealing to eat. Understanding the nature of the changes that occur and knowing how to control them allows bakers to manipulate formulas and procedures where necessary to create consistently attractive, well-textured loaves.

To successfully bring loaves from the proofer through their bake cycle and onto the cooling rack, you must master a number of skills:

1. Recognize when loaves and rolls are ready to be baked.

2. Judge when to score bread, and when the depth or width of scoring must be adjusted.

3. Bake at an appropriate temperature range for a given loaf's size and shape.

4. Decide when to use steam, and how much steam to use.

5. Judge the level of doneness.

6. Cool the loaves enough to ensure their structure is firm, their crumb is sufficiently dried, and they can be packed without damage to either product or shelf life.

Recognizing When Loaves Are Ready to Be Baked

Knowing when shaped breads are ready to be baked is critical to successful baking, and all the remaining steps for baking loaves and rolls are useless if you don't start with breads that are proofed properly. To review the proofing process and the characteristics of completely proofed loaves, review *Chapter 7*.

Scoring Loaves

When loaves are loaded into the oven and the door is closed, they go through what is actually the last, brief stage of dough fermentation. Yeast cells in the dough can withstand temperatures only to about 139°F, but it will take some time before the center of the loaf reaches this point.

As the heat in the oven increases, the loaves undergo a phenomenon known as *oven spring* (sometimes called *oven kick*). During oven spring, the yeast cells ferment the dough in an accelerated fashion. A large amount of CO_2 gas is generated within the loaf in a short period, causing sudden growth in the loaf and tremendous pressure on its exterior. The intensely dry heat of the oven can form a skin on the loaf that can restrict its ability to expand and accommodate the increase in its CO_2

content. If this happens, the final crumb may become tighter than we prefer, and a lack of extensibility in the skin of the loaf may cause it to distort or rupture due to its inability to stretch and grow in a controlled fashion.

To help the loaves grow in a controlled, attractive manner and to ensure they have an open crumb structure, we sometimes slash their surface with a sharp knife or razor blade to coax the intense gas pressure in the direction we want it to go. This process of slashing loaves before baking them is called *scoring*. Not all loaves must be scored before they are baked. Pan loaves, especially, often go without scoring because they are surrounded on the bottom and sides by the pan itself, and this allows the loaves within to expand fully without rupturing.

Food historians cannot be certain about the origins of scoring, but it may have come about as a way of individual bakers marking their loaves before baking them in a communal oven. In any case, bakers eventually realized that by planning *how* they score the loaves, they could help ensure the even appearance and open crumb they were looking for. In the photograph in Figure 8.1a, you will see two bâtards. The one on the right doesn't have any scoring, and the one on the left has been scored with a straight cut that runs just under the skin of the loaf. Notice in Figures 8.1b and 8.1c how just one cut down the center of the loaf makes a significant difference in the volume, crumb structure, and overall attractiveness of the loaf.

Figure 8.1a Two loaves about to be loaded into a deck oven. The left one is scored and the right one is not.

Figure 8.1b The same two loaves after 10 minutes of baking. The right one is scored and the left one is not.

Figure 8.1c The same two loaves cut open to illustrate the effect of proper scoring on both exterior appearance and interior crumb structure.

Figure 8.2a Baguettes scored three different ways. Only the center loaf is scored properly.

Figure 8.2b The same three baguettes after baking. Only the center loaf was scored properly.

If scoring is done carelessly, or the pattern used doesn't relieve enough pressure inside the loaf, then the bread takes on a distorted shape that limits its expansion, compresses the crumb, and creates an unappealing exterior appearance. Like it or not, customers take appearance into consideration when purchasing bread, and they usually avoid distorted loaves even if their eating quality is fine. Figures 8.2a and 8.2b show baguettes scored three different ways. Only the center loaf is scored properly, with cuts that overlap by about one-third and are not too diagonal.

Notice how the different methods of scoring loaves can make a considerable difference in their final appearance. The "sausage cut" on the loaf at the top of the photo is too diagonal to allow the loaf to expand evenly, which causes the baguette to blow out noticeably. The loaf at the bottom of the photo has cuts that are well formed and not too diagonal, as does the loaf in the center, but they do not overlap, so the loaf still bakes into a distorted, irregular shape.

In the real world of bakery production, it is often not possible for all breads to be perfectly proofed before they are baked. Sometimes you may need to take a batch from the proofer a bit early to prevent backups in production, or you find your oven isn't large enough to hold all the bread you think is ready for baking.

You should keep these considerations in mind as you determine the length, type, and depth of scoring you select for each batch. For instance, when loading a batch of boules (round French loaves), you might typically score them with a simple cross shape. However, if they are underproofed, you can score them with slashes a bit wider or deeper than normal to help accommodate the unusually high potential for further growth brought about by underproofing. This may help prevent a *blowout,* which occurs when the loaves break open in an unattractive way. Conversely, if the loaves have been in the proofer too long and seem fragile or bloated already, you might try scoring with shorter or shallower cuts.

Small rolls are often not scored at all. Part of the reason is that the heat penetrates them quickly and they usually expand well enough before a skin or crust might form. Another practical reason, though, is that rolls are often produced by the hundreds or thousands, and trying to score each of them individually is both tedious and time-consuming. There may be some benefit to scoring rolls, and some excellent bakers still choose to do it, but the time involved, the degree of improvement seen, and the price charged for rolls are factors to be considered when deciding whether to do so. Generally, if rolls are scored, bakers use either a single slash across the center of the roll or a simple cross shape.

Baking Temperature

Ideally, when we bake bread of any type or size, we want the exterior of the product to be browned just to our preferences and the center of the loaf to be baked completely. With this in mind, at what temperature should we bake bread?

To answer this question, we must consider these two factors about the dough we have prepared:

1. The level of sugar present in the dough
2. The physical size and shape of the loaves or rolls

To a certain degree, the level of browning on the outside of a loaf can be adjusted to suit your preferences or those of your customers. Still, we do want to brown the crust enough to benefit from the aromas associated with caramelization, and we must create enough structure in the exterior to withstand the forces of gravity. A large sandwich loaf, especially, can be so tall that if the sides of the loaf aren't browned enough, they will not be able to support the weight of the crown.

Two kinds of browning in bread during the bake concern us:

Maillard browning, which is the browning that results from proteins reacting with sugars.

Caramelization, which is the browning that results from sugars breaking down under heat.

Maillard browning is named after the scientist who discovered the process itself, and it can occur at fairly low oven temperatures (it can even occur at room temperature in a bag of dried milk over a long period). We can see evidence of Maillard browning just a short time after bread is inserted into the oven, when the crust reaches a temperature of only 140–150°F. Caramelization of sugars in the crust doesn't become noticeable until breads reach 320–340°F on their exterior, which occurs much later in the baking process.

SUGAR CONTENT

The more sugar present in dough, the faster the loaves made with it will brown. Note we didn't say they *bake* much faster, just they *brown* faster. This is one of the challenges presented when you include sugar in sizable quantities in a dough formula.

If the formula includes more than 4–5% sugar, you may have to reduce the bread's baking temperature compared to the same bread made with a lower sugar level (or no sugar at all). Otherwise, the outside of the loaf can brown excessively before the inside is completely baked. For example, if you have a round loaf of lean white dough that bakes normally at 450°F for 35–40 minutes, you may need to bake it at 400–425°F if you adjust the formula by adding considerable sugar.

WEIGHT OF THE LOAF OR ROLL

Typically, if we bake a load of baguettes scaled at 375g each at 475°F or so, it might take 20–25 minutes for them to be browned well on the outside and baked enough on the inside. If we take the same dough used to make these baguettes and make 60g round rolls instead, we will find they bake much faster. So, will simply pulling the rolls that are smaller in shape and size from the oven earlier always give us the best possible rolls? The answer is that it probably will not.

Practically speaking, when we say that a loaf or roll is done inside, we mean it has solidified to a point where it is no longer raw. Technically, this means the proteins in the dough have coagulated and the starches have gelatinized completely under heat. In addition, much of the water that was originally in the dough is evaporated as solidification occurs.

When proteins have coagulated and starches have gelatinized sufficiently, all movement of liquid water in the dough stops, and the dough begins to become rigid in its structure. How quickly this process occurs depends largely on how far the center of the loaf is from its exterior. Long, narrow loaves like baguettes can be completely baked in 20–25 minutes, but even smaller rolls will bake significantly faster—perhaps in 12–15 minutes.

The baking process for different-sized breads is further complicated when the crust doesn't *brown* as fast as the faster *bake* time in the bread's interior. Remember, we want the outside of the loaf or roll to be browned to our liking at precisely the same time the inside finishes baking. Underbrowned rolls may be done inside, but the lack of browning means their aromas and flavor will not be as nice as those of a properly browned roll. So, when possible, it is better to bake small rolls made from any given dough at a much higher temperature than standard loaves made from the same dough. If a baguette made from a particular dough bakes at 475°F for 23 minutes, you would probably need to bake rolls made from the same dough at 500°F or higher to get them to brown soon enough and avoid the risk of overbaking and drying them out.

Overbaking occurs when a product such as a loaf or roll is baked so long that it is too dry in its crumb and crust. It is then less enjoyable to eat, and its shelf life is shortened considerably. The occurrence of overbaking is not always obvious if you judge bread by color alone; it can happen in rolls or loaves that have taken on little color at all. A baker, then, must anticipate that overbaking might occur, and check loaves and rolls by feel as well as by sight. If you notice breads aren't coloring well before they are done inside, then the baking temperature for that particular product probably should be increased. On the other hand, if coloration occurs before the inside is done, then the baking temperature should be reduced.

SHAPE OF THE LOAF OR BREAD

Another factor that affects the appropriate temperature and length of time to bake a particular loaf is its shape or dimensions. As mentioned previously in this chapter, the time it takes for the innermost part of a loaf to be done depends on the distance between the outside of a loaf and its center. For this reason, a 1-pound round loaf will take longer to bake completely than a baguette of the same weight. Likewise, a short bâtard scaled at the same weight as a full-length baguette will require more time than the baguette to bake fully. Thus, short or round loaves are sometimes baked at lower temperatures than baguettes made from the same dough, as it takes longer for the interior to bake and you don't want the crust to brown before the inside is done.

CONSIDER THE PROOFING AND RETARDING METHODS USED

One more point to consider when choosing a baking temperature is whether the loaves were proofed conventionally for 1–3 hours or retarded for an extended period (see *Chapter 7*). Retarded loaves can ferment for a long time at a cool temperature and have a slow rate of yeast activity. The amount of sugar converted from starch by amylase (see *Chapter 5*) may accumulate faster than the yeast can consume it, which leaves more sugar in the retarded loaves than in conventionally proofed loaves. This extra sugar will cause the loaves' crusts to brown more rapidly, in the same way that adding sugar at the time of mixing would. For this reason, you may want to bake retarded loaves at a somewhat lower temperature than loaves that are proofed conventionally. The recommended difference in temperature between the two may be 10–20°F lower for the retarded loaves.

Using Steam

As we mentioned previously, when loaves enter an oven, the intensely dry heat can cause a skin to form on their surface. This skin can restrict the ability of the loaf to expand in reaction to the buildup of CO_2 in the dough. If that happens, the loaf might contort or burst such that the finished product appears misshapen and unattractive. This limiting of expansion also has a negative effect on the texture of the crumb, which can be too close or dense if it isn't able to expand normally during oven spring.

Scoring can relieve this pressure to a large degree, but even well-scored loaves won't always grow in an attractive manner if they are loaded into a hot, dry oven chamber. If we load these loaves into a humid, steam-filled oven cavity instead, their skins don't form as quickly and they can achieve greater volume.

Ovens Used in Bread Baking

The "best" oven for bread baking can be difficult to determine. First, we describe the ovens you'll encounter in most bakeshops, and then we discuss which kinds are best suited to which types of bread baking.

The most common type of oven in many restaurants and cafés is a typical *range oven* that might be found under the stovetop on any cook's line. These are similar in many ways to conventional home ovens, except they are usually bigger. They are really designed more to service the needs of sauté cooks than they are to fill the requirements of a bakeshop, but some bakers still use them. They rely mostly on the heat of *radiation* to do their job, where the gas or electric elements heat a solid metal plate at the oven's bottom, and this heat radiates toward whatever is placed on the oven's racks. The strength of the range oven is its simplicity, as the moving parts are few to none and qualified service technicians are easy to find. However, it has at least three weaknesses: It is too small to accommodate much product at any one time, it generally has no steam contraption to use after you load your bread into it, and you must retrofit it with stones if you want to mimic the bottom heat created by a deck oven.

Another common oven in restaurants and many bakeshops is the *convection oven*, which may be located on cook's lines, in the prep area, or anywhere baking and pastry work takes place. Styles include one- or two-door models located singly on a steel table or stacked on top of one another in two or three levels. Sometimes they have a steam generator (which makes them a so-called combination or "combi" oven), but usually they don't. The heat they generate is carried efficiently through the oven chamber by electrically powered fans, and this movement of energy through air currents is called *heat of convection*. Because the air currents carry heat so efficiently when compared to the radiant heat of conventional ovens, the baking temperature for any bread might be as much as 25–50°F lower than it would in a conventional oven while delivering the finished product in the same amount of time.

The great thing about convection ovens is that they use less energy and can be stacked so as to create lots of baking capacity in very little floor space. Their weaknesses: They usually don't have a steam generator, and the forced air currents that transmit the heat of the oven also dry the surface of the bread quickly. A dry surface on bread that has just entered the oven restricts growth during oven spring

Ovens Used in Bread Baking (Continued)

and tends to reduce the browning of the crust, which means less flavor and fewer nice aromas. Varieties like challah, croissants, and Danish that are egg-washed before baking can do well in a convection oven, but most hearth-type loaves, like baguettes, need steam and generally do not bake well there.

A subset of convection ovens that works fairly well with some types of bread are *rack ovens*—so called because they can accept one, two, or even four entire speed racks full of product (depending on oven size and design). Unlike typical convection ovens, rack ovens are generally equipped with a steam generator, as they are designed for use in bakeries and bread baking is an assumed use. They are convenient to load and unload, as you simply insert specially built racks full of product right as they come out of a proofer, and little time is spent transporting bread into or out of the oven. This makes rack ovens well suited to baking rolls, Danish, croissants, challah, and most pan breads. See Figure 8.3.

The downside of rack ovens is their dependence on convection currents to transfer heat to the product, a problem when you are trying to make breads that were intended to be baked on a stone hearth. Special baguette pans are

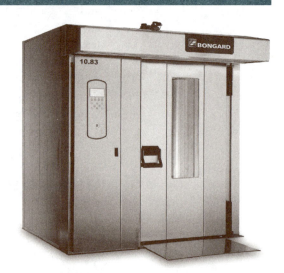

Figure 8.3 This rack oven is designed to accommodate heat-resistant speed racks full of product. The rack(s) rotates within the oven as heated air is blown by powerful fans. Courtesy of French Baking Machines (FBM).

designed with perforations along their length and ends that are open to recreate the shape of traditional baguettes as much as possible. Still, the lack of direct contact between a hearth loaf and any real hearth usually makes for less pop in the loaves during oven spring, so the degree of oven spring itself is reduced noticeably. This leads to less openness in the crumb structure, and a dimpled bottom crust (from the perforations) that seems to suggest the bread was factory-made. Less bottom heat can also lead to less definition in the scoring, as growth in the loaf is more even all over and less directed toward the cuts. Many high-volume bakeries choose to use rack ovens for reasons of convenience, limited floor space, or matters of staffing or workflow. Nevertheless, their use in producing hearth breads such as baguettes is at least a partial compromise.

Another common oven in bakeries that specialize in pan breads is a *revolving oven*, so called because it features a number of shelves that rotate in a motion like that of a Ferris wheel. Bread pans attached by straps in units of four or five loaves each are loaded side by side onto the shelves, which often accommodate ten or more straps. When a shelf is filled with pans, the oven operator turns on the motor that makes the shelves revolve. He then either stops the motor to load another shelf when it is level with the oven door, or he closes the door and lets the loaves within complete their bake while they rotate around the oven.

This type of oven works with radiant heat like a conventional oven, with burners or elements at the bottom of the unit. Unlike most conventional ovens, though, it carries the pans of bread or rolls in a rotation around the oven's cavity, which promotes an even bake with less need for rotating the pans by hand. If you aim to make lots of pan bread, this oven does the best job of fitting the most loaves in the least space with the most even bake. It also does a great job on challah, rolls, buns, and laminated pastries. Unfortunately, it does a relatively poor job of baking hearth loaves. Rotating ovens generally lack steam generators, and a lack of steam makes for poor crust on hearth loaves. Even if you retrofit a rotating oven with a steam apparatus, the large cavity in the oven (up to 10 feet high) encourages the steam to go right to the ceiling, and the loaves often see little benefit from the attempt. Some owners have tried installing tiles or stones on the shelves, but the ovens are rarely designed for this, and the bother and expense of fitting rotating shelves with stones may make the prospect of making do with this option seem unwise in the long run.

The last category of oven we examine is the *deck oven*, sometimes called a *hearth oven*. Basically, deck ovens are distinguished by the presence of a stone or composite (concrete) hearth in the bottom of the oven cavity. The gas or electric heating elements are located either beneath the deck or in positions both over and under the deck. Most deck ovens transmit their most intense heat through the hearth itself coming in contact with the loaves of bread. This method of heat transfer—where the heat source and the baked product come in direct contact with one another—is called *heat of conduction*. See Figure 8.4.

Ovens Used in Bread Baking (Continued)

Well-designed deck ovens have considerable mass that helps them hold their heat and recover quickly after they are loaded with bread. They also provide direct contact with the loaves being baked, and this heat of conduction leads to exceptional oven spring. The cavities are not high—usually 12–18 inches. Modern hearth ovens are usually equipped with a steam apparatus if they are designed to bake bread, but those designed for baking pizzas rarely have the steam option. They are called *deck ovens* because they are typically arranged in sets of three or four, stacked one on top of the other, somewhat resembling the decks on a ship.

The advantage of using a hearth oven is that you can make certain traditional European breads in a manner that closely resembles the practices of bakers from past centuries. Such breads are usually called *hearth breads*, and they get their name from the practice of placing the loaves directly on the hearth as they bake. The intense bottom heat from the stone hearth pushes the gases generated during oven spring toward the top of a loaf, and this helps the free-form loaves maintain good height as they bake. It also helps create a sort of wild, open crumb in loaves made from wet, underdeveloped dough.

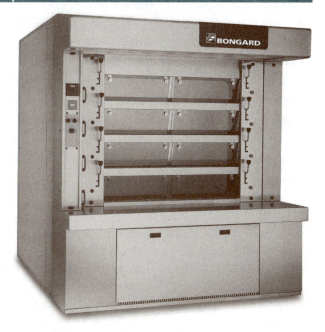

Figure 8.4 One type of steam-injected deck oven. Courtesy of French Baking Machines (FBM).

It is difficult to recreate traditional French, German, or Italian breads without a hearth oven. The lack of bottom heat in other oven types produces a more homogenous crumb structure, and the cuts made during scoring do not open as dramatically. Also, as steam-equipped deck ovens have smaller cavities, they tend to ensure that steam condenses on the outside of the loaves and not only on the ceiling of the oven.

One subset of ovens that fall into the hearth oven category is wood-fired ovens made from stone or bricks. The appeal of these ovens is that they duplicate in most ways the exact manner in which traditional European loaves were baked in past centuries. A baker starts some wood burning either in a chamber just beneath the deck or on the deck itself. The fire builds in intensity until glowing embers are produced; these transfer their heat to the floor and surrounding walls through both radiant and conductive heat methods. When the walls and floor are judged hot enough, the embers are removed and the oven's floor is swept and then mopped to remove the ash. Loaves are then loaded into the oven with a baker's peel and the oven's door closed for the remainder of the bake.

Many artisan bakers swear that wood-fired deck ovens produce just the right combination of conductive and radiant heat for baking hearth loaves. They may be right, as these ovens essentially duplicate a baking method used by the craftsmen who created these breads. The wild crumb, the crackly crust, and the slightly smoky flavors left by the residue of ash are qualities that may not be precisely recreated by the modern manufactured deck ovens of today.

Still, these testaments to the past can be difficult to control. There are no knobs for adjusting the heat directly, and steam comes only indirectly from mopping the deck before loading. Controlling the oven amounts to a science, so training employees to handle the process of loading and baking can take weeks. The order of baking is determined by the oven in most cases—baguettes and rolls are best baked when the oven is at its hottest, and gradually larger or fatter loaves are loaded into the chamber as it cools through the day. Learning how to fire the oven and when it needs refiring demands much from the baker who chooses to use it.

When these ovens are mastered, the breads they produce can almost transport us to a time long ago when people were much more of a participant in the cycle of food production. Their simple use of wood fire seems to ground them in tradition, and their appeal to artisan bakers is not surprising. Still, it is debatable whether their use today does much more than evoke imagery of past centuries, whatever their other advantages may be. Arguably, the artisanship in the term *artisan baker* applies more to the baked products and their quality than it does to the authenticity of the method chosen for baking. Certain subtle qualities may make loaves baked in wood-fired ovens slightly different from

Ovens Used in Bread Baking (Continued)

those made in modern deck ovens, but different isn't necessarily better, and practical considerations of baking capacity, technical mastery, and considerable inconvenience may outweigh the emotional boost we experience when we use ancient methods to make really great bread.

So which oven to choose? The answer depends on the type of bread you usually produce, the volume of sales you anticipate, your budget, and how much value you place on recreating ancient methods of production. A bakery that produces mostly pan breads and rolls can do very well with a rack oven or rotating oven. Wood-fired ovens are great for small to medium-sized bakeries that focus on hearth breads, if you don't mind the technical challenges of using them.

Bakers who wish to produce traditional hearth breads in quantity may want to choose a steam-injected deck oven.

And, of course, if you plan to produce all types of bread in significant quantity (and your budget allows), having both a deck oven and a rack oven gives you the advantages of both.

When commercial ovens were constructed that used indirect heat from coal, gas, or electricity, bakers noticed their design didn't always encourage the retention of steam in the oven during the early bake. Oven builders responded to bakers' needs by installing steam generators to provide moisture when it was needed, and they placed vents in the oven as well to evacuate the steam when it was no longer required.

You might be wondering, *Why not just leave the steam in the oven for the entire bake?* We limit the use of steam because the extended presence of steam can reduce the rate of caramelization on the bread's crust, and a baking chamber that is always humid reduces the amount of water that exits the loaves during baking. If we don't release the steam well before the end of the bake, we inhibit the ability of the crust to brown sufficiently, and we might end up with crusts that turn soft because the loaves retained too much water during the bake.

The quality of the crust in hearth loaves is enhanced by exposing the loaves to steam for the first 5–10 minutes of baking. This initially humid environment coats the loaves with moisture and prevents the formation of a crust before the loaf has a chance to expand. It also insulates the loaves from the intensity of the oven's heat during this period. Last, the steam encourages the gelatinization of starches on the outside of the loaf, which speeds the conversion of starch to sugar on the exterior and promotes the creation of a crisp, nicely browned crust.

It is important to note that not all types of loaves need steam to start their baking. Loaves like challah, for instance, usually contain sugar and eggs, so they are baked at a lower temperature (350–375°F) for slower browning, with no steam. The reduced temperature reduces the intensity of heat during the initial bake, and the egg wash that is applied to these loaves just before baking also insulates the loaves from the initial drying effect of the heat.

Most loaves baked in standard bread pans have their bottoms and four sides enclosed, leaving only the crown to crust over from contact with the hot dry air in the oven. These loaves also typically contain fats and sweeteners, so their baking temperature is not as high as for most hearth loaves, and they don't need steam as much to insulate them from dry oven heat.

How to Judge the Doneness of Bread

When is a loaf of bread done baking?

A loaf is done when the crust has browned enough to give flavor and structure to the loaf and the inside has baked enough that it is solid and free of raw aftertaste. It should also be free of excessive moisture that could later soften the crust of the hearth bread as it cools, and there should be no residual flavor of alcohol remaining from the fermentation of the dough. Color and outward appearance alert experienced bakers that it is time to unload a batch from the oven.

You might use other tools to decide if bread has baked enough. Many experienced bakers remove a hearth loaf from the oven and tap its bottom to test for a hollow sound. That is not an easy skill to master with consistency, and it may require a lot of trial and error before you become confident that your judgment (and hearing) is accurate. This doesn't mean the technique can't be used, but rather, if pinpoint precision is necessary, only experienced bakers can be relied on to make an accurate judgment.

Tradition-minded artisan bakers might cringe as they read this, but you can approach this scientifically and reduce the question to one of what the interior temperature of a fully baked loaf should be. This is the method many chefs use to determine when a roast beef is done, and there is no good reason why the same tool can't be used to determine doneness in loaves—that is, to measure the temperature reached when proteins have coagulated and starches have gelled enough to firm the interior of a loaf and eliminate its raw nature.

By pulling a loaf from a deck or a bread pan and carefully inserting a pocket thermometer in its bottom, you can easily read its interior temperature. If you do this only once to the loaf, there is no noticeable damage to its whole structure and the loaf remains quite salable. Operators who will not sell loaves that are scarred from a probe can use the probed loaf for sampling or eat it themselves.

This isn't to say that every loaf or even every batch should be "temped" to be certain the loaves are done. An oven operator who bakes the same type of breads every day quickly learns by sight and feel whether most breads are done. Still, certain types of bread, including challah, brioche, and stollen, can brown a great deal before they have finished baking. It is wise to check the interior temperature of one of those loaves before removing an entire batch from the oven. Loaves that are brown outside but underbaked inside will obviously be unappealing to eat; in addition, they can collapse when pulled from the oven. Being precise about the interior temperature ensures you won't lose an entire batch of loaves whose doneness is hard to judge by appearance or feel.

So, what temperature indicates a done loaf? The answer to this question is open to debate because even the technique of measuring interior temperature in loaves is not widely accepted. Still, many bakers agree that about 200°F is acceptable as an indicator of interior doneness. If you want the loaves to be browner when they have reached this temperature, you can certainly keep baking them, within reasonable limits. Some traditional Italian varieties, such as ciabatta and pane pugliese (see the *Appendix of Formulas*), are still fairly wet inside when their interior temperature reaches 200°F, and this excess moisture might soften the crust of the loaves as they cool. Baking these loaves longer so they reach 210°F or so helps them lose enough moisture to have a crisp crust. The same is true for many French breads, such as baguettes and boules.

The Importance of Cooling Bread after Baking

Many people assume that when a loaf of bread is out of the oven, it has finished baking. In most cases, this is simply not so. If we think of baking bread as a process of transformation from raw dough to finished loaf, we should recognize that baking hasn't quite finished when the loaf leaves the oven.

When the starches gelatinize and proteins coagulate within the dough under the heat of the oven, their ability to capture and hold moisture is significantly reduced.

Excess water that isn't tied up with the starches and proteins begins to evaporate from the loaf as it bakes, which is fortunate, because it allows the loaf to dry and become stable and palatable.

The evaporation process does not end when the loaf is unloaded from the oven. It continues for 1–3 hours, depending upon the size and shape of the loaves. If the baker is not careful to encourage cooling and evaporation, soggy or gummy bread may result.

Loaves taken from the oven must be cooled on a multi-tiered wire rack large enough to provide space between the loaves. Crowding the loaves as they cool on the rack traps the exiting steam and causes them to soften and destabilize. Crowding also extends the amount of time it takes for the loaves to cool. Examples of both properly and improperly spaced loaves cooling on a rack are illustrated in Figure 8.5.

In many cases, slicing loaves before they are cool enough results in tearing the loaf and possibly jamming the blades on an automatic slicer. If a loaf has not cooled, its crumb structure is not rigid enough to withstand vigorous slicing, and it may be ruined.

Bread eaten hot from the oven rarely shows the flavors and textures present when the loaf is cooled. Some aromas, such as that from baked yeast, might be accentuated in warm bread, but the practice of eating warm bread seems to be rooted in the *need* to heat bread that lacks much other flavor. The complexity of flavor experienced when we eat long-fermented breads usually trumps any positives of eating bread before it has cooled. The gumminess of hot bread detracts from the enjoyment of eating it, and some dieticians also feel that hot bread is less digestible.

Having said this, a few varieties of bread (a true minority) are enjoyable when they are eaten warm. Soft-dough pretzels are one example. Pizza is another example, and some small breads like brioche rolls, croissants, and buttery yeast rolls seem more enticing when warm. Bagels might fit this classification as well.

Baguettes are often eaten warm, but they can benefit from being cooled completely and then reheated in a hot oven just before eating. This process allows the baguette's crumb to firm completely while providing the tasty experience of eating this crusty bread warm. Once bread or rolls are reheated, however, their shelf life is brief, so it is important to serve them immediately.

Figure 8.5 On the upper shelf, loaves are well spaced and have enough room for steam to escape as they cool. On the lower shelf, loaves are crowded and steam cannot escape without softening the sides of the adjacent loaves.

Dan Leader

Owner and Operator, Bread Alone, Boiceville, New York

There's a lot of discussion among artisan bakers today about whether the term *artisan* can legitimately be applied to their bread, or if the term itself can be defined adequately. Dan Leader, who owns and operates the seminal Bread Alone bakery in Boiceville, New York, established his business in 1983, long before the term was coined.

He attended the University of Wisconsin, but during his senior year he decided to become a chef, and he enrolled at the Culinary Institute of America. Not long after graduating, he found employment at notable restaurants in the New York metropolitan area. He found promotion quickly and often, which culminated in his selection as Chef de Cuisine at the Water Club. While he enjoyed the recognition he received from working in this high-profile position, he found he was gradually drifting away from the sort of food he truly loved—beautiful but simple preparations focused more on flavor and aroma than on stunning appearance.

While working as a chef, Dan occasionally vacationed in France. He sought simple but wonderful places to eat, and his wanderings led him to traditional bakeries where breads were still made by hand, fermented with natural levain, and baked in wood-fired ovens. As he returned to visit these bakeries, he realized he wanted to become a baker himself; he wanted to recreate these traditionally made loaves back home. He decided to leave New York City to start his own bakery in upstate New York, in the Catskill Mountains.

Deciding just what was important in recreating these breads was not an easy task, and Dan will tell you himself that it took years of trial and error to figure out which factors were essential and which overrated. He struggled with a temperamental home-built stone oven at first, and he soon discovered that making great bread on a consistent basis involves more precise scaling of ingredients than is normal for someone with a chef's background. His travels in France eventually led him to Andre LeFort, who had rebuilt the ovens for the famous Lionel Poilâne, and together they decided to construct two wood-fired brick ovens at the bakery in the Catskills. These ovens were modeled on those commonly used in traditional French bakeries, and they produced loaves more consistent in their bake and more closely resembling the breads Dan was trying to recreate. Dan later added more modern steam-injected deck ovens alongside those beautiful brick models, but the underlying lesson in selecting them remained the same: Bread baking can be fun and should be simple, but it should always be approached professionally if you aim to be a professional.

Two more points characterize Dan's baking philosophy—an emphasis on naturally leavened breads and on all-natural ingredients featuring organically grown, stone-milled flour. In his opinion, ordinary flour yields ordinary bread. Dan's passion for baking and the success of his business are also expressed in his two books about his craft: *Bread Alone* (William Morrow, 1993) and *Local Breads* (W.W. Norton, 2007).

IMPRESSIONS OF ARTISAN BREAD BAKING AS AN INDUSTRY

Did you have any preconceptions about the artisan bread business (or any aspect of the bread business) that were altered by your industry experience?

There really was no artisan bread business when I started out, just some aging hippies and war resisters who were gardening and eating tofu. Traditional bread-baking techniques didn't really become "artisan" until I was quite well established.

Can we define artisan *bread? If so, what makes it distinctive, in your opinion?*

I can't really define it, but like the judge said, "I know it when I see it."

What are your thoughts on the future of the artisan bread business?

I hope artisan bread continues to be best served in the realm of the small business. It takes a lot of control and know-how to build an artisan bakery into a large commercial format. However, even if it is done, and done well, there will always be a place for the local bakery in the myriad towns and villages of America, Canada, South America, and Europe.

Summary

Baking, like fermentation, is a process of transformation. We start with flowing, fermented dough that has aromas of alcohol, and we change it into a solid, light-textured mass with excellent eating qualities and enticing, more complex aromas.

The first skill to be mastered in successful baking is carried over from successful proofing: knowing how to judge when breads are inflated enough to load into the oven. The next important skill is to properly score the loaves, if necessary, to allow them to expand in an attractive fashion that ensures good volume and a light-textured crumb. The chosen baking temperature determines whether or not the loaf will achieve a balance of good caramelization and a properly baked interior. Smaller breads need less baking time than larger ones, and loaves that are short and wide require more baking than those that are long and narrow. The ideal baking temperature for smaller breads is usually higher than for larger ones, as caramelization must occur faster given the short bake time for the interior.

Loading your oven with steam at the beginning of the bake can allow full expansion of hearth loaves before a crust forms, and it encourages the gelatinization of starches so conducive to crisp, crusty bread. Steam must be evacuated from the oven once the crust has formed, though, to encourage the drying of the bread and the caramelization of the crust. Finally, when bread has been unloaded from your oven, it must be allowed to cool sufficiently for the loss of steam to occur and the crust to remain crisp and stable.

Key Terms

baking	*convection oven*
oven spring	*heat of convection*
scoring	*rack ovens*
blowout	*revolving oven*
Maillard browning	*deck oven*
caramelization	*hearth oven*
overbaking	*heat of conduction*
range oven	*hearth breads*
radiation	

Questions for Review

1. What is *oven spring*?

2. Why do we score loaves before baking them? Do all loaves need scoring?

3. Should we always score the same type of bread the same way, no matter what? Why?

4. Does improper scoring lead to defects in bread aside from an ugly appearance?

5. What are the two types of browning that concern us as bread bakers?

6. Why is it advisable to bake a small 2-oz roll at a higher temperature than a large loaf?

7. Why shouldn't we just leave steam in an oven during the entire bake cycle?

8. How can we judge the doneness of a loaf of bread?

9. When does the baking of bread actually end?

Much of the bread discussed in this text is hard-crusted in nature and baked on a hot stone in a specialized oven to ensure its resemblance to rustic breads produced in European ovens from generations past.

1. Is this sort of bread superior to softer varieties? Is it always better to use crusty breads when pairing bread with dinner or selecting it for sandwiches? Can breads inspired by different traditions be considered artisan-style breads?

2. For some bakers, the concept of using a wood-fired brick oven to bake their bread is an integral part of baking in a manner that maintains artisan practices from centuries past. Still, do you think anything about baking with a wood-fired oven makes it better than making bread in a steam-injected, gas-fired deck oven? Be specific in your answer, and ask yourself what might motivate a baker to use an oven that is more challenging to operate than its more modern counterparts. Keep in mind that comparative bread quality can be hard to define and that more than one answer is possible.

Lab Exercise & Experiment

Refer to the formula for Pullman bread. Mix the dough as you would normally, but, instead of making loaves from the dough, opt for shaping 2-oz (60g) pieces into round rolls.

Pre-heat two ovens or decks to different temperatures: 375°F in one and 425°F in the other. If you are using convection ovens, you may wish to use temperatures 25–50°F lower, depending on their characteristics.

Shape and proof the rolls as you would normally, and space them evenly on at least 2 trays. When all of the rolls are proofed sufficiently, place one tray in one oven and the second tray in the other. If you have more trays, add them evenly to either oven, but do not place more product into one oven than you do in the other; that might affect the outcome of the experiment.

Bake each tray until it appears brown enough to be done.

You will undoubtedly find that the rolls in the 425°F oven are browned first, but the differences between the two sets of rolls will likely be more than just that. After all rolls have been taken from the oven, allow them to cool at least 30 minutes before sampling them. Do not sample them while they are warm.

What differences do you detect? What affect did the difference in temperature have on the ability of the rolls to retain their palatability? Should we bake smaller products like rolls at different temperatures than we do larger products? If we change the size of a roll or loaf, should we also change its bake time or temperature, if we are able? How would you change it?

PULLMAN BREAD (PAIN DE MIE)

	Metric		U.S. Measure		Formula Baker's %
	(1X)	**(4X)**	**(1X)**	**(4X)**	
	5-Qt Mixer	**20-Qt Mixer**	**5-Qt Mixer**	**20-Qt Mixer**	
STRAIGHT DOUGH					
Bread flour	900g	3600g	2 lb 4.0oz	9 lb 0.0oz	**100%**
Water	540g	2160g	1 lb 5.6oz	5 lb 6.4oz	**60%**
Butter, softened	72g	288g	2.9oz	11.5oz	**8%**
Sugar	45g	180g	1.8oz	7.2oz	**5%**
Milk powder	54g	216g	2.2oz	8.6oz	**6%**
Salt	20g	79g	0.8oz	3.2oz	**2.2%**
Instant yeast	9g	36g	0.4oz	1.4oz	**1%**
TOTAL YIELD	**1640g**	**6559g**	**4 lb 1.6oz**	**16 lb 6.4oz**	

Variation:

You can use the straight dough above as the basis for an adjusted dough that utilizes a sponge or old dough (see *Chapter 4*). Both pre-ferments are easy to prepare and practically risk-free to use. They add strength to what is already a strong dough, but the flavor is improved noticeably at pre-fermented flour levels of 25–40%.

GOAL TEMPERATURE: 77°F (25°C). See directions for determining correct water temperature in *Chapter 4*.

MIXING METHOD: Use the intensive mix method, described on p. 196.

FERMENTING: About 1 hour.

SCALING: for 13-in. Pullman pan: 32 oz; 17-in. Pullman pan: 44 oz; 9 × 4-in. bread pan: 30 oz. Some variation may result from differences in dough strength or peculiarities of pan size.

SHAPING: Shape as long logs for the Pullman pans and short logs for the standard, open-topped bread pans. Spray both the pans and their lids on the inside surface with pan release before placing shaped dough portions in them.

PROOFING:

1. Slide the lids onto the Pullman pans but leave an opening of about 1 in. or so to monitor the proof. When the crowns of the dough portions reach within ½ in. of the lid, close the lids and bake the Pullman loaves.

2. For open-topped pans, allow the crowns of the loaves to rise above the rim of the pan.

3. The loaves are usually proofed fully 50–70 minutes after being placed in a proofer set to 80°F and 80% humidity.

BAKING:

1. 380–400°F for 45–60 minutes for the closed-top Pullmans (350–370°F for a convection or rack oven); 350–375°F for 30–35 minutes for the open-topped bread pans (310–330°F for a convection or rack oven).

2. The sides of the loaves must be golden brown to support the weight of the crowns.

3. Differences in ovens can produce different temperatures and bake times—be conservative and check loaves earlier than their anticipated finish time.

COOLING:

1. After baking is complete, empty the loaves from their pans immediately or their sides will soften.

2. Cool completely before slicing, and wrap completely after cooling.

chapter

9

Rich and Laminated Doughs

Learning Outcomes:

- Define what is meant by a rich dough.

- Define lamination as it applies to bread baking.

- Understand how laminating bread dough creates different textures than mixing fat directly into the dough.

- Identify the reason laminated dough is generally stronger than rich dough that hasn't been laminated.

- Identify the common ingredient differences between croissant dough and Danish dough.

- See how using pre-ferments in laminated dough formulas helps provide better flavor and/or extensibility.

- Define plasticity as it applies to fats typically used in dough lamination.

- Define butter block, base dough, and turns as they apply to laminating bread dough.

- Distinguish between a single fold and a double fold, and become familiar with their alternative names.

- Understand how to laminate bread dough used to make various products.

- Fabricate various laminated pastries from croissant and Danish dough.

The Effects Ingredients Have on Dough

Rich Dough Defined

A rich dough is generally one that is high in fat and sometimes high in eggs or sugar. Doughs that have little or no fat are often referred to as *lean doughs*.

Effects of Fat on Dough

As we mentioned in *Chapter 4,* the introduction of fat into bread dough has several noticeable effects:

1. It coats and literally shortens the strands of gluten, creating what is known as the *shortening effect.* If the fat is a liquid, such as olive oil, this effect can create a silky texture in bread. If it is a solid, such as butter, it can create textures ranging from soft to crumbly or flaky, depending on the quantity used and how much it is worked into the dough.

2. It interferes with the bonding of gluten strands, thereby reducing dough strength and increasing dough tenderness.

3. It can add to the flavor of the dough if the fat has a noticeable taste (such as butter or olive oil), and it can affect mouthfeel either pleasantly (as with butter or olive oil) or unpleasantly (as with any fat that doesn't melt in the mouth, such as vegetable shortening).

Effects of Eggs on Dough

Whole eggs have both proteins (in the whites and yolks) and fats (in the yolk), with the bulk of their composition being water. The effects of the proteins more or less overwhelm the effects of the fats on the dough, so eggs are *net tougheners,* which means their overall effect on dough structure is to strengthen rather than tenderize it. The albumin in egg whites captures and holds gases in much the same way gluten does, and the emulsifiers in the egg yolks help keep added fats suspended within and distributed throughout the moisture in the dough.

Effects of Sugar on Dough

Sugar interferes with gluten formation in bread dough, so, with regard to dough structure, it always acts as a tenderizer. At levels of more than 12% of the flour weight, this tenderizing effect can seriously slacken the dough. At the same level there is also a noticeable slowing of the rate of fermentation and, from this point on, the rate of fermentation continues to slow as the sugar levels are increased. Sugar's hygroscopic (water-drawing) qualities create these effects.

If you want to include large quantities of fat or sugar in your bread dough, then you must accept the effects of these ingredients on the dough and take measures to incorporate them without seriously damaging the strength of the dough.

Strategies for Turning Lean Dough into Rich Dough

Adding Sugar

1. As we mentioned before, high levels of sugar can negatively affect both dough strength and fermentation activity. When adding large amounts of sugar to bread dough, it is usually a good idea to do so in 3 or 4 increments during the mixing period. By holding back most of the sugar until *after* the gluten bonds have formed, you can minimize the destabilizing effect of sugar on dough strength. Adding water with every addition of sugar helps the crystals dissolve into the dough as easily as possible.

2. Fermentation, on the other hand, can't be improved by adding sugar in stages, so you must increase the level of yeast in dough to make up for the slower CO_2 production that occurs with high concentrations of sugar. It isn't unusual to see levels of instant yeast totaling 2–3% of flour weight to counteract the negative effects of sugar levels greater than 12%.

Adding Fat

1. You have two options for incorporating large amounts of fat into a bread dough: Either strengthen the dough before mixing it in directly, or use a laminating method that separates the dough from the fat it supports.

Why Not Just Add the Fat to the Dough?

When bakers first added large amounts of butter to bread dough, they noticed that while the flavor and tenderness of the dough was enhanced, the effects on the dough texture, structure, and final volume were not always what they wanted. Because adding fat to dough causes its gluten strands to shorten (see *Chapter 4*), the strength of the dough is much less, and its volume is lessened as well. The crumb becomes somewhat dense and compacted—like a biscuit or scone, in some respects. Biscuits and scones can be wonderful, but if that is not what you're trying to create, you must find ways to add lots of fat to dough without adversely affecting its structure and volume.

INCREASING STRENGTH IN DOUGHS WITH LARGE QUANTITIES OF FAT

One technique for reinforcing the strength and volume of the bread dough when a large amount of butter is added is to replace with eggs much of the water or milk used to hydrate the dough. The albumin (egg white) of an egg can capture and hold air much like gluten does, so using a lot of whole egg in a dough rich with butter helps it retain a light, airy texture and good volume. Brioche and its variations (*kugelhopf*, *stollen*, *pannetone*, and *pan' doro*, among others) are all products that evolved from ways to get a lot of butter into a bread product without sacrificing strength or volume.

Another strategy for maximizing the strength of dough that must accept large amounts of fat is to develop the dough's gluten before the fat is actually added to the dough. Fat's tenderizing effects are much less destabilizing if the dough's gluten network is established ahead of time.

Lamination is yet another option, though it was almost certainly developed first as a way to make pastry dough and was not typically used in bread making until the late nineteenth or early twentieth century.

Lamination Defined

When we say that we want to *laminate* bread dough, we mean we want to encase a large amount of butter in bread dough and put it through a series of folds that yield distinct alternating layers of dough and butter. You are probably familiar with some common applications of dough laminates, such as croissants and Danish pastries. Another is laminated brioche dough. Puff pastry is also a type of laminated dough, and its lamination process can be similar to croissant or Danish dough. However, puff pastry has no yeast or any other leavener aside from steam, and as such is not generally regarded as bread in the conventional sense. It is classified as a pastry, and so is mostly in the domain of pastry chefs.

In fact, as the crafts of bread baking and pastry making evolved in France, one significant legal point of distinction was that members of the bread guild were supposed to make only breads, pastries, and cakes that contained manufactured yeast or levain as an ingredient. Pastry chefs were not allowed (at least technically) to include yeast in their products. For this reason, different versions of the croissant evolved over time; the first was simply rolled into a crescent from a yeasted sweet dough that was not laminated. In the early 1920s, bakers in Paris decided to combine the crescent-shaped sweet roll idea with the concept of puff pastry, and the Parisian croissant was born.

It is interesting to speculate about why the bakers decided to do that. To find an answer, we should examine the effects of lamination on the texture and volume of bread dough.

If you look at puff pastry, you will see that a plain, basic unleavened dough is rolled out into a square or rectangle and then used to wrap a large amount of butter—sometimes as much as 100% of the weight of the flour in the dough—so as to surround the butter layer completely with dough on all sides.

This dough-wrapped square of butter is rolled out to a dimension about 3 times as long as it is wide. It is then treated as if it had three equal-sized segments from end to end, and it is folded like a letter. The segment on one end is folded over the segment in the middle, and then the remaining segment is folded over the other two, leaving a seam along one side. The dough is allowed to relax for a period, and then the process is repeated. Each set of folds is called a series of *turns*, and this particular method of folding is called a *single fold*. Puff pastry usually undergoes six sets of single folds, or turns, before it is completed.

When the six sets of turns are completed, the dough features thousands of alternating layers of dough and butter. When carefully cut segments of this layered dough are rolled out and cut again into different shapes, they can be baked, either with or without fillings. What happens when they are baked can be quite dramatic, as the dough pieces often achieve a final height 7 or 8 times the original.

What causes the rise in height—even though the dough contains no eggs, yeast, or other leaveners—is steam. Because the dough and butter are maintained

Origins of the Croissant

The legend surrounding the birth of the croissant is well known in baking circles, though its relationship to modern croissants is sometimes misunderstood. In the late seventeenth century, the Ottoman Turks laid siege to the city of Vienna, in Austria. Plans were hatched by the Turks to tunnel under the city's walls and catch its defenders as they slept. As they were digging their tunnels, the Turks did not realize the noise from their picks and shovels could be heard by bakers who typically worked in basement bakeries throughout the night. The bakers reported what they heard to Austrian soldiers within the city, and the Turks were trapped. Not long thereafter, the Turkish sultan withdrew from Austria and ended the siege— a military reversal that was never overcome.

The Emperor of Austria-Hungary awarded some recognition to the bakers who sounded the alarm. It isn't clear whether he commissioned them to create a baked product to honor the occasion or if they created the product to honor their emperor, but the bakers produced a sweet yeasted roll in the shape of a crescent. The shape was significant because it purposely mocked the crescent symbol on the Turkish flag.

This is now referred to as the *Viennese croissant*, but it was not quite the same roll we see in French cafés today. The Viennese version was made from dough that was not laminated, and that was how croissants were made through the time Viennese bakers in Paris made the roll popular during the World's Fair of 1889.

By the early 1920s, some bakers in Paris were using yeast in laminated dough to create crescent rolls that were both light and flaky, and the Parisian croissant was born. Since then, laminated croissant dough has also been paired with chocolate to make a square, flaky version of pain au chocolat (sometimes referred to as *chocolatines*), and croissants filled with other sweet items like almond cream or raspberry jam now appear all over the Western world.

in separate, continuous layers, the steam they generate during baking causes a significant separation of the layers. The butter is eventually absorbed by the dough as it bakes, but before that happens, the starches and proteins in the dough firm up enough that the steam pockets between the layers remain. This causes the final product to develop a flaky texture. The flakiness can be compared to the flakiness in pie dough, except in pie dough the steam pockets created by fat pieces during baking are relatively irregular and coarse. The flakiness of layers in laminated dough is finely textured and continuous in its nature, not broken-up like pie dough.

When Polish bakers immigrated to Paris, they brought with them the small, rolled, crescent-shaped sweet breads that were traditional since the fifteenth century. We don't know who was inspired to use laminated dough to make the rolled crescents, but the combination was embraced widely in Paris about the same time the baguette was taking the city by storm, in the early 1920s.

The combination of flakiness from lamination and even lighter texture from a yeasted dough made the Parisian croissant superior in its appeal when compared to either plain sweet dough or non-yeasted puff pastry. So, by using a lamination method to incorporate large amounts of fat into bread dough, we maintain the strength of the dough and the height of the final product, and we create both flakiness and lightness in the product.

BASE DOUGH, BUTTER BLOCK

We should pause here and define terms used commonly in the process of laminating bread dough. The dough we make in the mixer that is later layered with butter is called the *base dough* (*detrempe* in French). The large mass of butter we enclose with dough is called a *butter block* (*beurrage* in French). Usually the base dough contains some butter to allow for better extensibility of the dough during the rolling or sheeting process, but the weight of that butter rarely exceeds 10% of the weight of the flour used, and it is not really considered from a structural standpoint when analyzing the physical aspects of lamination.

PRODUCTS FROM LAMINATED DOUGH

The most common products made in bakeshops today from laminated dough are croissants and Danish. There is also a less widespread tradition of laminating brioche dough in France. That may seem outlandish, as brioche dough often incorporates a large amount of butter directly. Bakers who choose to make laminated brioche often use somewhat less fat in the base dough to compensate for the fat that is folded in during lamination. Nevertheless, there are examples of brioche with a full complement of butter enclosing a separate butter block, and the results can be surprisingly light and feathery. Even though brioche contains a lot of eggs and fat already, the process of laminating it is similar to that used for croissant and Danish dough.

The Lamination Process

We discuss common differences among croissant, laminated brioche, and Danish dough a bit later; here we explain the lamination process they share.

BASE DOUGH IS MIXED

First, the base dough is mixed using the improved mixing method (see *Chapter 4*)—that is, the dough is mixed on first speed for 4–5 minutes to hydrate the flour and to incorporate all ingredients evenly, followed by 2–3 minutes of mixing on second speed. The hydration of the dough is generally not high—a percentage in the high 50s to low 60s is most frequent, depending on the strength of the bread flour used.

There is a common misconception among bakers that the base dough should be mixed very little because the dough will later undergo a folding process that can develop the gluten. While it is certainly true that the folding process increases gluten development and that excessive strength in the base dough can lead to extensibility problems, gluten development in the dough must be sufficient before lamination to provide the strength for good height and proper volume in the final product.

Several strategies are available for ensuring extensibility while allowing more initial gluten development. One is to use a liquid pre-ferment as an ingredient in the base dough. Liquid pre-ferments (see *Chapter 5*) have high levels of enzyme activity, and the protease they add to the base dough supports extensibility. Either poolish or liquid levain can do the job here; use enough poolish to pre-ferment perhaps 15–20% of the flour in the dough, or enough liquid levain to pre ferment 10–12%. Other amounts can be made to work, of course, but you must experiment with the quantity used and be certain to employ your skills in baker's math (see *Chapter 3*) to track the changes in formulation from one batch to another.

You could use active dry yeast instead of instant or compressed yeast to increase the quantity of dead yeast cells in the dough, which in turn increases the amount of glutathione (see *Chapter 2*). *Glutathione* is a protein fragment that works in a manner similar to the enzyme protease to weaken protein bonds and make dough more extensible.

Finally, employing an autolyse period during the mixing process (see *Chapter 4*) allows maximum enzyme development in the dough and may provide greater extensibility. If you prefer not to interrupt production with an autolyse period, it is still possible to scale your ingredients for a base dough the day before, combine the flour and liquid (with no salt, yeast, or fat) and allow them to rest at room temperature, covered, and then mix the entire dough with all ingredients the next day.

The base dough is often placed directly in the refrigerator after mixing to control its fermentation and make it more easily handled during lamination. It might be better to establish some degree of fermentation activity before placing the dough in the cooler— perhaps for 30 minutes. Also, to provide for the acids that would be lost through such abbreviated bulk fermentation, using a pre-ferment is recommended. In any case, the dough should be just about as cold as the butter before proceeding with lamination, and it should be held in the refrigerator until just before rolling out or sheeting.

STEP #1: CREATE YOUR BUTTER BLOCK

The quantity of butter to be layered in during lamination should not be determined casually. It is usually 25–35% of the weight of the base dough when making croissants or Danish. More butter than that is not commonly used, but if you do decide to use more, you must perform additional sets of folds on the dough to keep the butter layers from being too thick. We discuss the reasons for this later when we discuss performing the folds, or *turns*.

Your butter should be quite cold when you start to form the butter block for lamination. Your base dough should be cold and firm as well, and left in the refrigerator until the butter block is finished.

Procedure for Forming and Plasticizing a Butter Block

1. Cut 1-pound butter prints into thick slices and distribute them over a piece of parchment paper, forming a square. Cover the square with another piece of parchment.

2. Pound the surface of the paper-covered butter block with a rolling pin that has no ball bearings. Rotate the block occasionally as you do so, and turn it over occasionally as well to ensure the butter is plasticized evenly (see Figure 9.1).

3. Check the level of plasticity occasionally by running the whole block over the edge of your workbench, bending the block as you do so. When you are able to bend the block easily without cracking it, and it can still be separated easily from the paper, it is probably ready for being enclosed in dough (see Figures 9.2a and 9.2b).

Your goal here is to soften the butter and increase its plasticity without getting it so warm and soft that it smears or even melts. You must pound the butter block with some degree of force, applying that force equally across the surface of the square as you beat it with the entire length of the rolling pin. Because it is natural for differences in thickness or plasticity to develop in different parts of the block as you pound it, try rotating the paper-covered butter block under your pin as you strike it. You should occasionally turn the block over altogether and then resume the process. Usually, after only 2–3 minutes of pounding the block and rotating it as you do, you will find the plasticity is acceptable.

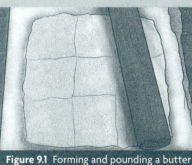
Figure 9.1 Forming and pounding a butter block.

Figure 9.2a A well-plasticized butter block can be bent easily without breaking.

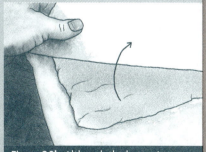
Figure 9.2b Although the butter is now pliable, it still separates easily from the parchment.

What do we mean by *plasticity*? You saw the term in *Chapter 4* applied to dough structure, but it means much the same thing when applied to butter. Plasticity is the quality of a solid mass that allows it to be shaped easily and to hold that shape. Butter's natural range of plasticity is fairly narrow compared to other solid fats like shortening, lard, and margarine. Some bakers have observed that when plasticizing butter, you should stop pounding it when it reaches approximately 60°F, and you should complete the lamination of the butter and dough before it reaches around 70°F. Other bakers do not approve of using temperature to measure butter's plasticity, possibly because they have enough experience that they don't need to. Instead, they observe other physical signs that the butter is sufficiently plasticized. In Figures 9.2a and 9.2b, notice that the butter block, when properly plasticized, can be pulled tightly and bent over the edge of a baker's bench easily without cracking or breaking. Still, it is firm enough to be a pliable solid; it is not soft or squishy, and it can still be easily peeled away from the paper beneath it.

One key aspect of successful lamination is making certain, first of all, that both butter and base dough are cold—usually the same temperature—before you proceed.

Your goal in plasticizing your butter block is to make it malleable enough to have the same consistency as the cold dough. One common misperception about lamination is that the butter and the dough should be the same temperature throughout the lamination process. That is not precisely true—they should be about the same temperature *before* you plasticize the butter block; when you pound the block, its temperature will rise from the heat caused by friction. Just be certain that one is as easily molded or bent as the other, or you will have problems getting the layers to remain uninterrupted as you roll out or sheet the combined dough. If the butter is harder than the dough, it will crack and possibly puncture the dough layers surrounding it as you roll it. If it is too soft, it will seep between dough layers or move about under them like a liquid rather than a solid, leaving thick layers in some spots and practically no butter in others.

High-volume bakeries often plasticize the butter for their pastries in a planetary mixer. They then roll out portions of their base dough separately and place the appropriate weight of butter on top of the dough before proceeding with enclosure of the butter and the lamination process.

Once the butter is pounded (or mixed) to the same consistency as the cold base dough, you may proceed with encasing the butter block. Roll out your base dough into a square about ½ inch thick—the outer dimensions vary with the weight of the base dough.

STEP #2: ENCLOSE THE BUTTER BLOCK

Procedure for Enclosing the Butter Block

1. Roll out your base dough into a square of the proportions shown in Figure 9.3a. Lay the butter block on top of it so the corners of the butter block are just shy of the edges of the dough and so it rests at a 45-degree angle to the dough's edges.

2. Fold the corners of the dough toward the middle of the butter block, and then seal the seams between them. The corners of the dough, when folded inward, should overlap and completely envelop the butter block in a sealed covering of dough (see Figures 9.3b and 9.3c).

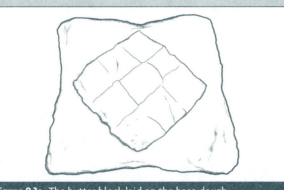

Figure 9.3a The butter block laid on the base dough.

Figure 9.3b Folding in the corners of the dough to make a package.

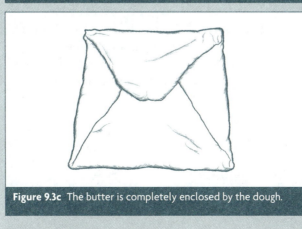

Figure 9.3c The butter is completely enclosed by the dough.

STEP #3: ROLL OUT AND FOLD THE DOUGH

Now you begin to actually perform turns on the dough-and-butter package. Large-scale production of laminated pastries demands the use of a mechanical sheeter. If you work in a small shop, though, you can perform the operation by hand with a rolling pin. There are two basic ways to perform turns on the dough, and we describe them here.

The Single-Fold Laminating Technique

Procedure for Performing a Single Fold

1. Whether you use a sheeter or a pin, roll out the dough (with the butter encased inside) to a thickness of about ⅓ inch and to outer dimensions where the piece is about 2½ times as long as it is wide.

2. With the long sides of the piece oriented from left to right (top and bottom of the rectangle; see Figure 9.4a), mentally divide the piece into three segments, as you would to fold a letter.

3. Fold one of the segments on the end over the center segment (see Figure 9.4b), and then fold the segment that remains over the other two (see Figure 9.4c). This is one set of single folds.

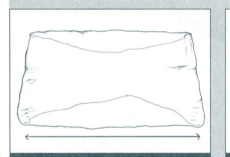

Figure 9.4a The dough package is rolled out or sheeted prior to performing the turns. Divide it mentally into thirds.

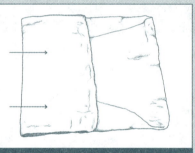

Figure 9.4b One-third of the length is folded over the center.

Figure 9.4c The remaining third of the dough is folded over the other two sections.

Typically, when the butter block is 25–30% of the weight of the base dough, the entire lamination process requires three sets of single folds. If the butter is 35–40%, the process would probably require four sets of single folds, and for 50%, probably six sets (this is typical for puff pastry, which depends completely on steam for leavening and needs the extra layers).

The Double-Fold Laminating Technique

Procedure for Performing a Double Fold

1. To perform a double fold, roll your dough a bit longer than you would for a single-fold maneuver—3–3½ times as long as it is wide (see Figure 9.5a).

2. Bring one edge from a short side toward the middle, but stop short of that precise spot; rest the edge a few inches off center.

3. Bring the other edge over to meet the one at rest. The dough is now folded as in Figure 9.5b.

4. Finish the double-fold maneuver by folding the new left edge over to meet the new right edge

(see Figure 9.5c). Try to keep the entire dough shaped as a nearly perfect rectangle as you perform the folds, and keep the edges and corners squared as you go. Before making any fold, make certain the top surface of the dough is free of excess flour—use a bench brush or dry pastry brush to sweep it away—which can interfere with proper sealing and show up later as white streaks in the finished products.

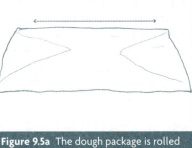

Figure 9.5a The dough package is rolled out or sheeted prior to performing the turns. Divide it mentally into fourths.

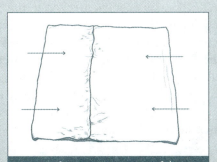

Figure 9.5b Once one-quarter of the length is folded toward the center of the dough, the opposite end is folded to meet the first end. The ends don't meet *precisely* in the center of the dough, so you avoid creating areas of laminated dough that have no butter and no laminations as you make additional turns.

Figure 9.5c One-half of the dough is then folded over the remaining half.

The term *single fold* is straightforward enough, but the term *double fold* is really a misnomer. Some bakers think the double fold produces twice as many layers as the single fold, but this notion is incorrect. The double fold actually provides 1½ times as many layers as does a set of single folds. Still, it can be a time-saver. Two sets of double folds provide the same number of layers as three sets of single folds.

Another possible point of confusion for bakers is that several terms are applied to each of the two basic methods of doing turns. The single fold is also known variously as the *3-fold* (because you mentally divide it into three sections before folding), the *tri-fold*, and the *letter fold*. The double fold is also called the *4-fold* (four imaginary sections) and the *book-fold*. Other terms may be used in some bakeries, but all that is important is that you know how to execute the two basic methods and learn to call them by whichever term is preferred by your employer or instructor.

STEP #4: DECIDE HOW MANY FOLDS YOU NEED

You shouldn't assume when laminating your dough that more folds will produce superior results or that fewer folds implies an inferior level of quality. The number of folds assigned to a given laminated dough aren't arbitrarily chosen; they are related to how much butter must be encased within the dough. When the butter weighs 25–30% of the weight of the base dough, three sets of single folds produce enough alternating layers of butter and dough that the laminations will remain distinct, while the dough layers will still absorb the butter as it melts.

If you enclose more butter than that and don't use any more folds than before, the butter layers will be thicker, and some of the butter will run between the dough layers as it melts instead of being completely absorbed by the dough. When you see bakers pouring off melted butter from a pan of croissants, you will know they are using croissant dough with butter layers that are too thick. That is an obvious waste of money. To avoid the waste, either add a set of folds to help thin the butter layers or use less butter to begin with.

On the other hand, using too many sets of folds thins the butter layers so much they can disappear altogether. In this case, the butter layers simply meld with the surrounding dough, and the lamination (or layering) is practically gone. When you eat a croissant that seems too bready and isn't flaky, it may have been made with either too many folds or not enough butter to maintain distinct layers.

There is certainly flexibility within these parameters for figuring a correct number of layers for your dough. Just the same, be certain you understand how changing the number of folds or altering the butter quantity can affect the product, and experiment to find the range that works for you.

Differences Between Croissant Dough and Danish Dough

If you look at the formulas for croissant and Danish dough in the *Appendix of Formulas* (pp. 212–214), you will see that many of the ingredients for them are similar. However, important differences do exist, and you should become familiar with them.

First, Danish dough is generally richer in butter and/or sugar. The size of the butter block in many Danish formulas is 30–35% of the weight of the base dough, while in a croissant formula, the proportion is usually a bit less—25–30%. The sugar level in croissants is often only 6–8% of the flour weight, while in Danish dough we can see levels at or above 12%.

Danish usually contains whole eggs in its formulation, while croissants usually don't (or they contain much less). When this is the case and both varieties of dough are made in the same bakery, you often see a richer yellow color in the Danish from the egg yolks in the dough.

Last, some bakers follow the tradition of adding one spice or another (often cardamom) to Danish dough. Generally, less is added than you can easily taste, but it does create a subtle complexity in the final dough aromas, and the tiny grains of the spice help bakers distinguish Danish from croissant dough that may be stored in the same cooler or on the same speed rack.

Some Caveats in Working with Laminated Dough Products

Always keep your base dough and butter cold until the moment you begin to work with them. When you start to plasticize the butter, it will increase in temperature, but make certain it is the same *consistency* as the colder base dough—that is, has the same degree of pliability—and you should have an easier time maintaining proper layers in the dough.

Be certain you brush all excess flour from the dough surface before folding the dough.

Keep laminated dough in the refrigerator until just before sheeting it for further use.

If you egg-wash the pastries you make from laminated dough, avoid allowing the egg mixture to drip down the cut edges of the dough. Egg wash can dry quickly in the oven, and if enough drips down the sides, it can act like a thin wrapper that keeps the layers in the dough from expanding.

Shaping Croissants and Danish

When you are ready to cut and shape pastries from your laminated dough, roll out the dough and cut pieces as you wish. The photographs in Figures 9.6–9.11 provide ideas to get you started.

Figure 9.6 Steps in forming a plain croissant.

Figure 9.7 Steps in forming a filled croissant.

Figure 9.8 Steps in forming a Danish pinwheel.

Figure 9.9 Steps in forming a Danish pocket.

Figure 9.10 Steps in forming a Danish diamond.

Figure 9.11 Steps in forming a Danish snail.

ARTISAN BAKER PROFILE

Craig Ponsford

Owner and Founder of Artisan Bakers in Sonoma, California

Craig Ponsford did what few American bakers have done: He went to Paris and earned a gold medal for his baguette at the Coupe de Monde de la Boulangerie. He achieved that as a member of a three-man U.S. team that was trained and sent to the competition in 1996 by the Bread Bakers Guild of America. Since then, Craig has devoted much of his time to supporting the mission of the Guild in educating bakers about the craft of traditional bread baking.

Craig is a 1991 graduate of the California Culinary Academy in San Francisco. He honed his skills as an artisan by working for bakeries in the San Francisco Bay area, including Glenn Mitchell's Grace Baking Company, and in 1992 he and his family opened their own bakery, Artisan Bakers, in Sonoma County.

The bakery was well received, and his business grew steadily. In an effort to learn more about his craft, he attended the Coupe de Monde bread competition in Paris in both 1992 and 1994 as an observer. By 1995 he had become a member of the Bread Bakers Guild of America, and it was the Guild that selected Craig to compete in the Baguette and Specialty Breads category for Team USA in the 1996 Coupe de Monde. While training for the competition, Craig came under the guidance of Didier Rosada (see the baker profile in *Chapter 7*), a master baker from France who was living in the United States and soon to become the head instructor at the National Baking Center in Minneapolis, Minnesota. Craig credits Didier's expertise in both the science of fermentation and the shaping of French breads for his win. He also insists the fundamental techniques he acquired from Didier transformed his bakery's bread immeasurably.

Craig's many years of service within the Guild as an actively involved board member were recognized in 2002, when he was elected board chairman, a position he still holds. He is still active in the selection and coaching of team members for the Coupe de Monde, and he was an international judge at the Le Saffre Coupe, held in Argentina in 2007.

Your instructor may also demonstrate additional techniques. The final thickness of the laminated dough after sheeting or rolling may depend on the look you are trying to achieve. Croissant dough might be sheeted to a thickness of 5–7mm, while Danish dough is often rolled out a bit thinner—perhaps 4–5mm. Be careful not to roll the dough so thin that the laminations are damaged.

Croissants are generally not glazed after baking, but Danish pastries often are. An apricot glaze applied just as the Danish come out of the oven gives them an appealing shine and extends their shelf life through most of a day. Using a warm fondant or simple icing to stripe the Danish while they are still warm is also an attractive option.

Summary

Dough lamination is the process of encasing a large mass of butter with dough and putting it through a series of folds to create distinct alternating layers of dough and butter. These layers provide flakiness to baked products made from the dough.

Parisian-style croissants came about as a union of the crescent-shaped, yeasted sweet roll made in Vienna and the concept of laminated puff pastry. Danish dough used to make other sweet pastries generally has more butter and sugar than croissant dough, and, unlike most croissant formulas, Danish usually contains eggs. Puff pastry is also laminated, and its assembly is similar to that of croissant or Danish dough, but because it contains no yeast or chemical leaveners, it is not generally classified as a bread product.

Laminated dough generally is stronger than conventional enriched dough containing the same amount of butter. This is because the layers of dough that alternate with the layers of butter don't contain much butter before they are baked. In this manner, the dough's gluten strands are not weakened as much, and they can exhibit the strength associated with lean dough. The pastries made from laminated dough thus achieve great height even though they support a good deal of solid fat.

Key Terms

laminate	*butter block*
turns	*glutathione*
single fold	*plasticity*
base dough	*double fold*

Questions for Review

1. The lamination process uses a lot of fat and seems to require a lot of time. Why not just simplify the process by adding all the fat to the base dough as it is mixed?

2. If a croissant dough procedure requires three sets of single folds, how many double folds would be required to get the same number of layers?

3. What is a good way to describe *plasticity* as it applies to laminating dough with solid fat?

4. What are some common differences in formulation between croissant and Danish dough?

Questions for Discussion

1. Bakers and their customers love the taste of butter, of course, so it is the preferred type of fat for use in croissant dough. Still, many bakery owners feel butter is so expensive they would have to charge a price for their pastries that is higher than customers would accept. They use margarine instead, or some combination of butter and margarine, so they can laminate their pastry dough but charge a more affordable price.

   Is that an acceptable notion for a bakery that aspires to make the best artisan breads available to their customers? Would it be any more acceptable if their customers knew about the margarine and could make up their own minds about it? Many bakeries in France do just that.

2. Bakeries often freeze trays of laminated dough for future use or fabricate the pastries and freeze them, thawing them later as needed for daily baking. Properly frozen dough or pastries show little or no sign of their having been frozen when the pastries are baked.

   Some artisan shops make a point of not having freezers on the premises to promote the idea that their processes are all-natural. Are bakeries that freeze raw product violating any concept of artisan baking? What about freezing finished product? Is there any difference? When does the use of modern technology compromise the philosophy of artisan bread baking?

Lab Exercise & Experiment

Use the formula for croissants below, and, if you have no liquid levain, either make the straight dough or use a poolish instead. Make two equal-sized batches of croissant dough with 5-quart tabletop mixers. Laminate the base dough for each batch as directed, but substitute sticks of margarine (not the spreadable kind in a tub) for butter when laminating one of the batches.

Do the same number of turns when performing the lamination for each dough, and refrigerate them precisely the same way before later sheeting and cutting the laminated dough into triangles. Roll the triangles into crescents as you would normally, but keep the croissants with margarine on separate trays. Keeping the identity of each type secret after panning them (the instructor can manage this) lends an extra level of credibility to the product test that follows. Proof and bake each batch in exactly the same manner.

After the croissants have cooled (and letting them cool is important here), the instructor should have each student take a piece of each type of croissant and compare them for flavor, flakiness, aroma, and mouthfeel. Can you tell them apart? Which has the best degree of flakiness, and which has the best flavor and aroma? Are the answers to these two questions the same? What impact would your answers have on your decision to pay much more for butter than for margarine when deciding how to laminate your croissants? If you decide butter is worth the expense, how would you justify it to an employer who wants to run the lowest cost possible?

CROISSANTS WITH LIQUID LEVAIN

	Metric		U.S. Measure		Formula Baker's %
	(1X)	(4X)	(1X)	(4X)	
	5-Qt Mixer	20-Qt Mixer	5-Qt Mixer	20-Qt Mixer	
STRAIGHT DOUGH					
Bread flour	750g	3000g	26.0oz	6 lb 8.0oz	100%
Milk	390g	1560g	13.5oz	3 lb 6.1oz	52%
Water	75g	300g	2.6oz	10.4oz	10%
Sugar	75g	300g	2.6oz	10.4oz	10%
Butter, unsalted (mixed into dough)	30g	120g	1.0oz	4.2oz	4%
Salt	20g	78g	0.7oz	2.7oz	2.6%
Instant yeast	8g	30g	0.3oz	1.0oz	1.0%
Butter block (unsalted)	375g	1500g	13.0oz	3 lb 4.0oz	50%
TOTAL YIELD	**1722g**	**6888g**	**3 lb 11.7oz**	**14 lb 14.8oz**	
					Pre-Ferment Baker's %
Liquid Levain					
Bread flour	*75g*	*300g*	*2.6oz*	*10.4oz*	*100%*
Water	*75g*	*300g*	*2.6oz*	*10.4oz*	*100%*
Ripe levain (not used in final dough)	*38g*	*198g*	*1.3oz*	*5.2oz*	*50%*
Subtotal	*188g*	*798g*	*6.5oz*	*26.13*	
	5-Qt Mixer	20-Qt Mixer	5-Qt Mixer	20-Qt Mixer	
ADJUSTED DOUGH					
Bread flour	675g	2700g	1 lb 7.4oz	5 lb 13.6oz	
Milk	390g	1560g	13.5oz	3 lb 6.1oz	
Water	0g	0g	0.0oz	0.0oz	
Sugar	75g	300g	2.6oz	10.4oz	
Butter, unsalted (mixed into dough)	30g	120g	1.0oz	4.2oz	
Salt	20g	78g	0.7oz	2.7oz	
Instant yeast	7g	30g	0.3oz	1.0oz	
Liquid levain (from above)	150g	600g	5.2oz	1 lb 4.8oz	
Butter block (unsalted)	375g	1500g	13.0oz	3 lb 4.0oz	
TOTAL YIELD	**1722g**	**6888g**	**3 lb 11.7oz**	**14 lb 14.8oz**	

NOTE: This bread may be made using only the ingredients and quantities listed for the straight dough, if you want dough with less flavor and somewhat less extensibility. If, instead, you prepare a levain using the quantities specified above, subtract those ingredient weights from the straight dough to arrive at the quantities listed for the adjusted dough. Mix and hold the levain, covered but slightly vented, at 70°F for 12 hours before mixing the final dough.

Pre-Fermented Flour:	10%
Hydr. of Pre-Ferment:	100%

Variation:

You can use essentially the same ingredient weights as the ones specified above together with most of the same procedures to make a dough that substitutes poolish—at the same weight—for liquid levain.

GOAL TEMPERATURE: 77°F (25°C). See directions for determining correct water temperature in *Chapter 4*.

MIXING METHOD:

1. Use the improved mix method. *Do not mix the butter block into the dough.*

2. Mix all ingredients except the butter block into a base dough for about 5 minutes on first speed and 2–3 minutes on second speed until the dough is lightly developed.

FERMENTATION: Form the dough into a square shape or place it in a square-bottomed container and bulk ferment, covered or wrapped, for 1 hour at room temperature. Then label and refrigerate overnight.

ENCLOSING BUTTER BLOCK: See the procedure illustrated in the text and drawings in *Chapter 9*, p. 145.

LAMINATING (Turns):

1. Begin to perform either 3 sets of single turns or 2 sets of double turns on the dough (see text and illustrations in *Chapter 9*, pp. 146–147).

2. Rest the dough when necessary for 15–20 minutes between sets. Generally, no more than 2 sets of turns can be accomplished without allowing for rest time.

3. After the turns are completed, wrap the dough completely and chill for an extended period in the refrigerator to allow the laminated dough to relax. Usually, the laminated dough rests at least 12 hours or overnight before being sheeted and cut into shapes.

SCALING:

1. Using a rolling pin or sheeter, roll out the dough to a rectangular sheet, generally 5–7 mm thick, though you can choose the thickness you wish.

2. Cut into triangles or rectangles in any size you like. 2–3 oz (50–80 g) is common for a croissant, but you can make them larger for sandwiches or smaller for buffets.

SHAPING: Roll triangles into the classic crescent shape (see *Chapter 9*). Fill rectangular pieces and roll them into cylinders. About 12 average-size items per parchment-covered tray is normal.

PROOFING: 45 minutes–1 hour at 78–80°F and 80% humidity. If the croissants are cold when they enter the proofer, the proofing time may be somewhat longer. Be especially careful

about the temperature during the proofing of the pastries. If the temperature climbs over 80°F, you may inadvertently melt the butter before the pastries are baked, and many of the layers will be lost. Setting the proof temperature just a bit below 80°F is a safer bet.

BAKING:

1. Carefully but quickly egg-wash the pastries just before inserting them into the oven. Be careful not to allow an excessive amount of egg wash to drip over the cut edges of the dough; this can harden in the oven and restrict the ability of the laminated pastries to rise during oven spring.

2. 20–25 minutes at 400–425°F in a conventional oven, with the trays double-panned if you are using a deck oven. Set convection or rack ovens 25–50°F lower. Your oven may vary from these estimates.

COOLING: Most large bakeries allow croissants and Danish to cool right on the pans used for baking them, but if you have enough space, you can certainly remove them from the trays and cool them on a wire rack.

chapter *10*

Creating Dough Formulas

Learning Outcomes:

- Understand the difference between a recipe and a formula.

- Define the term *balance* as it applies to bakery formulas.

- Identify the typical range of usage of water, salt, and yeast in balanced dough formulas.

- Use baker's percentage to recognize problems with unbalanced dough formulas.

- Resize a batch size of bread dough to a larger or smaller batch size while ensuring the dough remains unchanged.

- Recognize the limitations that ingredients, methods, equipment, and storage space place on production.

Formulation: How Can We Design Our Own Reliable Bread Dough?

By this time, you have learned a bit about bread ingredients, successfully mixed bread dough, recognized when it is ready for division, and shaped a number of loaves. You may have even determined when proofing is complete or performed the loading and baking of loaves in an oven. Do you think you're ready to run a bakery?

Of course, you're obviously not, but being inexperienced is only part of it.

Until now, you have been relying on formulas and procedures devised by other people—by either this author or your instructing chef. Would you be able to create them yourself? Or if something went wrong with the scaling of a batch, could you figure a way to save it and end up with the same dough you wanted? If late orders require a larger batch of baguette dough, can you rework the formula without making more loaves than you need?

It is possible, of course, to work in a bakery or pastry shop your entire life without knowing how to do those things, but it is unlikely your career would advance beyond performing work designed by someone else. Being the head baker or pastry chef in any shop demands that you know how formulas are created and why they are designed the way they are.

Occasionally, for a number of reasons, a formula or procedure requires adjustment. The dough looks too dry as it mixes. It rises too quickly. Or it moves too slowly. Learning how to recognize the need for changes and coming up with reliable solutions to ever-changing production scenarios requires a lot of experience, but it also demands a thorough understanding of how these processes—ingredient selection, mixing, fermenting, shaping, and baking—all affect each other.

When a bread dough contains too much of one ingredient or not enough of another, it is said to be *out of balance*, or *not in balance*. Too little water, for instance, keeps some of the gluten in the flour from forming, and it slows the rate of fermentation in a way you may not anticipate. Too much salt can slow fermentation as well, or be too assertive in the flavor profile. An excess of yeast makes bread dough ferment too quickly and may force you to divide and shape it before you want to. Whenever the ingredients in a bread dough cause it to perform in an unexpected way, the dough is said to be out of balance. Dough formulas that yield bread that performs as expected are said to be *balanced*.

This isn't to suggest you can predict everything in an artisan-run bakery. Industrial bread makers gave up on that challenge decades ago. Unfortunately, they adopted the use of chemical conditioners to artificially control their dough and thereby hedge their bet. We can usually direct a dough the way we want without resorting to methods that sacrifice flavor (and personal health), but this requires study of the natural fermentation process and insights into how to manipulate it.

To create your own recipes for bread, it can be helpful to follow a logical routine that provides a sound, predictable starting point; this can be altered later as you refine your bread formula. Select your ingredients, create a formula in which they are balanced, and develop a procedure to mix, ferment, and bake them that accommodates the limitations of your staffing, your facility, and your equipment.

Choose Your Ingredients

You probably sensed that formulas weren't just random combinations of ingredients, but you may not realize just how precisely many of the ingredient ratios specified in balanced formulas actually are. Following is a list of points, categorized by ingredient, to guide you in making sensible ingredient selections:

1. Choose your flour.
    a. All-purpose flour, bread flour, or high-gluten flour? The higher the protein content of your flour, the longer you must mix it to obtain the desired level of gluten development. That risks overoxidation and a loss of carotenoid pigments. Higher protein can also give bread a rubbery consistency that is not appropriate for every type of bread. Very low protein, however, often results in poor loaf volume, so the middle ground represented by bread flour from winter wheat is usually the best choice for rustic hearth breads.
    b. Whole wheat, whole rye, a mixture of flours, or what? French law defines pain ordinaire (baguette dough) as being made from white flour, but there are no such restrictions in North America, and we can customize our flour choices as we like. Higher-extraction flours have higher ash levels and more destabilizing bran, however, so choosing flours high in bran (like whole wheat and rye) has a negative effect on loaf volume. Many customers appreciate the addition of natural fiber present in bran, though, so as long as you understand bran's effects on loaf structure, you can use higher-extraction flours with great success.

2. Determine your hydration. How wet should your bread dough be? That depends on the texture and height you desire for your bread. Doughs that are very wet, such as ciabatta and *pane pugliese*, have wildly open crumb structures but fairly low, flat profiles. What you may gain in voluptuous mouthfeel comes hand in hand with a fairly rustic, inelegant outward appearance. That's fine if it is what you were expecting, but you might not want to design a highly hydrated dough if precise shaping is your goal.

    At the other extreme, drier doughs such as challah and Pullman bread produce loaves with tight, closed crumb structure and a homogenous, possibly cottony mouthfeel. Their firm nature makes dough handling easy and produces loaves with shapes that are easy to manipulate. This lack of moisture can also shorten shelf life, though, so these breads should be wrapped after cooling.

    Baguettes represent a midpoint in dough hydration, featuring (ideally) a reasonably open crumb structure with irregularly sized holes and a texture that is definitely noticeable as you chew it. The dough is just firm enough, however, to be shaped much more effectively than ciabatta dough, so it can yield loaves that rise high and are as pretty on the outside as they are on the inside.

3. How much salt? The range of salt used in modern bread formulas is generally restricted by limits of taste and by the impact of salt on the rate of fermentation. A proportion of 2% of flour weight is most common, but you have a little room to adjust that figure to your personal tastes. A baguette dough that is handmade instead of machine-mixed, and therefore fermented a long time to develop maturity, sometimes has a salt level of only 1.7–1.8%. The reasoning here is that the complex aromas and flavors that can result from long fermentation might be masked a bit by salt levels of 2% or higher.

    On the other hand, some bakers in Paris and elsewhere use salt levels at 2.2% of total flour weight. Whether that difference is subtle or sinful is entirely a matter of taste, both literally and figuratively. In any case, you should avoid using salt levels that make your bread dough taste noticeably salty, in the opinion of your customers. The salt is there to enhance the natural flavors of the bread, not to mask them.

4. How much yeast, and what kind? If you want your dough to rise slowly and benefit from longer fermentation, precisely controlling the quantity of yeast in the formula is critical to your success. First, decide what kind of yeast to use. Compressed yeast, instant yeast, and active dry yeast all have their adherents and their pluses and minuses. A lean dough leavened with various levels of instant yeast at an ambient temperature of about 77°F may exhibit the following peak fermentation times:

   - 0.3%   3-4 hours
   - 0.4-0.5%   1½–2 hours
   - 0.7 %   1 hour
   - 1%   30-45 minutes

   To get the proper percentages for compressed (fresh) yeast, divide the instant yeast percentage by a factor of 0.4. For example, to get a fermentation of 3-4 hours using compressed yeast, divide 0.3% by 0.4 for a compressed yeast percentage of 0.75%.

   To get the proper percentage for active dry yeast, multiply the instant yeast percentage by a factor of 1.25. For example, to get a fermentation of 3-4 hours using active dry yeast, multiply 0.3% by 1.25 for an active dry yeast percentage of 0.375 percent, or about 0.4% when rounded up.

   The above percentages are estimates at best. Differences in weather, room temperature, humidity, enzyme activity in your dough, and even elevation above sea level can affect the rate at which your dough reaches peak fermentation.

5. Fat or no fat? If you want to add silkiness or tenderness to your dough, then solid fats like butter or liquid fats like olive oil can do the job. The range of textures that can be obtained by altering the fat levels in your dough are represented by breads like challah and Pullman bread at one end and brioche and pannetone on the other. More fat can mean more tenderness, but it can also mean weak dough from too much shortening of the gluten strands. One strategy for maintaining dough strength while adding a large amount of fat to your dough is to hold back the fat and add it toward the end of the mixing cycle, when gluten strength has already been developed and the structural impact of fat can be minimized.

   Any fat content of less than 10% of flour weight probably won't complicate the mixing process much, and the fat can be added up front with the other dough ingredients.

6. Sugar, and how much? Sugar is a tenderizer, like fat, and significant quantities of it can make a bread dough slacken and lose strength. At 12% of flour weight or less, this effect of sugar on dough strength is of less concern, so the entire amount can be added at the start of the mix cycle. At levels greater than 12% of flour weight, however, it is advisable to add the sugar in two or three stages over the course of the entire mix cycle. That gives the gluten strands in the dough time to develop more completely before much sugar is added, and more dough strength can be retained.

   That critical level of 12% is also applicable to sugar's effects on yeast activity and fermentation rate in bread dough. At levels lower than 12%, sugar increases the rate of fermentation as yeast feed quickly on it, but at levels greater than 12%, the hygroscopic nature of sugar crystals denies too much water to the yeast cells in the dough, and fermentation is noticeably slowed. A dough with more than 12% sugar in its formula, then, usually has higher than normal yeast levels to compensate for the slowing caused by the high levels of sugar.

Create a Formula, Not Just a Recipe

We define a *formula* as a list of ingredients contained in a bread dough that lists both the weights of the ingredients used *and* the mathematical relationship between them. A recipe may be contained within a formula, even if it is not identified as such, but the important point to remember when distinguishing a formula from a recipe is that a formula is defined mathematically and is therefore more precise in meaning than a simple list of quantities used. For example, see Table 10.1.

Table 10.1 Baguette Dough Recipe versus Formula

BAGUETTE DOUGH #1		BAGUETTE DOUGH #2		
INGREDIENTS	Weight (g)	INGREDIENTS	Weight (g)	%
Bread flour	1377	Bread flour	1377	100%
Water	1060	Water	1060	77%
Salt	28	Salt	28	2%
Instant yeast	10	Instant yeast	10	0.7%
TOTAL BATCH	2475g	TOTAL BATCH	2475g	

Baguette Dough #1 is a recipe—a list of ingredients and their measurements to be used in mixing a batch of dough at a specific size. A recipe can be useful, and this one does give carefully specified weights (instead of inaccurate volume measurements), but the weights refer only to the batch size specified. The table for Baguette Dough #2, on the other hand, illustrates a dough *formula*. The percentages listed to the right of the ingredient weights represent a mathematical definition of the dough's composition.

In the table for Baguette Dough #2, even if we change the batch size, its relative ingredient proportions remain the same, so its characteristics of flavor, texture, and appearance should remain identical as well. Expressing ingredient lists as formulas instead of as recipes locks in the characteristics desired by the designer of that dough.

DETERMINE YOUR PROCEDURE

When you have established your ingredient list and you know what proportions you wish to use, you can decide which procedures you will use to mix the dough, ferment it, and shape it before baking.

HOW LONG TO MIX?

You probably recall that how you mix a dough can affect its flavor, texture, and appearance as much as its list of ingredients can. The three mixing methods described in *Chapter 4* are really just touchstones to guide you in analyzing formulas and deciding how to manipulate them. An infinite set of combinations of first-speed mixing and second-speed mixing (including the option of *no* second-speed mixing) is available to you as you design your own formulas. Still, it is important to review how altering mix times affects dough.

◆ 4-5 minutes on first speed for incorporation

For instance, a period of 4-5 minutes on first speed is necessary for almost any dough to give its flour particles time to completely absorb water and form its initial gluten bonds. Dough formulas with a lot of low-gluten flour, like rye, can probably get by with a shorter first-speed mixing period. Procedures that feature an autolyse type of extended rest period allow for enough passive gluten formation that the first-speed mixing time can often be shortened to 3 minutes.

◆ Enough second-speed mixing to develop the gluten as needed—no more, and no less, keeping in mind that long bulk fermentation increases dough strength as well

With a lean dough, especially, which has no flavorings like butter or sugar to hide behind, you may wish to maximize the flavor you can obtain from the flour alone. Less mixing preserves the carotenoid pigments that provide aroma and flavor components to simple breads. Mixing only on first speed for 10-15 minutes (the short mix method) maximizes flavor, but it provides the least strength to the dough and requires long fermentation (3-5 hours) to develop maturity (see *Chapter 4*). It provides the most open crumb of any mixing method, but there are times when that characteristic is not an advantage (as when making pan breads for sandwiches).

Mixing 4-5 minutes on first speed and perhaps 8 minutes or longer on second speed gives a lot of mechanically produced strength to a dough, so it requires much less fermentation time to reach maturity. The long mixing at high speed destroys most of the carotenoid pigments, though, so this method leaves you with a dough that provides little flavor. This intensive method isn't the best choice for lean breads, but doughs high in fat or sugar may require intensive mixing to provide enough strength for the fragile, rich dough.

Compromise methods like the improved mix method feature 4-5 minutes of first-speed mixing followed by short periods of second-speed mixing (3-5 minutes) that develop the gluten significantly without destroying the carotenoid pigments in the dough. Maturity can be reached in only 1½-2 hours, or even less time if a large amount of pre-ferment is used, so bread can still be shaped and baked in a reasonable period. If you want a bread with a reasonably open crumb that has a creamy crumb color, good taste, and a nice appearance in a reasonable time, this method can work for you.

To some degree, the options for mix time can be limited by your ingredients. If you use large amounts of fat and sugar, for instance, you must adopt a method that is fairly intensive or you won't develop enough strength in the dough to support all that weight. If you desire a long fermentation to get maximum flavor, you are limited to either the short mix or improved mix. Choosing the intensive method would develop so much strength in the dough mechanically that you wouldn't want to allow much fermentation or risk making the dough too strong to shape.

HOW MUCH FERMENTATION IS ENOUGH? DO I NEED A PRE-FERMENT?

You need to allow enough time for the yeast to inflate the dough and give it a light texture. Large quantities of yeast (1% or more of instant yeast) can do the job for a lean dough in as little as 30-60 minutes, but that shorter period does not allow the bacteria enough time to produce the organic acids that provide most of a lean dough's strength and flavor. When you accelerate gas formation from yeast activity, you reduce strength and flavor.

Using smaller quantities of manufactured yeast or the wild yeast from a levain allows you to slow the process and obtain the dough maturity and flavor you want, but you still must monitor the dough's fermentation and take it to the bench when it has reached optimal gas development.

Typical bulk fermentation time is 1½–2 hours for doughs mixed using the improved mix method, though you can shorten that to 1 hour if you use enough pre-ferment. The more old-fashioned short mix method requires 3–5 hours, depending on whether or not you use a pre-ferment in your formula. Intensively mixed doughs usually ferment no more than 30–60 minutes before they are divided and shaped. By using synthetic dough conditioners, you can shorten the fermentation time to almost nothing, but that should be your first clue that you need to review the comments about flavor development above and in *Chapter 4*.

Pre-ferments such as poolish, sponge, biga, old dough, and levain can give you a way to shorten bulk fermentation by providing the acids needed to obtain dough strength and flavor early in the final dough's bulk fermentation. Pre-ferments must be mixed diligently ahead of time, and some are difficult to produce in a consistent manner (such as poolish), but the advantages they offer in shortened workflow and complex flavor profiles may outweigh the inconvenience of adding them to your production list. In any case, if you (a) need to shorten your bulk fermentation time, (b) don't want to sacrifice flavor, and (c) don't want to use synthetic dough conditioners, your best option is to use a pre-ferment.

If you elect to use a pre-ferment, you must consider *all* of its effects on the finished dough, including its impact on dough structure, strength, handling characteristics, appearance, flavor, and aromas. You can't just pick and choose among the qualities of a pre-ferment; they all come wrapped in the package.

For instance, a biga is fairly firm, easy to prepare and maintain, and provides great flavor to any bread made with it. To wet doughs like ciabatta and pane pugliese, its firmness contributes good acidity and strength. For baguette dough, though, the extra strength provided by a biga can provide too much elasticity, and it may be difficult to extend the baguettes during shaping. Poolish and liquid levain can grant you more extensibility, though these pre-ferments have their own limitations. For more information about pre-ferments and their effects, see *Chapter 5*.

HOW LONG SHOULD YOU PROOF YOUR LOAVES, AND WHEN SHOULD YOU AIM TO BAKE THEM?

Proofing is one of the important defined periods of fermentation in any professional shop, but its only purpose is to reinflate loaves to an optimal point after they are shaped. If you are baking bread made with manufactured yeast, and it was mixed within the last few hours, it will probably proof in 90 minutes or less. It may even proof in less than 60 minutes if the temperature in your proofer (or bakery) exceeds 80°F. Keep an eye on how rapidly a dough reaches maturity during its bulk fermentation. If it is ready for division fairly early, then it is likely the loaves made from it will proof quickly as well.

Exceptions to these guidelines abound, of course. Small rolls usually take no more than 30–60 minutes to proof. Bread leavened exclusively with levain (using no manufactured yeast) can take 2–4 hours at 80°F, depending on the yeast activity present in the levain itself.

And, of course, by placing the loaves on a covered rack and locating the rack in a refrigerator, you can slow proofing considerably. It is not unusual these days to see artisan-style bakeries that start their day at the relatively late hour of 5 or 6 A.M. They can do this because they don't need to get up earlier—the loaves they'll bake that day are already waiting for them in the walk-in.

These bakers start by baking the loaves shaped and held from the day before, mix dough while the oven is being loaded, and later shape the loaves that will be baked tomorrow after they are held in the refrigerator. This convenient practice, called *retardation*, does have practical limitations.

The first limitation is space in the refrigerator. A one- or two-door reach-in refrigerator can do in a pinch, but it will hold only limited amounts of bread and probably won't work in a high-production environment. Larger walk-in refrigerators and specialized retarder-proofers can generally hold more bread, but even they can become a bottleneck. Matching your refrigeration capacity to likely production has an important effect on your ability to take advantage of retarding in managing your workflow.

The challenges of retarding finished loaves revolve mostly around controlling CO_2 gas production and guarding against excessive enzyme activity in the dough used to make the bread. Strategies for controlling gas production include reducing the amount of yeast used, limiting bulk fermentation to 30 minutes, and finding the precise temperature that will provide just enough inflation by morning when you need it. This discovery process might require extensive testing and failure. There is no way for even the most experienced baker to predict the yeast levels, bulk fermentation times, and retarding temperatures that will yield loaves that are ready when wanted without practical advance testing.

If your loaves just can't make it through until morning when you're there to bake them, consider adding a tiny amount of ascorbic acid to give them extra strength. There is some controversy in France and elsewhere about how authentically "artisan" bread can be when synthetic substances of any sort are added, but ascorbic acid is really just man-made vitamin C, and the tiny amounts recommended for retarding bread (about 20 parts per million, or 20 ppm) are completely burned off during the course of baking.

HOW BIG SHOULD THE LOAVES OR ROLLS BE, AND HOW LONG SHOULD YOU BAKE THEM?

If you are formulating a bread to meet the requirements of a certain restaurant account, you must work closely with the chef or manager at that account to find a specified product weight and shape that meets the restaurant's needs.

Keep these important points in mind:

◆ A short, fat loaf or a round loaf at a given weight takes longer to bake than a long, thin loaf at the same weight made with the same dough. It may also require a lower temperature to achieve the same level of doneness without developing too much color.

◆ The smaller the loaf or roll your account requests from you, the more time it will take you to divide and shape the entire batch of dough. A loaf that weighs 8 oz can't be priced at half the amount you charge for a 1-lb loaf. The labor to make two 8-oz loaves is about twice that of making one 16-oz loaf, so the price of the 8-oz loaf shouldn't be much lower.

ARTISAN BAKER PROFILE

Christy Timon and Abe Faber

Clear Flour Bread, Boston, Massachusetts

Clear Flour Bread isn't the largest bakery in the greater Boston metropolitan area, but, if reviews are any indication, it may well be the best. It has garnered "Best Bread" and "Best Bakery" awards from *Boston Magazine, Cooking Light,* and the *Boston Globe,* which characterized the operation as a "bread mecca."

The operation is owned and operated by Christy Timon and Abram Faber, who met in 1983 when Abe was hired as a part-time delivery driver for Christy's bakery. He was a recent graduate of the Massachusetts College of Art and looking for a way to supplement his artist income, while Christy had already been operating her bakery for about a year. Abe's limited role soon grew into a full-time job that included being a baker, business manager, and maintenance man.

Christy, who has a B.A. from the University of Wisconsin, had gained considerable experience working in baking and pastry at restaurants around Madison and, eventually, the Boston area. She started a catering business in Brookline, Massachusetts, in the early 1980s, and the breads she baked for use in that business became a big selling point. Some restaurants around town asked her to begin baking her breads in large enough quantity to sell them separately, and this business eventually grew enough to add a retail storefront and product lines that included croissants, brioche, and pastry items.

Both Christy and Abe, who are now married, feel strongly about their role as operators of a neighborhood bakery that focuses on servicing a local market. They do not claim that being smaller makes their bread better or that mechanization in large bakeries makes for inferior product. They simply enjoy making the bread more than they do managing the business, and they prefer the bakery be manageable enough to allow them to do that. Their commitment to encouraging the emergence of similar neighborhood bakeries is evident in the startups operated by their former employees (see Artisan Baker Profile: Alison

Pray) and their enthusiastic support of the Bread Bakers Guild of America, where Abe serves as vice chairman. Abe provides insight into their baking and business philosophy:

IMPRESSIONS OF ARTISAN BREAD BAKING AS AN INDUSTRY

Can we define artisan bread? If so, what makes it distinctive, in your opinion?

I don't think there really is such a thing as "artisan bread." The fact that the baker is an artisan, and that he aspires to practice a craft using the highest possible level of knowledge and hand skills, doesn't necessarily make a great loaf of bread. Just like bread made by factory methods doesn't necessarily produce a bad loaf. The bread must stand on its own regardless of the techniques used for its creation.

Like a lot of operators, you and Christy are married and have kids. How do you balance work and family life? Do you think this is something that just about any married couple can do for a living?

It is very hard. You have to really love what you do and be enriched by it because it is definitely not an 8-hour workday or a 5-day workweek. I don't think we have ever reached any kind of perfect equilibrium with work and family life. It is difficult to be in a profession where every single holiday means working right through the night to bring food to other families' celebrations while forgoing your own. If it's enjoyable on a daily basis, though, somehow it all works out. Christy and I actually enjoy the work. If you like to work in your bakery (as opposed to just liking the *idea* of operating a bakery), then this is a career for you!

You and Christy spend a lot of time working with the Bread Bakers Guild of America. Why is this work important to you?

It is important to us because, while we want to focus on our local community as neighborhood bakers, we and the BBGA want to assist in offering high-quality, affordable bread education to as many aspiring bakers as we can.

What are the intangibles that keep you in this business?

Of course, I love when a food-aware customer seeks out our bakery because she heard we made something great. But it makes me even happier when people who don't know much about food just happen to wander in and, for the first time in their lives, taste these breads made only with traditional, time-honored methods. And they come back again and again.

Something pleasantly subversive has occurred in their life: Making a separate trip for a loaf of bread is now a worthwhile endeavor. And this may lead to other changes. Maybe they'll consider buying cheese directly from a cheesemonger, or great-tasting eggs

from a farmer who raises the chickens. These are forms of consumerism that will ultimately prove more sustainable for us and the world we live in.

So, my overall message is that old cliché about acting locally by always thinking globally as well. And I feel lucky to have found a way, through baking, to a measure of success in both those areas.

Do you have any pearls of wisdom for the bakery and pastry students reading this book?

Work hard to learn first how your teacher or employer is asking you to practice your craft, and get it down perfectly. Only after that should you allow your own creativity to shine through or add your own personal take on the craft. You must learn the basics first.

Summary

Creating your own breads is fun and challenging, but it cannot be a casual process if you plan to produce them consistently well in a predictable time frame. While you can employ your creative instincts for ideas, you must also approach the process scientifically or risk failure on a large scale. Take advantage of your experience and the principles you have learned in ingredient selection, dough mixing, fermentation, and baking to increase the likelihood of your formulas being balanced and practical to produce.

Recognize that using formulas to design new breads instead of relying upon standard recipes will lock in the characteristics you intended for that dough. By establishing mathematical relationships between the flour in a formula and all other ingredients, you can change batch size without altering the characteristics of the bread. The consistency of the product can be assured if the ingredient quantities are derived from the original percentage relationships.

There are practical limitations to what sorts of bread you can create by altering ingredients or procedures. That should not discourage you from trying new ideas, but your experiments in bread design require a firm foundation in the basics if they are to succeed.

Key Terms

balance   *formula*   *recipe*

Questions for Review

1. What are some common reasons for a bread dough to require changes in its ingredients or associated procedures?

2. What is the essential difference between a bread recipe and a bread formula?

3. What are the most common considerations when determining the type of flour (or flours) you will use? Will the choice of flour affect other aspects of dough production in any way?

4. What sorts of abnormalities are easy to recognize when you glance at a formula, and how is it possible to immediately recognize them?

5. How do fats and sugar challenge us when designing our own bread formulas?

6. Does one preferred mix method make the best bread in most cases?

7. What limitations are there in retarding finished loaves of bread overnight before baking them the next day?

Questions for Discussion

Given the challenges that confront us when we try to keep our production day organized, is it justifiable to consider using chemical conditioners when making artisan-style bread? Why or why not?

Lab Exercises & Experiments Using Baker's Percentage

*T*he following two exercises utilize worksheets designed to help you develop formulas manually. These can be copied from the text or downloaded from the book's companion website (www.wiley.com/college/dimuzio) and printed as hard copies. A baker may wish to use these worksheets before settling on a final formula and entering the data into a computer spreadsheet for archiving or general access to employees. The first exercise contains one pre-ferment, so the worksheet is designed specifically for that purpose. The second exercise is an example of a dough with *two* pre-ferments, which, while less common in practice, is seen in some bakeries and also at competitions.

If you wish to design a straight dough with no pre-ferment at all, you would use the first three columns only to make your computations.

If you want to design a formula with more than two pre-ferments (rarely seen outside of competitions), you can design your own worksheet and borrow elements from the worksheet designed for two pre-ferments.

For both of these worksheets, the underlying process is the same:

Determine what ingredients will be in the straight dough of a particular batch size you have chosen. Decide if you want to use a pre-ferment; then, if you do decide to use a pre-ferment, figure out what ingredients are in it and subtract those ingredient weights from the original straight dough to get the weights for the version of the dough that includes the pre-ferment.

Creating Your Formula:

1. Decide what batch size you want to create first, and then select the relative percentages assigned to the ingredients. Based on your experiences with other bread formulas, think about the primary and secondary effects contributed by the ingredients you choose.

2. Total these percentages and convert the total to a decimal number to find the percentage sum.

3. Divide the batch size by the percentage sum to find the weight of total flour in the batch size you've chosen.

4. Find the weights for all individual ingredients in the straight dough by multiplying the total flour weight in the batch by the percentages you chose for them.

5. If you are using a pre-ferment, decide how much of the total flour in the formula you wish to ferment ahead of time in percentage terms.

6. Multiply the total flour in the batch by the percentage of pre-fermented flour you'd prefer, and write that figure as the weight of flour in your pre-ferment.

7. Multiply the flour weight in your pre-ferment by the hydration rate of your pre-ferment to obtain the weight of water in your pre-ferment.

8. List any salt or yeast in your pre-ferment, if measurable.

9. Total the weight of ingredients in the pre-ferment, and write them in the appropriate box.

10. Subtract the weight of any ingredients in the pre-ferment from their corresponding weights in the straight dough. The remaining weights, plus your pre-ferment weight, make up the ingredient list for the new, adjusted dough.

EXERCISE 1

You wish to design your own baguette dough, and you already maintain a liquid levain every day, so you would prefer to use that as a pre-ferment to keep your bulk fermentation time to a minimum. You arbitrarily decide to make the first batch size at 6000g.

The ingredient list and the overall percentages you think will work well are as follows:

Bread flour	100%
Water	69%
Salt	2%
Instant yeast	0.4%

Your liquid levain is maintained at 100% hydration, and you decide, based on figures supplied by an experienced baker, to try pre-fermenting only 11% of the total flour weight in the formula. This is because you want the strength and flavor provided by the acids in the liquid levain but you don't want the baguettes to taste sour, and you are wary of the higher levels of enzymes that would be contributed by a larger quantity of liquid levain.

Guided by the worksheet for one pre-ferment on p. 171, use the desired batch size and percentages you've chosen to find the ingredients for both the straight dough and the adjusted dough for the batch you wish to make. The results are listed on the worksheet printed below, which you have filled in by hand.

Design Worksheet for Formulas with 1 Pre-Ferment

PRODUCT _Baguette w/ Liquid Levain (6000g Batch)_

INGREDIENTS	BAKER'S % (STRAIGHT DOUGH)		STRAIGHT DOUGH	MINUS	PRE-FERM. (OPTIONAL)	EQUALS	ADJUSTED DOUGH METRIC (G)	OR	ADJUSTED DOUGH U.S. (OZ)
Bread flour	100%	→	3501g	–	385g	=	3116g	OR	6 lb 14.0oz
Water	69%	→	2416g	–	385g	=	2031g	OR	4 lb 8.0oz
Salt	2%	→	70g	–	0g	=	70g	OR	2.5oz
Instant yeast	0.40%	→	14g	–	0g	=	14g	OR	0.5oz
		→		–		=		OR	
		→		–		=		OR	
		→		–		=		OR	
		→		–		=		OR	
		→		–		=		OR	
		→		–		=		OR	
		→		–		=		OR	
		→		–		=		OR	
		→		–		=		OR	
		→		–		=		OR	

Pre-Ferment _Liquid Levain_	↓↓↓	↓↓↓	Subtotal → 770g	Pre-Ferm. Weight 6001g	OR	Pre-Ferm. Weight 1 lb 11.0oz

	↓↓↓	↓↓↓		↓↓↓		↓↓↓
Percentage Sum		Batch Weight		Adj. Dgh. Wt.		Adj. Dgh. Wt.
171.40%		6001g	‹--These totals should be the same--›	6001g	OR	13 lb 4.0oz

Percentage Sum (sum of all baker's percents × 0.01) = _1.714_

Total Flour (batch weight / percentage sum) = _3501g_ = 100%

Hydration of Pre-Ferment _100%_   **% Pre-Ferm. Flour** _11%_   **x Total Flour =** _385g_

PROCEDURE: _____

1st speed: _5 min_   Divide: _400g pieces_

2nd speed: _3–4 min_   Rest time: _20 min_

Water temp.:   Shape:

Final dough temp.:   Proof: _60–90 min_

Bulk ferment: _2 hrs @ 75°F_   Bake time/temp.: _20–25 min @ 475°F_

1. The math is correct. You made the batch listed in the adjusted dough column, and, while the bread was enjoyable, you decide the loaves are still too sour and you want to adjust the liquid levain quantity downward. You decide to try it with only 9% pre-fermented flour, using the same type of liquid levain. Using a blank worksheet, determine the new weights for the same-sized batch in both the pre-ferment column and in the adjusted dough.

   Note the straight dough percentages and weights do not change—just the amount of levain used and the adjusted weights in the last column.

2. You decide you like the flavor profile at 9% pre-fermented flour, but the baguettes now seem less extensible during the shaping period, so again you decide to modify the formula by increasing the percentage of water and making them less elastic. You want to go from 69% overall hydration to 70%. Use a blank worksheet and, borrowing whatever figures you need from the one used before, figure out what changes will occur in the worksheet and the figures represented.

EXERCISE 2

You want to develop a completely different dough for your French boule, this time using two pre-ferments to add an unusual degree of complexity to the formula. You make these two pre-ferments every day anyway, so the inconvenience of needing two pre-ferments to make the dough will be minimal.

You decide to mix a 7,000g batch of dough.

The two pre-ferments you have selected are liquid levain and sponge.

The ingredient list and the overall percentages you think will work well are as follows:

Bread flour	100%
Water	69%
Salt	2%
Instant yeast	0.4%

Your liquid levain is maintained at a 100% hydration, and you decide, based on figures supplied by an experienced baker, to try pre-fermenting only 8% of the total flour weight in the formula with the liquid levain. This is because you want the flavor and complexity provided by the acids in the liquid levain, but you don't want the baguettes to taste at all sour.

You make your sponge every day about 24 hours before you first need it. Its hydration rate is always 60%, and the measurement of manufactured yeast in it is so tiny it isn't worth tracking in the formula. You like the balance of strength and flavor offered by a sponge, so you decide arbitrarily to pre-ferment 10% of the total flour in the dough with the sponge.

Taking the batch size you have chosen, the ingredient list above, and the percentages associated with them, you use the worksheet for two pre-ferments on p. 172 and come up with the following:

Design Worksheet for Formulas with 2 Pre-Ferments

PRODUCT _French Boules (7000g Batch)_

INGREDIENTS	BAKER'S % (STRAIGHT DOUGH)		STRAIGHT DOUGH	MINUS	PRE-FERM. #1 (OPTIONAL)	MINUS	PRE-FERM. #2 (OPTIONAL)	EQUALS	ADJUSTED DOUGH METRIC (G)	OR	ADJUSTED DOUGH U.S. (OZ)
Bread flour	100%	→	4060g	–	325g	–	406g	=	3329g	OR	
Water	70%	→	2842g	–	325g	–	244g	=	2273g	OR	
Salt	2%	→	81g	–	0g	–	0g	=	81g	OR	
Instant yeast	0.40%	→	16g	–	0g	–	0g	=	16g	OR	
		→		–		–		=		OR	
		→		–		–		=		OR	
		→		–		–		=		OR	
		→		–		–		=		OR	
		→		–		–		=		OR	
		→		–		–		=		OR	
		→		–		–		=		OR	
		→		–		–		=		OR	
		→		–		–		=		OR	
		→		–		–		=		OR	

Pre-Ferment #1 _Liquid Levain_	↓↓↓	Subtotal #1—› 650g		Pre-Ferm. 1 Weight 650g	OR	Pre-Ferm. 1 Weight
Pre-Ferment #2 _Sponge_	↓↓↓		Subtotal #2—› 650g	Pre-Ferm. 2 Weight 650g		Pre-Ferm. 2 Weight
	↓↓↓			↓↓↓		↓↓↓
	Total			Total		Total
	6999g	‹--These totals should be the same--›		6999g	OR	

Percentage Sum (sum of all baker's percents × 0.01) = _1.724_

Total Flour (batch weight / percentage sum) = _4060g_ = 100%

Hydration of Pre-Ferment #1 _100%_   **% Pre-Ferm. Flour #1** _8%_

Hydration of Pre-Ferment #2 _60%_   **% Pre-Ferm. Flour #2** _10%_

PROCEDURE: _____

1st speed: Divide:

2nd speed: Rest time:

Water temp.:   Shape:

Final dough temp.:   Proof:

Bulk ferment: Bake time/temp.:

1. What would the weights be if you had to use a scale that weighs in ounces only?

2. Does the percentage relationship of the ingredients change when the units of measurement change?

3. Take a blank copy of the above worksheet and refigure the metric quantities in the adjusted dough column for a dough that uses all the same ingredients but pre-ferments 11% of the total flour using the liquid levain. Which numbers change, and which do not? Why is this so?

Design Worksheet for Formulas with 1 Pre-Ferment

PRODUCT _____

INGREDIENTS	BAKER'S % (STRAIGHT DOUGH)		STRAIGHT DOUGH	MINUS	PRE-FERM. (OPTIONAL)	EQUALS	ADJUSTED DOUGH METRIC (G)	OR	ADJUSTED DOUGH U.S. (OZ)
		→		−		=		OR	
		→		−		=		OR	
		→		−		=		OR	
		→		−		=		OR	
		→		−		=		OR	
		→		−		=		OR	
		→		−		=		OR	
		→		−		=		OR	
		→		−		=		OR	
		→		−		=		OR	
		→		−		=		OR	
		→		−		=		OR	
		→		−		=		OR	

Pre-Ferment	↓↓↓	↓↓↓		Subtotal →	Pre-Ferm. Weight	OR	Pre-Ferm. Weight

↓↓↓	↓↓↓	↓↓↓	↓↓↓
Percentage Sum	Batch Weight	Adj. Dgh. Wt.	Adj. Dgh. Wt.

‹--These totals should be the same--›   OR

Percentage Sum (sum of all baker's percents × 0.01) = _____

Total Flour (batch weight / percentage sum) = _____ = 100%

Hydration of Pre-Ferment _____   **% Pre-Ferm. Flour** _____   **x Total Flour =** _____

PROCEDURE: _____

1st speed: Divide:

2nd speed: Rest time:

Water temp.:   Shape:

Final dough temp.:   Proof:

Bulk ferment: Bake time/temp.:

Design Worksheet for Formulas with 2 Pre-Ferments

PRODUCT _____

INGREDIENTS	BAKER'S % (STRAIGHT DOUGH)		STRAIGHT DOUGH	MINUS	PRE-FERM. #1 (OPTIONAL)	MINUS	PRE-FERM. #2 (OPTIONAL)	EQUALS	ADJUSTED DOUGH METRIC (G)	OR	ADJUSTED DOUGH U.S. (OZ)
		→		−		−		=		OR	
		→		−		−		=		OR	
		→		−		−		=		OR	
		→		−		−		=		OR	
		→		−		−		=		OR	
		→		−		−		=		OR	
		→		−		−		=		OR	
		→		−		−		=		OR	
		→		−		−		=		OR	
		→		−		−		=		OR	
		→		−		−		=		OR	
		→		−		−		=		OR	

Pre-Ferment #1   ↓↓↓   Subtotal #1—→   Pre-Ferm. 1 Weight   OR   Pre-Ferm. 1 Weight

Pre-Ferment #2   ↓↓↓   Subtotal #2—›   Pre-Ferm. 2 Weight   Pre-Ferm. 2 Weight

↓↓↓   ↓↓↓   ↓↓↓

Total   Total   Total

‹--These totals should be the same--›   OR

Percentage Sum (sum of all baker's percents × 0.01) = _____

Total Flour (batch weight / percentage sum) = _____ = 100%

Hydration of Pre-Ferment #1 _____   **% Pre-Ferm. Flour #1** _____

Hydration of Pre-Ferment #2 _____   **% Pre-Ferm. Flour #2** _____

PROCEDURE: _____

1st speed: Divide:

2nd speed: Rest time:

Water temp.:   Shape:

Final dough temp.:   Proof:

Bulk ferment: Bake time/temp.:

1

Flour Composition and Milling Technology

Elements of the Wheat Endosperm

Starch, a type of complex carbohydrate, makes up the majority of the wheat's endosperm. At the molecular level, it comprises long chains of sugar (*glucose*) molecules that are chemically bonded. There are two basic types of starch in wheat, *amylose* and *amylopectin*. Amylose constitutes around 25% of the wheat starch and forms long straight chains. Amylopectin amounts to about 75% of the wheat starch and can form a more complex set of branched chains within its structure. Both types are located within compact granules in the endosperm.

Because the granules are so compact, they resist penetration by other substances. At room temperature, they are not water-absorbent, but when they are heated, starch granules can absorb a lot of water. When they are milled, most of the starch granules (90% or more) remain intact and unbroken, and they are referred to as *native starch*. The remaining 10% of the granules that are broken are referred to as *damaged starch*. Native starch absorbs only about 40% of its own weight in water, but damaged starch can absorb its full weight or more.

The purpose of starch in a wheat berry is to supply food to the seedling that will grow if it is planted in the soil. The seedling can't feed directly on starch granules; they must be broken down into their component sugar molecules first. Luckily for the wheat seedling, there are also *enzymes* in the *endosperm*, and one called *amylase* can break chains of starch into sugar molecules as the berry is about to sprout.

Fortunately for bakers, amylase also breaks down the starch in flour; the yeast we use in bread dough, like the seedling from a wheat berry, can't feed on starch. Amylase turns the starch in flour into simple sugars. Because native starch granules are so resistant to water, they are also resistant to the effects of amylase and are not an optimal source of simple sugars for the yeast. The damaged starch, however, absorbs water easily, which makes it easy for the enzyme amylase to attack the damaged starch and convert it into sugars.

Keep in mind, this doesn't mean that more damaged starch in flour is always better for bread. Millers and bakers tend to agree that 7–10% starch damage is optimal.

173

More than 10% damaged starch results in more converted sugar in the dough and too swift a rate of fermentation. In addition, the excessive sugar levels make the dough fairly sticky and unpleasant to handle. Too little damaged starch can be just as undesirable. At levels of less than 7%, the comparative lack of converted sugars causes a significant reduction in the rate of fermentation.

Starch doesn't function only as food for yeast in bread dough; it is also an essential structural component for loaves of bread. It absorbs a considerable amount of water when the dough is mixed, but draws in even more moisture when the loaves are baked and the starch begins to *gelatinize*, or swell and solidify under heat. Sugars on the outside of the loaf that aren't consumed during fermentation caramelize and turn the crust brown.

Pentosans are another type of carbohydrate (a gum, specifically) found in the wheat endosperm at levels of about 2%, which isn't much. Pentosans are often overlooked, but they can absorb up to 15 times their own weight in water, so even a small presence of pentosans in flour can have a noticeable effect on dough consistency. Pentosans are present in much higher levels in rye flour, which can cause complications in making rye bread successfully. This subject is discussed in greater detail in *Chapter 4* and *Chapter 10*.

Protein is the substance that drives the most discussion about wheat flour. It is an organic compound comprised of chains of amino acids. Within the wheat berry, there are two general classifications of proteins, soluble and insoluble. *Soluble proteins*, which amount to around 20% of the total protein weight, are located in the germ and the vicinity of the endosperm that's near the bran layer. They are called *soluble* because they dissolve in water, and they are primarily globulins, albumins, and various enzymes. Their presence is reflected in flour's stated percentage of protein, but they do not contribute in any way to the formation of gluten.

Insoluble proteins account for the remaining 80% of the proteins in the endosperm. They do not dissolve in water. The two insoluble proteins present in wheat are *glutenin* and *gliadin*. Glutenin forms long, strong chains that seem to give wheat dough its strength, while gliadin strands bond to glutenin strands, possibly near their joints (the nature of bonding between glutenin and gliadin is not completely understood). In order to bond, the two proteins must be in the presence of water. As they bond, they form a more complex protein called *gluten*.

Gluten forms a web or fabric that captures and holds air bubbles formed in bread dough during mixing. As CO_2 gas is generated by the yeast, it migrates to the air bubbles already in the dough and increases their size. To a large degree, the glutinous web can accommodate the larger bubbles without their breaking, so the dough increases in size as it ferments. The rising that's so characteristic of leavened bread is due not only to the yeast producing CO_2 but also the wheat flour containing the insoluble proteins necessary to capture and hold the gas.

Cereal chemists believe glutenin provides the strength or elasticity characteristic of wheat dough, while gliadin seems to exhibit the extensibility that allows the dough to be stretched. While rye also contains both glutenin and gliadin in its endosperm, it doesn't contain enough glutenin to form the same amount of gluten as wheat. The same can be said for barley. For practical purposes, rye and barley flour are treated in formulas as if they had no gluten at all. Still, you should remember that the gliadin in rye and barley causes the same reaction as wheat does for people with gluten intolerance (celiac disease).

The most common test in North America for predicting the performance of wheat flour is done with a *faringraph*. Using this device in a laboratory environment, technicians measure the resistance of a dough sample to mechanical mixing. As the dough mixes, the faringraph generates a chart on paper that reflects the character-

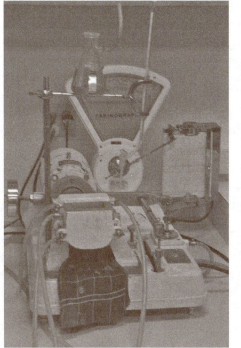

Figure A1.1 A farinograph. The small box with the tubes running to it is a small dough mixer. Notice the graph on the paper chart being generated on the right.

Figure A1.2 An alveograph. A technician uses the alveograph to inflate a small piece of dough into a bubble. Notice that, just above the dough bubble, a paper chart is being generated to reflect the air pressure necessary to inflate and finally break the bubble.

istics of its strength, its water absorption capacity, and its tolerance to long mixing. Historically, these have been the dough traits that concerned American bakers the most, so it should be no surprise that this is the device most used by American millers to evaluate the performance properties of flour. Figure A1.1 contains an illustration of a farinograph.

In Europe, it is more common for millers to use a machine called an *alveograph* (see Figure A1.2) to test for the protein qualities of most concern to bakers. Using this device, lab technicians blow air into a small piece of dough, creating a large bubble. The alveograph measures the resistance of the dough bubble to both inflation and rupture. It produces numerical values for the qualities of elasticity and extensibility in the dough, for the relationship between the two, and for the overall strength of the dough.

How Ash Content Is Determined

Lab technicians weigh a small sample of white flour and place it in a ceramic cup. They place the sample in a specially designed oven at a temperature of 900°F or more until all the organic matter is burned away, leaving only a small amount of powdery ash. This ash is composed of minerals like iron, sodium, copper, zinc, and potassium, most of which were present in the bran. The amount of ash left in the cup directly reflects the bran content of the original flour.

The weight of the ash divided by the weight of the original flour sample yields a percentage. For instance, 0.5g ash remaining in a cup that held 100g flour before burning has an ash level of 0.5%. This doesn't mean the flour contained actual ash, only that the ash remaining from a burned sample was at a specified level. That level can be used to predict the probable level of residual bran in the white flour.

A tiny quantity of bran may be desirable, as the minerals in the bran encourage fermentation, and the bran particles can interrupt some gluten bonds and aid in granting extensibility to dough that is too strong. On the other hand, if flour contains too much bran, too many gluten bonds are weakened, and the darker color of the bran gives the dough a grayish cast. For both structural and aesthetic reasons, too high an ash level is judged by millers and most bakers to be undesirable.

MEASURING THE ENZYME LEVEL IN FLOUR

The last test we discuss measures the enzyme level in a particular batch of flour. At the mill, technicians mix a fixed weight of flour into a measured amount of hot water, creating a *slurry*. The hot water in the slurry causes the starches in the flour to *gelatinize* or thicken. A metal probe is inserted into the mixture, and the amount of time it takes for the probe to fall to the bottom of the container is recorded. This number is referred to as the flour's *falling number*. Typically, wheat that is *sound* (has not sprouted) has a falling number of about 350 seconds before the probe passes through a slurry made from its flour.

The level of amylase in wheat berries increases as the wheat stalk nears the time it would go to seed and the berries sprout. A falling number lower than 200 seconds indicates that excessive levels of amylase accumulated in the wheat berries as they neared their harvest. The high amylase level causes the starch to break down into sugar more quickly, thereby making the slurry less thick and less likely to slow the probe. On the other hand, a falling number larger than 350 seconds indicates that the wheat crop being tested was probably harvested a bit early, further from the time that sprouting would occur. It probably would not contain enough amylase to sustain an acceptable rate or length of fermentation.

The falling number is used as an indicator of amylase levels in flour. Bakers prefer the falling number of their flour be in the mid-200s, but wheat growers can't allow their crops to accumulate that much amylase naturally without risking sprouting. To compensate for this, millers tend to add a measured amount of malted barley flour to the white flour to raise its amylase levels to a point where the falling number of the white flour is acceptable.

When barley or wheat is *malted*, the grain is allowed to sprout, dried in a low oven, and ground into a powder. Any grain can be used to make malt, but barley malt and wheat malt are the types most commonly used to increase amylase levels. Another option for millers is to use *fungal amylase*, which, as the name suggests, is derived from a type of fungus. Fungal amylase is sometimes preferred because it is specialized in its effects and has no other enzymes or sweeteners to complicate the overall fermentation. The chief drawback of using fungal amylase is that employees with certain allergies or sensitivities may develop a rash or other reaction when they work around flour that contains that source of enzyme.

ADDITIVES IN FLOUR

Before flour is packaged and sold, millers blend it with additives besides malt.

The Enrichment Process

The most common process is referred to as *enrichment*, which occurs when iron, thiamin, niacin, riboflavin, and folic acid are added to flour that would otherwise lack these natural vitamins and minerals because the bran was removed. Millers must provide enrichment by law, unless a customer specifically requests that they leave it out.

Oxidizers

Oxidizers are chemicals that add oxygen to dough, which increases dough strength and tolerance to long fermentation. *Ascorbic acid* is the synthesized form of vitamin C, and it is an example of an oxidizer. Because it is a vitamin, and because it is destroyed during baking, most bakers view it as a completely harmless way to add tolerance to long *proofing*, which is the final stage of fermentation for loaves just before baking them. It is generally used in quantities of 20 ppm (parts per million) or less.

Other oxidizers are more controversial, especially within the artisan baking community. *Potassium bromate* is perhaps the most infamous. Some bakers appreciate it because its strengthening characteristics become apparent only during the final proof and the early bake—long after shaping has taken place. It gives better volume and more attractive openings where the crust is cut. Unfortunately, it has been determined that potassium bromate can cause cancer in laboratory animals. California and Oregon have banned its use in flour sold without printed warnings, and it is similarly prohibited as an additive in a number of foreign countries.

Bleaching Agents

Historically, people in most of Western Europe and North America are raised to prefer white bread over whole-grain varieties, perhaps because it has a less bitter taste profile or because of its comparatively light texture. Bakers have inevitably responded by making more and more white bread, and millers obliged by offering flours treated with bleach to ensure the whitest possible color.

Benzoyl peroxide is added to some flours purely for the purpose of destroying the *carotene pigments* that give white flour a natural creamy hue. The chemical reaction caused by adding benzoyl peroxide not only makes the crumb seem artificially white but also destroys important aromas and subtle flavors that derive from those pigments. There are absolutely no practical advantages to its use, and there are suspicions about its dietary effects, so artisan bakers are generally discouraged from including benzoyl peroxide in the flours they use.

Chlorine dioxide (chlorine gas) is sometimes used as a bleaching agent. It has the same bleaching effects as benzoyl peroxide but also alters the starch in flour and gives it added strength. This doesn't have any practical use in the higher-protein flours used to make bread (although most bread flour is still bleached), but it can be useful in baking cakes. Cake flour has little gluten, so the structural advantages of chlorine-bleached flour seem to trump the concerns cake bakers have about using it. Almost all cake flours are bleached. Usually, the only alternative for cake bakers who don't want bleaching is to find the lowest-protein pastry flour available. Artisan bread bakers *never* use bleached flour—they prefer the ivory crumb, pronounced aromas, and pleasant flavors created with unbleached flour.

ADA

Azodicarbonamide (ADA) is classified as a bleaching agent, but it acts more like an oxidizer because it has significant effects on flour maturation. Soon after flour is milled, its performance characteristics in dough are generally characterized by too much extensibility and insufficient strength. The gradual absorption of oxygen from the air can eliminate the problem, but until it has aged 2–3 weeks, it is referred to in the trade as *green flour*. ADA can provide even green flour with enough strength to be used soon after milling, which means millers can spend less money storing flour too green to ship and use in baking. Most serious artisan bakers prefer to age their flour naturally for the time required to give it sufficient strength; they thus avoid using ADA, which merely speeds a perfectly natural process.

The Milling Process

Initially, turning grain into flour, or *milling* it, was done solely to create a meal or powder that more readily absorbed water. While this is still central to the process of milling, today's process is much more involved because bakers demand flours that meet stricter specifications. The procedure for getting from whole grain to white powder has become more technical and controlled.

Wheat grains are first cleaned and separated from foreign objects like stones, insects, and metal shards by running them through special sieves that remove particles different in size from the grain. Magnets are used to collect metal contaminants.

TEMPERING WHEAT GRAINS

To help achieve a clean separation between the bran on the outside and the endosperm on the inside, wheat grains are soaked in water for a period in a process called *tempering* or conditioning. Mills in North America usually temper wheat for 5–8 hours, while in France and other parts of Europe they may devote 24 or even 48 hours to this stage. After the grains are tempered, they undergo an additional period of cleaning.

The miller begins the process of tempering by soaking the grain in water to create a difference in consistency between the endosperm and its skin, with the skin becoming tougher and the endosperm softer. This makes it easier for corrugated steel rollers to scrape away the bran before the endosperm is broken apart or further reduced. If the tempering stage is too short or eliminated altogether, much of the bran clings to the endosperm as it's ground into a powder, yielding a flour sprinkled with tiny bits of bran that are difficult to remove.

The initial set of corrugated rollers is known as the *first break rollers*. If the tempering was effective, the grain breaks into a number of relatively large pieces, each with varying specific weights, and the bran is mostly separated from the endosperm. By directing strong air currents at the first break while the grain passes through, pieces with different weights are blown into different troughs, or streams, which, after further reduction into powder, are reassembled into flours that possess the specified protein and ash levels.

EXTRACTION RATE OF FLOUR

The percentage of flour that remains after all the separating and reduction is complete is called the flour's *extraction rate*. It is typical for the white flour made from the entire wheat berry—known as *straight flour*—to be 73–76% of the weight of the original wheat before milling, which is an extraction rate of 73–76%. Some white flours, called *patent flours*, have considerably lower extractions rates; these are quite low in ash because they are ground from fragments of the center of the berry, far away from the bran. The outer region of the endosperm can be ground into flour with a slightly grayish color; this is called *clear flour*. The patent flours cost more than straight flour or clear flour and are prized by some for their perceived purity of color and high protein, but they can be too strong for easy extension and have less of the minerals that microorganisms need during fermentation. Clear flours, though higher in protein and minerals, have less strength than straight or patent flours, and their darker color makes them good candidates for blending into some varieties of rye bread.

The ash level of a flour is primarily used to evaluate its bran content. In addition, it can be used as an indirect reflection of the flour's extraction rate. High ash levels indicate higher than normal levels of microscopic bran bits in the flour. The closer we get to the bran layer when milling, the more incidental bits of bran get into the flour, so the ash level is also higher.

Key Terms

starch	*sound*
glucose	*malted*
amylose	*fungal amylase*
amylopectin	*enrichment*
native starch	*oxidizers*
damaged starch	*ascorbic acid*
enzymes	*proofing*
endosperm	*potassium bromate*
amylase	*benzoyl peroxide*
gelatinize	*carotene pigments*
pentosans	*chlorine dioxide*
protein	*azodicarbonamide*
soluble proteins	*green flour*
insoluble proteins	*milling*
glutenin	*tempering*
gliadin	*first break rollers*
gluten	*extraction rate*
farinograph	*straight flour*
alveograph	*patent flours*
slurry	*clear flour*
falling number	

advanced
topic #

2

Advanced Baker's Percentage

Using Pre-Ferments in Formula Creation

In *Chapter 3,* we covered introductory mathematical concepts to help you predict dough characteristics, spot abnormalities in formulas, and create your own formulas for breads made from a straight dough.

You probably have experience using pre-ferments in bread making by now. Because pre-ferments utilize a portion of the flour and water within a formula, their presence on the list of ingredients can make creating a formula seem a bit more complicated than the straight dough formulas in *Chapter 3.* At the least, if we don't maintain a concise format for presenting the additional information that relates to pre-ferments, we won't be able to preserve our goal of getting the pertinent information in one snapshot.

Table A2.1 shows a list of ingredients for making a predetermined batch size for baguette dough: flour, water, yeast, and salt. The table lists the ingredients, their percentage relationships, and their individual weights.

TABLE A2.1 Ingredients Necessary to Create a Straight Dough for Baguettes

INGREDIENTS	BAKER'S %	STRAIGHT DOUGH
Bread flour	100%	1000g
Water	68%	680g
Salt	2%	20g
Instant yeast	0.7%	7g
TOTAL WEIGHT		1707g

Percentage Sum:	1.707 (170.7%)
Total Flour:	1000g

If you wanted to make a straight dough for baguettes, the ingredients illustrated in the table, measured as they are, would work well, as long as you use a classic direct method to ferment the dough (see *Chapter 5*) and allow at least 4–5 hours for the bulk fermentation. The baguettes from this dough will likely be flavorful and aromatic.

If you wish to make the same size batch of baguettes in less time, however, and didn't want to mix them intensively to mature the dough more quickly, you must use a pre-ferment. Most pre-ferments are mixtures of flour, water, and a small amount of yeast—much like baguette dough itself. Still, while the list of ingredients in the dough may not change much, the inclusion of a pre-ferment changes how we account for *total* flour and water in a formula.

We select poolish as our pre-ferment. If we used old dough (*pâte fermentée*) instead, we would have to account for the significant amount of salt and yeast present in that pre-ferment.

Table A2.2 shows how the inclusion of the poolish changes how we account for all the ingredients in the final, adjusted dough. The expanded table records the same information listed in Table A2.1 as well as the flour, water, and yeast set aside for the poolish. In the "Adjusted Dough" column on the far right of the table, we list the ingredients necessary to make our baguette dough by using the pre-ferment poolish and subtracting its ingredients from the flour and water in the original straight dough. Note that the amount of yeast in the poolish is so small (about an eighth of 1g) it doesn't measurably affect the total yeast in the formula. This is usually the case when we subtract the ingredients in a long-fermented sponge or poolish from a straight dough; the yeast quantity in the pre-ferment is so small we don't bother accounting for it when calculating the adjusted dough. Even when we do, as in Table A2.2, the effects on the calculation are so minuscule as to make their inclusion meaningless.

The major exception is when you decide to use old dough as your pre-ferment. Because old dough is simply leftover baguette dough, in most cases, its higher levels of yeast and its significant level of salt require that we account for those ingredients in the table's "Pre-ferment" column when subtracting the old dough's ingredients from the original straight dough.

Neither firm levain nor liquid levain has added yeast or salt, so their inclusion as a pre-ferment means you must list only their flour and water weights in the "Pre-Ferment" column before subtracting them from the straight dough.

TABLE A2.2 The Altered List of Ingredients Necessary to Make the Same Size Batch of Baguette Dough, But with the Inclusion of a Poolish

INGREDIENTS	BAKER'S %	STRAIGHT DOUGH	PRE-FERMENT	ADJUSTED DOUGH
Bread flour	100%	1000g	250g	750g
Water	68%	680g	250g	430g
Salt	2%	20g	0g	20g
Instant yeast	0.7%	7g	0.13g	7g (rounded)
Poolish	_____	_____	500g (rounded)	500g (rounded)
TOTAL WEIGHT		1707g		1707g

Percentage Sum:	1.707 (170.7%)		% Pre-Fermented Flour:	25%
Total Flour:	1000g		% Hydration of Pre-Ferm.:	100%

Which Pre-Ferment Should You Use?

How do we decide which pre-ferment to use, and how much should we use? These are questions you must decide for yourself, but the decision should not be arbitrary. You should take into account the unique characteristics of any given pre-ferment, the flavor profile you wish to achieve, the secondary effects that might complicate the process, or—as a more mundane consideration—which pre-ferments are practical to produce in your bakery. Factors like ambient temperature of the bakery, refrigeration capacity, and whether or not people are there around the clock can make some of those decisions for you. Sponge can be easy to mix and maintain, but it can make baguettes difficult to extend. Poolish is trickier to handle, and levain requires periodic feeding on a set schedule. For more guidance about the characteristics of individual pre-ferments, see *Chapter 5*.

Once you have decided what type of pre-ferment to use, you must calculate how much to use by deciding how much of the flour in the dough you wish to ferment ahead of time. In our case, we might decide to ferment 25% of the total flour in the dough by making it into a poolish. We enter the percentage of flour we wish to pre-ferment on a new line that appears to the bottom right of the expanded table in Table A2.2. Just below that entry, we enter the hydration rate for the poolish, which is 100% (meaning the water in the poolish is the same weight as the flour). The flour we wish to ferment ahead of time is borrowed from the total flour in the original straight dough, and the water used to hydrate the poolish is taken from the total water used in the original straight dough.

The two batches of dough illustrated in Tables A2.1 and A2.2 are the same size overall, and the percentage relationships between the ingredients in each dough is the same. For instance, bread flour is expressed as 100%, water as 68%, salt as 2%, and instant yeast as 0.7% for each version of the dough. The weights recorded in the "Straight Dough" column are also identical for the two formulas.

When we list the ingredient quantities for the poolish in the "Pre-Ferment" column and subtract them from the values in the "Straight Dough" column, we obtain the weights for each ingredient to be recombined later with the poolish to create our final, adjusted dough. The total weight of the dough after we recombine all ingredients (the total of the values in the "Adjusted Dough" column) are the same as if we had simply mixed all the ingredients in the original straight dough without bothering to pre-ferment anything.

When we decide to include a pre-ferment in our formula, then, and we wish the formula to give us the same size batch as the original straight dough version, we simply expand the original table that records the ingredients used. The new table is larger—and possibly a bit more intimidating—but the mathematical calculations used to figure the adjusted dough formula are straightforward. It's just a matter of subtraction. Once you understand what the number in each box represents, the logic of the final dough adjustments becomes obvious.

3

Controlling Fermentation: Living and Nonliving Players

Controlling Yeast Activity

Of the two major by-products of yeast fermentation, it is carbon dioxide gas (CO_2) we most wish to control. Of course, alcohol production proceeds hand in hand with CO_2 production, but the alcohol burns off when bread is baked, and its side effects in fermented dough generally pose no problem. As CO_2 accumulates in bread dough during fermentation, it migrates toward air cells that were created in the gluten fabric of the dough during the mixing process. These air cells grow in size as more CO_2 gas is generated by the yeast. The gluten can stretch and accommodate the growth of the air cells to a great degree without breaking, but it cannot do so indefinitely. Unless we intervene by deflating the dough mass or placing the loaves in an oven, the raw dough will continue to expand and finally collapse when the gluten strands can be stretched no further.

When a mass of dough or a finished loaf accumulates too much CO_2 gas and reaches the point of collapse, it has lost its ability to hold gas and is said to be *overproofed*. Overproofed loaves that collapse no longer exhibit the open air cells and light texture that characterize leavened bread. Overproofing is irreversible; the gluten structure of the dough or loaf is literally torn apart from too much gas pressure, and the gluten bonds cannot be repaired.

If we gain control over the rate of yeast fermentation, we can regulate the production of CO_2 and keep the gas from accumulating too rapidly before we are ready to shape loaves or bake the bread. We can then schedule our bread production to have fermented dough ready and finished loaves properly risen on a timetable that suits our needs. We can manipulate three factors in the creation of bread dough to control the fermentation activity of yeast: the time allowed for fermenting the dough, the temperature of the dough and its environment, and the hydration (water content) of the dough.

TIME, TEMPERATURE, AND HYDRATION

As time proceeds, yeast cells feeding on simple sugars use up those sugars and produce gradually more and more CO_2 and alcohol. If we reduce the time allowed for fermentation, we reduce the amount of sugars used up and limit the production of carbon dioxide. That doesn't necessarily mean we should make a habit of minimizing fermentation times in making bread dough (see "Controlling Bacterial Activity" below), but we should be aware of all the effects of shortened fermentation times.

For instance, when making loaves to be refrigerated overnight (see *Chapter 7* and *Chapter 10*), it is generally wise to limit bulk fermentation of the dough to 30 minutes or so, thereby ensuring that gases produced as the loaves slowly grow do not lead to overproofing.

Generally, as the temperature of a dough or pre-ferment increases, the rate of yeast fermentation also increases. If the same temperatures are lowered, the rate decreases by a similar proportion. Yeast cells can live at 33–138°F, but their optimal temperature for maximum gas and alcohol production is around 95°F. Some bakers proof their shaped loaves at 95° or higher to speed production, but when the loaves are that warm, the margin of error in judging their readiness for the oven is narrow. It is wiser to use a more moderate temperature—76–80°F—for both bulk fermenting the dough and for proofing the shaped loaves before baking.

Controlling Bacterial Activity

The presence or absence of lactic bacteria in bread dough is the factor with the greatest impact on the baked bread's flavor. The two types of lactic bacteria (see *Chapter 5*) prefer two entirely different environments, so if you can control the environment in which bread dough is fermented, you can control the levels of each type of bacteria in the dough.

TIME, TEMPERATURE, AND HYDRATION

The factors we monitor to control bacterial activity in bread dough are the same as for controlling yeast activity. As the time of fermentation increases, the level of bacteria increases—to a point. When all the sugars in a dough are used up, or when the acids from fermentation become too concentrated, the bacteria begin to die, but as long as fresh food and water are available and you don't wait too long, populations of bacteria increase. The speed at which they increase, though, is slow compared to yeast. Dough made from manufactured yeast generally must be fermented at least 3–4 hours to allow enough time for lactic bacteria to accumulate and contribute acids for flavor development.

Homofermentative bacteria increase dramatically between 70°F and 90°F. Heterofermentative bacteria thrive when the temperature is cooler—50–65°F. So higher temperatures during bulk fermentation and proofing tend to increase homofermentative bacteria and their primary by-product, which is mild lactic acid. Conversely, if we reduce ambient temperature during fermentation, we increase the numbers of heterofermentative bacteria, which produce both lactic and the sharper-flavored acetic acid. Higher temperatures produce a milder taste, while lower temperatures tend to create a more sour flavor profile.

Water levels in dough also effect bacterial activity. Homofermentative bacteria prefer dough that is wet, so adding water to a dough increases their number. Heterofermentative bacteria do better in drier environments, so reducing the water content of a dough or pre-ferment leads to an increase in their number and the quantity of acetic acid they produce.

Enzymes: Amylase and Protease

As wheat in a field gets closer to the time of going to seed, amylase is produced within the wheat kernel to degrade its starch granules into sugars that can be converted to energy for the future seedling. Farmers try to harvest their wheat crop before the levels of amylase in the wheat berries gets too high, which would result in bread dough with sticky handling qualities and a too-rapid fermentation. Millers test flour for amylase content and make corrections to it by adding either malted barley flour or fungal amylase (amylase created with a type of fungus). Their object in correcting the flour for amylase levels is to offer a product that ferments predictably and reliably every time it is used.

The enzyme protease generally does not require augmentation to be effective in bread dough. It is present naturally in flour in enough concentration to, if given time, gradually weaken the dough. Bakers count on that happening when they use an autolyse period while mixing dough (see *Chapter 4*) or when adding poolish or liquid levain (see *Chapter 5*) to it. These liquid pre-ferments contain so much water that, as they sit before use, their protease activity increases dramatically, and they can jump-start the process of protein degradation and make otherwise tight bread dough more extensible in less time.

Unfortunately, perhaps, protease continues to degrade the protein structure over time, and if you must hold finished raw loaves in a refrigerator overnight, the reduction in dough strength can lead to their collapse after they rise in the refrigerator. While protease has no direct effect on the process of fermentation, its weakening effect on long-fermented loaves can affect how long you can ferment them without risking collapse. As we suggested in *Chapter 2* with respect to changing ingredients, if you change the length of the fermentation you use to proof your bread, you not only affect when the loaves are ready for baking but also change the structure of the bread itself. Any modifications you adopt in formulating or fermenting your bread must respect not only the changes you intend (such as a more convenient bake time the next morning) but also the secondary changes (such as weakened structure) that may pose problems if they are not addressed.

The overall level of enzyme activity in dough (whether amylase, protease, or zymase) can be controlled to some degree by manipulating the same three environmental factors we use to control yeast and bacteria: time, temperature, and hydration. Longer fermentation times, naturally, allow for a greater effect of enzymes on the dough itself, and shorter times do the opposite. Higher temperatures tend to elevate the level of enzyme activity in bread dough, while lower ones usually reduce it (though not eliminate it entirely). Higher water levels allow for easier movement of enzymes in dough and so increase enzyme activity, while lower water levels characteristic of firm doughs and pre-ferments reduce enzyme activity considerably.

Decorative
Dough Pieces

Working with Decorative Dough

Pastry students often work with edible foodstuffs such as sugar, marzipan, and chocolate to create decorative items for cakes. Some students also advance to making entire artistic showpieces from the same materials.

The skills learned in those crafts can usually be applied to working with decorative bread dough. It is beyond the scope of this book to provide in-depth lessons in shaping decorative pieces with bread dough, but basic aspects of the process are illustrated.

Types of Decorative Dough

Decorative dough that contains yeast is referred to as *active decorative dough*. If it contains no yeast, it falls into the broad category of *dead dough*. Many lean, yeasted doughs from your regular repertoire can be shaped into leaves, flowers, or grapes, and they can sometimes be rolled into strands for weaving mats.

Problems can arise when using regular bread dough for these purposes. If you let the dough ferment for long, it will be full of gas. The gas that makes bread light in texture and enjoyable to eat may also distort the shape you made. In fact, for fairly elaborate woven pieces, the dough strands may grow significantly even as you work with them. To avoid this problem, most yeasted dough made for decorative purposes has far less yeast than dough made for eating loaves. Another option, of course, is to work with non-yeasted or dead dough.

There are still other considerations for formulating a decorative dough. Conventional bread flour is strong and often resistant to easy extension or shaping. For this reason, you might choose other flours to displace bread flour in whole or in part to make extensibility less problematic. A weaker white flour, such as all-purpose or pastry flour, might be better, or you might use a variety of rye flour called *white rye*. White rye is milled from the center of the rye berry and features less bran, so it is lighter in color, and rye flour's low gluten content helps make extension fairly easy. Other flours with no gluten can be included to make dough more extensible, and larger, irregularly ground pieces of bran in the mix can further degrade protein strength and make the dough easier to shape.

Decorative dough might not color well in the absence of long fermentation, so sugar is almost always added to its formulation. Sugar can have another beneficial effect in decorative dough: It tenderizes the dough and allows for greater extension and less elasticity.

Decorative dough should be drier than most bread dough to keep it from being sticky and unmanageable. There are times when you need to undo what you have just assembled or just want to try a certain arrangement to see how it would look without committing to it. Moist or sticky dough can make that difficult to achieve, so we aim to hydrate decorative dough—whether yeasted or dead—so it requires no flour at all on the bench surface as we work with it.

It is perfectly acceptable to work exclusively with one dough color, but many bakers prefer to explore other options for coloration. If you are looking for a mono-chromatic presentation, then, after baking, you may wish to apply caramel color to parts of your dead dough piece to highlight certain features or provide contrast. Yeasted decorative dough is almost always colored ahead of time if contrast is desired. Mixing in cocoa powder with the dough makes this option easy.

Other edible items you can use to color dead dough include fruit or vegetable powders, such as spinach powder or beet powder, which can be effective and are easily added during the mixing process. Spices can also be useful here—turmeric for a flat gold or yellowish color, chili powder or paprika for a reddish brown. Avoid using cayenne, as the volatile oils it contains are so concentrated you may experience discomfort while working with it.

Plain frozen spinach can be drained and its liquid used to make special syrups for coloring dough. Beet juice from canned beets or carrot juice can be made to work here, too. If you are interested in an unconventional look, dough pieces of different colors can be combined and reworked into one. This yields a marbled effect, which can be accentuated by further flattening, folding, and sheeting the dough a few times before using it.

Yeasted dough pieces must be proofed briefly to look attractive after they have been baked. If a shine is desired, you can apply egg wash to the surface before baking it.

Dead dough pieces are usually made from weaker dough than are yeasted decorative doughs. They depend more on starch than on gluten to hold the final piece together. If we bake dead dough pieces soon after we shape them, they may not lose enough moisture to ensure their structural stability. For this reason, it is common to allow a day or even longer for dead dough pieces to dry before baking (as long as you are not in a time-limited competition). A slow, steady rate of moisture evaporation before baking seems to reduce cracking as well.

Yeasted decorative pieces are baked almost like any other yeasted dough, but baking dead dough can be a bit different. Your goal with the dead dough piece is to dry it completely to make the starches quite rigid and strong enough to withstand gravity. It may swell a little in the oven, but it will not grow in size. It usually seems softer during baking than it was before it entered the oven, but after baking, if the pieces are not massive, they should continue to lose moisture as they cool and dry to sufficient hardness.

Following this text, in the *Appendix of Formulas*, are four formulas for decorative dough: two active doughs suitable for weaving flat centerpieces, and two dead

Figure A4.1a Making letters.

Figure A4.1b Assembling words.

Figure A.4.1c Pieces for plaque before assembly.

Figure A4.1d Rear view of finished product once assembly is complete.

doughs that can be used in creating rigid decorations or showpieces. Suggested baking temperatures and times are included with the formulas, and items that can be easily fashioned are illustrated.

Figures A4.1a–d illustrate steps in the technique for making a plaque with a cornucopia. Refer to the color insert following page 114 for additional steps in this process as well as a photo of the finished product.

Figures A4.2a–d illustrate the assembly of a dead dough centerpiece featuring a rooster with decorative flowers and feathers. Additional steps associated with the construction of this dead dough centerpiece are in the color insert following page 114.

Figure A4.2a Rooster pieces cut and baked.

Figure A4.2b Pieces for rooster centerpiece assembly.

Figure A.4.2c Rooster assembly.

Figure A4.2d Rear view of finished product once assembly is complete.

Appendix
of Formulas

An Introduction
to the Formulas

Batch Sizing and Formulation

In designing these formulas, we have selected batch sizes that maximize the capacity 5-quart bowls and 20-quart bowls on planetary mixers. Market feedback indicates these are the most common sizes used by baking and pastry students. Alternatively, if you need to create a different-sized batch, then *Chapter 3* and the *Advanced Topic #2* can instruct you in the methods for doing so.

All baker's percentages that pertain to the formula weights are listed just to the right of the straight dough ingredient quantities. The straight dough representation is listed for all formulas in case the instructor or student prefers to mix a straight dough (that is, with no pre-ferment) and has the time for a good, long bulk fermentation. In the case of dough leavened solely with levain (sourdough starter), however (see *Chapter 5*), using the straight dough representation requires adding manufactured yeast and will yield a dough that isn't actually a sourdough at all. Recommended adjustments for converting a sourdough to a straight dough with manufactured yeast are noted in formulas that require it.

If class time is short, you may want to make a pre-ferment ahead of time and mix the adjusted dough listed below many of the straight dough formulas. That should provide you with dough maturity in 1½–2 hours (except for most true sourdoughs, which can take twice that long).

If time is short and you *still* need to mix a straight dough, you should probably adopt the intensive mix method (see *Chapter 4*) and use an instant yeast percentage near 0.7% of the total flour weight in the formula. This method will certainly yield less flavor than the short mix or improved mix methods, but it should get your dough to maturity in 30–60 minutes. (See the description for these mixing methods below.)

The quantities of water listed in the formulas were based on using a bread flour with a protein level of 11%, milled from hard winter wheat, and stored in an air-conditioned environment. The age of the flour, the wheat used, its moisture level, and your particular storage conditions will create differences in characteristics from the ones we used here. You may need to adjust water levels by one or two percentage points to get the dough consistency you expect—no two runs of flour are completely alike.

SCALING

We started with fairly round flour weights in the straight doughs and then let the ingredient percentages (and any pre-ferment requirements) in the formula determine the other quantities. With the 5-quart batches, this meant the quantity of yeast in a pre-ferment might be very small. These smaller quantities are more easily measured in grams than in ounces, so we strongly suggest you use metric units in scaling dough whenever you are able.

If you're lucky enough to have a scale that measures in fractions of a gram, then you may have less trouble scaling minute quantities, but in the more likely event you don't, you can approximate the correct quantity by scaling an entire gram and then using a paring knife or other blade to cut it into halves, thirds, fourths, and so on. Even in this case, using grams instead of ounces as the unit of measurement will yield more accurate quantities of salt or yeast.

All the metric quantities are listed in grams rather than decimal kilograms because most of the quantities listed are not large, and getting U.S. students to feel comfortable with metric quantities seems easier when they don't have to keep moving decimal places back and forth. When all metric quantities are expressed simply as grams, with a few instances of fractions of a gram, getting through the math when developing formulas is easier.

The U.S. measurements are expressed in pounds and decimal ounces. One of the obvious disadvantages of the U.S. weight system is that (unlike the metric system) it is not based on units of 10 but rather on units of 16. This means that if we want to analyze or expand a U.S. formula using baker's percentage principles (see *Chapter 3*), we must mentally convert, for example, 4 lb 5.75 oz flour to 64 oz + 5.75 oz to 69.75 oz just for one ingredient, and then repeat that process for each ingredient in the formula before we're able to make use of the information. You might also need to make those conversions in your head before weighing the ingredients, depending on the capabilities of your scale.

On the other hand, 1,525 g flour need not be converted to any other expression as long as you have a scale that measures in grams. Also, even when you have converted all your pounds and ounces to decimal ounces, the prospect of scaling 0.06 oz yeast might be impractical or even impossible.

Mixing and Other Procedures

For most lean doughs, like baguettes or *pain au levain*, you have a choice of several mixing methods. For quick reference purposes, we describe the three classic mechanical methods for French breads below. For a more in-depth explanation of how these mixing methods differ, or why you might prefer one to another, consult *Chapter 4*. Eventually, you may choose to develop a hybrid method that doesn't exactly fit any definition we have given. That can work well, of course, but a thorough understanding of the three methods defined here will help you decide what mixing speeds or times to select and will help you predict changes in your dough if you alter the mixing process in any way.

To be certain you have control of the rate of fermentation, please take seriously the recommendations about calculating the proper water temperature. If you wildly guess at what water temperature to use (or use whatever temperature you have from the tap), you surrender much of the fermentation control you're trying to achieve, and consistent results are unlikely. The goal temperature for every dough is listed in its formula. A discussion of how to calculate the proper water temperature for mixing bread dough is located on page 54 in *Chapter 4*.

THREE METHODS FOR MIXING FRENCH-STYLE BREADS

Whichever mixing method you use, and whether or not you use a pre-ferment, the dough must reach maturity before it can be easily handled, so the times mentioned are only estimates.

Consult *Chapter 5* for a more in-depth discussion of dough maturity.

Short Mix Method

1. Mix 12–15 minutes on first speed. Empty the dough into a tub lightly sprinkled with flour and cover.

2. Bulk ferment 3–4 hours, depending on pre-ferment used, or 4–5 hours if using none (straight dough) or making a sourdough with no manufactured yeast.

3. Perform a set of stretch-and-folds on the dough every 15–20 minutes at least 4–5 times—more if necessary. The dough will gradually get smoother and stronger.

Intensive Mix Method

1. Mix 5 minutes on first speed, then 8–15 minutes on second speed. Empty the dough into a tub lightly sprinkled with flour and cover.

2. Bulk ferment 30 minutes if using a pre-ferment, or up to 60 minutes if using none (straight dough). The intensive method is not appropriate for a sourdough that uses no manufactured yeast.

3. The dough should not require any folds to achieve its strength.

Improved Mix Method

1. Mix 5 minutes on first speed, then 3–5 minutes on second speed. Empty the dough into a tub lightly sprinkled with flour and cover.

2. Bulk ferment 1–2 hours, depending on pre-ferment used, or up to 3 hours if using none (straight dough) or making a sourdough with no manufactured yeast.

3. Perform a set of stretch-and-folds after 20–30 minutes of fermentation. A second set is optional if the dough appears to need more strength, but be aware that more strength can mean less extensibility. The dough will improve noticeably in strength over the period of its bulk fermentation.

AFTER MIXING

After you have mixed your dough, you will generally follow these procedures to ferment, divide, shape, proof, and bake.

Scaling

◆ True baguettes are scaled at around 350 g (12 oz), but plumper versions (called *parisiennes*) are scaled at 500 g (18oz). Shorter, skinnier ones (*ficelles*) are scaled at 175 g (6 oz).

◆ A *bâtard* (log-shaped loaf) or *boulot* (oval loaf) is scaled at 400–1000 g (14 oz–2 lb 4 oz).

◆ *Boules* (rounds) can be anywhere from 200 g (7 oz) for a *petite boule* to 2,000 grams (5 lb) for a large *miche*.

◆ Rolls (*petits pains*) are typically scaled at 60–100 g (2–3 oz).

◆ Pan loaves are scaled according to the capacity of the bread pan. Lean white breads might be scaled at 1 lb 12 oz–2 lb for a 9-inch rectangular pan, while dense whole wheat breads need more dough to get the same volume—perhaps 2 lb–2 lb 4 oz. Smaller or larger pans require less or more dough respectively.

Proofing

◆ Proof *baguettes*, ideally, on floured, couche-covered boards, seam-side down, with large pleats between about 6 loaves per board. They can be proofed in perforated, scalloped pans if you bake in a convection or rack oven. Parchment-lined sheet pans can be used, but the baguettes can lose their symmetry and become a bit flat. Proof 60–90 minutes for most baguettes, or 2–3 hours for sourdough.

◆ *Bâtards* and *boulots* can be proofed either right-side up in pleated couche or upside-down in oblong proofing baskets. Parchment-lined sheet pans are usable, but the loaves often lose their symmetry and some of their height. Proof 60–90 minutes for most loaves, but 2–3 hours for sourdough.

◆ *Boules* made from moderately wet dough are easier to proof upside-down in round proofing baskets, but any strong dough can be shaped into rounds that are proofed seam-side down on floured proofing boards (for deck ovens) or directly on parchment-lined sheet pans. Proof 70–90 minutes for most boules, but 2–3½ hours for sourdough.

◆ For convenience, *rolls* are often proofed in a 4 × 5 or 5 × 6 arrangement on parchment-lined sheet pans. Some artisans prefer to proof them on boards or couche and bake them directly on the hearth of a deck oven. Rolls usually proof quickly—30–60 minutes in most cases, or 45–90 minutes for sourdough.

◆ All loaves and rolls are best proofed in a heat- and humidity-controlled proofer at about 80°F (27°C) and 80% humidity.

◆ If a proofer is not available, cover the rack holding the boards and keep it as close to 80°F (27°C) as possible. Putting water-soaked towels on a sheet tray and locating it directly under the bread-loaded trays can provide limited humidity.

Baking

◆ *Load and score loaves where appropriate.* Load the loaves on your peel or mechanical loader, score if appropriate (see *Chapter 8*), and place in the preheated oven (oven temperature varies by bread type; consult individual formulas for recommended baking temperatures).

◆ *Steam hearth breads before and after inserting the loaves.* Bread made from rich dough and many pan breads generally don't need steam, so check the steam recommendations in the formulas.

◆ *Baguettes*—Bake at 460–480°F (240–250°C), or 25–40°F less for convection or rack ovens.

◆ For baguettes, adjust oven temperatures to achieve the correct bake in 22–25 minutes. Shorter bake times tend to leave too much moisture in the baguettes, thus softening the crust; longer times may make for a thick crust and a dry interior.

◆ *Boules, bâtards, and boulots*—425–440°F (220–230°C) for 30–35 minutes or longer if necessary, or 25–40°F less for convection or rack ovens

◆ *Rolls*—450–500°F (235–260°C) for 12–18 minutes, depending on size and type, or 25–40°F less for convection or rack ovens.

◆ *Pan breads and loaves from rich dough*—350–375°F (175–190°C) or even less if premature browning is an issue, or 25–40°F less for rack or convection ovens. Check individual formulas for special baking temperatures.

Generally, the larger the loaf, the lower the temperature and the longer the bake time should be. For small loaves or rolls, the opposite is true.

Cooling

Cool (without crowding the loaves) on a rack with wire shelves. Cooling the loaves is an important part of the baking cycle. Accelerate cooling and reduce the chance of a soggy crust by spacing the loaves 1–2 inches apart as they cool.

BAGELS

	Metric		U.S. Measure		Formula Baker's %
	(1X)	**(4X)**	**(1X)**	**(4X)**	
	5-Qt Mixer	**20-Qt Mixer**	**5-Qt Mixer**	**20-Qt Mixer**	
STRAIGHT DOUGH					
High-gluten flour	1000g	4000g	2 lb 8oz	10 lb 0.0oz	**100.0%**
Water	600g	2400g	1 lb 8oz	6 lb 0.0oz	**60.0%**
Diastatic malt powder	3g	12g	0.1oz	0.5oz	**0.3%**
Salt	22g	88g	0.9oz	3.5oz	**2.2%**
Instant yeast	4g	16g	0.2oz	0.6oz	**0.4%**
TOTAL YIELD	**1629g**	**6516g**	**4 lb 1.2oz**	**16 lb 4.6oz**	
					Pre-Ferment Baker's %
Firm Levain					
High-gluten flour	*80g*	*320g*	*3.2oz*	*12.8oz*	*100.0%*
Water	*48g*	*192g*	*1.9oz*	*7.7oz*	*60.0%*
Ripe levain (not used in final dough)	*80g*	*320g*	*3.2oz*	*12.8oz*	*100.0%*
Subtotal	*128g*	*832g*	*5.1oz*	*1 lb 4.5oz*	
	5-Qt Mixer	**20-Qt Mixer**	**5-Qt Mixer**	**20-Qt Mixer**	
ADJUSTED DOUGH					
Bread flour	920g	3680g	2 lb 4.8oz	9 lb 3.2oz	
Water	552g	2208g	1 lb 6.1oz	5 lb 8.3oz	
Diastatic malt powder	3g	12g	0.1oz	0.5oz	
Salt	22g	88g	0.9oz	3.5oz	
Instant yeast	4g	16g	0.2oz	0.6oz	
Firm levain (from above)	128g	512g	5.1oz	1 lb 4.5oz	
TOTAL YIELD	**1629g**	**6516g**	**4 lb 1.2oz**	**16 lb 4.6oz**	

NOTE: This bread may be made using only the ingredients and quantities listed in the straight dough. If you made firm levain using the quantities specified above, you would subtract those ingredient weights from the straight dough to arrive at the quantities listed for the adjusted dough. Mix and hold the levain, covered but slightly vented, at 70°F for 12 hours before mixing the final dough.

Pre-Fermented Flour:	8%
Hydr. of Pre-Ferment:	60%

GOAL TEMPERATURE: 74°F (23°C).

MIXING METHOD: Improved mix—see p. 196.

BULK FERMENT: 30–60 minutes. If the dough is too warm, you may need to cover and refrigerate it until it reaches the goal temperature. Finished bagels are held in the refrigerator overnight, so don't let the dough develop too much gas before dividing and shaping.

SCALING: 4 oz (115 g). Cut the portions from narrow strips of dough. Have a couple of people scale the pieces as others shape them.

SHAPING:

1. Roll each portion into a strand about 10 inches long, deflating the dough as you do this.

2. Wrap one strand around the knuckles of your dominant hand, with the ends of the strand overlapping near your palm.

3. Roll the overlapped ends over and back against the bench to seal the bagel. Place the shaped bagels (12 per board) on a cornmeal-covered proofing board the size of a full sheet pan. Holes should be 2–2¼ inches wide.

4. Place the filled boards on a covered speed rack as you work.

PROOFING:

1. Place the covered rack in a refrigerated walk-in immediately, cinching the loose ends of the plastic covering the rack to minimize moisture loss, or zipping it tightly, if you have that sort of closure.

2. Hold under refrigeration overnight. Keep cold until just before boiling the next day.

BOILING:

1. The next day, prepare a large but shallow pot of boiling water—2–3 gallons—and add about 8 oz malt syrup, aiming to give the water an amber-colored appearance.

2. Prepare 1 parchment-covered sheet pan for every board of 12 bagels, and stack them near your work area.

3. Prepare a large ice-water bath to cool the bagels after they are boiled.

4. Assemble small cake pans full of sesame or poppy seeds, dried onions rehydrated in water, pretzel salt, or any combination of these.

5. After all preparations have been made, use a spider to drop 4 or more bagels at a time into the water, depending on the diameter of the pot. It's good to boil them for at least 1 full minute, or maybe 2 minutes, but take the proofing state of the bagels into consideration before you boil them. If the bagels proofed too much overnight, reduce their boiling time somewhat to prevent them from collapsing.

6. After boiling, chill immediately in the ice-water bath, drain for a few seconds, and top with seeds or onions (optional) before arranging them 12 per tray to a sprayed, parchment-lined sheet pan.

BAKING: 500°F for 15–20 minutes in a typical deck oven. Set convection or rack ovens 25–50°F cooler.

COOLING: Cool on a rack with wire shelves, or pile the bagels into a wire basket.

BAGUETTES—DIRECT METHOD

STRAIGHT DOUGH	Metric (1X) 5-Qt Mixer	Metric (4X) 20-Qt Mixer	U.S. Measure (1X) 5-Qt Mixer	U.S. Measure (4X) 20-Qt Mixer	Formula Baker's %
Bread flour	1000g	4000g	2 lb 3.0oz	8 lb 12.0oz	100%
Water	700g	2800g	1 lb 7.5oz	6 lb 2.0oz	70%
Salt	20g	80g	0.7oz	2.8oz	2%
Instant yeast	3g	12g	0.1oz	0.4oz	0.3%
TOTAL YIELD	**1723g**	**6892g**	**3 lb 11.3oz**	**15 lb 1.2oz**	

NOTE: The yeast quantity listed in the formula is intended for bakers who use the short mix method. A dough mixed with the intensive mix method should receive a yeast percentage around 0.7%, while the yeast percentage for an improved mix dough would be more appropriately set at 0.4%.

GOAL TEMPERATURE: 77°F (25°C).

MIXING METHOD: Short mix, intensive mix, or improved mix—see pp. 195–196.

BULK FERMENTATION: See directions associated with the mix method chosen, pp. 195–196.

SCALING: See options, p. 196.

SHAPING: See directions in *Chapter 6*.

PROOFING: See directions, pp. 196–197.

BAKING: See directions, p. 197.

COOLING: See directions, p. 198.

BAGUETTES WITH LIQUID LEVAIN

	Metric		U.S. Measure		Formula Baker's %
	(1X)	(4X)	(1X)	(4X)	
	5-Qt Mixer	20-Qt Mixer	5-Qt Mixer	20-Qt Mixer	
STRAIGHT DOUGH					
Bread flour	1000g	4000g	2 lb 3.0oz	8 lb 12.0oz	**100%**
Water	680g	2720g	1 lb 7.8oz	5 lb 15.2oz	**68%**
Salt	20g	80g	0.7oz	2.8oz	**2%**
Instant yeast	7g	28g	0.2oz	1.0oz	**0.7%**
TOTAL YIELD	**1707g**	**6828g**	**3 lb 11.7oz**	**14 lb 14.8oz**	
Liquid Levain					*Pre-Ferment Baker's %*
Bread flour	*100g*	*400g*	*3.5oz*	*14.0oz*	*100%*
Water	*100g*	*400g*	*3.5oz*	*14.0oz*	*100%*
Ripe levain (not used in final dough)	*66g*	*264g*	*2.3oz*	*9.2oz*	*66%*
Subtotal	*266g*	*1064g*	*9.3oz*	*2 lb 5.2oz*	
	5-Qt Mixer	20-Qt Mixer	5-Qt Mixer	20-Qt Mixer	
ADJUSTED DOUGH					
Bread flour	900g	3600g	1 lb 15.5oz	7 lb 14.0oz	
Water	580g	2320g	1 lb 4.3oz	5 lb 1.2 oz	
Salt	20g	80g	0.7oz	2.8oz	
Instant yeast	7g	28g	0.2oz	0.8oz	
Liquid levain (from above)	200g	800g	7.0oz	1 lb 12.0oz	
TOTAL YIELD	**1707g**	**6828g**	**3 lb 11.7oz**	**14 lb 14.8oz**	

NOTE: This bread may be made using only the ingredients and quantities listed for the straight dough, if enough time is available—probably 4–5 hours just for the bulk fermentation—but reduce the instant yeast percentage to about 0.3%. If, instead, you prepare a levain using the quantities specified above, subtract those ingredient weights from the straight dough to arrive at the quantities listed for the adjusted dough. Mix and hold the levain, covered but slightly vented, at 70°F for 12 hours before mixing the final dough.

Pre-Fermented Flour:	10%
Hydr. of Pre-Ferment:	100%

GOAL TEMPERATURE: 77°F (25°C).

MIXING METHOD: Short mix, intensive mix, or improved mix—see pp. 195–196.

BULK FERMENTATION: See directions associated with the mix method chosen, pp. 195–196.

SCALING: See options, p. 196.

SHAPING: See directions in *Chapter 6*.

PROOFING: See directions, pp. 196–197.

BAKING: See directions, p. 197.

COOLING: See directions, p. 198.

BAGUETTES WITH OLD DOUGH

	Metric		U.S. Measure		Formula Baker's %
	(1X)	**(4X)**	**(1X)**	**(4X)**	
	5-Qt Mixer	20-Qt Mixer	5-Qt Mixer	20-Qt Mixer	
STRAIGHT DOUGH					
Bread flour	1000g	400g	2 lb 3.0oz	8 lb 12.0oz	**100%**
Water	680g	2720g	1 lb 7.8oz	5 lb 15.2oz	**68%**
Salt	20g	80g	0.7oz	2.8oz	**2%**
Instant yeast	7g	28g	0.3oz	1.0oz	**0.7%**
TOTAL YIELD	**1707g**	**6828g**	**3 lb 11.8oz**	**14 lb 15.0oz**	
					Pre-Ferment Baker's %
Old Dough					
Bread flour	*250g*	*1000g*	*8.8oz*	*2 lb 3.0oz*	*100%*
Water	*170g*	*680g*	*6.0oz*	*1 lb 8.0oz*	*68%*
Salt	*5g*	*20g*	*0.2oz*	*0.7oz*	*2%*
Instant yeast	*2g*	*7g*	*0.1oz*	*0.3oz*	*0.7%*
Subtotal	*427g*	*1707g*	*15.1oz*	*3 lb 11.8oz*	
	5-Qt Mixer	20-Qt Mixer	5-Qt Mixer	20-Qt Mixer	
ADJUSTED DOUGH					
Bread flour	750g	3000g	1 lb 10.3oz	6 lb 9.0oz	
Water	510g	2040g	1 lb 1.9oz	4 lb 7.4oz	
Salt	15g	60g	0.5oz	2.1oz	
Instant yeast	5g	21g	0.2oz	0.7oz	
Old dough (from above)	420g	1707g	15.1oz	3 lb 11.8oz	
TOTAL YIELD	**1707g**	**6828g**	**3 lb 11.8oz**	**14 lb 15.0oz**	

NOTE: This bread may be made using only the ingredients and quantities listed for the straight dough, if enough time is available—probably 4–5 hours just for the bulk fermentation—but reduce the instant yeast percentage to about 0.3%. If you make old dough using the quantities specified above, subtract those ingredient weights from the straight dough to arrive at the quantities listed for the adjusted dough. Mix the old dough and ferment 3 hours at room temperature, or ferment 1 hour at room temperature and refrigerate until use.

Pre-Fermented Flour:	25%
Hydr. of Pre-Ferment:	100%

GOAL TEMPERATURE: 77°F (25°C).

MIXING METHOD: Short mix, intensive mix, or improved mix—see pp. 195–196.

BULK FERMENTATION: See directions associated with the mix method chosen, pp. 195–196.

SCALING: See options, p. 196.

SHAPING: See directions in *Chapter 6*.

PROOFING: See directions, pp. 196–197.

BAKING: See directions, p. 197.

COOLING: See directions, p. 198.

BAGUETTES WITH POOLISH

	Metric		U.S. Measure		Formula Baker's %
	(1X)	**(4X)**	**(1X)**	**(4X)**	
	5-Qt Mixer	**20-Qt Mixer**	**5-Qt Mixer**	**20-Qt Mixer**	
STRAIGHT DOUGH					
Bread flour	1000g	4000g	2 lb 3.0oz	8 lb 12.0oz	**100%**
Water	680g	2720g	1 lb 7.8oz	5 lb 15.2oz	**68%**
Salt	20g	80g	0.7oz	2.8oz	**2%**
Instant yeast	7g	28g	0.3oz	1.0oz	**0.7%**
TOTAL YIELD	**1707g**	**6828g**	**3 lb 11.8oz**	**14 lb 15.0oz**	
					Pre-Ferment Baker's %
Poolish					
Bread flour	*200g*	*800g*	*7.0oz*	*1 lb 12.0oz*	*100%*
Water	*200g*	*800g*	*7.0oz*	*1 lb 12.0oz*	*100%*
Instant yeast	*0.1g*	*0.4g*	*0.003oz*	*0.012oz*	*0.04%*
Subtotal	*400g*	*1600g*	*14.0oz*	*3 lb 8.0oz*	
	5-Qt Mixer	**20-Qt Mixer**	**5-Qt Mixer**	**20-Qt Mixer**	
ADJUSTED DOUGH					
Bread flour	800g	3200g	1lb 12.0oz	7 lb 0.0oz	
Water	480g	1920g	1lb 0.8oz	4 lb 3.2oz	
Salt	20g	80g	.7oz	2.8oz	
Instant yeast	7g	28g	.3oz	1.0oz	
Poolish (from above)	400g	1600g	14.0oz	3 lb 8.0oz	
TOTAL YIELD	**1707g**	**6828g**	**3 lb 11.8oz**	**14 lb 15.0oz**	

NOTE: This bread may be made using only the ingredients and quantities listed for the straight dough, if enough time is available—probably 4–5 hours just for the bulk fermentation—but reduce the instant yeast percentage to about 0.3%. If, instead, you make a poolish using the quantities specified above, subtract those ingredient weights from the straight dough to arrive at the quantities listed for the adjusted dough. Mix and hold the poolish, covered but slightly vented, at 70°F for 12 hours before mixing the final dough.

Pre-Fermented Flour:	20%
Hydr. of Pre-Ferment:	100%

GOAL TEMPERATURE: 77°F (25°C).

MIXING METHOD: Short mix, intensive mix, or improved mix—see pp. 195–196.

BULK FERMENTATION: See directions associated with the mix method chosen, pp. 195–196.

SCALING: See options, p. 196.

SHAPING: See directions in *Chapter 6*.

PROOFING: See directions, pp. 196–197.

BAKING: See directions, p. 197.

COOLING: See directions, p. 198.

BLEU CHEESE BREAD WITH TOASTED WALNUTS

	Metric		U.S. Measure		Formula Baker's %
	(1X)	**(4X)**	**(1X)**	**(4X)**	
	5-Qt Mixer	20-Qt Mixer	5-Qt Mixer	20-Qt Mixer	
STRAIGHT DOUGH					
Bread flour	650g	2600g	1 lb 6.0oz	5 lb 8.0oz	**90%**
Whole wheat flour	72g	288g	2.6oz	10.0oz	**10%**
Water	520g	2079g	1 lb 2.5oz	4 lb 6.6oz	**72%**
Salt	14g	58g	0.5oz	2.0oz	**2%**
Instant yeast	0g	0g	0.0oz	0.0oz	**0%**
Bleu cheese, crumbled	253g	1011g	8.6oz	2 lb 2.3oz	**35%**
Walnut halves and pieces, toasted	181g	722g	6.1oz	1 lb 8.5oz	**25%**
TOTAL YIELD	**1690g**	**6758g**	**3 lb 9.3oz**	**14 lb 5.3oz**	

					Pre-Ferment Baker's %
Liquid Levain					
Bread flour	*144g*	*578g*	*4.9oz*	*1 lb 3.6oz*	*100%*
Water	*144g*	*578g*	*4.9oz*	*1 lb 3.6oz*	*100%*
Ripe levain (not used in final dough)	*72g*	*381g*	*2.5oz*	*9.8oz*	*50%*
Subtotal	*360g*	*1537g*	*12.3oz*	*3 lb 1.0oz*	
	5-Qt Mixer	20-Qt Mixer	5-Qt Mixer	20-Qt Mixer	
ADJUSTED DOUGH					
Bread flour	506g	2022g	1 lb 1.1oz	4 lb 4.4oz	
Whole wheat flour	72g	288g	2.5oz	10.0oz	
Water	376g	1502g	12.7oz	3 lb 3.0oz	
Salt	14g	58g	0.49oz	2.0oz	
Instant yeast	0g	0g	0.0oz	0.0oz	
Bleu cheese, crumbled	253g	1011g	8.6oz	2 lb 2.3oz	
Walnut halves and pieces, toasted	181g	722g	6.1oz	1 lb 8.5oz	
Liquid levain (from above)	288g	1155g	9.8oz	2 lb 7.2oz	
TOTAL YIELD	**1690g**	**6758g**	**3 lb 9.3oz**	**14 lb 5.3oz**	

Pre-Fermented Flour:	20%
Hydr. of Pre-Ferment:	100%

NOTES:

1. This bread may be made using only the ingredients and quantities listed for the straight dough, if enough time is available—probably 4–5 hours just for the bulk fermentation—but add perhaps 0.3% instant yeast. However, the dough would not be pain au levain because there would be no levain. If, instead, you make a levain using the quantities specified above, subtract those ingredient weights from the straight dough to arrive at the quantities listed for the adjusted dough. Mix and hold the levain, covered but slightly vented, at 70°F for 12 hours before mixing the final dough.

2. Add the walnuts toward the end of the mixing process *on first speed only*, after the dough is developed. Do not add bleu cheese crumbles directly to the dough during mixing, or they will break up and make the dough too short. When the dough (minus the cheese) has finished mixing, take it to the bench and stretch it without tearing it into a rough rectangle. Spread most of the cheese crumbles over the dough, fold it as you would for a laminated dough, and then perform one or two more sets of folds during the bulk fermentation.

Options:

1. You can add up to 0.07% instant yeast to the dough without changing the nature of this bread, but any more turns it into something other than true pain au levain.

2. You can add dried apples or pears at 15% and reduce walnuts to 20% and bleu cheese to 25%. The dried apples are absorbent, so increase water in the dough to keep its original consistency.

GOAL TEMPERATURE: 77°F (25°C).

MIXING METHOD: Short mix, intensive mix, or improved mix—see pp. 195–196.

BULK FERMENTATION: See directions associated with the mix method chosen, pp. 195–196.

SCALING: Boule, bâtard, or boulot: 400–650 g. Allow 20 minutes for pre-shapes to relax.

SHAPING: This bread is not ideal for making baguettes—the loaves are rough-textured and would tend to come out too flat. A boule, bâtard, or boulot shape (see *Chapter 6*) is recommended.

PROOFING: See directions, pp. 196–197.

BAKING:

1. The cheese in these loaves sometimes sticks to the oven deck, so you may wish to place parchment over your loader or peel before transferring the loaves to the oven.

2. Ideal baking temperature for the loaves in a deck oven is 425–440°F (220–230°C), depending on your oven's characteristics, 25–40°F less for convection or rack ovens.

3. Load the loaves on your peel or mechanical loader, score appropriately (see *Chapter 8*), and place in the pre-heated oven with ample steam.

COOLING: See directions, p. 198.

BRIOCHE WITH LIQUID LEVAIN

	Metric		U.S. Measure		Formula Baker's %
	(1X)	**(4X)**	**(1X)**	**(4X)**	
STRAIGHT DOUGH	5-Qt Mixer	20-Qt Mixer	5-Qt Mixer	20-Qt Mixer	
Bread flour	750g	3000g	1 lb 11.0oz	6 lb 12.0oz	**100%**
Whole eggs	390g	1560g	14.0oz	3 lb 8.0oz	**52%**
Water	75g	300g	2.7oz	10.8oz	**10%**
Sugar	113g	450g	4.1oz	1 lb 0.2oz	**15%**
Salt	20g	78g	0.7oz	2.8oz	**2.6%**
Instant yeast	14g	54g	0.5oz	1.9oz	**1.8%**
Butter, sliced or broken into pieces	308g	1230g	11.1oz	2 lb 12.3oz	**41%**
TOTAL YIELD	**1668g**	**6672g**	**3 lb 12.1oz**	**15 lb 0.2oz**	
					Pre-Ferment Baker's %
Liquid Levain					
Bread flour	*75g*	*300g*	*2.7oz*	*10.8oz*	*100%*
Water	*75g*	*300g*	*2.7oz*	*10.8oz*	*100%*
Ripe levain (not used in final dough)	*38g*	*198g*	*1.4oz*	*5.40*	*50%*
Subtotal	*188g*	*798g*	*6.8oz*	*27.0oz*	
ADJUSTED DOUGH	5-Qt Mixer	20-Qt Mixer	5-Qt Mixer	20-Qt Mixer	
Bread flour	675g	2700g	24.3oz	6 lb 1.2oz	
Whole eggs	390g	1560g	14.0oz	3 lb 8.2oz	
Water	0g	0g	0.0oz	0.0oz	
Sugar	113g	450g	4.1oz	1 lb 0.2oz	
Salt	20g	78g	0.7oz	2.8oz	
Instant yeast	14g	54g	0.5oz	1.9oz	
Liquid levain	150g	600g	5.4oz	1 lb 5.6oz	
Butter, sliced or broken into pieces	308g	1230g	11.1oz	2 lb 12.3oz	
TOTAL YIELD	**1668g**	**6672g**	**3 lb 12.1oz**	**15 lb 0.2oz**	

NOTES:

Pre-Fermented Flour:	10%
Hydr. of Pre-Ferment:	100%

1. This bread may be made using only the ingredients and quantities listed for the straight dough, if desired. Add water as necessary to create a firm, supple, but not crumbly dough. If you use a levain, then hold it, covered but slightly vented, at 70°F for 12 hours before mixing the final dough.

2. Add butter toward the end of the mixing process, *on first speed only*, after the dough is developed. Add sugar in 3 stages to allow for better gluten development and dough strength.

Options:

You may substitute honey for all or part of the sugar. Keep in mind that honey is only about 80% solids, and the 20% that is water should be subtracted from the formula's straight dough and adjusted dough water weight figures. Further water adjustments may be necessary.

You may increase the percentage of butter in the formula to 45–50%, but you may need to use higher percentages of egg and flour to keep the same dough consistency, strength, and definition.

GOAL TEMPERATURE: 77°F (25°C). See *Chapter 4* for directions for determining correct water temperature.

MIXING METHOD:

1. *Hold back all of the butter* and most of the sugar, leaving about one-third of the sugar in with the other ingredients. Mix those other ingredients for 5 minutes on first speed, add half the remaining sugar, then mix another 4 minutes on second speed.

2. Add any remaining sugar and mix until the dough is fully developed—probably another 4–8 minutes—for a total of 8–12 minutes of second-speed mixing. The dough will be sticky from the high sugar levels but not actually wet.

3. When the dough can be sheeted easily in a windowpane test, add the butter in pieces to the dough and incorporate by mixing *on first speed only* until the butter is evenly absorbed. It is normal for the dough to appear as if it shreds apart after you add the butter. Don't panic—all will be well again.

FERMENTATION: When the butter is completely and evenly incorporated (no lumps), empty the dough into a tub lightly sprinkled with flour; cover. Bulk ferment for 1 hour and then cover well and refrigerate for 12 hours or overnight. If the dough is more than 2°F over the goal temperature, you may wish to shorten the bulk fermentation.

SCALING:

1. *Pan loaves*—14–16 oz (400–450 g) per 8-inch bread pan.

2. For a large Parisian-style *grande tête* (a round loaf with a topknot, proofed and baked in a fluted pan)—14–16 oz (400–450 g), with 20–25% of that reserved for the topknot.

3. *Petite brioche* (rolls) with a topknot (smaller versions of the grande tête)—1¾–2¼ oz (50–60 g).

SHAPING: For illustrations of different brioche shapes, see the color inserts in this book.

1. *Pan loaves*—For a nice look, divide into 3 strands and braid before panning (*brioche Vendenne*), or divide into 6 pieces, round the pieces as if for rolls, and place them in a staggered arrangement in the bottom of the bread pan (*brioche Nanterre*). A simple log shape is fine for loaves used in sandwiches.

2. Parisian-style *grande tête*:

   a. Round the smaller piece first, and then form this round into a cone shape.

   b. Round the larger piece, leaving the seam at its base.

   c. Use two fingers to drive a cone-shaped hole through the large round at its center point, on top of the crown down through its center point at the bottom.

   d. Place the pointed end of the shaped brioche cone in through the top hole and down through the bottom hole, pulling the tail through by an inch or so to help secure it. Place into a large fluted mold (spray first with pan release), seam-side down, and proof.

3. *Petite brioche* (rounds) with a topknot (see an illustration of this technique in the color insert following page 114):

   a. Round the portion as you would for any roll. Turn the roll on its side 90 degrees so the bottom seam is visible. Place your small finger at a spot about one-third of the way down from the crown, and roll back and forth gently to create a narrow neck between the crown and the base of the roll—it will take on the shape of a bowling pin.

   b. Create a deep hole all around the base of the topknot's neck. Push the neck down into the hole. Place the roll into a small fluted mold and proof.

PROOFING: As we explained in *Chapter 9*, very rich doughs like brioche should be given about a three-quarter proof only.

1. *Pan loaves*: 1½–2 hours or more, depending on how cold the dough is entering the proofer.

2. *Grand tête*: 2–2½ hours.

3. *Petite brioche*: about 1 hour, or slightly longer for very cold dough.

BAKING:

1. Egg-wash the loaves and rolls before baking, but use a light touch or the egg can cause sticking problems when removing brioche from the pans later. The butter, sugar, and eggs in this dough will make the loaves and rolls brown prematurely if the temperature for baking is too high.

2. Bake rolls at 400°F for 10–15 minutes, and bake 14–16 oz loaves at 360–375°F, depending on your oven's characteristics, for 30–35 minutes. Set convection or rack ovens 25–50°F lower.

3. The sides of any pan loaf must be browned sufficiently to hold up the crown of that loaf, and the interiors must be baked thoroughly to ensure loaf stability. Using a pocket thermometer to check the interior temperature at the center of one loaf may be wise before you commit to pulling all loaves from the oven. The butter, sugar, and eggs in this dough can make the loaves and rolls brown prematurely if the temperature for baking is too high, and then the interior can still be underdone while the outside looks ready.

COOLING: Cool by removing the loaves or rolls from their molds and spacing them apart on a wire rack.

CHALLAH (NORMAL)

STRAIGHT DOUGH	Metric (1X) 5-Qt Mixer	Metric (4X) 20-Qt Mixer	U.S. Measure (1X) 5-Qt Mixer	U.S. Measure (4X) 20-Qt Mixer	Formula Baker's %
Bread flour	650g	2600g	1 lb 6.0oz	5 lb 8.0oz	65%
High-gluten flour	350g	1400g	12.0oz	3 lb 0.0oz	35%
Water	330g	1320g	11.2oz	2 lb 12.9oz	33%
Whole eggs	150g	600g	5.1oz	1 lb 4.4oz	15%
Egg yolks	60g	240g	2.0oz	8.2oz	6%
Vegetable oil	80g	320g	2.7oz	10.9oz	8%
Sugar	70g	280g	2.4oz	9.5oz	7%
Salt	20g	80g	0.7oz	2.7oz	2%
Instant yeast	7g	28g	0.2oz	0.95oz	1%
TOTAL YIELD	**1717g**	**6868g**	**3 lb 10.4oz**	**14 lb 9.5oz**	

NOTE: The yeast quantity listed in the formula is intended for bakers who use the short mix method. A dough mixed with the intensive mix method should receive a yeast percentage around 0.7%, while the yeast percentage for an improved mix dough would be more appropriately set at 0.4%.

GOAL TEMPERATURE: 77°F (25°C). You may have to use water as cold as possible to arrive anywhere close to the goal temperature. See directions for calculating correct water temperature in *Chapter 4*.

MIXING METHOD: Choose the intensive mix method (p. 196), but be careful not to overmix or overheat the dough. If the dough is too warm after mixing, cover tightly and hold in a refrigerator until it cools sufficiently.

FERMENTATION: 45–60 minutes.

SCALING: Scale all your strands first and then roll them all, or have a team work on scaling and rolling strands simultaneously, braiding loaves as they go.

1. Four-strand loaf—6 oz (170 g) per strand.
2. Three-strand loaf—8 oz (225 g) per strand.
3. Knotted rolls, 1½–3 oz (45–85 g) per small strand.

SHAPING:

1. Drawings that demonstrate braiding techniques are in *Chapter 6* on pp. 96–99.

2. Three loaves per parchment-covered full sheet tray is recommended, spaced evenly on the tray. Egg-wash loaves immediately both after panning and then just before going into the oven to get a superb shine.

PROOFING: 60–75 minutes at 80°F and 80% humidity. Allow space for growth during proofing between trays on the rack.

BAKING:

1. 350–375°F (175–190°C), or even less if premature browning is an issue; 25–40°F less for rack or convection ovens.

2. When ready (see *Chapter 7*), load the trays into the oven. No scoring is necessary, and no steam should be used, but remember to egg-wash the loaves a second time just before baking them.

3. You may wish to double-pan the loaves if you are baking in a deck oven—too much bottom heat can cause excessive browning on the bottoms of the loaves.

COOLING: Cool (without crowding the loaves) on a rack with wire shelves.

CHALLAH (SWEET)

STRAIGHT DOUGH	Metric		U.S. Measure		Formula Baker's %
	(1X)	(4X)	(1X)	(4X)	
	5-Qt Mixer	20-Qt Mixer	5-Qt Mixer	20-Qt Mixer	
Bread flour	650g	2600g	1 lb 6.0oz	5 lb 8.0oz	65%
High-gluten flour	350g	1400g	12.0oz	3 lb 0.0oz	35%
Water	330g	1320g	11.2oz	2 lb 12.9oz	33%
Whole eggs	150g	600g	5.1oz	1 lb 4.4oz	15%
Egg yolks	60g	240g	2.0oz	8.2oz	6%
Vegetable oil	80g	320g	2.7oz	10.9oz	8%
Sugar	120g	480g	4.1oz	1 lb 0.3oz	12%
Salt	20g	80g	0.7oz	2.7oz	2%
Instant yeast	7g	28g	0.2oz	0.95oz	1%
TOTAL YIELD	**1767g**	**7068g**	**3 lb 12.1oz**	**15 lb 0.3oz**	

NOTE: The yeast quantity listed in the formula is intended for bakers who use the short mix method. A dough mixed with the intensive mix method should receive a yeast percentage around 0.7%, while the yeast percentage for an improved mix dough would be more appropriately set at 0.4%.

GOAL TEMPERATURE: 77°F (25°C). You may have to use water as cold as possible to arrive anywhere close to the goal temperature. See directions for calculating correct water temperature in *Chapter 4*.

MIXING METHOD: Choose the intensive mix method (p. 196), but be careful not to overmix or overheat the dough. If the dough is too warm after mixing, cover tightly and hold in a refrigerator until it cools sufficiently.

FERMENTATION: 45–60 minutes.

SCALING: Scale all your strands first and then roll them all, or have a team work on scaling and rolling strands simultaneously, braiding loaves as they go.

1. Four-strand loaf—6 oz (170 g) per strand.
2. Three-strand loaf—8 oz (225 g) per strand.
3. Knotted rolls, 1½–3 oz (45–85 g) per small strand.

SHAPING:

1. Drawings that demonstrate braiding techniques are in *Chapter 6* on pp. 96–99.

2. Three loaves per parchment-covered full sheet tray is recommended, spaced evenly on the tray. Egg-wash loaves immediately both after panning and then just before going into the oven to get a superb shine.

PROOFING: 75–90 minutes or sometimes longer at 80°F and 80% humidity. Allow space for growth during proofing between trays on the rack.

BAKING:

1. 330–350°F (165–176°C) or even less if premature browning is an issue; 25–40°F less for rack or convection ovens.

2. When ready (see *Chapter 7*), load the trays into the oven. No scoring is necessary, and no steam should be used, but remember to egg-wash the loaves a second time just before baking them.

3. You may wish to double-pan the loaves if you are baking in a deck oven—too much bottom heat can cause excessive browning on the bottoms of the loaves.

COOLING: Cool (without crowding the loaves) on a rack with wire shelves.

CHRISTMAS STOLLEN

	Metric		U.S. Measure		Formula Baker's %
	(1X)	**(4X)**	**(1X)**	**(4X)**	
	5-Qt Mixer	**20-Qt Mixer**	**5-Qt Mixer**	**20-Qt Mixer**	
STRAIGHT DOUGH					
Bread flour	550g	2200g	19.0oz	4 lb 12.0oz	**100%**
Water	127g	506g	4.4oz	1 lb 1.5oz	**23%**
Whole eggs	116g	462g	4.0oz	1 lb 0.0oz	**21%**
Sugar (add in 3 stages)	160g	638g	5.5oz	1 lb 6.0oz	**29%**
Milk powder (high heat)	28g	110g	1.0oz	3.8oz	**5.0%**
Salt	11g	44g	0.4oz	1.5oz	**2.0%**
Instant yeast	10g	40g	0.3oz	1.4oz	**1.85%**
Vanilla extract	8g	33g	0.3oz	1.1oz	**1.5%**
Almond extract	8g	33g	0.3oz	1.1oz	**1.5%**
Cardamom	2g	7g	0.1oz	0.2oz	**0.3%**
Butter, sliced or broken (add after dough is developed, as with brioche)	220g	880g	7.6oz	1 lb 14.4oz	**40%**
After butter is incorporated:					
Toasted almonds, half ground and half in large pieces	149g	594g	5.1oz	1 lb 4.5oz	**27%**
Candied lemon peel	11g	44g	0.4oz	1.5oz	**2%**
Candied orange peel	11g	44g	0.4oz	1.5oz	**2%**
Dark raisins	94g	374g	3.2oz	12.9oz	**17%**
Golden raisins	94g	374g	3.2oz	12.9oz	**17%**
Dried cherries	94g	374g	3.2oz	12.9oz	**17%**
TOTAL YIELD	**1689g**	**6756g**	**3 lb 10.3oz**	**14 lb 9.4oz**	

					Pre-Ferment Baker's %
Sponge					
Bread flour	*138g*	*550g*	*4.8oz*	*19.0oz*	*100%*
Water	*83g*	*330g*	*2.9oz*	*11.4oz*	*60%*
Instant yeast	*0.1g*	*0.6g*	*0.01oz*	*0.02oz*	*0.1%*
Subtotal	*221g*	*880g*	*7.6oz*	*1 lb 14.4oz*	
	5-Qt Mixer	**20-Qt Mixer**	**5-Qt Mixer**	**20-Qt Mixer**	
ADJUSTED DOUGH					
Bread flour	413g	1650g	14.3oz	3 lb 9.0oz	
Water	44g	176g	1.5oz	6.1oz	
Whole eggs	116g	462g	4.0oz	1 lb 0.0oz	
Sugar, granulated	160g	638g	5.5oz	1 lb 6.0oz	
Milk powder (high heat)	28g	110g	1.0oz	3.8oz	
Salt	11g	44g	0.4oz	1.5oz	
Instant yeast	10g	40g	0.3oz	1.4oz	
Sponge (from above)	220g	880g	7.6oz	1 lb 14.4oz	
Vanilla extract	8g	33g	0.3oz	1.1oz	
Almond extract	8g	33g	0.3oz	1.1oz	
Cardamom	2g	7g	0.1oz	0.2oz	
Butter, sliced or broken (add after dough is developed, as with brioche)	220g	880g	7.6oz	1 lb 14.4oz	
After butter is incorporated:					
Toasted almonds, half ground and half in pieces	149g	594g	5.1oz	1 lb 4.5oz	
Candied lemon peel	11g	44g	0.4oz	1.5oz	
Candied orange peel	11g	44g	0.4oz	1.5oz	
Dark raisins	94g	374g	3.2oz	12.9oz	
Golden raisins	94g	374g	3.2oz	12.9oz	
Dried cherries	94g	374g	3.2oz	12.9oz	
TOTAL YIELD	**1689g**	**6756g**	**3 lb 10.3oz**	**14 lb 9.4oz**	

NOTES:

1. This bread may be made using only the ingredients and quantities listed for straight dough, if desired. Add water as necessary to create a firm, supple, but not crumbly dough.

2. If you use the sponge, then hold it, covered but slightly vented, at 70°F for 24 hours before mixing the final dough.

3. You will need additional butter for brushing the loaves hot out of the oven, and powdered sugar (preferably 6X, or doughnut sugar) to dredge them after they are well cooled.

Options:

1. You may substitute honey for all or part of the sugar. Keep in mind that honey is only about 80% solids, and the 20% that is water should be subtracted from the formula's straight dough and adjusted dough water weight figures. Further water adjustments may be necessary.

2. You may enclose a 1 oz (30 g) piece of almond paste, shaped like a cigar, when rolling the dough portions.

3. The raisins in the Stollen may be soaked overnight in rum or a mixture of rum and water.

Pre-Fermented Flour:	25%
Hydr. of Pre-Ferment:	60%

GOAL TEMPERATURE: 77°F (25°C). See directions for calculating correct water temperature in *Chapter 4*.

MIXING METHOD:

1. Choose the intensive mixing method (p. 196), but *hold back all of the butter* and most of the sugar, leaving about one-third of the sugar in with the other ingredients.

2. Mix those other ingredients for 5 minutes on first speed, add half of the remaining sugar, then mix another 4 minutes on second speed. Then add any remaining sugar and mix until the dough is fully developed—probably another 4–8 minutes, for a total of 8–12 minutes of second-speed mixing. The dough will be sticky from the high sugar levels but not actually wet.

3. When the dough can be sheeted easily in a windowpane test, add the butter in pieces to the dough and incorporate by mixing on *first speed only* until the butter is evenly absorbed. It is normal for the dough to appear as if it shreds apart after you add the butter. Don't panic—all will be well again.

4. When the butter has been incorporated evenly (no lumps), add the ground almonds and almond pieces to the mixer bowl and incorporate them on first speed. Then add all dried and candied fruits and mix in on first speed just until evenly distributed.

FERMENTATION:

1. Empty the dough into a tub lightly sprinkled with flour; cover. Bulk ferment for 1 hour and then cover well and refrigerate for 12 hours or overnight.

2. If the dough is more than 2°F over the goal temperature, you may wish to shorten the bulk fermentation.

SCALING: 24 oz (680 g) per loaf. Cut portions into square shapes as much as possible.

SHAPING:

1. If the dough portions are still cold after scaling, allow them to warm a bit until the dough is easily folded.

2. Take each square of dough and begin rolling one side toward the other (wrap the almond paste cigar in the dough as you roll it, if using this option). Stop short of the opposite end as you roll the dough, and leave this seam open and exposed, looking like a blanket sticking under a well-wrapped baby (which is what it is supposed to represent).

3. Place on parchment-lined sheet pans, 3 loaves per tray, spacing evenly.

PROOFING:

1. 2–3 hours when held at 80°F and 80% humidity.

2. As we explained in *Chapter 9*, very rich doughs like Stollen should be given only a three-quarter proof. If a controlled proofer is not available, cover the rack holding the boards and keep as close to 80°F as possible.

BAKING:

1. 350°F in a conventional or deck oven. Double-pan the trays if using a deck oven to avoid overbrowning the bottoms. 25–40°F less for convection or rack ovens.

2. This bread browns easily because of its high sugar and butter content, so be certain to spot-check the interior temperature of one of the loaves before you remove them from the oven, or you may find you have underbaked them.

3. After removing from the oven, brush the loaves heavily with butter and then roll them in granulated sugar.

COOLING: Cool completely on a wire rack. After they have cooled completely, dredge the loaves in powdered sugar (preferably 6X sugar, or doughnut sugar) and wrap in plastic bags.

CIABATTA WITH BIGA

	Metric		U.S. Measure		Formula Baker's %
	(1X)	**(4X)**	**(1X)**	**(4X)**	
	5-Qt Mixer	20-Qt Mixer	5-Qt Mixer	20-Qt Mixer	
STRAIGHT DOUGH					
Bread flour	900g	3600g	2 lb 1.0oz	8 lb 4.0oz	**100%**
Water	720g	2880g	1 lb 10.4oz	6 lb 9.6oz	**80%**
Salt	18g	72g	0.7oz	2.6oz	**2%**
Instant yeast	4g	14g	0.1oz	0.5oz	**0.4%**
TOTAL YIELD	**1642g**	**6566g**	**3 lb 12.2oz**	**15 lb 0.8oz**	
					Pre-Ferment Baker's %
Biga					
Bread flour	315g	1260g	11.55oz	2 lb 14.2oz	100%
Water	189g	756g	6.9oz	1 lb 11.7oz	60%
Instant yeast	0.3g	1g	0.01oz	0.05oz	0.1%
Subtotal	504g	2017g	1 lb 2.5oz	4 lb 10.0oz	
	5-Qt Mixer	20-Qt Mixer	5-Qt Mixer	20-Qt Mixer	
ADJUSTED DOUGH					
Bread flour	585g	2340g	1 lb 5.5oz	5 lb 5.8oz	
Water	531g	2124g	14.8oz	4 lb 13.9oz	
Salt	18g	72g	0.7oz	2.6oz	
Instant yeast	4g	14g	0.1oz	0.5oz	
Biga (from above)	504g	2016g	1 lb 2.5oz	4 lb 10.0oz	
TOTAL YIELD	**1642g**	**6566g**	**3 lb 12.2oz**	**15 lb 0.8oz**	

NOTE: This bread may be made using only the ingredients and quantities listed for the straight dough, if enough time is available—probably 4–5 hours just for the bulk fermentation—but reduce the instant yeast percentage to about 0.3%. If, instead, you prepare a biga using the quantities specified above, subtract those ingredient weights from the straight dough to arrive at the quantities listed in the adjusted dough. Mix and hold the biga, covered but slightly vented, at 70°F for 24 hours before mixing the final dough.

Pre-Fermented Flour:	35%
Hydr. of Pre-Ferment:	60%

GOAL TEMPERATURE: 77°F (25°C). See directions for determining correct water temperature in *Chapter 4*.

MIXING METHOD:

1. **Mixing by hand:**

   a. Cut the biga into a number of small pieces. Add it with some of the water to a plastic tub of appropriate size and soften the pieces by squeezing them with your hands.

   b. Add all the remaining ingredients and mix with your hands until they are homogenous. The dough will be wet—don't add any extra flour.

   c. Cover the tub and allow the mixture to rest for about 15 minutes.

   d. After the rest period, give the mixture a set of folds as you would for any baguette dough, even though the dough may seem unmanageable. Repeat these rest periods and sets of folds 4 or 5 times, until the dough seems to have more elasticity and less fluidity.

2. **Mixing by machine:**

   a. **Short mix:** 12–15 minutes on first speed. Empty the dough into a tub lightly sprinkled with flour and cover. Bulk ferment for 3 hours. Perform a set of stretch-and-folds on the dough every 15–20 minutes, a total of 4 or 5 times. The dough will gradually get smoother and stronger.

   b. **Improved mix:** Use the double hydration method discussed in *Chapter 4*. Hold back 10–15% of the total water in the formula so the consistency of the dough is like that of a typical baguette dough. Mix about 5 minutes on first speed followed by 3–5 minutes on second speed. Then add the remaining water and incorporate *on first speed only*—probably 2–4 additional minutes. Place the dough in a covered tub lightly sprinkled with flour. Bulk ferment for 2–3 hours, giving the dough a set of stretch-and-folds every 15 minutes or so, perhaps 3 or 4 times.

SCALING:

1. Gently empty the tub of dough onto a well-floured bench and rearrange it so its shape is rectangular and its thickness is the same throughout.

2. Cut a strip of dough as wide as you want your loaves to be. Then cut for length.

3. Keep the dough portions as rectangular as you can and rest them temporarily on floured proofing boards as you proceed. Keep the proofing boards with the portions covered as you proceed.

4. Standard loaves—16–18 oz (450–525 g).

5. Rolls (ciabattine)—3–4 oz (90–120 g).

SHAPING: The portions are not so much shaped as they are stretched slightly. Stretch each loaf into a rectangle 8–10 inches long and place on well-floured couche with pleats between each row of two loaves. With this bread, you may wish to leave any small pieces of dough sitting on top of the larger rectangle because the loaves will be flipped upside-down just before loading them in the oven.

PROOFING: 45 minutes at 80°F and 80% humidity. If a proofer is not available, cover the rack holding the boards and keep as close to 80°F as possible.

BAKING:

1. In a deck oven—475–500°F (245–260°C).

2. Load the ciabatta on your peel or mechanical loader, flipping them upside-down as you do so to expose the attractive veined look of the flour clinging to the underside.

3. Insert the loaves with a few seconds of steam. No scoring is necessary.

4. 25–30 minutes for loaves, 12–15 minutes for rolls. Be sure to vent the oven after the first 10 minutes of baking. Shorter bake times tend to leave too much moisture in the loaves and will soften the crust; longer times may make for a thick crust and a dry interior.

COOLING: Cool (without crowding the loaves) on a rack with wire shelves.

CROISSANTS WITH LIQUID LEVAIN

	Metric		U.S. Measure		Formula Baker's %
	(1X)	**(4X)**	**(1X)**	**(4X)**	
	5-Qt Mixer	**20-Qt Mixer**	**5-Qt Mixer**	**20-Qt Mixer**	
STRAIGHT DOUGH					
Bread flour	750g	3000g	26.0g	6 lb 8.0oz	**100%**
Milk	390g	1560g	13.5oz	3 lb 6.1oz	**52%**
Water	75g	300g	2.6oz	10.4oz	**10%**
Sugar	75g	300g	2.6oz	10.4oz	**10%**
Butter, unsalted (mixed into dough)	30g	120g	1.0oz	4.2oz	**4%**
Salt	20g	78g	0.7oz	2.7oz	**2.6%**
Instant yeast	8g	30g	0.3oz	1.0oz	**1.0%**
Butter block (unsalted)	375g	1500g	13.0oz	3 lb 4.0oz	**50%**
TOTAL YIELD	**1722g**	**6888g**	**3 lb 11.7oz**	**14 lb 14.8oz**	
					Pre-Ferment Baker's %
Liquid Levain					
Bread flour	*75g*	*300g*	*2.6oz*	*10.4oz*	*100%*
Water	*75g*	*300g*	*2.6oz*	*10.4oz*	*100%*
Ripe levain (not used in final dough)	*38g*	*198g*	*1.3oz*	*5.2oz*	*50%*
Subtotal	*188g*	*798g*	*6.5oz*	*26.13*	
	5-Qt Mixer	**20-Qt Mixer**	**5-Qt Mixer**	**20-Qt Mixer**	
ADJUSTED DOUGH					
Bread flour	675g	2700g	1 lb 7.4oz	5 lb 13.6oz	
Milk	390g	1560g	13.5oz	3 lb 6.1oz	
Water	0g	0g	0.0oz	0.0oz	
Sugar	75g	300g	2.6oz	10.4oz	
Butter, unsalted (mixed into dough)	30g	120g	1.0oz	4.2oz	
Salt	20g	78g	0.7oz	2.7oz	
Instant yeast	7g	30g	0.3oz	1.0oz	
Liquid levain (from above)	150g	600g	5.2oz	1 lb 4.8oz	
Butter block (unsalted)	375g	1500g	13.0oz	3 lb 4.0oz	
TOTAL YIELD	**1722g**	**6888g**	**3 lb 11.7oz**	**14 lb 14.8oz**	

NOTE: This bread may be made using only the ingredients and quantities listed for the straight dough, if you want dough with less flavor and somewhat less extensibility. If, instead, you prepare a levain using the quantities specified above, subtract those ingredient weights from the straight dough to arrive at the quantities listed for the adjusted dough. Mix and hold the levain, covered but slightly vented, at 70°F for 12 hours before mixing the final dough.

Pre-Fermented Flour:	10%
Hydr. of Pre-Ferment:	100%

Variation:

You can use essentially the same ingredient weights as the ones specified above together with most of the same procedures to make a dough that substitutes poolish—at the same weight—for liquid levain.

GOAL TEMPERATURE: 77°F (25°C). See directions for determining correct water temperature in *Chapter 4*.

MIXING METHOD:

1. Use the improved mix method. *Do not mix the butter block into the dough.*

2. Mix all ingredients except the butter block into a base dough for about 5 minutes on first speed and 2–3 minutes on second speed until the dough is lightly developed.

FERMENTATION: Form the dough into a square shape or place it in a square-bottomed container and bulk ferment, covered or wrapped, for 1 hour at room temperature. Then label and refrigerate overnight.

ENCLOSING BUTTER BLOCK: See the procedure illustrated in the text and drawings in *Chapter 9*, p. 145.

LAMINATING (Turns):

1. Begin to perform either 3 sets of single turns or 2 sets of double turns on the dough (see text and illustrations in *Chapter 9*, pp. 146–147).

2. Rest the dough when necessary for 15–20 minutes between sets. Generally, no more than 2 sets of turns can be accomplished without allowing for rest time.

3. After the turns are completed, wrap the dough completely and chill for an extended period in the refrigerator to allow the laminated dough to relax. Usually, the laminated dough rests at least 12 hours or overnight before being sheeted and cut into shapes.

SCALING:

1. Using a rolling pin or sheeter, roll out the dough to a rectangular sheet, generally 5–7 mm thick, though you can choose the thickness you wish.

2. Cut into triangles or rectangles in any size you like. 2–3 oz (50–80 g) is common for a croissant, but you can make them larger for sandwiches or smaller for buffets.

SHAPING: Roll triangles into the classic crescent shape (see *Chapter 9*). Fill rectangular pieces and roll them into cylinders. About 12 average-size items per parchment-covered tray is normal.

PROOFING: 45 minutes–1 hour at 78–80°F and 80% humidity. If the croissants are cold when they enter the proofer, the proofing time may be somewhat longer. Be especially careful about the temperature during the proofing of the pastries. If the temperature climbs over 80°F, you may inadvertently melt the butter before the pastries are baked, and many of the layers will be lost. Setting the proof temperature just a bit below 80°F is a safer bet.

BAKING:

1. Carefully but quickly egg-wash the pastries just before inserting them into the oven. Be careful not to allow an excessive amount of egg wash to drip over the cut edges of the dough; this can harden in the oven and restrict the ability of the laminated pastries to rise during oven spring.

2. 20–25 minutes at 400–425°F in a conventional oven, with the trays double-panned if you are using a deck oven. Set convection or rack ovens 25–50°F lower. Your oven may vary from these estimates.

COOLING: Most large bakeries allow croissants and Danish to cool right on the pans used for baking them, but if you have enough space, you can certainly remove them from the trays and cool them on a wire rack.

DANISH DOUGH WITH LIQUID LEVAIN

	Metric		U.S. Measure		Formula Baker's %
	(1X)	**(4X)**	**(1X)**	**(4X)**	
	5-Qt Mixer	20-Qt Mixer	5-Qt Mixer	20-Qt Mixer	
STRAIGHT DOUGH					
Bread flour	725g	2900g	1 lb 9.0oz	6 lb 4.0oz	100%
Milk	218g	870g	7.5oz	1 lb 14.0oz	30%
Whole eggs	145g	580g	5.0oz	1 lb 4.0oz	20%
Water	73g	290g	2.5oz	10.0oz	10%
Sugar	87g	348g	3.0oz	12.0oz	12%
Butter, unsalted (mixed into dough)	58g	232g	2.0oz	8.0oz	8%
Salt	18g	73g	0.6oz	2.5oz	2.5%
Instant yeast	12g	46g	0.4oz	1.6oz	1.5%
Butter block (unsalted)	363g	1451g	12.5oz	3 lb 2.0oz	50%
TOTAL YIELD	**1699g**	**6790g**	**3 lb 10.5oz**	**14 lb 10.1oz**	
					Pre-Ferment Baker's %
Liquid Levain					
Bread flour	*58g*	*232g*	*2.0oz*	*8.0oz*	*100%*
Water	*58g*	*232g*	*2.0oz*	*8.0oz*	*100%*
Ripe levain (not used in final dough)	*29g*	*153g*	*1.0oz*	*2.0oz*	*50%*
Subtotal	*145g*	*617g*	*5.0oz*	*1 lb 2.0oz*	
	5-Qt Mixer	20-Qt Mixer	5-Qt Mixer	20-Qt Mixer	
ADJUSTED DOUGH					
Bread flour	667g	2668g	1 lb 7.0oz	5 lb 12.0oz	
Milk	218g	870g	7.5oz	1 lb 14.0oz	
Whole eggs	145g	580g	5.0oz	1 lb 4.0oz	
Water	15g	58g	0.5oz	2.0oz	
Sugar	87g	348g	3.0oz	12.0oz	
Butter, unsalted (mixed into dough)	58g	232g	2.0oz	8.0oz	
Salt	18g	73g	0.6oz	2.5oz	
Instant yeast	12g	46g	0.4oz	1.6oz	
Liquid levain (above)	116g	464g	4.0oz	1 lb 0.0oz	
Butter block (unsalted)	363g	1451g	12.5oz	3 lb 2.0oz	
TOTAL YIELD	**1699g**	**6790g**	**3 lb 10.5oz**	**14 lb 10.1oz**	

NOTE: This bread may be made using only the ingredients and quantities listed for the straight dough, if you wish. The dough will have less flavor and somewhat less extensibility. If, instead, you prepare a levain using the quantities specified above, subtract those ingredient weights from the straight dough to arrive at the quantities listed for the adjusted dough. Mix and hold the levain, covered but slightly vented, at 70°F for 12 hours before mixing the final dough.

Pre-Fermented Flour:	8%
Hydr. of Pre-Ferment:	100%

GOAL TEMPERATURE: 77°F (25°C). See directions for determining correct water temperature in *Chapter 4*.

MIXING METHOD:

1. Use the improved mix method. *Do not mix the butter block into the dough.*

2. Mix all ingredients except the butter block into the base dough for about 5 minutes on first speed and 2–3 minutes on second speed until the dough is lightly developed.

FERMENTATION: Form the dough into a square shape or place it in a square-bottomed container and bulk ferment, covered or wrapped, for 1 hour at room temperature. Then label and refrigerate overnight.

ENCLOSING BUTTER BLOCK: See the procedure illustrated in the text and drawings in *Chapter 9*, p. 145.

LAMINATING (Turns):

1. Begin to perform 2 sets of single turns and 1 set of double turns on the dough (see text and illustrations in *Chapter 9*, pp. 146–147).

2. Rest the dough when necessary for 15–20 minutes between sets. Generally, no more than 2 sets of turns can be accomplished without allowing for rest time.

3. After the turns are completed, wrap the dough completely and chill for an extended period in the refrigerator to allow the laminated dough to relax. Usually, the lami-

nated dough rests at least 12 hours or overnight before being sheeted and cut into shapes.

SCALING:

1. Using a rolling pin or sheeter, roll out the dough to a rectangular sheet, generally 4–6 mm thick, though you can choose the thickness you wish.

2. Cut into 4-in. (10 cm) squares for diamonds and pockets. Strips can be cut from a folded rectangular sheet for snails. 2 oz (50–60 g) is common for a danish, but you can make them larger or smaller as you wish.

SHAPING: See the illustrations for shaping types of danish in *Chapter 9*, pp. 149–150. About 12 average-sized items per parchment-covered tray is normal.

PROOFING: 45 minutes–1 hour at 78–80°F and 80% humidity. If the Danish are cold when they enter the proofer, the proofing time may be somewhat longer. Be especially careful about the temperature during the proofing of the pastries. If the temperature climbs over 80°F, you may inadvertently melt the butter before the pastries are baked, and many of

the layers will be lost. Setting the proof temperature just a bit below 80°F is a safer bet.

BAKING:

1. Carefully but quickly egg-wash the pastries just before inserting them into the oven. Be careful not to allow an excessive amount of egg wash to drip over the cut edges of the dough—this can harden in the oven and restrict the ability of the laminated pastries to rise during oven spring.

2. 20–25 minutes at 400–425°F in a conventional oven, with the trays double-panned if you are using a deck oven. Set convection or rack ovens 25–50°F lower. Your oven's idiosyncrasies may cause variations from these estimates—check early.

COOLING: Most large bakeries allow Danish to cool right on the pans used for baking them, but if you have sufficient space, you can certainly remove them from the trays and cool them on a wire rack.

DARK ACTIVE DOUGH (DECORATIVE)

	Metric		U.S. Measure		Formula Baker's %
	(1X)	**(4X)**	**(1X)**	**(4X)**	
	5-Qt Mixer	**20-Qt Mixer**	**5-Qt Mixer**	**20-Qt Mixer**	
STRAIGHT DOUGH					
Bread flour	900g	3600g	2 lb 0.0oz	8 lb 0.0oz	**100%**
Sugar	36g	144g	1.28oz	5.1oz	**4%**
Salt	14g	58g	0.5oz	2.1oz	**1.6%**
Vegetable shortening	54g	216g	1.9oz	7.7oz	**6%**
Instant yeast	2g	7g	0.06oz	0.3oz	**0.2%**
Whole milk	558g	2232g	1 lb 3.8oz	4 lb 15.4oz	**62%**
Dark cocoa powder	90g	370g	3.2oz	12.8oz	**10%**
TOTAL YIELD	**1654g**	**6617g**	**3 lb 10.8oz**	**14 lb 11.3oz**	

MIXING METHOD:

1. Place all ingredients in the mixing bowl and mix for 5 minutes on low speed and 3–5 minutes on second speed. Unlike with dead dough, we are looking to develop the gluten in this decorative dough. The consistency should be firm and smooth but still supple and not crumbly.

2. After mixing, wrap the dough tightly and allow to rest about 15 minutes in the refrigerator before dividing and shaping. Refrigerate until use to control yeast activity, and keep covered on the bench to avoid skin forming.

PROOFING:

1. Allow finished centerpieces to relax in the refrigerator overnight or to proof in an enclosed, humidified proofer at about 80°F and 80% humidity until visibly puffy, 30–60 minutes.

2. You may wish to egg-wash your piece before or after proofing.

BAKING: In general, 25–35 minutes at 350°F will work fine in a deck oven. Set convection and rack ovens 25–50°F lower, depending on the characteristics of the oven.

COOLING: On a wire rack.

DELI-STYLE RYE BREAD

	Metric		U.S. Measure		Formula Baker's %
	(1X)	**(4X)**	**(1X)**	**(4X)**	
	5-Qt Mixer	20-Qt Mixer	5-Qt Mixer	20-Qt Mixer	
STRAIGHT DOUGH					
High-gluten flour	700g	2800g	1 lb 10.0oz	6 lb 8.0oz	**80%**
Medium rye flour	200g	800g	8.0oz	2 lb 0.0oz	**20%**
Water	612g	2448g	1 lb 7.1oz	5 lb 12.5oz	**68%**
Salt	18g	72g	0.7oz	2.7oz	**2%**
Instant yeast	5g	22g	0.2oz	0.8oz	**0.6%**
Caraway seeds	18g	72g	0.7oz	2.7oz	**2%**
TOTAL YIELD	**1553g**	**6214g**	**3 lb 10.7oz**	**14 lb 10.7oz**	
					Pre-Ferment Baker's %
Rye Sour					
Medium rye flour	*180g*	*720g*	*6.8oz*	*1 lb 11.2oz*	*100%*
Water	*144g*	*576g*	*5.4oz*	*1 lb 5.8oz*	*80%*
Ripe levain (not used in final dough)	*9g*	*36g*	*.3oz*	*1.4oz*	*5%*
Subtotal	*324g*	*1296g*	*12.2oz*	*3 lb 1.0oz*	
	5-Qt Mixer	20-Qt Mixer	5-Qt Mixer	20-Qt Mixer	
ADJUSTED DOUGH					
High-gluten flour	520g	2080g	1 lb 3.2oz	4 lb 12.8oz	
Medium rye flour	200g	800g	8.0oz	2 lb 0.0oz	
Water	468g	1872g	1 lb 1.7oz	4 lb 6.7oz	
Salt	18g	72g	0.7oz	2.7oz	
Instant yeast	5g	22g	0.2oz	0.8oz	
Rye sour (from above)	324g	1296g	12.2oz	3 lb 1.0oz	
Caraway seeds	18g	72g	0.7oz	2.7oz	
TOTAL YIELD	**1553g**	**6214g**	**3 lb 10.7oz**	**14 lb 10.7oz**	

NOTE: You can make this bread using only the ingredients and quantities listed for the straight dough, but the dough will have much less flavor and will not properly be sourdough rye, as no sour culture will be used. Rye flour usually must be acidified to control excess amylase activity. If, instead, you prepare a rye sour using the quantities specified above, subtract those ingredient weights from the straight dough to arrive at the quantities listed for the adjusted dough. Mix and hold the rye sour, covered but slightly vented, at 70°F for 15 hours before mixing the final dough.

Pre-Fermented Flour:	20%
Hydr. of Pre-Ferment:	80%

Option:
You may add ground caraway seed instead of whole seeds.

GOAL TEMPERATURE: 80°F (27°C). See directions for determining correct water temperature in *Chapter 4*.

MIXING METHOD:

1. *Warning:* Rye mixes for much less time than all-white dough. Mix 3 minutes on first speed, then 3–4 minutes on second speed.

2. Significant gluten development will be evident, but even a small proportion of rye means the dough may be stickier than normal white bread. Do not try to eliminate the stickiness by adding flour.

3. Empty the dough into a tub lightly sprinkled with flour; cover.

FERMENTATION: Bulk ferment for 45–60 minutes. The dough will gain substantial strength during bulk fermentation.

SCALING: This dough is not ideal for making baguettes—the loaves tend to come out too flat. Boules, bâtards, boulots: 14–22 oz (400–650 g). Allow 10 minutes for pre-shapes to relax.

SHAPING: Use a small degree of tension when making the final shapes, but don't use too much force or the dough may tear.

PROOFING: Boules, bâtards, and boulots may be proofed seam-side down on couche with pleats or seam-side up in baskets. The shaped loaves should proof sufficiently within

45–60 minutes when held at 80°F and 80% humidity. Rye bread can proof quickly, so be sure to check on the loaves earlier than you expect most breads to be ready.

BAKING:

1. 430–450°F, depending on your oven's characteristics. Rack or convection ovens might be better set at 400–425°F.

2. When they are ready (see *Chapter 7* for a discussion of proofing), load the loaves on your peel or mechanical loader, score appropriately (see *Chapter 8*), and place in the pre-heated oven with ample steam. Generally, rye loaves should not be scored too deeply. Patterns like the sausage cut or shallow cross-cuts work well.

3. After 10 minutes of baking, be certain to open the oven vents. You may wish to decrease the temperature by about 25°F to allow for an extended bake.

4. Adjust oven temperature to achieve the correct bake in 35–45 minutes. Shorter bake times tend to leave too much moisture in the loaves and will soften the crust.

COOLING: Cool (without crowding the loaves) on a rack with wire shelves.

DOUBLE RAISIN BREAD WITH TOASTED WALNUTS

	Metric		U.S. Measure		Formula Baker's %
	(1X)	**(4X)**	**(1X)**	**(4X)**	
	5-Qt Mixer	**20-Qt Mixer**	**5-Qt Mixer**	**20-Qt Mixer**	
STRAIGHT DOUGH					
Bread flour	600g	2400g	1 lb 5.0oz	5 lb 4.0oz	**90%**
Whole wheat flour	67g	267g	2.3oz	9.3oz	**10%**
Water	480g	1921g	1 lb 0.8oz	4 lb 3.2oz	**72%**
Salt	13g	53g	0.5oz	1.9oz	**2%**
Instant yeast	0g	0g	0.0oz	0.0oz	**0%**
Dark raisins	167g	667g	5.8oz	1 lb 7.3oz	**25%**
Golden raisins	167g	667g	5.8oz	1 lb 7.3oz	**25%**
Walnut halves and pieces, toasted	167g	667g	5.8oz	1 lb 7.3oz	**25%**
TOTAL YIELD	**1661g**	**6642g**	**3 lb 10.0oz**	**14 lb 8.3oz**	
					Pre-Ferment Baker's %
Liquid Levain					
Bread flour	133g	533g	4.7oz	1 lb 2.7oz	100%
Water	133g	533g	4.7oz	1 lb 2.7oz	100%
Ripe levain (not used in final dough)	67g	267g	2.33oz	9.4oz	50%
Subtotal	333g	1333g	11.73oz	2 lb 14.8oz	
	5-Qt Mixer	**20-Qt Mixer**	**5-Qt Mixer**	**20-Qt Mixer**	
ADJUSTED DOUGH					
Bread flour	467g	1867g	1 lb 0.3oz	4 lb 1.3oz	
Whole wheat flour	67g	267g	2.3oz	9.3oz	
Water	347g	1388g	12.1oz	3 lb 0.5oz	
Salt	13g	53g	0.5oz	1.9oz	
Instant yeast	0g	0g	0.0oz	0.0oz	
Dark raisins	167g	667g	5.8oz	1 lb 7.3oz	
Golden raisins	167g	667g	5.8oz	1 lb 7.3oz	
Walnut halves and pieces, toasted	167g	667g	5.8oz	1 lb 7.3oz	
Liquid levain	266g	1066g	9.4oz	2 lb 5.4oz	
TOTAL YIELD	**1661g**	**6642g**	**3 lb 10.0oz**	**14 lb 8.3oz**	

NOTE: This bread may be made using only the ingredients and quantities listed for the straight dough, if enough time is available—probably 4–5 hours just for the bulk fermentation—but you would need to add perhaps 0.3% instant yeast to do so, and the dough would not properly be pain au levain because there would be no levain. If, instead, you prepare a levain using the quantities specified above, subtract those ingredient weights from the straight dough to arrive at the quantities listed for the adjusted dough. Mix and hold the levain, covered but slightly vented, at 70°F for 12 hours before mixing the final dough.

Pre-Fermented Flour:	20%
Hydr. of Pre-Ferment:	100%

Options:

1. You may add up to about 0.07% instant yeast to the dough without changing the nature of this bread, but any more turns it into something other than true pain au levain.

2. You may substitute any dried fruit or any toasted nut variety you like, or leave out whatever you don't. Variations such as apricots with hazelnuts, cherries with pecans, or apples (or pears) with walnuts can be used with success. Toasted walnuts or hazelnuts alone make a bread that goes well with many cheeses. You may need to vary the water content of the dough, as some dried fruits are more absorbent than others.

GOAL TEMPERATURE: 77°F (25°C).

MIXING METHOD: Short mix or improved mix—see pp. 195–196. Hold back the nuts and raisins. Add the nuts during the last minute of mixing, and then the raisins, using first speed only.

BULK FERMENTATION: Explained in mixing methods described on pp. 195–196.

SCALING: See options, p. 196.

SHAPING: This dough is not ideal for shaping baguettes. See directions in *Chapter 6*.

PROOFING: See directions, pp. 196–197, for sourdough.

BAKING: See directions, p. 197.

COOLING: See directions, p. 198.

FOCACCIA WITH BIGA

	Metric		U.S. Measure		Formula Baker's %
	(1X)	**(4X)**	**(1X)**	**(4X)**	
	5-Qt Mixer	**20-Qt Mixer**	**5-Qt Mixer**	**20-Qt Mixer**	
STRAIGHT DOUGH					
Bread flour	925g	3700g	2 lb 0.0oz	8 lb 0.0oz	**100%**
Water	666g	2664g	1 lb 7.0oz	5 lb 12.3 oz	**72%**
Extra-virgin olive oil	92g	370g	3.2oz	12.8oz	**10%**
Salt	18g	74g	0.6oz	2.60oz	**2%**
Instant yeast	6g	26g	0.2oz	0.8oz	**0.7%**
TOTAL YIELD	**1707g**	**6834g**	**3 lb 11.0oz**	**14 lb 12.5oz**	
					Pre-Ferment Baker's %
Biga					
Bread flour	*278g*	*1110g*	*9.6oz*	*2 lb 6.4oz*	*100%*
Water	*167g*	*666g*	*5.8oz*	*1 lb 7.1oz*	*60%*
Instant yeast	*0.3g*	*1g*	*0.01oz*	*0.04oz*	*0.1%*
Subtotal	*445.3g*	*1777g*	*15.41oz*	*3 lb 13.54oz*	
	5-Qt Mixer	**20-Qt Mixer**	**5-Qt Mixer**	**20-Qt Mixer**	
ADJUSTED DOUGH					
Bread flour	647g	2590g	1 lb 6.4oz	5 lb 9.6oz	
Water	499g	1998g	1 lb 1.2oz	4 lb 5.1oz	
Extra-virgin olive oil	92g	370g	3.2oz	12.8oz	
Salt	18g	74g	0.6oz	2.6oz	
Instant yeast	6g	26g	0.2oz	0.9oz	
Biga (from above)	445g	1776g	15.4oz	3 lb 13.5oz	
TOTAL YIELD	**1707g**	**6834g**	**3 lb 11.0oz**	**14 lb 12.5oz**	

NOTE: This bread may be made using only the ingredients and quantities listed for the straight dough, if enough time is available—probably 4–5 hours just for the bulk fermentation—but reduce the instant yeast percentage to about 0.3%. If, instead, you prepare a biga using the quantities specified above, subtract those ingredient weights from the straight dough to arrive at the quantities listed for the adjusted dough. Mix and hold the biga, covered but slightly vented, at 70°F for 24 hours before mixing the final dough.

Pre-Fermented Flour:	30%
Hydr. of Pre-Ferment:	100%

Option:

You may mix small quantities of chopped fresh herbs directly into the dough if you wish, probably 0.4% of the flour weight. Rosemary, thyme, or marjoram are sometimes used.

GOAL TEMPERATURE: 77°F (25°C). See directions for determining correct water temperature in *Chapter 4*.

MIXING METHOD: Either hand mixing or the short mix is recommended (pp. 195–196).

Hand mixing:

1. Cut the biga into a number of small pieces. Add it with some of the water to a plastic tub of appropriate size and soften the pieces by squeezing them with your hands. Then add all the remaining ingredients and mix with your hands until they are homogenous.

2. The dough will be wet—don't add extra flour. Cover the tub and allow the mixture to rest for about 15 minutes.

3. After the rest period, give the mixture a set of folds as you would for any baguette dough, even though the dough may seem unmanageable. Repeat these rest periods and sets of folds 4 or 5 times until the dough seems more elastic and less fluid.

SCALING:

1. For the 1X-sized batch, dump the dough onto a floured bench and stretch a bit to fit a half-size sheet pan well coated with olive oil.

2. For larger batches, cut the dough into large rectangles of 1700 g and treat as explained above.

TOPPING:

1. Brush the top of the focaccia with additional oil. Sprinkle with coarse-grained salt, if you like, and freshly ground black pepper.

2. Other topping options include thinly sliced tomatoes and zucchini, caramelized onion, or roasted garlic (press garlic pieces into the dough to prevent burning).

3. Cheese is also an option, but the "less is more" philosophy may be appropriate here, as the emphasis should be on the taste and texture of the bread, not the toppings.

PROOFING: Proof until puffy, around 45 minutes if the goal temperature was met when mixing the dough.

BAKING: 30–40 minutes in a 425°F deck oven. If your oven has excessive bottom heat, consider double-panning the focaccia before baking them.

COOLING: Cool in the pans, as the bottoms will be oily.

HEARTY SOURDOUGH RYE

	Metric		U.S. Measure		Formula Baker's %
	(1X)	(4X)	(1X)	(4X)	
	5-Qt Mixer	20-Qt Mixer	5-Qt Mixer	20-Qt Mixer	
STRAIGHT DOUGH					
Medium rye flour	510g	2040g	1 lb 2.0oz	4 lb 8.0oz	**51%**
High-gluten flour	490g	1960g	1 lb 1.0oz	4 lb 4.0oz	**49%**
Water	680g	2720g	1 lb 7.8oz	5 lb 15.2oz	**68%**
Salt	20g	80g	0.7oz	2.8oz	**2%**
Instant yeast	6g	24g	0.2oz	0.8oz	**0.6%**
TOTAL YIELD	**1706g**	**6824g**	**3 lb 11.7oz**	**14 lb 14.8oz**	
					Pre-Ferment Baker's %
Rye Sour					
Medium rye flour	*350g*	*1400g*	*12.3oz*	*3 lb 1.0oz*	*100%*
Water	*280g*	*1120g*	*9.8oz*	*2 lb 7.2oz*	*80%*
Ripe levain (not used in final dough)	*18g*	*70g*	*0.6oz*	*2.5oz*	*5%*
Subtotal	*648g*	*2590g*	*1 lb 6.7oz*	*5 lb 10.6oz*	
	5-Qt Mixer	20-Qt Mixer	5-Qt Mixer	20-Qt Mixer	
ADJUSTED DOUGH					
Medium rye flour	160g	640g	5.8oz	1 lb 7.0oz	
High-gluten flour	490g	1960g	1 lb 1.0oz	4 lb 4.0oz	
Water	400g	1600g	14.0oz	3 lb 8.0oz	
Salt	20g	80g	0.7oz	2.8oz	
Instant yeast	6g	24g	0.2oz	0.8oz	
Rye sour (from above)	630g	2520g	1 lb 6.1oz	5 lb 8.2oz	
TOTAL YIELD	**1706g**	**6824g**	**3 lb 11.7oz**	**14 lb 14.8oz**	

NOTE: You can make bread using only the ingredients and quantities listed for the straight dough, but the dough will have much less flavor and will not properly be sourdough rye, as no sour culture will be used. Rye flour usually must be acidified to control excess amylase activity. If, instead, you prepare a rye sour using the quantities specified above, subtract those ingredient weights from the straight dough to arrive at the quantities listed for the adjusted dough. Mix and hold the rye sour, covered but slightly vented, at 70°F for 15 hours before mixing the final dough.

The higher levels of rye flour in this formula will make for a loaf that is significantly more dense than the "Deli-style" rye. This is closer to the rye breads commonly found in Europe.

Pre-Fermented Flour:	35%
Hydr. of Pre-Ferment:	80%

Options:

1. Add caraway seed at a rate of 2% of the total flour weight, but leaving out the caraway can be interesting too. The true flavor of the rye can then be dominant.

2. Add toasted walnuts at a rate of 20–30% of the total flour weight, but do not combine with caraway. Walnut rye goes especially well with cheeses.

GOAL TEMPERATURE: 80°F (27°C). See directions for determining correct water temperature in *Chapter 4*.

MIXING METHOD:

1. *Warning:* Rye mixes for much less time than all-white dough. Mix 3 minutes on first speed, then 3 minutes on second speed.

2. Some gluten development will be evident, but even a small proportion of rye means the dough may be stickier than normal white bread. Do not try to eliminate the stickiness by adding flour.

3. Empty the dough into a tub lightly sprinkled with flour; cover.

FERMENTATION: Bulk ferment for 30–45 minutes. The dough will gain substantial strength during bulk fermentation.

SCALING: This dough is not ideal for making baguettes—the loaves tend to come out too flat. Boules, bâtards, or boulots: 14–22 oz (400–650 g). Allow 10 minutes for pre-shapes to relax.

SHAPING: Use some tension when making the final shapes, but don't use too much force or the dough may tear.

PROOFING: Boules, bâtards, and boulots may be proofed seam-side down on couche with pleats or seam-side up in baskets. The shaped loaves should proof sufficiently within 45–60 minutes when held at 80°F and 80% humidity. *Rye bread can proof very quickly,* so be sure to check on the loaves earlier than you would most breads.

BAKING: 430–450°F, depending on your oven's characteristics. Rack or convection ovens might be better set at 400–425°F.

1. Load the loaves on your peel or mechanical loader, score appropriately (see *Chapter 8*), and place in the preheated oven with ample steam. Generally, rye loaves should not be scored too deeply. Patterns like the sausage cut or shallow cross-cuts work well.

2. After 10 minutes of baking, be certain to open the oven vents. You may wish to decrease the temperature by about 25°F to allow for an extended bake.

3. Adjust oven temperatures to achieve the correct bake in 35–45 minutes. Shorter bake times tend to leave too much moisture in the loaves and will soften the crust.

COOLING: Cool (without crowding the loaves) on a rack with wire shelves.

HONEY WHOLE WHEAT BREAD

	Metric		U.S. Measure		Formula Baker's %
	(1X)	**(4X)**	**(1X)**	**(4X)**	
	5-Qt Mixer	20-Qt Mixer	5-Qt Mixer	20-Qt Mixer	
STRAIGHT DOUGH					
Whole wheat flour, high protein	900g	3600g	1 lb 15.0oz	7 lb 12.0oz	**100%**
Water	540g	2160g	1 lb 2.6oz	4 lb 10.4oz	**60%**
Honey	207g	828g	7.1oz	1 lb 12.5oz	**23%**
Salt	18g	72g	0.6oz	2.5oz	**2%**
Instant yeast	18g	72g	0.6oz	2.5oz	**2%**
Vital wheat gluten	18g	72g	0.6oz	2.5oz	**2%**
TOTAL YIELD	**1701g**	**6804g**	**3 lb 10.6oz**	**14 lb 10.4oz**	

Variation:

You can add a mixture of seeds like sesame, poppy, and sunflower to the dough for a more complex flavor and texture. Add seeds to the above formula at a rate of 12% of the flour weight, and increase the vital wheat gluten to 3%. You will probably need to add a bit more water as well.

GOAL TEMPERATURE: 77°F (25°C). You may find the friction factor for an intensively mixed dough like this is much higher than normal—possibly by 8–15°F.

MIXING METHOD: Use the intensive mix (p. 196). Check that the dough's moisture looks appropriate within the first minute of mixing and adjust if necessary.

SCALING:

1. For 9-in. bread pans, probably 2 lb 2 oz (975 g), and proportionally less for smaller pans.

2. This dough is usually baked in standard American-style bread pans, so the portions should be cut in square shapes as much as possible and then lightly pre-shaped into cylinders.

3. The final size of the loaves depends a lot on how completely you are able to develop the gluten, so some variation in loaf size and the appropriate weight for your pans is to be expected.

SHAPING:

1. Logs for rectangular bread pans.

2. Rounds for parchment-covered sheet pans, in which case you may wish to score them just before proofing (dense loaves of whole wheat or rye can sometimes be scored ahead of time).

PROOFING: Proof, ideally, in a humidity- and temperature-controlled proofer for 50–75 minutes at 80°F and 80% humidity.

BAKING:

1. Ideal baking temperature for the full-sized loaves in a conventional oven is about 350°F, depending on your oven's characteristics. Rack or convection ovens might be better set at 310–325°F.

2. When ready, load the trays into the oven. No scoring is necessary, and no steam should be used.

3. If using a deck oven, you may wish to double-pan the loaves to ensure they don't receive too much bottom heat and overbrown on the bottom.

COOLING: Empty the loaves from their pans as soon as they come out of the oven, or their sides and bottoms will soften too much to support their crowns. Cool (without crowding the loaves) on a rack with wire shelves.

PAIN AU LEVAIN WITH FIRM LEVAIN

	Metric		U.S. Measure		Formula Baker's %
	(1X)	**(4X)**	**(1X)**	**(4X)**	
	5-Qt Mixer	**20-Qt Mixer**	**5-Qt Mixer**	**20-Qt Mixer**	
STRAIGHT DOUGH					
Bread flour	900g	3600g	2 lb 0.0oz	8 lb 0.0oz	**90%**
Whole wheat flour	100g	400g	3.6oz	14.2oz	**10%**
Water	680g	2720g	1 lb 8.2oz	6 lb 0.7oz	**68%**
Salt	20g	80g	0.7oz	2.8oz	**2%**
Instant yeast	0g	0g	0.0oz	0.0oz	**0%**
TOTAL YIELD	**1700g**	**6800g**	**3 lb 12.5oz**	**15 lb 1.8oz**	
					Pre-Ferment Baker's %
Firm Levain					
Bread flour	300g	1200g	10.7oz	2 lb 10.7oz	100%
Water	180g	720g	6.4oz	1 lb 9.6oz	60%
Ripe levain (not used in final dough)	300g	1200g	10.7oz	2 lb 10.7oz	100%
Subtotal	780g	2554g	1 lb 11.7oz	6 lb 15.0oz	
	5-Qt Mixer	**20-Qt Mixer**	**5-Qt Mixer**	**20-Qt Mixer**	
ADJUSTED DOUGH					
Bread flour	600g	2400g	1 lb 5.3oz	5 lb 5.3oz	
Whole wheat flour	100g	400g	3.6oz	14.2oz	
Water	500g	2000g	1 lb 1.8oz	4 lb 7.1oz	
Salt	20g	80g	0.7oz	2.8oz	
Instant yeast	0g	0g	0.0oz	0.0oz	
Firm levain	480g	1920g	1 lb 1.1oz	4 lb 4.3oz	
TOTAL YIELD	**1700g**	**6800g**	**3 lb 12.5oz**	**15 lb 1.8oz**	

NOTE: This bread may be made using only the ingredients and quantities listed for the straight dough, if enough time is available—probably 4–5 hours just for the bulk fermentation—but you would need to add perhaps 0.3% instant yeast to do so, and the dough would not properly be pain au levain because there would be no levain. If, instead, you prepare a levain using the quantities specified above, subtract those ingredient weights from the straight dough to arrive at the quantities listed for the adjusted dough. Mix and hold the levain, covered but slightly vented, at 70°F for 12 hours before mixing the final dough.

Pre-Fermented Flour:	30%
Hydr. of Pre-Ferment:	60%

Option:

You may add up to about 0.07% instant yeast to the dough without changing the nature of this bread, but any more turns it into something other than true pain au levain.

Variations:

See a list of variations on basic pain au levain on pp. 224–225.

GOAL TEMPERATURE: 77°F (25°C).

MIXING METHOD: Short mix, intensive mix, or improved mix—See pp. 195–196.

BULK FERMENTATION: See directions associated with the mix method chosen—pp. 195–196, for sourdough.

SCALING: See options, p. 196.

SHAPING: See directions in *Chapter 6.*

PROOFING: See directions, pp. 196–197, for sourdough.

BAKING: See directions, p. 197.

COOLING: See directions, p. 198.

PAIN AU LEVAIN WITH LIQUID LEVAIN

	Metric		U.S. Measure		Formula Baker's %
	(1X)	**(4X)**	**(1X)**	**(4X)**	
	5-Qt Mixer	**20-Qt Mixer**	**5-Qt Mixer**	**20-Qt Mixer**	
STRAIGHT DOUGH					
Bread flour	900g	3600g	2 lb 0.0oz	8 lb 0.0oz	**90%**
Whole wheat flour	100g	400g	3.6oz	14.2oz	**10%**
Water	680g	2720g	1 lb 8.2oz	6 lb 0.7oz	**68%**
Salt	20g	80g	0.7oz	2.8oz	**2%**
Instant yeast	0g	0g	0.0oz	0.0oz	**0%**
TOTAL YIELD	**1700g**	**6800g**	**3 lb 12.5oz**	**15 lb 1.8oz**	
					Pre-Ferment Baker's %
Liquid Levain					
Bread flour	*200g*	*800g*	*7.1oz*	*1 lb 12.5oz*	*100%*
Water	*200g*	*800g*	*7.1oz*	*1 lb 12.5oz*	*100%*
Ripe levain (not used in final dough)	*100g*	*400g*	*3.6oz*	*14.2oz*	*50%*
Subtotal	*500g*	*2000g*	*1 lb 1.8oz*	*4 lb 7.1oz*	
	5-Qt Mixer	**20-Qt Mixer**	**5-Qt Mixer**	**20-Qt Mixer**	
ADJUSTED DOUGH					
Bread flour	700g	2800g	1 lb 8.9oz	6 lb 3.6oz	
Whole wheat flour	100g	400g	3.6oz	14.2oz	
Water	480g	1920g	1 lb 1.1oz	4 lb 4.3oz	
Salt	20g	80g	0.7oz	2.8oz	
Instant yeast	0g	0g	0.0oz	0.0oz	
Liquid levain	400g	1600g	14.2oz	3 lb 8.9oz	
TOTAL YIELD	**1700g**	**6800g**	**3 lb 12.5oz**	**15 lb 1.8oz**	

Pre-Fermented Flour:	20%
Hydr. of Pre-Ferment:	100%

NOTE: This bread may be made using only the ingredients and quantities listed for the straight dough, if enough time is available—probably 4–5 hours just for the bulk fermentation—but you would need to add perhaps 0.3% instant yeast to do so, and the dough would not properly be pain au levain because there would be no levain. If, instead, you prepare a levain using the quantities specified above, subtract those ingredient weights from the straight dough to arrive at the quantities listed for the adjusted dough. Mix and hold the levain, covered but slightly vented, at 70°F for 12 hours before mixing the final dough.

Option:

You may add up to about 0.07% instant yeast to the dough without changing the nature of this bread, but any more turns it into something other than true pain au levain.

Variations:

See a list of variations on basic pain au levain below.

GOAL TEMPERATURE: 77°F (25°C).

MIXING METHOD: Short mix, intensive mix, or improved mix—see pp. 195–196.

BULK FERMENTATION: See directions associated with the mix method chosen—pp. 195–196, for sourdough.

SCALING: See options, p. 196.

SHAPING: See directions in *Chapter 6*.

PROOFING: See directions, pp. 196–197, for sourdough.

BAKING: See directions, p. 197.

COOLING: See directions, p. 198.

VARIATIONS ON PAIN AU LEVAIN:

The basic pain au levain dough can be modified in many ways to create breads very different from the original. You can use either of the preceding formulas for pain au levain, keeping in mind that the one using firm levain is more sharply acidic than the one made with liquid levain.

Walnuts:

- These are a common addition, and walnut levain bread is often served with cheese in France.

- Use an amount equal to 25% or more of the weight of the flour. Other nut options are hazelnuts or pecans.

- Toasting the nuts in an oven (and then cooling them) before use brings out wonderful aromas and complex flavors.

- Add only in the last minute or two of mixing, on first speed only.

Olives (pitted, of course):

- Olives are sometimes added to this basic dough at 25–35% of the weight of the flour.

- Drain the olives well before use—even a day ahead of time if possible. The brine can color the dough purple or gray if mixed in for too long a time, so add the olives at the last minute or so.

- Many bakers toss the olives with flour just before adding them.

- You may want to reduce the salt in the formula to 1.5% instead of the usual 2% so the saltiness of the olive bread won't be overwhelming.

- Fresh rosemary, thyme, or herbes de Provence can be used in conjunction with the olives.

Cracked Grains:

- Alternative grains add flavor, texture, and more complex aromas to pain au levain. Using added grains at 25% or more is common.

- You can purchase 6-grain or 9-grain preassembled mixtures from bakery purveyors, or, if you have the storage space, you can keep individual containers of cracked grains or seeds like wheat, rye, barley, millet, oats, and flax and customize the mixture yourself.

- Generally, you'll want to create a soaker by mixing the grains with a quantity of water (equal to or greater than the weight of grains) a day or so ahead of time. This water is a separate quantity from that used to hydrate the flour in the formula and should not be subtracted from the water in the standard formula or considered in evaluating the overall hydration of the dough. If possible, add the soaker toward the end of the mix time to reduce the risk of damaging the gluten structure.

PAIN DE CAMPAGNE

	Metric		U.S. Measure		Formula Baker's %
	(1X)	**(4X)**	**(1X)**	**(4X)**	
	5-Qt Mixer	20-Qt Mixer	5-Qt Mixer	20-Qt Mixer	
STRAIGHT DOUGH					
Bread flour	900g	3600g	1 lb 11.0oz	6 lb 12.0oz	**90%**
Medium rye flour	100g	400g	3.0oz	12.0oz	**10%**
Water	680g	2720g	1 lb 4.4oz	5 lb 1.6oz	**68%**
Salt	22g	88g	0.7oz	2.6oz	**2.2%**
Instant yeast	3g	12g	0.1oz	0.4oz	**0.5%**
TOTAL YIELD	**1705g**	**6820g**	**3 lb 3.2oz**	**12 lb 12.6oz**	

Options:

You could use a pre-ferment to make this dough, if you wish. With sponge, biga, or old dough, limit pre-fermented flour in the formula to 35% or less. The high enzyme levels in poolish make it less risky at 25% or less. Firm levain works reliably up to 30% or so, but liquid levain can create stickiness at anything above 18–20%.

The use of any pre-ferment reduces significantly the time necessary for the dough to reach maturity.

GOAL TEMPERATURE: 77°F (25°C).

MIXING METHOD: Short mix, intensive mix, or improved mix—see pp. 195–196.

BULK FERMENTATION: See directions associated with the mix method chosen—pp. 195–196.

SCALING: See options, p. 196.

SHAPING: See directions in *Chapter 6.*

PROOFING: See directions, pp. 196–197.

BAKING: See directions, p. 197.

COOLING: See directions, p. 198.

PAIN RUSTIQUE—HAND METHOD

	Metric		U.S. Measure		Formula Baker's %
	(1X)	**(4X)**	**(1X)**	**(4X)**	
	5-Qt Mixer	20-Qt Mixer	5-Qt Mixer	20-Qt Mixer	
STRAIGHT DOUGH					
Bread flour	600g	2400g	2 lb 2.0oz	8 lb 8.0oz	**100%**
Water	450g	1800g	1 lb 9.5oz	6 lb 6.0oz	**75%**
Salt	13g	53g	0.8oz	3.0oz	**2.2%**
Instant yeast	2g	8g	0.1oz	0.5oz	**0.4%**
TOTAL YIELD	**1065g**	**4261g**	**3 ib 12.4oz**	**15 lb 1.5oz**	

GOAL TEMPERATURE: 77°F (25°C). See directions for determining correct water temperature in *Chapter 4*.

MIXING BY HAND:

1. Add all the ingredients and mix with your hands until they are homogenous. The dough will be wet—don't add extra flour.

2. Cover the tub and allow the mixture to rest for about 15 minutes.

3. After the rest period, give the mixture a set of folds as you would any baguette dough, even though the dough may seem unmanageable. Repeat these rest periods and sets of folds 4 or 5 times until the dough seems to be more elastic and less fluid.

SCALING:

1. Gently empty the tub of dough onto a well-floured bench and rearrange the dough so its shape is rectangular and its thickness the same throughout.

2. Cut a strip of dough as wide as you want your loaves to be. Then cut for length. Keep the dough portions as rectangular as you can and rest them temporarily on floured proofing boards as you proceed. Keep the proofing boards with the portions covered as you proceed.

3. Standard loaves—8–16 oz (450–525 g).

SHAPING:

1. The portions are not so much shaped as they are stretched slightly. Stretch each loaf into a rectangle 8–10 inches long and place on well-floured couche with pleats between each row of 2 loaves.

2. With this bread, you may wish to leave any small pieces of dough sitting on top of the larger rectangle because the loaves will be flipped upside-down just before loading them in the oven.

PROOFING: 45 minutes at 80°F and 80% humidity. If a proofer is not available, cover the rack holding the boards and keep as close to 80° as possible.

BAKING:

1. In a deck oven—475–500°F (245–260°C).

2. Load the ciabatta on your peel or mechanical loader, flipping them upside-down as you do so to expose the attractive veined look of the flour clinging to the underside.

3. Insert the loaves with a few seconds of steam. No scoring is necessary.

4. 25–30 minutes for loaves, 12–15 minutes for rolls. Be sure to vent the oven after the first 10 minutes of baking. Shorter bake times tend to leave too much moisture in the loaves and will soften the crust; longer times may make for a thick crust and a dry interior.

COOLING: Cool (without crowding the loaves) on a rack with wire shelves.

PANE PUGLIESE WITH BIGA

	Metric		U.S. Measure		Formula Baker's %
	(1X)	**(4X)**	**(1X)**	**(4X)**	
	5-Qt Mixer	20-Qt Mixer	5-Qt Mixer	20-Qt Mixer	
STRAIGHT DOUGH					
Bread flour	950g	3800g	2 lb 1.0oz	8 lb 4.0oz	**100%**
Water	722g	2888g	1 lb 9.1oz	6 lb 4.3oz	**76%**
Salt	19g	76g	0.7oz	2.6oz	**2%**
Instant yeast	4g	15g	0.1oz	0.5oz	**0.4%**
TOTAL YIELD	**1695g**	**6779g**	**3 lb 10.9oz**	**14 lb 11.5oz**	
					Pre-Ferment Baker's %
Biga					
Bread flour	*333g*	*1330g*	*11.6oz*	*2 lb 14.2oz*	*100%*
Water	*200g*	*798g*	*6.9oz*	*1 lb 11.7oz*	*60%*
Instant yeast	*0.3g*	*1g*	*0.01oz*	*0.05oz*	*0.1%*
Subtotal	*532g*	*2830g*	*1 lb 2.5oz*	*4 lb 10.0oz*	
	5-Qt Mixer	20-Qt Mixer	5-Qt Mixer	20-Qt Mixer	
ADJUSTED DOUGH					
Bread flour	618g	2470g	1 lb 5.5oz	5 lb 5.8oz	
Water	523g	2090g	1 lb 2.2oz	4 lb 8.6oz	
Salt	19g	76g	0.7oz	2.6oz	
Instant yeast	4g	15g	0.1oz	0.5oz	
Biga (from above)	532g	2128g	1 lb 2.5oz	4 lb 9.9oz	
TOTAL YIELD	**1695g**	**6779g**	**3 lb 10.9oz**	**14 lb 11.5oz**	

NOTE: This bread may be made using only the ingredients and quantities listed for the straight dough, if enough time is available—probably 4–5 hours just for the bulk fermentation—but reduce the instant yeast percentage to about 0.3%. If, instead, you prepare a biga using the quantities specified above, subtract those ingredient weights from the straight dough to arrive at the quantities listed for the adjusted dough. Mix and hold the biga, covered but slightly vented, at 70°F for 24 hours before mixing the final dough.

Pre-Fermented Flour:	35%
Hydr. of Pre-Ferment:	60%

GOAL TEMPERATURE: 77°F (25°C). See directions for determining correct water temperature in *Chapter 4.*

MIXING METHOD: Improved mix (p. 196), with the following modifications:

1. Use the double hydration method discussed in *Chapter 4.* Hold back 10–15% of the total water in the formula so the consistency of the dough is like that of a typical baguette dough. Mix about 5 minutes on first speed followed by 3–5 minutes on second speed. Then add the remaining water and incorporate *on first speed only*—probably 2–4 additional minutes.

2. Place the dough in a covered tub lightly sprinkled with flour. Bulk ferment for 2–3 hours, giving the dough a set of stretch-and-folds every 15 minutes or so, perhaps 3 or 4 times.

SCALING:

1. Gently empty the tub of dough onto a well-floured bench and rearrange the dough so its shape is rectangular and its thickness the same throughout.

2. Cut a strip of dough as wide as you want your square portions to be. Then cut your squares from the strip.

3. Rest the squares temporarily on floured proofing boards as you proceed. Keep the proofing boards with the portions covered as you go.

4. Standard loaves—24–32 oz (675–900 g).

SHAPING:

1. Round the portions gently but with some tension, pulling the skin toward the base of the loaf as you turn the dough in your hand. Use flour as needed to prevent sticking.

2. Turn the loaf over quickly so its seam is showing on top. Sprinkle flour liberally over the seam so it will not easily seal.

3. Turn the loaf back to seam-side down and either proof in floured baskets or on a well-floured proofing board.

PROOFING: 60–75 minutes at 80°F and 80% humidity. If a proofer is not available, cover the rack holding the boards and keep as close to 80° as possible.

BAKING:

1. In a deck oven—425–440°F (220–230°C), 25–40°F less for convection or rack ovens.

2. Load the loaves on your peel or mechanical loader by flipping them upside-down. As you do so, you will expose the attractive veined look of the flour clinging to the underside and allow the seams to open.

3. If the seams do not appear to open on some loaves, you can score them lightly.

4. 50–70 minutes with steam in the first 10 minutes of the bake. Be sure to vent the oven after the first 10 minutes. Shorter bake times tend to leave too much moisture in the loaves and will soften the crust; longer times may make for a thick crust and a dry interior.

COOLING: Cool (without crowding the loaves) on a rack with wire shelves.

PIZZA DOUGH WITH BIGA

	Metric		U.S. Measure		Formula Baker's %
	(1X)	(4X)	(1X)	(4X)	
	5-Qt Mixer	20-Qt Mixer	5-Qt Mixer	20-Qt Mixer	
STRAIGHT DOUGH					
Bread flour	1000g	4000g	2 lb 3.0oz	8 lb 12.0oz	**100%**
Water	650g	2600g	1 lb 6.8oz	5 lb 11.0oz	**65%**
Salt	22g	88g	0.8oz	3.1oz	**2.2%**
Instant yeast	4g	16g	0.1oz	0.6oz	**0.4%**
TOTAL YIELD	**1676g**	**6704g**	**3 lb 10.7oz**	**14 lb 10.6oz**	
					Pre-Ferment Baker's %
Biga					
Bread flour	200g	800g	7.0oz	1 lb 12.0oz	100%
Water	120g	480g	4.2oz	1 lb 0.8oz	60%
Instant yeast	0.2g	422g	0.01oz	14.8oz	0.1%
Subtotal	320g	1281g	11.2oz	2 lb 12.8oz	
	5-Qt Mixer	20-Qt Mixer	5-Qt Mixer	20-Qt Mixer	
ADJUSTED DOUGH					
Bread flour	800g	3200g	1 lb 12.0oz	7 lb 0.0oz	
Water	530g	2120g	1 lb 2.6oz	4 lb 10.2oz	
Salt	22g	88g	0.8oz	3.1oz	
Instant yeast	4g	16g	0.1oz	0.6oz	
Biga (from above)	320g	1280g	11.2oz	2 lb 12.8oz	
TOTAL YIELD	**1676g**	**6704g**	**3 lb 10.7oz**	**14 lb 10.6oz**	

NOTE: This bread may be made using only the ingredients and quantities listed for the straight dough. If, instead, you prepare a biga using the quantities specified above, subtract those ingredient weights from the straight dough to arrive at the quantities listed for the adjusted dough. Mix and hold the biga, covered but slightly vented, at 70°F for 24 hours before mixing the final dough.

Pre-Fermented Flour:	20%
Hydr. of Pre-Ferment:	60%

GOAL TEMPERATURE: 75°F (24°C). See directions for determining correct water temperature in *Chapter 4*. Keep in mind that when mixing only on first speed, the friction factor will be much less than when using second speed.

MIXING METHOD: 10 minutes on first speed. Empty the dough into a tub lightly sprinkled with flour; cover.

FERMENTATION: 15 minutes rest period.

SCALING:

1. 7 oz (200 g) pieces for the classic size served around Naples, Italy, which produces a 9–10-in. pizza. Scale at larger sizes if you wish.

2. Round all portions and set them in the bottom of a lightly floured, large, but shallow plastic tub with a well-fitting lid. Leave several inches between the rounds to allow for growth and relaxation overnight.

3. Cover the tub with the lid and refrigerate at least several hours and preferably overnight.

SHAPING:

1. Take a portion straight from the refrigerator and stretch it gently over a clenched hand, using gravity to assist you and turning the portion in your hand as you go.

2. Keep the thickness fairly even as you do so. The recommended 7-oz piece should make a 9–10-in. shell.

PROOFING: None.

TOPPING:

1. Place the stretched round on a cornmeal- or semolina-covered peel and top immediately with tomatoes or sauce (2 oz for the 7-oz dough shell).

2. Quickly add cheese, fresh basil, or anything else you choose. True Italian pizza is never overloaded with toppings, so we encourage you to hold back somewhat and let yourself actually taste the crust.

3. Load the pizza immediately, or it may start to stick to the peel.

BAKING:

1. Get your deck oven about as hot as you safely can—600–700°F is fine, if that's possible. Go with 550°F if you can't go hotter.

2. In a very hot oven, a pizza can bake in as little as 2–3 minutes. At 550°F, it will probably take at least 2–3 minutes longer than that, 5–6 minutes total.

3. Be conservative the first time you do this and check the bake early to avoid burning. Slide the pizzas directly on the stone deck when you load them into the oven and retrieve them with the peel as well.

COOLING: This is one of the few breads actually best eaten hot from the oven. No cooling necessary.

PULLMAN BREAD (PAIN DE MIE)

	Metric		U.S. Measure		Formula Baker's %
	(1X)	(4X)	(1X)	(4X)	
	5-Qt Mixer	20-Qt Mixer	5-Qt Mixer	20-Qt Mixer	
STRAIGHT DOUGH					
Bread flour	900g	3600g	2 lb 4.0oz	9 lb 0.0oz	100%
Water	540g	2160g	1 lb 5.6oz	5 lb 6.4oz	60%
Butter, softened	72g	288g	2.9oz	11.5oz	8%
Sugar	45g	180g	1.8oz	7.2oz	5%
Milk powder	54g	216g	2.2oz	8.6oz	6%
Salt	20g	79g	0.8oz	3.2oz	2.2%
Instant yeast	9g	36g	0.4oz	1.4oz	1%
TOTAL YIELD	**1640g**	**6559g**	**4 lb 1.6oz**	**16 lb 6.4oz**	

Variation:

You can use the straight dough above as the basis for an adjusted dough that utilizes a sponge or old dough (see *Chapter 4*). Both pre-ferments are easy to prepare and practically risk-free to use. They add strength to what is already a strong dough, but the flavor is improved noticeably at pre-fermented flour levels of 25–40%.

GOAL TEMPERATURE: 77°F (25°C). See directions for determining correct water temperature in *Chapter 4*.

MIXING METHOD: Use the intensive mix method, described on p. 196.

FERMENTING: About 1 hour.

SCALING: For 13-in. Pullman pan: 32 oz; 17-in. Pullman pan: 44 oz; 9 × 4-in. bread pan: 30 oz. Some variation may result from differences in dough strength or peculiarities of pan size.

SHAPING: Shape as long logs for the Pullman pans and short logs for the standard, open-topped bread pans. Spray both

the pans and their lids on the inside surface with pan release before placing shaped dough portions in them.

PROOFING:

1. Slide the lids onto the Pullman pans but leave an opening of about 1 in. or so to monitor the proof. When the crowns of the dough portions reach within ½ in. of the lid, close the lids and bake the Pullman loaves.

2. For open-topped pans, allow the crowns of the loaves to rise above the rim of the pan.

3. The loaves are usually proofed fully 50–70 minutes after being placed in a proofer set to 80°F and 80% humidity.

BAKING:

1. 380–400°F for 45–60 minutes for the closed-top Pullmans (350–370°F for a convection or rack oven); 350–375°F for 30–35 minutes for the open-topped bread pans (310–330°F for a convection or rack oven).

2. The sides of the loaves must be golden brown to support the weight of the crowns.

3. Differences in ovens can produce different temperatures and bake times—be conservative and check loaves earlier than their anticipated finish time.

COOLING:

1. After baking is complete, empty the loaves from their pans immediately or their sides will soften.

2. Cool completely before slicing, and wrap completely after cooling.

ROSEMARY OLIVE OIL BREAD

	Metric		U.S. Measure		Formula Baker's %
	(1X)	**(4X)**	**(1X)**	**(4X)**	
	5-Qt Mixer	20-Qt Mixer	5-Qt Mixer	20-Qt Mixer	
STRAIGHT DOUGH					
Bread flour	1000g	4000g	2 lb 2.0oz	8 lb 8.0oz	**100%**
Water	680g	2720g	1 lb 7.1oz	5 lb 12.5oz	**68%**
Extra-virgin olive oil	40g	160g	1.4oz	5.4oz	**4%**
Rosemary leaves, chopped	5g	20g	0.2oz	0.7oz	**0.5%**
Salt	20g	80g	0.7oz	2.7oz	**2%**
Instant yeast	7g	28g	0.2oz	1.0oz	**0.7%**
TOTAL YIELD	**1752g**	**7008g**	**3 lb 11.6oz**	**14 lb 14.3oz**	
					Pre-Ferment Baker's %
Old Dough					
Bread flour	250g	1000g	8.5oz	2 lb 2.0oz	100%
Water	170g	680g	5.8oz	1 lb 7.1oz	68%
Salt	5g	20g	0.2oz	0.7oz	2%
Instant yeast	2g	7g	0.1oz	0.2oz	0.7%
Subtotal	427g	1707g	14.5oz	3 lb 10.0oz	
	5-Qt Mixer	20-Qt Mixer	5-Qt Mixer	20-Qt Mixer	
ADJUSTED DOUGH					
Bread flour	750g	3000g	1 lb 9.5oz	6 lb 6.0oz	
Water	510g	2040g	1 lb 1.3oz	4 lb 5.4oz	
Extra-virgin olive oil	40g	160g	1.4oz	5.4oz	
Rosemary leaves, chopped	5g	20g	0.2oz	0.7oz	
Salt	15g	60g	0.5oz	2.0oz	
Instant yeast	5g	21g	0.2oz	0.7oz	
Old dough (from above)	427g	1707g	14.5oz	3 lb 10.0oz	
TOTAL YIELD	**1752g**	**7008g**	**3 lb 11.6oz**	**14 lb 14.3oz**	

NOTE: This bread may be made using only the ingredients and quantities listed for the straight dough, if enough time is available—probably 4–5 hours just for the bulk fermentation—but reduce the instant yeast percentage to about 0.3%. If you make old dough using the quantities specified above, subtract those ingredient weights from the straight dough to arrive at the quantities listed for the adjusted dough. Mix the old dough and ferment 3 hours at room temperature, or ferment 1 hour at room temperature and refrigerate until use.

Pre-Fermented Flour:	25%
Hydr. of Pre-Ferment:	100%

GOAL TEMPERATURE: 77°F (25°C).

MIXING METHOD: Short mix, intensive mix, or improved mix—see pp. 195–196.

BULK FERMENTATION: See directions associated with the mix method chosen—pp. 195–196.

SCALING: See options, p. 196.

SHAPING: See directions in *Chapter 6*.

PROOFING: See directions, pp. 196–197.

BAKING: See directions, p. 197.

COOLING: See directions, p. 198.

RYE DEAD DOUGH (DECORATIVE)

	Metric		U.S. Measure		Formula Baker's %
	(1X)	**(4X)**	**(1X)**	**(4X)**	
	5-Qt Mixer	20-Qt Mixer	5-Qt Mixer	20-Qt Mixer	
STRAIGHT DOUGH					
White rye flour	1000g	4000g	2 lb 3.0oz	8 lb 12.0oz	**100%**
Syrup for dead dough (see separate formula)	670g	2680g	1 lb 7.5oz	5 lb 14.0oz	**67%**
TOTAL YIELD	**1670g**	**6680g**	**3 lb 10.5oz**	**14 lb 10.0oz**	

NOTE: This dough has a grayish cast from the color of the white rye. You may substitute medium rye, but the color will be much darker and you may need to add more syrup than specified above. This dough can be colored with cocoa, spinach powder, or spices like turmeric and paprika. To color with a spice or powder, subtract an amount of flour equivalent to the weight of the powder, and then add a bit less or more syrup as needed. To color with molasses or caramel color, subtract the weight of the liquid from the weight of the syrup normally used in the formula.

MIXING METHOD:

1. 3–5 minutes on first speed only is probably sufficient. Dead dough should be mixed just until the ingredients are evenly combined and can form a smooth mass. If you mix beyond this point, you increase the likelihood that the cut and shaped pieces made from the dough will blister noticeably on baking.

2. Add more syrup if necessary before the dough is completely mixed to achieve a consistency that is firm but smooth and not sticky.

3. Small batches of dead dough are easily mixed by hand in a mixing bowl.

4. You *must* keep this dough well covered during use or storage, or it will form a skin and become too dry to use.

FERMENTATION: None.

SCALING: Scale to any size you need, but be careful to keep the pieces covered with plastic. Keep the dough mass you are cutting from covered as well.

BAKING:

1. Any pieces made from this dough should be allowed to dry for 1–2 days before baking, if possible. Pieces that are well dried before baking lose their moisture more slowly and are less susceptible to cracking. In competitions, you will probably have to bake your pieces the same day you form them.

2. Use low heat—about 250°F—to thoroughly bake the pieces and dry them without browning them much. You're concerned here with getting the starches to gelatinize and set so as to form a rigid structure.

3. You may not need to bake every piece you make (flowers can often be left without baking), as they may dry to hardness without it, but for any piece designed to support weight or act as a structural component, thorough baking is necessary.

4. Baking times of 1–2 hours—or even longer—are not uncommon, depending on the size and weight of the piece. Very small items bake much more quickly.

COOLING: The pieces will sometimes seem a bit soft on leaving the oven, but items that are thin or narrow harden on cooling.

SAN FRANCISCO-STYLE SOURDOUGH BREAD

	Metric		U.S. Measure		Formula Baker's %
	(1X)	**(4X)**	**(1X)**	**(4X)**	
	5-Qt Mixer	20-Qt Mixer	5-Qt Mixer	20-Qt Mixer	
STRAIGHT DOUGH					
Bread flour	1000g	4000g	2 lb 3.0oz	8 lb 12.0oz	**100%**
Water	680g	2720g	1 lb 7.8oz	5 lb 15.2oz	**68%**
Salt	20g	80g	0.7oz	2.8oz	**2%**
Instant yeast	0g	0g	0.0oz	0.0oz	**0%**
TOTAL YIELD	**1700g**	**6800g**	**3 lb 11.5oz**	**14 lb 14.0oz**	
					Pre-Ferment Baker's %
Firm Levain					
Bread flour	*300g*	*1200g*	*10.5oz*	*2 lb 10.0oz*	*100%*
Water	*180g*	*720g*	*6.3oz*	*1 lb 9.2oz*	*60%*
Ripe levain (not used in final dough)	*300g*	*1200g*	*10.5oz*	*2 lb 10.0oz*	*100%*
Subtotal	*780g*	*3120g*	*1 lb 11.3oz*	*6 lb 13.2oz*	
	5-Qt Mixer	20-Qt Mixer	5-Qt Mixer	20-Qt Mixer	
ADJUSTED DOUGH					
Bread flour	700g	2800g	1 lb 8.5oz	6 lb 2.0oz	
Water	500g	2000g	1 lb 1.5oz	4 lb 6.0oz	
Salt	0g	0g	0.0oz	0.0oz	
Instant yeast	480g	1920g	1 lb 0.8oz	4 lb 3.2oz	
Firm levain	427g	1707g	14.5oz	3 lb 10.0oz	
TOTAL YIELD	**1700g**	**6800g**	**3 lb 11.5oz**	**14 lb 14.0oz**	

NOTE: This bread may be made using only the ingredients and quantities listed for the straight dough, if enough time is available—probably 4–5 hours just for the bulk fermentation—but you would need to add perhaps 0.3% instant yeast to do so, and the dough will not properly be a sourdough because no sour culture is used. If, instead, you prepare a levain using the quantities specified above, subtract those ingredient weights from the straight dough to arrive at the quantities listed for the adjusted dough. Mix and hold the levain, covered but slightly vented, at 70°F for 12 hours before mixing the final dough.

Pre-Fermented Flour:	30%
Hydr. of Pre-Ferment:	60%

Option:

You may add up to about 0.07% instant yeast to the dough without changing the nature of this bread, but any more turns it into something other than true sourdough.

GOAL TEMPERATURE: 77°F (25°C).

MIXING METHOD: Short mix, intensive mix, or improved mix—see pp. 195–196.

BULK FERMENTATION: See directions associated with the mix method chosen—pp. 195–196, for sourdough.

SCALING: Sourdough is not ideal for making baguettes—the loaves tend to come out too flat. See other options, p. 196.

SHAPING: See directions in *Chapter 6*.

PROOFING: See directions, pp. 196–197, for sourdough.

BAKING: See directions, p. 197.

COOLING: See directions, p. 198.

SICILIAN SEMOLINA BREAD

	Metric		U.S. Measure		Formula Baker's %
	(1X)	**(4X)**	**(1X)**	**(4X)**	
	5-Qt Mixer	20-Qt Mixer	5-Qt Mixer	20-Qt Mixer	
STRAIGHT DOUGH					
Bread flour	600g	2400g	1 lb 4.0oz	5 lb 0.0oz	**60%**
Durum flour (finely ground semolina)	400g	1600g	13.3oz	3 lb 5.4oz	**40%**
Water	680g	2720g	1 lb 6.7oz	5 lb 10.7oz	**68%**
Olive oil	40g	160g	1.3oz	5.3oz	**4%**
Salt	20g	80g	0.7oz	2.7oz	**2%**
Instant yeast	4g	16g	0.1oz	0.5oz	**0.4%**
TOTAL YIELD	**1744g**	**6976g**	**3 lb 10.1oz**	**14 lb 8.6oz**	
					Pre-Ferment Baker's %
Biga					
Bread flour	350g	1400g	11.7oz	2 lb 14.7oz	100%
Water	210g	840g	7.0oz	1 lb 12.0oz	60%
Instant yeast	0.4g	1.4g	0.01oz	0.05oz	0.1%
Subtotal	560.4g	2241.4g	1 lb 2.71oz	4 lb 10.75oz	
	5-Qt Mixer	20-Qt Mixer	5-Qt Mixer	20-Qt Mixer	
ADJUSTED DOUGH					
Bread flour	250g	1000g	8.3oz	2 lb 1.3oz	
Durum flour (finely ground semolina)	400g	1600g	13.3oz	3 lb 5.4oz	
Water	470g	1880g	15.7oz	3 lb 14.7oz	
Olive oil	40g	160g	1.3oz	5.3oz	
Salt	20g	80g	0.7oz	2.7oz	
Instant yeast	4g	16g	0.1oz	0.5oz	
Biga (from above)	560g	2240g	1 lb 2.7oz	4 lb 10oz	
TOTAL YIELD	**1744g**	**6976g**	**3 lb 10.1oz**	**14 lb 8.6oz**	

Pre-Fermented Flour:	35%
Hydr. of Pre-Ferment:	100%

NOTES:

1. This bread may be made using only the ingredients and quantities listed for the straight dough, if enough time is available—probably 4–5 hours just for the bulk fermentation—but you would need to use perhaps 0.3% instant yeast to do so. If, instead, you prepare a biga using the quantities specified above, subtract those ingredient weights from the straight dough to arrive at the quantities listed for the adjusted dough. Mix and hold the biga, covered but slightly vented, at 70°F for 12 hours before mixing the final dough.

2. Coarser semolina granules can be substituted for the finer flour, but a much longer autolyse of 30–45 minutes would be advisable.

GOAL TEMPERATURE: 77°F (25°C). See directions for determining correct water temperature in *Chapter 4*.

MIXING METHOD: Improved mix (p. 196), with the following modifications:

1. Mix 3 minutes on first speed, then cover the mixer bowl with plastic sheeting and allow the mixture to rest 20–30 minutes—this is known as an autolyse period. Add water if the dough appears too dry.

2. After the autolyse period, continue mixing 3–4 minutes on second speed. Be careful not to overmix—semolina does not tolerate overmixing well.

3. Empty the dough into a tub lightly sprinkled with flour; cover.

FERMENTATION:

1. Bulk ferment for 2–3 hours.

2. Perform a set of stretch-and-folds after 20 minutes of fermentation. A second set is optional if the dough appears to need more strength. The dough will improve noticeably in strength over the period of bulk fermentation.

SCALING: 20 oz (570 g) for football-shaped loaves. Pre-shape the portions as rounds and allow them to relax for 15 minutes before final shaping.

SHAPING:

1. See *Chapter 6* for illustrations on shaping a boulot or football from a round pre-shape.

2. Alternatively, pre-shape the portions as cylinders and, after 15–20 minutes, extend them into long strands, like a baguette, which can then be coiled into an S-shape.

3. In Sicily, these loaves are often moistened on top before proofing and dipped into a container of sesame seeds, but this is entirely optional.

PROOFING:

1. Proof in floured, pleated couche, 4–6 loaves per board, or use long proofing baskets.

2. 60 minutes or so at 80°F and 80% humidity. If a proofer is not available, cover the rack holding the boards and keep as close to 80°F as possible.

BAKING:

1. In a deck oven—425–440°F (220–230°C). Rack or convection ovens might be better set at 25–40°F less.

2. When they are ready (see the discussion of proofing in *Chapter 7*), load the loaves on your peel or mechanical loader, score as for boulots, and place in the preheated oven with ample steam.

3. 30–40 minutes. Be sure to vent the oven after the first 10 minutes of baking. Shorter bake times tend to leave too much moisture in the loaves.

COOLING: Cool (without crowding the loaves) on a rack with wire shelves.

SYRUP FOR DEAD DOUGH

	Metric		U.S. Measure		Formula Baker's %
	(1X)	**(4X)**	**(1X)**	**(4X)**	
	5-Qt Mixer	20-Qt Mixer	5-Qt Mixer	20-Qt Mixer	
Water	300g	1200g	10.3oz	2 lb 9.0oz	**100%**
Sugar	300g	1200g	10.3oz	2 lb 9.0oz	**100%**
Glucose or corn syrup	105g	420g	3.6oz	14.4oz	**35%**
TOTAL YIELD	**705g**	**2820g**	**1 lb 8.1oz**	**6 lb 0.4oz**	

METHOD:

1. Mix all the ingredients together in a saucepan and bring just to a boil. Do not allow the syrup to boil for any time afterward, or the balance of water and sugar will be different from that specified above.

2. Allow the syrup to cool completely (to about room temperature or lower) before using. Do not use while the syrup is still warm. Stirring the finished syrup while the pot is in an ice bath can expedite the cooling process when necessary, but the syrup may also be prepared ahead a day or two.

WHITE ACTIVE DOUGH (DECORATIVE)

	Metric		U.S. Measure		Formula Baker's %
	(1X)	**(4X)**	**(1X)**	**(4X)**	
	5-Qt Mixer	**20-Qt Mixer**	**5-Qt Mixer**	**20-Qt Mixer**	
STRAIGHT DOUGH					
Bread flour	1000g	4000g	2 lb 2.0oz	8 lb 8.0oz	**100%**
Sugar	40g	160g	1.4oz	5.4oz	**4%**
Salt	13g	52g	0.4oz	1.8oz	**1.6%**
Vegetable shortening	60g	240g	2.0oz	8.2oz	**6%**
Instant yeast	2g	8g	0.1oz	0.3oz	**0.2%**
Whole milk	600g	2400g	1 lb 4.4oz	5 lb 3.8oz	**60%**
TOTAL YIELD	**1715g**	**6860g**	**3 lb 10.3oz**	**14 lb 9.2oz**	

MIXING METHOD:

1. Place all ingredients in the mixing bowl and mix for 5 minutes on low speed and 3–5 minutes on second speed. Unlike with dead dough, we are looking to develop the gluten in this decorative dough. The consistency should be firm and smooth but still supple and not crumbly.

2. After mixing, wrap the dough tightly and allow to rest about 15 minutes in the refrigerator before dividing and shaping. Keep in the refrigerator until use to control yeast activity, and keep covered on the bench to avoid skin forming.

PROOFING:

1. Allow finished centerpieces to relax in the refrigerator overnight or proof them a bit in an enclosed, humidified proofer at about 80°F and 80% humidity until visibly puffy, 30–60 minutes.

2. You may wish to egg-wash your piece before or after proofing.

BAKING: In general, 25–35 minutes at 350°F in a deck oven. Set convection and rack ovens 25–50°F lower, depending on the characteristics of the oven.

COOLING: On a wire rack.

WHITE DEAD DOUGH (DECORATIVE)

	Metric		U.S. Measure		Formula Baker's %
	(1X)	**(4X)**	**(1X)**	**(4X)**	
	5-Qt Mixer	20-Qt Mixer	5-Qt Mixer	20-Qt Mixer	
STRAIGHT DOUGH					
White AP flour or strong pastry flour	1000g	4000g	2 lb 3.0oz	8 lb 12.0oz	**100%**
Syrup for dead dough (see separate formula)	670g	2680g	1 lb 7.5oz	5 lb 13.8oz	**67%**
TOTAL YIELD	**1670g**	**6680g**	**3 lb 10.5oz**	**14 lb 9.8oz**	

NOTE: This dough can be colored with cocoa, spinach powder, or spices like turmeric and paprika. To color with a spice or powder, subtract an amount of flour equivalent to the weight of the powder, and then add a bit less or more syrup as needed. To color with molasses or caramel color, subtract the weight of the liquid used from the weight of the syrup normally used in the formula. This dough is stronger and a bit less extensible than the rye dead dough due to the higher gluten levels in white flour.

MIXING METHOD:

1. 3–5 minutes on first speed only is probably sufficient. Dead dough should be mixed just until the ingredients are evenly combined and can form a smooth mass. If you mix beyond this point, you increase the likelihood that the cut and shaped pieces made from the dough will blister noticeably on baking.

2. Add more syrup if necessary before the dough is completely mixed to achieve a consistency that is firm but smooth and not sticky.

3. Smaller batches of dead dough are easily mixed by hand in a mixing bowl.

4. You *must* keep this dough well covered during use or storage, or it will form a skin and become too dry to use.

FERMENTATION: None.

SCALING:
Scale to any size you need, but be careful to keep all pieces covered with plastic. Keep the dough mass you are cutting from covered as well.

BAKING:

1. Pieces made from this dough should be allowed to dry for 1–2 days before baking, if possible. Pieces that are well dried before baking lose their moisture more slowly and are less susceptible to cracking. In competitions, you will probably have to bake your pieces the same day you form them.

2. Use low heat—about 250°F—to thoroughly bake the pieces and dry them without browning them much. You're concerned here with getting the starches to gelatinize and set so as to form a rigid structure.

3. You may not need to bake every piece you make (flowers can often be left without baking), as they often dry to hardness without it, but for any piece designed to support weight or act as a structural component, thorough baking is necessary.

4. Baking times of 1–2 hours—or even longer—are not uncommon, depending on the size and weight of the piece. Very small items bake much more quickly.

COOLING:
The pieces sometimes seem a bit soft on leaving the oven, but items that are thin or narrow harden on cooling.

Glossary

A

acetic acid An organic acid produced by heterofermentative bacteria. It is relatively sharp in its sourness and is found in such food products as vinegar and bread dough.

active decorative dough A type of decorative dough made using manufactured yeast. Sometimes referred to as *live dough* when used for decorative dough showpieces.

active dry yeast The first form of dried yeast commercially available to bakers. Because it has had most of its moisture removed, the yeast can be held in factory-sealed packages for as long as a year after the date of manufacture. It must be rehydrated in a small amount of warm water to resuscitate the yeast cells before its use in bread dough, and the large number of dead yeast cells present from the manufacturing process produce significant quantities of glutathione. Glutathione causes some degradation of the gluten bonds in bread dough, which can be either an advantage or disadvantage, depending on the type of dough you are trying to create.

ADA Azodicarbonamide: a flour additive, classified as a bleaching agent, that acts more like an oxidizer because it has significant effects on flour maturation. When added to flour—even "green" (nonaged) flour—it can allow bakers to obtain greater strength in their dough and more volume in their loaves.

additives Substances added to flour before it is marketed to bakers. They can range from the innocuous addition of vitamins and minerals, known as *enrichment*, to enzymes like amylase, to more controversial substances like bleach, bromates, and other conditioners.

alcohol The liquid produced by yeast as a by-product of fermentation.

alveograph A piece of equipment designed to analyze the protein qualities of wheat flour, used more commonly in Europe than in the United States. Specifically, it measures the resistance of a specifically sized dough bubble to inflation and rupture.

alveoli The holes or air cells that form in the crumb of bread dough after it is baked. Wetter doughs generally produce larger alveoli, while drier doughs tend to ensure smaller alveoli. The size of the alveoli can also be affected by how long the dough is mixed or how roughly it is handled during the shaping of the loaves.

amylase The enzyme responsible for the breakdown of starch into simple sugars.

amylopectin One of the two basic types of starch in wheat flour. It constitutes around 75% of the starch in wheat, and, at the molecular level, it forms a complex set of branched chains.

ascorbic acid The scientific name for vitamin C. In its synthetic form, it is often used as a flour additive to provide strength and elasticity to bread dough.

ash content Literally, the amount of ash left from a 50g sample of flour incinerated in a specially designed oven. The ash mostly comprises minerals, and because the minerals in wheat are located in the bran, a measurement of ash can be used to determine the level of bran left in white flour after it is milled.

autolyse The rest period for bread dough sometimes used by bakers after a short initial period of mixing on first speed. Its length is usually 15–30 minutes, and it is usually followed by a short period of mixing on second speed to achieve further gluten development. Its purpose is to allow for passive gluten development, which minimizes the oxidation of the dough, as well as the development of enhanced enzyme activity to aid in the development of extensibility for shaping.

azodicarbonamide See *ADA*.

B

bacteria Simple one-celled organisms placed in the Monera Kingdom, as they have no cell nucleus. In bread dough, we try to propagate homofermentative and heterofermentative types of lactic bacteria, which feed on sugars and produce mostly lactic and acetic acids as their primary by-products.

baguette Literally, "stick" or "wand" in French. A long loaf of lean white bread, narrow in diameter and generally 25–30 inches in length. It has evolved into the iconic symbol of traditional French bread baking, but it has been commonly produced only since the 1920s.

baker's math An alternate name for the term *baker's percentage*.

baker's percentage A method of using numeric relationships to present a brief snapshot of the characteristics likely to be present in a dough or batter formula. Generally, the total weight of the flour is assigned the value of 100%. Every other ingredient weight in the formula is then expressed as a percentage of the total flour weight. For instance, if a formula contains 10 lb bread flour and 7 lb water, the flour would be assigned the value of 100%, and the water would be assigned the value of 70%. We can use baker's percentage to resize or troubleshoot formulas, to predict their dough characteristics, and to check whether the formula is in balance.

banneton The French term for baskets specifically designed to hold raw shaped loaves of bread as they proof. The loaf is generally placed seam-side up (that is, upside-down) in the basket to allow the baker to flip it easily onto an oven peel before loading into the oven.

base dough The American term for what the French call a *detrempe*. In dough lamination, the dough made from all ingredients except the butter block.

bâtard The French term for a log-shaped or cylindrical loaf of bread, somewhat plump and significantly shorter than a baguette. It may be slightly elongated or short and fat.

benzoyl peroxide A bleaching agent used purely for the purpose of destroying the yellowish carotene pigments naturally present in white flour. In the process, it produces an extremely white color in the flour, but it also destroys the aromas and subtle taste associated with any bread made from the flour.

beta carotene An orange to yellow pigment found, for instance, in vegetables like carrots, in egg yolks, and in the endosperm of grains like wheat. In bread dough made from wheat flour, carotene pigments are responsible not only for excellent crumb color but also for subtle aromas and flavors developed during fermentation. Overoxidation of bread dough can destroy its carotene pigments.

biga A firm pre-ferment made of flour, water, and manufactured yeast where the water is 50–55% the weight of the flour. It is similar in some ways to sponge, but it usually is drier and has more yeast. Historically, this pre-ferment was used by Italian bakers to provide strength to breads made with high hydration or from weak bread flour. The term is sometimes used today by Italian bakers to refer to almost any pre-ferment.

bleaching agent Any of a number of chemical additives to flour, such as benzoyl peroxide or chlorine dioxide, designed to destroy the natural carotene pigments and to produce an extremely white color in the flour.

blow-out A condition in baked loaves of bread where the loaf has either been underproofed before baking or was inappropriately scored, producing a rupture in the loaf that creates an unattractive appearance. Longer proofing or proper scoring can alleviate the internal pressure in a loaf that causes this rupture.

boule Literally, "ball" in French. In bread baking, a round loaf of bread.

boulot The French term for a short, oval loaf of bread with slightly tapered ends.

bran The outer seed coat of a wheat berry, constituted mostly of cellulose and indigestible by humans. It provides valuable dietary fiber for people, though, and all of the minerals in the wheat berry are located in the bran. White bread flour is milled to remove most of the bran before the flour is packaged.

Bread Bakers Guild of America A nonprofit organization that promotes education in the field of artisan bread baking through its sponsorship of seminars, its publication of informative newsletters, and by providing a forum for communication between members who see baking as a craft that must be developed and supported.

brotform The German term for a basket specially designed to hold loaves of bread as they proof before baking.

bulk fermentation See *primary fermentation*.

butter block The square layer of butter enclosed by dough in the first stage of dough lamination, before the turns are begun. Called *beurrage* in French.

by-products When applied to fermentation, the elements that remain after fermentation has completed its process of breaking down organic matter. The primary by-products of yeast fermentation are alcohol and carbon dioxide, while those of bacterial fermentation are lactic and acetic acid.

C

caramelization The browning that results from the breakdown of sugars under intense heat.

carbon dioxide The gas produced by yeast as a by-product of fermentation.

carotene pigments See *beta carotene*.

carotenoid pigments See *beta carotene*.

chlorine dioxide A bleaching agent used for destroying the carotene pigments in white flour. This creates an intensely white color in the flour, but it also eliminates the subtle aromas and flavors associated with those pigments.

clear flour Flour ground from particles of the wheat endosperm lying near the bran. It tends to be grayish in color and, while high in protein, has somewhat less strength than patent flour due its lower level of gluten-forming proteins and its higher levels of ash. It once was used commonly in rye breads because it was cheap and its dark color posed no problem.

compressed yeast A solid form of fresh yeast marketed in individually wrapped blocks, usually 1 or 2 lb in size, with 1–3 dozen blocks per case. Like all forms of fresh yeast, it is highly perishable and must be kept in refrigerated storage. Its usable shelf life is about 21 days after the date of manufacture if it is stored properly.

conditioning When applied to the milling of wheat, the process of soaking wheat berries in water before grinding them into flour. The goal is to create a difference in texture between the bran (which becomes tougher) and the endosperm, making it easier to separate the bran from the endosperm during milling.

couche A long cloth made from canvas linen, usually pleated and set on plywood proofing boards to hold loaves of bread as they proof. These loaves are baked free-form, so they benefit from the temporary support of the pleats in the couche. Generally, couche must be floured so the loaves don't stick to the cloth.

cream yeast A liquid form of fresh yeast used in large industrial bakeries.

crumbled yeast A solid form of fresh yeast like compressed yeast in consistency, but not formed into blocks. It is, instead, marketed as crumbles in large bags.

D

damaged starch The starch that results from broken starch granules in the milling process. It is generally no more than 10% of the starch in wheat flour, but it can have dramatic effects on the characteristics of the dough and its rate of fermentation.

dead dough In French, *pâte morte*. Bread dough made with no yeast, usually for decorative purposes.

decorative dough Bread dough made for decorative purposes only.

degradation When applied to bread dough, a breaking down of the structure in dough as it ages, brought on by the action of enzymes such as protease.

direct method A traditional method of making baguette dough without a pre-ferment. The leavener is manufactured yeast, and all ingredients are mixed together at once, but, unlike many straight doughs, this one is fermented for a long time, and thus necessitates either the short or the improved mix method.

double fold A technique for folding dough during the lamination process, alternatively known as the *book fold* and the *4-fold*. The actual number of layers created is only 1½ times the number created by the so-called single-fold technique, so the term is a misnomer.

double hydration A mixing technique used by some bakers to shorten the mix time for superhydrated doughs by holding back some of the water and beginning the mixing procedure as if they were aiming for the same moderately wet consistency of baguette dough. After the baguette-type dough is mixed to a moderate level of development, such as with the improved mix, the remaining water is slowly added to the dough until it is completely incorporated, using only low speed.

durum A type of very hard wheat, generally used to make couscous, semolina, or durum flour for use in making pasta. Semolina is made of larger granules of durum wheat, while durum flour is more finely ground. The endosperm of durum wheat is fairly yellow in color due to a large presence of carotene pigments. Semolina and durum flour are also used in some formulas for bread dough, especially in traditional breads from Sicily and southern Italy.

E

elaboration The final feeding of flour and water a sourdough culture receives to enable it to grow in size and leavening power before it is incorporated into bread dough. Typically, a reserved piece of culture or leftover sourdough receives one to three feedings before it receives its final elaboration.

elasticity The tendency for a substance, such as bread dough, to snap back to its original position after it is stretched. Not to be confused with extensibility.

endosperm The largest portion of the wheat berry, comprising starch, proteins, pentosans, and sugars. When separated from the bran and the germ during milling, it is further ground into dust and forms the basis of white flour.

enrichment In baking, the addition of vitamins and minerals to white flour that has lost them due to the separation of the bran and germ from the endosperm.

enzymes Naturally occurring chemical catalysts that break down organic substances like proteins, starches, and sugars. Generally, individual enzymes break down very specific substances. For instance, zymase breaks down sugar into alcohol and carbon dioxide, but it has no effect on starch or proteins.

esters Substances produced when the acids from bacterial fermentation encounter the alcohol produced by yeast fermentation. They are thought to be responsible for a significant portion of the pleasant aromas generated in bread dough.

extensibility The ability of a substance, such as bread dough, to be stretched easily without tearing or retracting to its original shape.

extraction rate The weight of flour that actually remains from milling after all the grinding, separating, and reduction are performed, divided by the weight of the grain before grinding. For instance, if we get 65 lb bread flour from 100 lb wheat berries, that flour has an extraction rate of 65%.

F

falling number A number that reflects the time it takes for a specially designed probe to reach the bottom of a container filled with a slurry of flour and water. It is, indirectly, a reflection of the amount of amylase present in the flour. Numbers higher than 325–350 indicate a lower-than-average level of amylase, while numbers lower than 200–225 indicate a too-high amylase level. A lower number means a shorter time for the probe to drop, indicating elevated levels of amylase are causing the starches in the slurry to break down too quickly and thin the mixture. High amylase levels in flour can cause accelerated fermentation rates and sticky handling qualities in dough made from it. Low amylase levels can lead to extended periods of fermentation. Mills attempt to correct the amylase levels in flour to 250–300 before it is shipped out for delivery.

farinograph A laboratory device that measures the resistance of a dough sample to mechanical mixing. It is commonly used in the United States to aid in predicting the protein characteristics of flour made from wheat.

farro The Italian term for emmer, a type of wheat of ancient origin. The name is also sometimes applied to spelt. Wild forms of emmer grew in parts of the Middle East since before recorded history, and the first domesticated wheat was probably a type of emmer. Emmer does not produce good yields when compared to more modern strains of wheat, and the flour produced from it is much weaker, so it is not commonly found in bread anymore.

fermentation The breakdown of organic substances in the presence of yeast, bacteria, or mold.

Fertile Crescent An area of the Middle East loosely defined as being around the Tigris and Euphrates rivers, in present-day Iraq. In 8000 B.C., it became the cradle of human civilization when the Sumerians developed organized agricultural methods for growing grain. These more efficient grain production methods allowed more Sumerians to gravitate toward professions other than food gathering, including administration, the military, and craftsmanship—including baking.

final proof The designated period of fermentation that occurs after loaves are shaped and in which they inflate to a large degree as they await their insertion into an oven.

firm levain A firm pre-ferment made from flour, water, and a piece of naturally inoculated culture or leftover sourdough. When using North American flour, it is usually hydrated at a rate of 55–60%. Its dry consistency generally produces a sharper degree of sourness than that produced by liquid levain.

first break The first set of corrugated rollers through which wheat berries pass before milling. The berries are broken into relatively large pieces, then further separated and sorted for milling into flour.

flip-board A narrow, lightweight wooden board used for transferring loaves such as baguettes from their pleated couche to the loader or oven peel that will place them in the oven.

flour The powder or particles that result from the crushing or milling of starchy seeds, grains, tubers, or legumes.

formula A list of ingredients contained in a bread dough that includes both the weights of the ingredients used and the mathematical relationship between them.

free water Any water in a bread dough that is not truly absorbed or fixed by the starches, proteins, and other dry elements in the formula. Ciabatta, for instance, which is a type of superhydrated dough, has a great deal of free water.

fresh yeast The term applied by the baking industry to any manufactured yeast not intensively dehydrated before packaging. The most common form available to bakers is compressed yeast, which has the consistency of clay and is sold in wrapped blocks. Other forms used in large industrial plants are cream yeast, which is liquid in form, and crumbled yeast, which is similar to compressed yeast in consistency but not formed into blocks.

fungal amylase Amylase derived from the growth of a fungal base. It is sometimes used instead of malted barley flour to adjust the amylase levels of bread flour. Its advantages over malt are that the amylase itself is fairly isolated and does not produce any of the other secondary reactions that might result from using a comparatively complex ingredient like malted barley.

G

gelatinization The swelling of starches that occurs when they absorb water under heat.

germ The area of the wheat berry that contains the embryonic wheat plant. It also contains most of the naturally occurring oils in the seed, so it is often removed during milling to prevent rancidity from developing in flour.

gliadin One of the two simpler proteins that combine in the presence of water to form gluten. It is thought to provide the extensibility exhibited by gluten. Found in significant quantity in wheat, rye, and some other grains.

glucose The simple sugar consumed by yeast to produce alcohol and carbon dioxide.

glutathione A protein fragment present in both dead yeast cells and any milk, liquid or dry, that has not been heated to at least 180°F (82°C). Glutathione has destructive effects on protein bonds that are similar to those of the enzyme protease.

gluten A complex protein formed by the union of two simpler proteins, glutenin and gliadin, in the presence of water. It has properties of both elasticity and extensibility, and its unique web-forming characteristics enable it to hold gases produced during fermentation. It is present in small quantities in a number of grains, but only wheat contains enough gluten-forming proteins to make it the preferred grain for making bread flour.

glutenin One of the two simpler proteins that combine in the presence of water to form gluten. It is thought to provide the elasticity exhibited by gluten. Found in relatively large quantity in wheat and much lower quantity in some other grains.

granules The individual compact structures formed by native starch in wheat flour and the wheat endosperm. Unless these hard structures are broken open, their ability to absorb water without heat is limited to about 40% of their own weight, and they are less susceptible to degradation from the enzyme amylase.

green flour White flour that is not aged before its shipment or use in bread dough. Generally, white flour made from wheat develops better baking qualities and handling characteristics if it is allowed to age and passively oxidize 2–3 weeks before use.

guild An organization of professionals within a legally recognized and sanctioned craft, such as bread baking or pastry work. In the medieval and Renaissance periods in Europe, guilds worked to protect the standards of their craft, and they regulated any worker's entrance to their profession. In that role, they guided aspiring guild members' progress through apprenticeship to mastery of the craft.

H

hard wheat Wheat that is high in protein, and, by implication, high in gluten-forming proteins. It is used to mill bread flour and high-gluten flour, and it is blended with soft wheat flour to make some varieties of all-purpose flour.

heterofermentative bacteria The type of lactic bacteria that produces both lactic acid and acetic acid as by-products of bacterial fermentation. They prefer cooler and drier environments than do homofermentative bacteria, although they can survive under other conditions.

high-heat dried milk A type of dried milk marketed to bakers who want to be certain that glutathione has been deactivated in the product. The milk is heated to at least 180°F before it is dried and packaged. Not all dried milk is of the high-heat variety, and standard pasteurization does not deactivate glutathione.

homofermentative bacteria The type of lactic bacteria that produces only lactic acid as a by-product of bacterial fermentation. These bacteria prefer moist, warm environments, although they will survive under less than ideal conditions.

hydration rate The weight of water in a dough formula divided by the weight of total flour in a formula, expressed as a percentage. For instance, a dough with 7 lb water and 10 lb flour has a hydration rate of 70%.

hygroscopic The characteristic associated with ingredients like salt or sugar that means they absorb water away from their environment. This is why salt and sugar are used as preservatives to inhibit microbial growth in some foods. The same tendency to inhibit microbial growth can also limit the activity of yeast and bacteria in bread dough if a dough formula does not take these effects into account.

I

improved mix A mechanical mixing method for bread dough characterized generally by 3–5 minutes of low-speed mixing followed by 3–5 minutes of high-speed mixing. A rest period called an *autolyse* often appears between the low- and high-speed mixing intervals. The improved mixing method aims to retain much of the good crumb color, pleasant aromas, and fine flavor associated with the short mix method while achieving more gluten development and greater volume in less time. After the dough is mixed, it usually requires one or two sets of folds before reaching maturity in 1–2 hours.

insoluble proteins Proteins that do not dissolve in water, such as glutenin and gliadin.

instant dry yeast A type of dry yeast designed to be mixed in with the flour in a formula before any liquid is added. Because it does not require a separate period of rehydration or resuscitation before use, it is more convenient than active dry yeast and is often preferred. It has the same benefits of easy storage and long shelf life as does active dry yeast, and because it contains fewer dead yeast cells, there is less glutathione.

intensive mix A mechanical mixing method for bread dough characterized by 3–5 minutes of low-speed mixing followed by 8–15 minutes of high-speed mixing. The gluten is almost completely developed in this mixing method, so only a brief (if any) bulk fermentation period is required after mixing. The intensive mix method aims to shorten the production time of baguettes as much as possible, and by completely developing the gluten it maximizes the potential volume of the loaves. The hard mixing and rough handling incorporates a lot of oxygen, though, and produces a baguette that is excessively white in crumb color, close-textured, and bland in flavor. For some varieties, such as brioche, challah, and certain pan breads, the intensive method is actually preferred because the strong dough and close crumb it provides are seen as advantages.

intermediate proof The designated period of fermentation that occurs after dough is divided and pre-shaped into portions and before it undergoes final shaping. Also known as *bench proofing*. Its usual length is 15–30 minutes, and its primary purpose is to allow the pre-shaped portions to relax enough to allow further shaping without tearing or overworking the dough.

L

lactic acid An organic acid produced by both homofermentative bacteria and heterofermentative bacteria. It is relatively mild in its sourness and may be found in such food products as milk, yogurt, and bread dough.

lactic bacteria The collective term for the two bacteria most commonly propagated in bread dough during fermentation: homofermentative bacteria and heterofermentative bacteria.

laminate In bread making, to enclose a layer of butter completely with dough and then put the dough-and-butter sandwich through a series of folds to create a mass of dough with hundreds of alternating layers of dough and butter.

liquid levain A liquid pre-ferment made from flour, water, and a piece of naturally inoculated culture or leftover sourdough. When made with North American flour, it is usually hydrated at a rate of 100–125%. Its liquid consistency generally produces a milder level of sourness than that produced by firm levain, and it is much more enzyme-active.

M

Maillard process The browning of proteins that occurs in their reaction with sugars, which can be accelerated under heat. It is named after the French scientist who identified the process. While it is most noticeable in the early stages of a loaf's crust browning in an oven at 140–150°F, it can also be observed in milk powder stored at room temperature for long periods.

malt A powder made from grains that are first sprouted and then toasted until dry. The powder contains the sugar maltose and is rich in the enzyme amylase. It is also marketed as a syrup.

malted Describes grains that are first sprouted and then toasted until dry. The grain most commonly used is barley, and the next most common is wheat.

Marie Antoinette The queen of France during the French Revolution, executed along with her husband, Louis XVI. She was reputed to have commented that the starving citizens of France, who could find no bread, should instead eat brioche (widely mistranslated as "cake").

maturity A stage of development in bread dough where the dough has sufficient strength and handling characteristics to be easily divided and shaped into loaves. Maturity can be developed either manually (through hand kneading), mechanically, chemically (through fermentation or chemical additives), or any combination of these.

milling The process of grinding grains such as wheat into flour.

N

native starch The starch located in granules not broken during the milling of wheat flour. Because the hard granules of native starch are not damaged, they do not absorb as much water as damaged starch. Native starch usually constitutes 90% or more of the starch in bread flour.

natural pre-ferment Typically, any mixture of flour and water inoculated with a natural sourdough (levain) culture. The term in English is *sourdough*, in French *levain*, in German *Sauerteig*, in Italian *lievito naturale*, and in Flemish *desem*.

Neolithic man The term archaeologists use for the people of the late Stone Age. Human civilization at this time was characterized by people living in villages and depending largely on domesticated animals and plants for their food. The extraction of metals from ore to make advanced tools had not yet occurred. Different parts of the world advanced into and out of the Neolithic period at somewhat different times; the earliest Neolithic civilization may have developed around 8000 B.C. in what is today Iraq. This area passed into the Bronze Age by about 3500 B.C.

O

old dough The American term for the French pre-ferment *pâte fermentée*. It is usually just leftover baguette dough, as the ingredients in baguette dough are also present in almost every bread dough. Old dough may also be made as a dedicated batch of dough and reserved in its entirety for use in other dough making—often the next day. If it is to be fermented more than 1–2 hours, it should subsequently be refrigerated until use.

organic acids The collective term for the acids produced by bacteria during fermentation. Bakers are most concerned with two of them: lactic acid and acetic acid.

osmotolerant yeast A strain of instant dry yeast specially marketed for use with doughs that are low in moisture or high in sugar, such as brioche and Danish dough. It is also thought by some bakers to be more tolerant of freezing than standard instant dry yeast.

oven peel A long-handled, flat tool made from wood, with one end in the shape of a spade. It is used to load loaves into an oven and to retrieve them after they are baked.

oven spring The dramatic and rapid growth that occurs in loaves of bread during their first few minutes in a preheated oven. It is due to the accelerated level of fermentation that takes place during the sudden increase in temperature inside the loaf.

overbaking Baking a loaf of bread or a pastry to the point where it is too dry and becomes unpalatable. This can happen without obvious exterior signs, so bakers should be vigilant and not rely on appearance alone to judge when a product is completely baked.

overmixing Mixing a dough so long the links between its gluten strands are torn or the dough becomes much too extensible. In this condition, a bread dough cannot be made into shapes that hold their form, and its ability to hold gases and rise as it should is seriously impaired.

overproofed Describes a bread or yeast-leavened pastry that either collapses during the proofing period or is so over-inflated with carbon dioxide that it collapses shortly after being loaded into the oven.

oxidizers Chemical additives in white flour that add oxygen to dough during mixing and that increase dough strength and tolerance to long fermentation. Ascorbic acid, the synthesized form of vitamin C, functions as an oxidizer in bread dough and poses no threat to human health, but at the other extreme is potassium bromate, which is banned in Europe and Canada because of evidence it causes cancer in laboratory animals.

P

pain viennoise The French term for bread leavened with manufactured yeast only. It is contrasted with *pain française*, which is leavened with a sourdough culture and represented the traditional bread of France long before baking methods using manufactured yeast were brought by Viennese bakers.

pâte fermentée French term for reserved bread dough saved for use as a pre-ferment in a later batch of bread dough. Also called old dough. For the sake of simplicity, bakers usually use baguette dough for *pâte fermentée*, but other doughs can be reserved and utilized to strengthen and flavor subsequent batches.

patent flour A U.S. designation for white flour that is extremely low in ash because it is milled from endosperm particles at the center of the wheat berry.

pentosans A type of complex carbohydrate found in some types of plants, such as wheat and rye. It can absorb many times its own weight in water, but when it does so it is structurally weak. When a dough high in pentosans, such as rye bread, is mixed more than a few minutes, the pentosans can rupture and render their absorbed water back into the mix, making the dough wetter in consistency than before.

percentage sum The sum of all the ingredient percentages listed in a formula. In its raw form, it is expressed as a percentage, but to use it in mathematical calculations, we divide it by 100 to obtain a decimal number. For instance, a percentage sum of 170.3% is typically expressed 1.703.

plasticity The ability of a substance to be manipulated and molded into a desired shape different from its original form. The term can be applied to bread dough.

poolish A type of pre-ferment characterized by equal weights of flour and water together with a small amount of manufactured yeast. It is the most difficult type of pre-ferment to produce with the same level of quality day after day, and it is rarely fermented longer than 12–15 hours. Still, it is used often in the production of baguettes, as it produces good flavor and is high in enzymes that create extensibility. Its name reflects its origin with Polish bakers who immigrated to Paris.

potassium bromate An oxidizer once commonly added to bread flour, though it is now banned in Europe for being a suspected carcinogen, and it carries such stringent warning labels in California and Oregon that it is not as common as it once was. It features a delayed action in the mixing and baking process, where it boosts the height of loaves only after they are placed in the oven.

pre-ferment A mixture of flour and water that contains either a natural culture or manufactured yeast and that is fermented from a few hours up to a day or more before it is used as an ingredient for bread dough. The purpose of making the mixture so far ahead of final dough mixing is to allow it to acquire a significant amount of organic acids from bacterial fermentation. This acidic pre-ferment (which isn't necessarily sour) can provide maturity, strength, and flavor to the final dough while minimizing the time needed for bulk fermentation.

pre-fermentation An optional period of fermentation that can precede the mixing of the final bread dough. A quantity of flour and water may be mixed with either manufactured yeast or a natural culture to allow for the development of organic acids in the pre-ferment.

pre-ferments with manufactured yeast A mixture of flour, water, and a small amount of manufactured yeast. If it is allowed to ferment ahead of the time it will be used as an ingredient in a bread dough. Examples are poolish, sponge, biga, and old dough (*pâte fermentée*), which also contains salt.

primary effect The effect on dough or bread characteristics intended by adding a certain ingredient or when altering a given procedure. It is often contrasted with the secondary or unintended effects that accompany changes in ingredients or alterations in procedure. For instance, you might add sugar to a dough formula to sweeten the flavor of a bread (a primary or intended effect), but in quantities greater than 12% of the weight of the flour, the sugar addition can also noticeably weaken the dough structure and slow the rate of fermentation (in this case secondary or unintended effects).

primary fermentation Bulk fermentation. The period of fermentation that commences just after the dough is mixed and during which it is allowed to mature before its division into portions. This is the period in which maturity develops, strength is built, and flavor is obtained.

proofer An enclosed cabinet with temperature and humidity controls that is used to hold loaves of bread as they proof before baking.

proofing In bread baking, the period of fermentation between the final shaping of bread loaves and their placement in an oven. The period may last 30 minutes to a few hours or more, depending on the type of bread being proofed, and it may be extended even longer if the loaves are refrigerated in a process called *retarding*. The main purpose of proofing is to reinflate the loaves to an appropriate level before baking them, to assure lightness and proper texture.

protease The enzyme that breaks down protein chains.

protein An organic compound composed of chains of amino acids.

R

red wheat A term applied to wheat varieties with a dark, reddish-brown bran surrounding their wheat berries. Whole wheat flour milled from red wheat has a noticeably reddish-brown color.

retarding When applied to bread baking, the use of refrigeration to delay the process of proofing loaves of bread.

Romans The people who occupied the classical city of Rome and its surrounding dominions in southern Italy. Their domination of Italy evolved into complete control of the entire Mediterranean region and adjoining lands between 200 B.C. and A.D. 400. They learned naturally leavened bread-baking techniques from the Egyptians and the Greeks, and they spread these techniques throughout most of western Europe.

rye One of the first domesticated grains. It grows easily in cold, damp climates not considered ideal for growing wheat. It became a preferred domesticated grain in northern, central, and eastern Europe. It is reasonably high in gliadin but low in glutenin, so it provides little gluten to bread dough.

S

saccharomyces cerevisiae The species of yeast that includes those selected by manufacturers for domestication and use in the food and beverage industry. Its wild form can also be found in sourdough cultures (in French, *levain*).

scoring The practice of slashing the surface of loaves of bread before they are baked. It may serve a decorative purpose, but it is often primarily intended to relieve the gas pressure within a loaf of bread as it bakes in a manner that ensures maximum expansion and loaf symmetry.

secondary effect An unintended effect on dough or bread characteristics that accompanies primary or intended effects. See *primary effect*.

semolina The large granules ground from durum wheat.

short mix One of the three defined mixing methods for French bread dough. It features 12–15 minutes of low-speed mixing and must be followed by many folds and an extended period of bulk fermentation—up to 5 hours—for the dough to reach maturity. This was the most common mechanical mixing method in France from the 1920s through the mid-1950s.

shortening effect The shortening of gluten strands that results from their being surrounded by fat in bread or pastry dough. Whether this is an advantage or disadvantage depends on how much tenderization (and possible destabilization) the baker wishes to produce in the dough.

single fold A technique for folding dough during the lamination process, also known as the *letter fold* and the *3-fold*. Generally, a laminated dough designed for making croissants has a butter block that is 25–30% of the weight of the base dough, and it receives three sets of single folds. Any dough with a larger butter block requires gradually more sets of folds, until you get to puff pastry, which may have a butter block that is 50–75% of the weight of the base dough and usually receives at least six sets of single folds.

slurry A mixture of water and a thickener, such as starch or flour, with a liquid consistency.

soaker A mixture of cracked or whole grains and water left to soften for a time before final use in bread dough.

soft wheat Wheat low in protein and, by implication, low in gluten-forming proteins. It is used to mill pastry flour and cake flour, and it is blended with hard wheat flour to make some varieties of all-purpose flour.

soluble proteins Proteins that dissolve in water, such as albumins. The proteins glutenin and gliadin are *not* water soluble and hence are called *insoluble proteins*.

sound Describes wheat berries that did not sprout before milling.

spelt A somewhat primitive form of wheat still used in bread making. The gluten formed when using spelt flour tends to be somewhat weak, and the dough is often less tolerant to mixing than dough made with modern wheat flour.

sponge A pre-ferment made from flour, water, and manufactured yeast where the water is about 60% of the weight of the flour. This firm pre-ferment is easy to make and has a much wider window of usability than more fragile pre-ferments like poolish. It is more acidic than poolish, though not really sour, and it produces greater strength in doughs.

spring wheat Wheat planted in the spring and harvested in late summer or early autumn.

starch A type of complex carbohydrate that constitutes the majority of the wheat berry's endosperm. At the molecular level, it comprises long chains of sugar (glucose) molecules that are chemically bonded.

straight dough A dough mixed without a pre-ferment or starter.

streams The troughs carrying particles of different weight during the flour milling process. By directing strong air currents at the first break while the grain passes through, pieces with different weights are blown into different troughs, which, after further reduction into powder, can be reassembled later into flours that possess required specifications deemed for protein and ash level.

Sumerians The people who as early as 8000 B.C. inhabited and ruled the geographic area surrounding the Tigris and Euphrates rivers, most of which is now Iraq. They are known for developing the first signs of organized agriculture, and they are thought to have created the first nation-state largely due to the society they developed when fewer people were needed to gather grain for bread.

superhydrated Describes bread doughs containing large amounts of free water. Examples: ciabatta, pane pugliese, and a number of other classic Italian breads.

T

tempering See *conditioning*.

tenacity Resistance to stretching or distortion.

total flour The total of the combined weights of flours in a dough formula. If there is only one type of flour in the formula, its weight and the weight of total flour in the formula are the same. But, for instance, if a formula calls for 8 lb bread flour and 2 lb rye flour, total flour is 10 lb.

traditional mix Also known as *short mix*. A mechanical dough-mixing method characterized by 12–15 minutes of mixing on low speed only, with no period of second-speed or high-speed mixing. It is meant to emulate the type of mixing a dough receives when mixed by hand, which features minimal initial gluten development and many subsequent sets of folds to strengthen the dough while minimizing its mechanical oxidation. The lack of gluten development often results in baguettes with low volume and an undramatic appearance, but by minimizing the mechanical agitation of the dough the baker obtains excellent crumb color, a wide-open and irregular crumb structure, maximum flavor, and the best possible shelf life.

turns The series of folds a dough undergoes as it is being laminated. One set of single folds or one set of double folds is referred to as one set of turns.

V

viscoelastic Describes bread dough that displays properties of both a liquid and a solid—that is, it exhibits strength and elasticity while still flowing outward (albeit slowly). By mixing the dough, altering its hydration, or allowing it to rest and ferment, we can manipulate its viscoelastic properties.

viscosity Thickness or resistance to flow in a liquid. Bread dough generally has this characteristic, though doughs at different rates of hydration will exhibit different degrees of viscosity.

W

wheat berry The seed of the wheat plant after it is husked. It contains all of the bran or seed coat, the endosperm, and the germ.

wheat bran The outer seed coat of the wheat berry, comprising mostly cellulose, which is indigestible. It is a good source of dietary fiber, however, and it contains all the minerals present in the wheat berry.

white rye A type of rye flour with most of its bran removed. It is milled from the center of the rye berry. It has a lighter color than other forms of rye and is sometimes called *light rye*. It is often used in formulas designed to create high-rising, light-textured rye breads such as those found in delis and sandwich shops. It is thought by many artisan bakers to have less flavor than either medium or dark rye flours.

white wheat Any wheat variety whose berry is surrounded by a white or ivory-colored bran. Whole wheat flour milled from white wheat has a much lighter color than other whole wheat flours and is often judged less bitter than whole wheat flour from red wheat.

whole wheat flour Flour milled from the entire wheat berry, including the bran, germ, and endosperm.

winter wheat Wheat planted in autumn, allowed to go dormant during the winter, and then harvested in late spring or early summer.

Y

yeast One-celled organisms that are part of the Fungi Kingdom. The different species of yeast that we prefer in bread dough consume sugars to produce alcohol and carbon dioxide as by-products.

Z

zymase The enzyme produced by yeast cells that breaks down glucose (a simple sugar) into alcohol and carbon dioxide.

Bibliography

Alford, Jeffrey, and Naomi Duguid. *Flatbreads and Flavors*. New York: William Morrow, 1995.

Amendola, Joseph. *The Bakers' Manual*. 2nd ed. New York: Ahrens, 1967.

Bilheux, Roland, Alain Escoffier, Daniel Hervé, and Jean-Marie Pouradier. *Special and Decorative Breads*. Paris: Compagnie Internationale de Consultation Education et Media; New York: Van Nostrand Reinhold, 1989.

Calvel, Raymond, James MacGuire, and Ronald Wirtz. *The Taste of Bread*. Gaithersburg, MD: Aspen, 2001.

Child, Julia, and Simone Beck. *Mastering the Art of French Cooking*. Vol. 2. New York: Knopf, 1979.

Collister, Linda, and Anthony Blake. *The Bread Book*. New York: Lyons, 1993.

Couet, Alain, and Eric Kayser, with Bernard, Isabelle, and Valerie Ganachaud, Daniel Hervé, Leon Megard, and Yves Saunier. *Special and Decorative Breads*. Vol. 2. Paris: Compagnie Internationale de Consultation Education et Media; New York: Van Nostrand Reinhold, 1990.

Dannenberg, Linda. *Paris Boulangerie Pâtisserie*. New York: Clarkson Potter, 1994.

David, Elizabeth. *English Bread and Yeast Cookery*. Newton, MA: Biscuit, 1994.

Dupaigne, Bernard. *The History of Bread*. New York: Abrams, 1999.

Field, Carol. *Celebrating Italy*. New York: William Morrow, 1990.

———. *The Italian Baker*. New York: Harper & Row, 1985.

Figoni, Paula. *How Baking Works*. 2nd ed. Hoboken, NJ: John Wiley & Sons, 2008.

Glezer, Maggie. *Artisan Baking Across America*. New York: Artisan, 2000.

Hamelman, Jeffrey. *Bread: A Baker's Book of Techniques and Recipes*. Hoboken, NJ: John Wiley & Sons, 2004.

Heads of Department, Craft School Richemont. *Swiss Bakery*. Lucerne: Craft School Richemont, 2001.

Jacob, H.E. *Six Thousand Years of Bread: Its Holy and Unholy History*. New York: Lyons & Burford, 1944.

Kaplan, Stephen Laurence. *Good Bread Is Back*. Durham, NC: Duke University Press, 2006.

Kline, L., and T.F. Sugihara. "Microorganisms of the San Francisco Sour Dough French Bread Process." *Applied Microbiology* (March 1971): 459–465.

Leader, Dan. *Bread Alone*. New York: William Morrow, 1993.

Leonard, Thom. *The Bread Book*. Brookline, MA: East West Health Books, 1990.

McGee, Harold. *On Food and Cooking*. New York: Charles Scribner's Sons, 1984.

MacGuire, James. "The Baguette." *The Art of Eating* (2006 Number 73 and 74): 40–51.

Ortiz, Joe. *The Village Baker*. Berkeley, CA: Ten Speed Press, 1993.

Pyler, E.J. *Baking Science and Technology*. Chicago: Siebel, 1973.

Rambali, Paul. *Boulangerie*. New York: Macmillan, 1994.

Scherber, Amy, and Toy Kim Dupree. *Amy's Bread*. New York: William Morrow, 1996.

Silverton, Nancy. *Breads from the La Brea Bakery*. New York: Villard, 1996.

Index